RECOGNIZING THE ROMANTIC NOVEL

NEW HISTORIES OF BRITISH FICTION, 1780–1830

LIVERPOOL ENGLISH TEXTS AND STUDIES, 53

RECOGNIZING THE ROMANTIC NOVEL

NEW HISTORIES OF BRITISH FICTION, 1780–1830

EDITED BY
JILLIAN HEYDT-STEVENSON
AND
CHARLOTTE SUSSMAN

LIVERPOOL UNIVERSITY PRESS

First published 2008 by
Liverpool University Press
4 Cambridge Street
Liverpool
L69 7ZU

British Library Cataloguing-in-Publication data
A British Library CIP record is available

ISBN 978-1-84631-162-8 cased

Typeset by XL Publishing Services, Tiverton
Printed and bound by Biddles Ltd, King's Lynn

For Henry and Jacob Green
and
Will Heydt-Minor

Contents

Acknowledgements

We would first of all like to thank our contributors for their enthusiasm and commitment to this volume.

Our graduate students were instrumental in helping us prepare this volume: our gratitude and respect goes to Nathan K. Hensley (Duke), Peter Hutchings (Princeton), John Leffel, Terry Francis Robinson, Michele Speitz (Colorado) and Courtney Wennerstrom (Indiana).

Our colleagues in the field were also essential as we designed and thought through ideas for the volume. Anne Mellor was especially helpful: she stimulated our ideas and sharpened our focus. James Chandler, Mary Favret, Deidre Lynch, and Ian Balfour encouraged and supported this project in its various stages with their intellectual generosity. Jeffrey Cox and John Allen Stevenson were kind enough to read through versions of our essay and preface, and for their interest and suggestions we are particularly grateful.

We would like to thank our respective Romantic Novel seminars at both Duke (2006) and the University of Colorado (2005 and 2006) for engaging in the thoughtful and serious quest to understand the ideas the Romantic novel yielded and the pervasive influence it exerted.

The English Departments at Colorado and Duke offered financial and intellectual support for the development of this volume.

Many thanks are due to our editor, Anthony Cond, for making this volume possible, and we are indebted to him and to our anonymous readers who offered valuable suggestions for structuring the volume and integrating the various essays.

Notes on Contributors

Miranda Burgess is Associate Professor of English at the University of British Columbia. She works on Romantic-period literary history and on the histories of genre, print culture, nationalism/transnationalism, and reading. Her book *British Fiction and the Production of Social Order, 1740–1830* (Cambridge, 2000) explored the uses of genre change in developing theories of British society and nationhood. She is completing a manuscript, *Romantic Transport: Reading, Feeling, and Literary Form, 1790–1830*, about the media contexts of Romantic affect and their sources in contemporary problems of transnational exchange, with a special focus on Ireland.

Ian Duncan is Professor of English at the University of California, Berkeley. He is the author of *Modern Romance and Transformations of the Novel: The Gothic, Scott, Dickens* (Cambridge, 1992) and *Scott's Shadow: The Novel in Romantic Edinburgh* (Princeton, 2007). Other books include a co-edited collection of essays, *Scotland and the Borders of Romanticism* (Cambridge, 2004), and editions of Walter Scott's *Ivanhoe* (Oxford, 1996) and *Rob Roy* (Oxford, 1998), James Hogg's *Winter Evening Tales* (Edinburgh, 2002), and a co-edited anthology, *Travel Writing 1700–1830* (Oxford, 2005).

Markman Ellis is Professor of Eighteenth-Century Studies in the School of English at Queen Mary, University of London. He is the author of *The Coffee House: A Cultural History* (2004), *The History of Gothic Fiction* (2000) and *The Politics of Sensibility* (1996). He is currently working on a study of intellectual networks in 1750s' London.

Michael Gamer is Associate Professor of English at the University of Pennsylvania, author of *Romanticism and the Gothic: Genre, Reception, and Canon Formation* (Cambridge, 2000), and editor of Horace Walpole's *Castle of Otranto* (Penguin, 2002) and Charlotte Smith's *Manon L'Escaut* and *The Romance of Real Life*, Volume 1 of Pickering and Chatto's *Works of Charlotte Smith* (2005). With Jeffrey Cox he co-edited the *Broadview Anthology of Romantic Drama* (2003), and with Dahlia Porter he has edited *Lyrical Ballads 1798 and 1800* (Broadview Press, 2008). He has also published a number of additional essays in *PMLA, Novel, ELH, Nineteenth-Century Contexts, Studies in Romanticism*, and other journals on popular culture, national collections, the novel, pornography, authorship, and dramas of spectacle.

Ina Ferris is Professor of English at the University of Ottawa. Her publications include a critical edition of Charlotte Smith's *The Old Manor House* (Pickering and Chatto, 2006), *The Romantic National Tale and the Question of Ireland* (Cambridge, 2002) and *The Achievement of Literary Authority: Gender, History, and the Waverley Novels* (Cornell, 1991). She is currently working on a project on the culture of the book in the Romantic period.

Jillian Heydt-Stevenson is Associate Professor in the Departments of English and Comparative Literature/Humanities at the University of Colorado, Boulder. She is the author of *Austen's Unbecoming Conjunctions: Subversive Laughter, Embodied History* (2005), Associate Editor of *Last Poems*, Cornell Wordsworth Series (1999), and the author of essays on Austen, Coleridge, Wordsworth, and the aesthetic movement of the picturesque. She is currently working on Thing Theory in French and British Romantic Literature.

Mary L. Jacobus is Professor of English at Cambridge University. Her first book, *Tradition and Experiment in Wordsworth's Lyrical Ballads, 1798* (1976) was followed by an edited collection, *Women Writing and Writing about Women* (1979); *Reading Woman: Essays in Feminist Criticism* (1986); *Body/Politics: Women and the Discourses of Science* (1989), co-edited with Evelyn Fox Keller and Sally Shuttleworth; *Romanticism, Writing, and Sexual Difference: Essays on* The Prelude (1994); *First Things: The Maternal Imaginary in Literature, Art, and Psychoanalysis* (1996); *Psychoanalysis and the Scene of Reading* (1999); and *The Poetics of Psychoanalysis: In the Wake of Klein* (2005).

Saree Makdisi is Professor of English and Comparative Literature at UCLA. He is the author of *Romantic Imperialism* (Cambridge, 1998); *William Blake and the Impossible History of the 1790s* (Chicago, 2003); and *Palestine Inside Out: An Everyday Occupation* (Norton, 2008). He is currently completing work on a book tentatively called *Radical Afterlives: Britain, 1798–1870*.

Laura Mandell is Associate Professor of English at Miami University, Ohio. She is the author of *Misogynous Economies: The Business of Literature in Eighteenth-Century Britain* (1999) and General Editor of the Poetess Archive (http://unixgen.muohio.edu/~poetess). She has published numerous articles about women writers in *MLQ*, *The Wordsworth Circle*, and *Studies in Romanticism*. She has recently finished a manuscript titled 'Standing Apart: The Untapped Potential of Enlightenment Feminism', and she is currently working on a manuscript titled 'Technologies of Emotion from Punchcutting to Photography'.

Suzie Asha Park is Assistant Professor of English at Eastern Illinois University. She completed her degree at the University of California at Berkeley, and has published work in *European Romantic Review* and *Eighteenth Century: Theory and Interpretation*. Her current book project theorizes 'compulsory narration' in the light of the rise of information culture in the eighteenth and nineteenth centuries.

Charlotte Sussman is Associate Professor of English at Duke University. She is the author of *Consuming Anxieties: Consumer Protest, Gender and British Slavery, 1713–1833* (2000) as well as articles on Samuel Richardson, Charlotte Smith, Walter Scott and Mary Shelley. She is currently working on a project entitled 'Imagining the Population: British Literature in an Age of Mass Migration'.

Helen Thompson is Associate Professor of English at Northwestern University. Her book *Ingenuous Subjection: Compliance and Power in the Eighteenth-Century Domestic Novel* was published by the University of Pennsylvania Press in 2005. She is presently working on a project about subject–object relations and empiricism.

Preface

Despite their diversity of approaches, the essays in this volume challenge us to rethink our ideas of the novel as a genre, and of the literary movement known as Romanticism. They propose that the Romantic-era novel was characterized by a fierce concern with the interpenetration among political structures, literary forms and genres, and individual subjectivity. Furthermore, they argue that the Romantic-era novel was engaged on the level of both form and content with re-imagining community, as the nature of sociality changed in a newly mobile, urban world. Such re-imagining came from a number of different perspectives, including the utopianism of the Jacobin novel, the nightmarish vision of gothic conspiracy, and the scepticism that questioned even 'enlightened' social structures; yet all these narrative strategies encouraged readers to see the world anew.

The last decade has produced ground-breaking new work on the Romantic-era novel. This scholarship has generally followed two different, though hardly mutually exclusive, trends: the recovery of little-read authors who were popular in their day, but who have slipped into obscurity in our own; and the recovery of long-ignored political and cultural contexts for Romantic-era fiction. The essays in the present collection contribute to both approaches. Some add to our understanding of authors such as Mary Hays, who, until recently, were unknown to most readers. More, however, follow the second path, and ask how previously unexplored contexts can help us recognize Romantic-era novels in new and fuller ways. For this reason, some of the authors discussed in this collection may seem familiar, at least at first glance. But the goal of these essays is to demonstrate that even writers such as Jane Austen or Walter Scott, whom we are accustomed to seeing isolated in a spotlight of celebrity, can look quite different when the busy stage of the Romantic-era novel is more fully illuminated behind them. Thus, the essays in this volume also re-examine the edifice of criticism that surrounds Romantic-era novels and their authors. Markman Ellis reminds us in his essay for this volume that there was significant tension during the Romantic era between the cognitive work of enlightenment, and the more theatrical trope of illumination. We are well aware of invoking that connotation here, and in order to demonstrate the impact of the 're-illumination' these essays carry out we briefly discuss below the critical history of some of the authors who show up more than once in our table of contents: Frances Burney, Jane Austen, and James Hogg.

Frances Burney has been so successfully recovered by a ground-breaking crew of feminist literary historians that her work, particularly her first novel, *Evelina*, is now required reading in many undergraduate literature classes.[1] A counterpoint to the mopey *Clarissa*, and a more broadly satiric precursor to *Pride and Prejudice*, *Evelina* has been welcomed for its strongly feminine, perhaps even feminist, perspective on the eighteenth century. It is hard to remember that for generations Burney, despite the popularity she enjoyed in her own lifetime, remained unread. Even today, her work beyond *Evelina* is still unfamiliar to most readers. The two essays on Burney included in this volume ask us to rethink not only our relatively new familiarity with this author, but also the place she has come to hold in histories of the British novel. Addressing Burney's less widely read later fiction, Helen Thompson focuses on *Cecilia, or Memoirs of an Heiress* (1782), and Suzie Asha Park looks at *The Wanderer; or Female Difficulties* (1814), a novel neglected in our own time and unpopular in Burney's own. Together, Thompson and Park bolster the argument for Burney's centrality to the novel of the period, but see that centrality as springing from her implicit critique of Enlightenment ideals, rather than from her progressive voice. They contest the way the 'Burney school' has been used to prop up certain critical narratives about the late-eighteenth-century novel. Thompson, in her essay on *Cecilia*, takes aim at the Habermasian idea that popular literacy in general, and the novel in particular, helped 'pacify' the public sphere by inculcating manners and managing class differences. Park, in "'All Agog to Find Her Out": Compulsory Narration in *The Wanderer*', evaluates more recent claims by feminist critics such as Deidre Lynch and Claudia Johnson that the novel, formally, cultivates an understanding of subjectivity as 'depth'. Park treats Burney's novel as a limit-case of the Romantic belief in freedom of expression. The essay argues that *The Wanderer* gives us a way to think about where and why the freedom to tell one's story seamlessly becomes the *obligation* to tell one's story. The sceptical Burney illuminated by Park and Thompson has important implications for our understanding of the Romantic-era novel, exemplifying its interrogation of Enlightenment cultural narratives and eighteenth-century generic conventions.

In scholarly discussions, coterie gatherings, or films, Jane Austen has become arguably the most central writer – whether poet or novelist – to contemporary popular and critical understandings of the Romantic era. Yet not very long ago, the notion of Austen as a representative for this period would have been considered ludicrous. Fortunately, however, the moment has passed when she could be considered dissociated from her time and labelled as wilfully ignorant of her era's major literary and political developments. Recently scholars have situated Austen not only as someone aware of her historical moment, but also as a writer who can and should be called a Romanticist, rather than, say, an Augustan.[2] But there is still work to be done to re-immerse Austen in the Romantic period. Because of this, we have included three new essays on this novelist in our volume, all of which reintegrate her as a Romantic-era novelist in relation to contemporaneous writing in other genres, particularly poetry.

We also want to focus on one of the most controversial topics in Austen criticism: the novelist's relationship to empire. In order to better highlight the polemical nature of this debate we have chosen two essays that address the same novel, *Mansfield Park*, but that offer opposing viewpoints on the subject. In 'Austen, Empire and Moral Virtue', Saree Makdisi argues that *Mansfield Park*'s treatment of slavery, far from exposing the novelist's subversive tendencies, instead fits seamlessly into Britain's turn-of-the-century plan to fortify and renew the empire. This new imperialism uses as its tool a subjectivity that depends upon a self-regulating 'morality', self-control and good behaviour. Paradoxically inherited from the radicals of the 1790s, this subjectivity becomes the most effective apparatus for maintaining social and economic order both at home and in the colonies. In contrast, Miranda J. Burgess suggests that through Fanny *Mansfield Park* lodges a complaint against empire and its injustices. In her essay, subjectivity, rather than fuelling empire, in fact enables one to remember and empathize with the historical vestiges of imperial conquest.

Burgess's argument, in addition to providing an alternative point of view to Makdisi's, also provides a bridge between his essay and Mary Jacobus's, which also explores Austen's engagement with Romantic poetry. Jacobus argues for a thoroughly Romantic Austen, one steeped in – not oblivious to or contemptuous of – the poetry of the eighteenth and early nineteenth centuries. Like Burgess, who contends that *Mansfield Park* makes a case that literary writing and reading preserve the memorials that allow a questioning of Britain's imperial history, Jacobus is concerned with the way that allusions to Romantic poetry provide a historical and national 'unconscious' by allowing a critique of imperialism to surface through quotation in ways that *Persuasion* has been said to ignore. Here, in our volume's third treatment of subjectivity in Austen, Jacobus examines how allusions in *Persuasion* create an 'interstitial' space 'where subjectivities blur and new meanings emerge'. In doing so, Jacobus shows compellingly how Austen's poetic allusions give us access to Anne Elliot's private thoughts but do not wrest the character or novel from an investigation of history itself.

One of the new contexts that has revealingly re-illuminated study of the Romantic-era novel has been a theorization of the relationships between England, Scotland, Ireland and Wales as 'internal colonialism'. These aesthetic and political interconnections generated a wave of imaginative energy that manifested itself in poetry, fiction and other forms of prose. As Katie Trumpener argues,

> English literature, so-called, constitutes itself in the late eighteenth and early nineteenth centuries through the systematic imitation, appropriation, and political neutralization of antiquarian and nationalist literary developments in Scotland, Ireland and Wales. The period's major new genres (ballad collection, sentimental and Gothic fiction, national tale, and historical novel), its central modes of historical scholarship and literary production, and even its notions of collective and individual memory have their origins in the cultural nationalism of the peripheries.[3]

Trumpener's work, along with that of others, has reopened interest in authors such as Sydney Owenson, Maria Edgeworth, and Charles Maturin. Another figure who has assumed new prominence in this recontextualization is the Scottish author James Hogg, whose best-known work, *The Private Memoirs and Confessions of a Justified Sinner*, is analysed by two of our contributors. Hogg was for a long time most notable as Walter Scott's wackier, more locally 'Scottish' contemporary. But the two essays included here show the depth of Hogg's engagement with the politico-ethical issues of the Romantic era, as well as the significance of his experiments with the generic conventions of the novel. Ina Ferris places *The Confessions* in relation to early-nineteenth-century debates about our access to and understanding of the past, by focusing on its engagement with the popular historical genre of 'secret histories'. She argues that Hogg's novel mounts a double-pronged critique of historical thought, attacking general history (as was conventional in secret histories) while also interrogating the motivating assumptions of secret history itself. On the one hand, as is often noted, the novel undermines the mediating concepts through which a modern mind makes sense of and surmounts the past to produce the present as the kind of synthesis exhibited most famously in the period by Scott's Waverley novels.[4] On the other – and this has been less often remarked – it places in question the antiquary's conviction that, once suspect mediating concepts have been ditched, the past can be authentically approached through the concreteness and intimacy of its fragmentary 'remains'. Continuing the project of situating Hogg on the larger stage of Romantic intellectual life, Ian Duncan argues in 'Sympathy, Physiognomy, and Scottish Romantic Fiction' that *Confessions of a Justified Sinner* puts significant moral pressure on the ambition to enter another person's thoughts and feelings, an ambition which was characteristic of the Enlightenment discourse of sentimentality. Hogg's novel mounts a powerful critique of the liberal politics of sympathy, revealing the will-to-power that charges its imaginary dynamic of sentimental exchange. The outsider's view of the cultural formations of the Scottish Enlightenment that the novel offers does not spare the dominant post-Enlightenment literary genre of the novel itself, and the modes of sympathetic identification activated in its reading. To understand the novelistic legacy of such ideas of sympathy, Duncan puts *The Confessions* in conversation with Walter Scott's *Redgauntlet*, published in Edinburgh in the same month as Hogg's novel. In the complexity of its representation, Scott's novel no less stringently than Hogg's recognizes the 'Romantic' crisis of an Enlightenment project: the emergence of modern uses of imagination and sentiment.

Although we have clustered together essays offering alternative readings of these individual novelists, we have otherwise arranged the essays in *Recognizing the Romantic Novel* in roughly chronological order. We believe such sequencing can tell us something about both the unity of the Romantic novel over this time-span, and the changes it underwent with each passing decade.

The deep, violent, political divisions of the 1790s have fostered a good deal of interest in the novels of those years. In this decade, the experimental drive and revisionary spirit of the Romantic-era novel are perhaps most clearly visible. Of the many aspects of generic exploration characterizing this decade, the essays included here focus on two: the British novel's growing, but not always comfortable, understanding of England's entanglement in the revolutionary upheavals of Europe; and its re-imagining of forms of community. More at ease with thinking of itself in the imperial and Atlantic context, England struggled to come to terms with

European revolutions in ways that shaped the seemingly disparate genres of the Godwinian 'philosophical romance' and the Radcliffian gothic. Laura Mandell's essay on the 'philosophical romances' of writers such as Mary Wollstonecraft and Mary Hays describes the fierce yearning, particularly among female intellectuals, for a 'revolution in female manners', in Wollstonecraft's phrase,[5] to accompany the political revolution occurring in France; such a revolution, Mandell demonstrates, would also restructure the novel as a genre. Utopian images of communities bound by sympathy and sincerity rather than tradition or blood ties also appear in Charlotte Smith's novel *The Banished Man*, discussed in the volume's final essay. Markman Ellis's essay on the gothic novels of the 1790s examines the conservative flip-side of this image, in which social relationships have already been remade by a secret conspiracy of 'illuminati', producing not a utopia, but a nightmarish vision of social mystification and coercion. Nor can these concerns be confined to the 1790s, as Mandell shows by tracing experimentation with the marriage plot from Mary Wollstonecraft to her daughter Mary Shelley and beyond.

During the Romantic era, historical context affected not only the shaping of characters in novels, but the very shaping of novels themselves. The facts of the French Revolution and the British government's subsequent censorship of authors distinguish the Romantic period from the eras preceding and following it not only because of the sheer drama of events, but also because of the powerful impact they had on print culture. This is perhaps most apparent in the post-Revolution decades: the later 1790s and the first decade of the nineteenth century. Anxious about the spread of revolutionary fervour, the government placed novels among the print media that might spread political radicalism. 'Terror was the order of the day; and it was feared that even the humble novelist might be shown to be constructively a traitor', Godwin states in the preface to *Caleb Williams*.[6] Amanda Gilroy and Wil Verhoeven point out how seriously the Jacobin novel was censured – it 'had jumped the genre boundary of "polite entertainment" and now it had to be disciplined and brought back in line, along with other types of inflaming fiction, such as the sentimental and the gothic novel'.[7] As William St Clair explains in *The Reading Nation*, the Seditious Societies Act of 1799, introduced at the height of the anti-Jacobin scare, and reasserted in 1811, was designed to prevent the circulation of 'cheap publications adapted to influence and pervert the public mind'.[8]

Thus, before such laws were in effect, we witness the thrilling release of revolutionary sympathies in Jacobin novels such as Charlotte Smith's

Desmond, wherein the freedom to critique the British state functions like an aphrodisiac upon the characters, and perhaps the readers as well. After their enactment, however, the sedition laws in their own ways roused indignation or encouraged productivity – whether in revolt against or in political compliance with them – while also creating a particular stylistic phenomenon: the novel as cipher. The difference between *Desmond* (1792) and Smith's later novel *The Old Manor House* (1794) is instructive: the later novel, though only two years later, was brought into a world made completely different by the violence of the Terror.[9] Consequently, it uses as its setting the American, not the French Revolution, a physical and temporal placement that, as Jacqueline Labbe points out, allowed Smith 'to factor in a liberal politics without being overtly political and to devise a narrative strategy [...] that permitted liberal critiques of conservative government while also shielding, to a certain extent, their applicability to the 1790s'.[10] Significantly, then, the radical novel was not eradicated, though it sometimes went 'underground' with radical ideas embedded in the genre.

Following Marilyn Butler, critics have often felt compelled to sort the novels of this era into Jacobin and anti-Jacobin camps. Yet the politics of the Romantic-era novel during these decades finally cannot be reduced to the formula of Jacobin vs. anti-Jacobin, or radical vs. conservative. To do so is to fall into the kind of ideological trap that the revolution itself thrust upon British citizens. In fact, multiple novels present a vertiginous co-mingling of conservative and more radical points of view. In his essay for this volume, for instance, Saree Makdisi argues that in certain issues during this period – such as slavery and women's education – a 'political and intellectual convergence occurs in which it is virtually impossible to distinguish putatively conservative from would-be radical voices'. One striking example of this intermixture of viewpoints occurs in Elizabeth Hamilton's *Translations of the Letters of a Hindoo Rajah* (1796), which can appear conservative at one moment – as in its treatment of female education – and radical the next – as in its pro-Indian stance.[11] A figure such as Edgeworth provides a challenging case for such coalescence, since it is unclear whether she combines competing political perspectives to harbour more fully radical opinions or whether the political indeterminacy we find in her ambiguous Irish allegories results instead from what W. J. McCormack and Kim Walker have termed her 'Kierkegaardian reluctance', 'prolific in unresolved balances, fragmentary or multiplied emblems'.[12] It seems more precise to say, with Robert Miles, that what 'underwrites the difference of the Romantic novel' – and what makes its politics somewhat jarring for us to read – 'is the historical inception of an awareness of ideology as ideology, an awareness the novel shares with some of the poetry of the Romantic era'.[13]

Yet the beginning of the nineteenth century was also an era of enormous changes in the literary field. This is the moment when more novels than poetry began to be published, as Garside, Raven and Schowerling demonstrate in their magisterial work on the subject.[14] In his essay for this volume, Michael Gamer examines how the great collectors of the late eighteenth and early nineteenth centuries shaped literary history by championing the novel. His findings suggest that the Romantic era might also be called an 'Age of Canonization', as it organized the legacy of the eighteenth-century novel. In particular, Anna Barbauld, in shaking up what had become a predictable canon by adding women novelists to her edition of *The British Novelists* (1810) and offering a canon (in Michael Gamer's words) 'epistolary in nature and dissenting in flavour', alters how we look at the novel from 1810 on. Her introductory essay is predicated on a flexible sense of what constitutes a novel, so much so that '"fictitious narrative", "romance", and "novel" [can] function', as Gamer points out, 'as interchangeable yet historically specific terms. Thus, the universal appeal of 'fictitious narrative' transcends divisions of class, gender, nationality, and historical period even as its various forms are expressive of specific peoples and cultural moments'.

The literary landscape changed again after the Battle of Waterloo in 1814, and several of the essays in this volume make a case for our careful reconsideration of this era, particularly, perhaps, the long neglected 1820s, a point when fiction became 'the dominant imaginative literary genre', and sales in poetry declined.[15] 'What a state England is in!' Shelley wrote to Leigh Hunt in 1819.[16] Napoleon's defeat, as Jeffrey Cox points out, resolved nothing, and left the country in political and economic shambles: intellectuals, poets, politicians, and others gathered around Leigh Hunt to 'contribute to the struggle to change their society through cultural acts [...] believ[ing] not only that politics shape poetics but that poetry can alter ideology'.[17] If the novels of the 1790s looked outward to negotiate England's relationship to revolutionary Europe, the novelists of the post-Napoleonic era turned inward, as did the Hunt Circle, to re-examine British national identity, only to re-encounter strangeness and difference there. As Ina Ferris writes in her essay for this volume, 'apparently esoteric matters of scholarship and antiquarianism took on a new charge and

assumed a public profile in post-Waterloo Britain. [...] [The] period after
Waterloo witnessed an inward turn that moved into the foreground
internal tensions within the (less than) United Kingdom. It is no accident
that Irish and Scottish novels flourished in these years nor that what they
tended to make political was the question of historiography itself'. Thus
the gothic novel of the 1820s differs from the gothic novel of the 1790s in
locating the supernatural on native soil, even as it also evidences generic
continuity in its fascination with the tension between secrecy and
illumination. The problem of historiography and antiquarianism also
shows up in Miranda Burgess's discussion of the importance of debates
over geographical knowledge to *Mansfield Park*. Indeed, the two essays
uncover an unexpected affinity between Hogg's macabre gothic and
Austen's delicate moral drama in the tension they illustrate between the
compelling fragments and remains of archives and the grand narratives of
national history.

Perhaps because its hyper-awareness of ideology often included a
responsiveness to the ideological ramifications of artistic form, the
Romantic novel has been particularly vulnerable to debates about aesthetic
value. As several essays in this volume show, these debates are always
politically charged. Laura Mandell, for example, reminds us that the story
of the incompatibility of good art with good politics is common, beginning
with attacks on socialist realism up to more recent attacks on aesthetic
ideology. Such evaluations have persistently linked aesthetic quality and
morality. We are familiar with the Romantic era's concerns about the
novel's deleterious effects, especially on women, but we should remember
that such concerns led not only to a condemnation of the genre but also
to defences of it: for example, as Michael Gamer explains, the select
collections of novels from James Harrison's *The Novelist's Magazine* (1779–
88) to Barbauld's *The British Novelists* (1810) emphasized the novel's
propriety, virtue, morality, and didacticism, as well as the pleasure it gave.
Barbauld finds that the novel is 'an epic in prose', and her focus on
nationalism links the novel to the glory of Britain.[18]

The collection begins with our own essay on 'The Ethical Experiments
of the Romantic Novel' – an attempt to wrestle with some of the questions
about genre and periodization opened up by the preceding essays. Critics
have often seen the novel as fracturing into a number of sub-genres during
the Romantic era – gothic, historical novel, national tale, Jacobin novel,
etc. Building on the essays in this volume, however, we hope to show that
the Romantic-era novel can be understood as a field, not simply a

heterogeneous mass of fictional forms. We point out the concerns that Romantic fiction shared with other writing of the era, especially poetry. Furthermore, we propose that the varieties of generic experimentation exhibited by the Romantic novel share some common aims and strategies, particularly in their interrogation of the generic conventions that govern representations of 'real life'. Supplementing these arguments are our brief analyses of novels by Charlotte Smith and Maria Edgeworth. We hope the essays in this volume will illuminate not simply the complexity and vitality of the Romantic novel, but also its ambitious quest for literary and cultural strategies that would remake 'things as they are'.

Notes

1 See, for example, these important books from the 'first wave' of Burney scholarship: Kristina Straub, *Divided Fictions: Fanny Burney and Feminine Strategy* (Lexington: University of Kentucky Press, 1987); Margaret Doody, *Frances Burney: The Life in the Works* (Newark, NJ: Rutgers University Press, 1988); Julia Epstein, *The Iron Pen: Frances Burney and the Politics of Women's Writing* (Madison: University of Wisconsin Press, 1989).

2 See, for example, Claudia Johnson, *Jane Austen: Women, Politics, and the Novel* (Chicago: University of Chicago Press, 1988); Deidre Shauna Lynch, *The Economy of Character: Novels, Market Culture, and the Business of Inner Meaning* (Chicago: University of Chicago Press, 1998) and Deidre Lynch, ed., *Janeites: Austen's Disciples and Devotees* (Princeton: Princeton University Press, 2000); Clifford Siskin, *The Work of Writing: Literature and Social Change In Britain 1700–1830* (Baltimore: Johns Hopkins University Press, 1998); Clara Tuite, *Romantic Austen: Sexual Politics and the Literary Canon* (Cambridge: Cambridge University Press, 2002); William H. Galperin, *The Historical Austen* (Philadelphia: University of Pennsylvania Press, 2003); William Deresiewicz, *Jane Austen and the Romantic Poets* (New York: Columbia University Press, 2004.

3 Katie Trumpener, *Bardic Nationalism* (Princeton: Princeton University Press, 1997), p. xi.

4 For a compelling recent reading along these lines, see Ian Duncan's 'Authenticity Effects: The Work of Fiction in Romantic Scotland', *South Atlantic Quarterly* 102.1 (2003), pp. 93–116.

5 *A Vindication of the Rights of Woman*, ed. Anne Mellor and Noelle Chao (New York: Longman, 2007), p. 65.

6 William Godwin, *Caleb Williams* (Peterborough, Ontario: Broadview Press, 2000), p. 56.

7 Amanda Gilroy and Wil Verhoeven, Introduction to 'The Romantic-Era Novel: A Special Issue', *Novel: A Forum on Fiction* 34.2 (Spring 2001), p. 153.

8 William St Clair, *The Reading Nation in the Romantic Period* (Cambridge: Cambridge University Presss, 2004), p. 311. Here St Clair is citing William B. Todd and Ann

Bowden, *Tauchnitz International, Editions in English 1841–1955: A Bibliographical History* (Bibliographical Society of America, 1988).

9 Charlotte Smith, *Desmond*, ed. Antje Blank and Janet Todd (Peterborough, Ontario: Broadview Press, 2001) and Charlotte Smith, *The Old Manor House*, ed. Jacqueline M. Labbe (Peterborough, Ontario: Broadview Press, 2002).

10 Jacqueline M. Labbe, Introduction to Smith, *The Old Manor House*, pp. 13, 27.

11 Elizabeth Hamilton, *Translations of the Letters of a Hindoo Rajah*, ed. Pamela Perkins and Shannon Russell (Peterborough, Ontario: Broadview Press, 1999).

12 W. J. McCormack and Kim Walker, Introduction, in *The Absentee*, ed. W. J. McCormack and Kim Walker (Oxford: Oxford University Press, 1988, 2001), p. (xxxviii).

13 Robert Miles, 'What is a Romantic Novel?', in Amanda Gilroy and Wil Verhoeven, eds., 'The Romantic-Era Novel: A Special Issue', *Novel: A Forum on Fiction* 34.2 (Spring 2001), p.186.

14 *The English Novel 1770–1829: A Bibliographical Survey of Prose Fiction Published in the British Isles*, 2 vols.; general eds. Peter Garside, James Raven, and Rainer Schöwerling, Vol. I: 1770–1799, ed. James Raven and Antonia Forster, and Vol. II: 1800–1829, ed. Peter Garside and Rainer Schöwerling (Oxford: Oxford University Press, 2000).

15 Peter Garside, 'The English Novel in the Romantic Era: Consolidation and Dispersal', in *The English Novel 1770–1829*, p. 48.

16 Percy Shelley to Leigh Hunt, 23 December 1819, in *Letters*, ed. Frederick L. Jones, 2 vols. (Oxford: Clarenden Press, 1964), Vol. 2, pp. 166–67. Quoted in James Chandler, *England in 1819: The Politics of Literary Culture and the Case of Romantic Historicism* (Chicago: University of Chicago Press, 1998), p. 85.

17 Jeffrey N. Cox, *Poetry and Politics in the Cockney School: Keats, Shelley, Hunt and their Circle* (Cambridge: Cambridge University Press, 1998), pp. 55, 61.

18 Anna Letitia Barbauld, 'On the Origin and Progress of Novel-Writing', in Barbauld, ed., *The British Novelists* (London, 1810), Vol. 1, p. 3.

CHAPTER ONE

'Launched upon the Sea of Moral and Political Inquiry': The Ethical Experiments of the Romantic Novel

JILLIAN HEYDT-STEVENSON
AND CHARLOTTE SUSSMAN

Although it is less often remarked upon than the other revolutions of the Romantic era, an epoch-making event occurred in the British literary field at the end of the eighteenth century and the beginning of the nineteenth: the novel quantifiably became the dominant literary genre of the day. Peter Garside demonstrates that in the first three decades of the nineteenth century 'out-put of fiction almost certainly overtook that of poetry, and the genre eventually gained new respectability',[1] triumphantly surpassing others. Garside, James Raven, and Rainer Schowerling have recorded entries for 1106 fiction titles between 1780 and 1799 and entries for 2256 fiction titles first published in Britain in the thirty years between 1800 and 1829.[2] Thus, as Clifford Siskin argues, the reasons for critics' ignorance or rejection of the Romantic novel do not arise from

> an inability to count, or a failure to connect genre to history, but rather [a failure to recognize] the connections that already do count. Our associations are firmly fixed: once we rise novelistically past Fielding, Richardson and Sterne, and the 1780s and 1790s come into view, critical attention shifts to the supposedly lyrical advent of Romanticism. But those were precisely the decades when the novel took off.[3]

And yet rather than the linear trajectory we have been schooled to expect by the arrow-like image of 'the rise of the novel', the novel during the Romantic-era 'took off' in all directions. It seemed to lose the coherence of a single genre, and to explode into a multiplicity of sub-genres: the gothic, the historical novel, the national tale, the oriental tale, the radical or 'Jacobin' novel, and the novel of manners, to name only some of the most studied. All of these subgenres have proved interesting in their own right, yet critics, both at the time and in our own day, have tended to view this passion for experimentation much as Pope imagined Colley Cibber's study in *The Dunciad* – as piled masses of failed literary forms: 'Nonsense precipitate, like running Lead, / That slip'd thro' Cracks and Zig-zags of the Head'.[4] Robert Kiely, for example, begins *The Romantic Novel in England* (1972) by announcing that during this period, 'some odd things happened to the English novel': it 'became, in some hands, wild and flamboyant, grotesque and luxuriously artificial, by turns. Some of the experiments were silly and artless, attempts to cater to a popular taste for the sensational', though he concedes that 'others [...] were deeply serious efforts to stretch or break through old conventions'.[5] As Amanda Gilroy and Wil Verhoeven say in their introduction to a special issue of *Novel*, 'The Romantic-era novel, rather than constituting the first great age of the popular novel in English, which it was, came to be seen as "problematic": post-Richardson and pre-Dickens, but otherwise a taxonomic challenge'.[6] This sense that the Romantic novel needs a taxonomist rather than a literary critic has made it particularly vulnerable to debates about what constitutes a good novel in both its own day and ours – debates in which the word 'good' refers to both aesthetic and moral success.

Thus at precisely the moment when the novel became the dominant literary genre, it also appeared to fracture into a multitude of sub-genres – fracture to such a degree that no one was quite sure what a novel was. It was recognizable – everyone knew it was not a poem or an essay – but it seemed too unstable to be denominated. Both the popularity and the variety of the Romantic novel have tended to flummox critics – producing embarrassment,[7] denigration, or simply silence. As Claudia Johnson has recently observed, when 'Jane Austen considered "the novel" as it looked to her at the end of the eighteenth and the outset of the nineteenth century, she saw the enabling plenitude of late-century writers such as Edgeworth, Burney and Radcliffe'. '[M]odern historians of the novel', however, 'see earlier "masters" like Richardson and Fielding, then see either a plethora of trash as Watt did, or (is this better or worse?) nothing in particular, as McKeon did'.[8] This vision of the Romantic-era novel as a 'plethora of trash' has tended to distract scholars – leading them down the paths of sub-generic definition and into the vexed project of trying to place novels into discrete political camps.

While not discounting such studies, many of which are superb, we would like to suggest a two-pronged approach that allows us to understand the Romantic novel as a field, not simply a heterogeneous mass of fictional forms. First, in order to further the integration of the novel into studies of the period, from which it has traditionally been excluded, we would like to point out the concerns that Romantic fiction shared with other writing of the era, especially poetry. Second, we would like to propose that the varieties of generic experimentation in Romantic novels share some common aims and strategies, particularly in their interrogation of the generic conventions that govern representations of 'real life'. We have dubbed such experimentation 'ethical' in order to emphasize the way that Romantic-era novelists saw revolutions in generic form not only as philosophical or aesthetic explorations, but also as a medium for re-thinking human action and human community. Recognizing such commonalities allows us to put different sub-genres of fiction into productive conversation with each other, and to understand the way they all critique and revise previous traditions.

The Case for *Romantic* Fiction

The Romantic period has been stubbornly defined almost wholly in terms of the poetry it produced, and until fairly recently in terms of six poets only. Under that rubric, the Romantic novel could not be considered as 'Romantic' at all. Early-nineteenth-century critics contributed to this exclusion of the novel from the 'Spirit of the Age' – Hazlitt, for example, condemned the genre for its focus on women and domesticity; for him, as Suzie Asha Park makes clear in her chapter in this volume, the genre is inferior to poetry since 'it fails to become substantial material for romantic contemplation – "the internal conception and contemplation of the possible workings of the human mind"'. Hazlitt, of course, was wrong, and several of the essays in this volume show how close were the concerns of poetry and prose during this era.

This commonality appears not only at the thematic level, but also in the remarkable interpenetration of forms visible in so many Romantic-era novels, a broad-ranging interdisciplinarity that conflates fiction and history, that includes ekphrasis, that demonstrates the mutual influence between the novel and the theatre, and that meshes elements from high and low culture in ways that we have traditionally been expected to ignore. The very phenomenon of incorporating poetry into novels reveals a certain redefinition of prose, one that includes texts within texts and requires a reader to think of novels and poems as genres that overlap and that are to be embraced as equals. The practice of beginning each chapter with a poetic epigraph runs from Radcliffe to Scott, and the use of embedded poetic allusions to express a character's innermost thoughts runs from Mary Wollstonecraft to Mary Shelley.[9] A single page of Charles Maturin's *Melmoth the Wanderer* (1820), for example, can hold up to five allusions to other works.[10] We might expect the elegantly spare prose of an author such as Austen to eschew these strategies, but as Mary Jacobus's essay for this volume demonstrates, she too relies on the imbrication of literature and consciousness. Recently, critics have begun to examine the allusiveness that stretches across Romantic poetry and prose, seeing it as key to the exploration of a new kind of consciousness.[11] Clearly, both poets and novelists were sensitive to their placement in that stream of literary tradition we call print culture, and one way they signalled their awareness was by including poetry in prose texts. As Katie Trumpener observes in *Bardic Nationalism* (1997), 'the concentration of sheer literariness' in such works 'results not only in many passages of great rhetorical intensity, but in a powerful evocation of the need for tradition'; it also functions, we would add, as an index of the novelists' anxiety about their place in that tradition.[12]

Along with this formal commonality, we see the themes traditionally associated with Romantic poetry also characterizing Romantic fiction: images of the sublime; the capacity for and fall from transcendence; an emphasis on the natural world as a critical space for revelation, danger, and salvation; acute sensitivity to ties between the body and mental states; liminal and subliminal spaces for exploration of sexuality; and of course the inwardness that Hazlitt lauds. What is unique, but not less 'Romantic', is the writers' use of these topics, supposedly reserved for the esteemed genres of epic or lyric, to conceptualize something domestic, such as whom one marries, rather than how one philosophizes about the purpose and form of poetry. The prevalent Romantic theme of loss, for example, those 'everlasting longings for the lost',[13] permeates prose as much as Romantic poetry. Whether we are discussing antiquarianism or Fanny Price's rumination on the ravishing and efflorescing qualities of time, as Miranda Burgess does in this volume, a focus on the past saturates writing of the period. Thus, we can connect the kind of contemplation of bygone days seen in Wordsworth's survey of the ruins of Tintern Abbey and Shelley's rumination on Ozymandias with the novelistic fascination with archivalism. In this volume, Ina Ferris and Markman Ellis argue that early gothic fiction 'typically framed its texts through a trope of scholarly retrieval, presenting itself as the rediscovery, translation, transcription, or piecing together of obscure documents from the past'.[14] The project of making the past speak was imagined as the work not only of the lyric poet and the gothic writer, but also as that of the emergent figure of the historical novelist, who was, in Scott's words, 'like Lucan's witch, at liberty to walk over the recent field of battle, and select for the subject of resuscitation by his sorceries, a body whose limbs had recently quivered with existence, and whose throat had but just uttered the last note of agony'.[15] In these practices, a concern with the affective power of the past intersects with what Georg Lukacs called the rise of historical consciousness in the novel.

At the same time as it engaged with historical difference, the novel, like the other literature of its day, grappled with Britain's immersion in the complex dynamics of a global empire. The Romantic period spans the years between the collapse of Britain's 'first empire' in the Americas after the American War of Independence and the consolidation of its 'second empire' in India, Africa and Australia. At the forefront of the ethical and political concerns of the day was the problem of slavery in Britain's Caribbean colonies. While fiction may not contain anything as overt and public as the debate over slavery and the slave trade carried out in poetry by Hannah More, Anna Barbauld and others, slavery and plantation life make innumerable oblique appearances in the Romantic novel – from Edgeworth's *Belinda* to Austen's *Mansfield Park* (as well as occasional overt appearances, as in William Earle's *Obi; Or the History of Three-Fingered Jack*). How to interpret the 'off-stage' presence of Antigua in Austen's novel has provoked much recent critical discussion – a debate to which Burgess and Makdisi contribute here. Closer to home, the vexed colonial relationships between England, Scotland, Ireland, and Wales generated a wave of imaginative energy that manifested itself in poetry, fiction and other forms of prose. Katie Trumpener has made a compelling case for the centrality of these aesthetic and political interconnections and her work, along with that of others, has reopened interest in authors such as Owenson, Edgeworth and Maturin, which has done much to reinvigorate the study of the Romantic novel.

Recent criticism has documented the ways in which the Near and Far East – territories at that point outside British colonial control – also excited the Romantic imagination. William Beckford's *Vathek* (1786), for example, continues the eighteenth-century tradition of the oriental tale. Yet, whereas earlier tales, in the manner of *Gulliver's Travels* or *Rasselas*, had used the imaginary 'East' as a place to site allegorical critiques of England, *Vathek* inaugurates an interest, on one hand, in the precise details of 'oriental' life and history, and, on the other, in the 'East' as a place of fantasy and experimentation (perhaps particularly sexual experimentation). The novel influenced the following generation of writers, especially Byron. He, like others, was struck by Beckford's commitment to representing life in the Near East not just in the tale's content, but also by adopting an 'oriental' style. And indeed, the generic possibilities of 'oriental' narratives like *A Thousand and One Nights* – their intricate framing, their magical happenings, their freedom from 'realist' time schemes, and their devaluation of character in favor of adventure – excited many Romantic writers of both poetry and prose; it is hard to find a Romantic-era novel that does not allude to some oriental tale. Yet the East, especially India, was also very much a real place during the Romantic period, and the subject of many more topical narrative mappings, including Owenson's *The Missionary* and Scott's *Guy Mannering*. Thus, the East was viewed with a kind of double vision: it provided an escape into an imaginary world of experimentation, even as the 'real' Orient was ever more mapped, colonized, and put under academic scrutiny.

At the same time that the novel turned outward to contemplate the sweep of history and geography, it also, like poetry, turned inward to interrogate the nature of selfhood. Even as Wordsworth traces the development of the self in *The Prelude*, and Keats and Shelley investigate the minute workings of the psyche in their odes, the Romantic novel, too, probes the nature of interiority. While one might argue that novels have always been concerned with representing individual interiority, the Romantic-era novel explores questions of selfhood particular to the age. For example, in a departure from the eighteenth-century novel, it is concerned not only with the effect of family and class on personality, but also with the impact of political systems on individual development. Godwin, for example, announces in the preface to *Caleb Williams* that he aims to 'comprehend, as far as the progressive nature of a single story would allow, a general review of the modes of domestic and unrecorded despotism by which man becomes the destroyer of man'.[16] This interest in the relationship between the individual psyche and its social milieu extended to an impassioned exploration of the impact of particular historical settings upon character. As Scott famously explains in *Waverley*, one's

capacity for both thought and action is dependent upon historical circumstances: Fergus McIvor 'possessed a character of uncommon acuteness,
fire and ambition, which, as he became acquainted with the state of the
country, gradually assumed a mixed and peculiar tone, that could only have
been acquired Sixty Years since'.[17] In its attribution of personality-shaping
agency to historical epoch, fiction may go beyond poetry to explore the
interface between individual interiority and the exterior world.

The Case for Romantic *Fiction*

In *Matilda*, Mary Shelley's dark tale of incestuous love, Matilda's father,
returning from a long journey after his wife's death to find a daughter who
'seemed to belong to a higher order of beings' – only then to fall in love
with her – describes himself as 'somewhat like one of the seven sleepers,
or like Nourjahad, in that sweet imitation of an eastern tale'.[18] It is telling,
yet also typical of characters in Romantic-era novels, that Matilda's father
feels that his life has moved out of the range, even out of the genre, of the
realist novel, and can only be understood through different generic
conventions – here, those of myth, or of the oriental tale. For many critics,
this has been the hallmark of Romantic fiction: its seeming wanton
destruction of the successful narrative paradigms put in place by the eighteenth-century novel. Kiely, for instance, argues that 'although romantic
novels do have structural patterns, character types, and situations in
common, their primary tendency is to destroy (or, at the very least, under-
mine) particular narrative conventions. Romantic novels thrive like
parasites on structures whose ruin is the source of their life'. The result, he
says dramatically, is 'a kind of literary sadism'.[19] Miles reiterates that the
'salient feature of the Romantic novel appears to be its failure to conform
to and remain within accustomed boundaries'.[20]

   And all agree that the primary narrative conventions that the Romantic
novel breaks down – or should we say breaks free of? – are those of
'realism'. Since Ian Watt's masterful study, *The Rise of the Novel* (1957), the
British novel has been defined in terms of its realism and topicality. Along
with literary historians, social theorists such as Benedict Anderson and
Jürgen Habermas have celebrated those qualities, and linked them to the
genre's ability to reflect a particular socio-cultural situation back to its
readers, allowing them to unite into 'imagined communities' (to use
Anderson's phrase).[21] For Habermas, 'the psychological novel', exempli-

fied by *Pamela* (1740), 'fashioned for the first time the kind of realism that allowed anyone to enter into the literary action as a substitute for his own':

> On the one hand, the empathetic reader repeated within himself the private relationships displayed before him in literature.[…] On the other hand, from the outset the familiarity (*Intimität*) whose vehicle was the written word, the subjectivity that had become fit to print, had in fact become the literature appealing to a wide public of readers.[22]

Thus, in most socio-historical studies of the novel, the genre's success is tied to its 'realism' – the formal qualities that allow it to reflect its own milieu accurately back to hungry readers. Twentieth-century critics come by such criteria honestly: topicality was the quality most often used to hierarchize narrative during the Romantic period as well. Yet more recent critics, pre-eminently Anderson, often take the privileging of realism one step further, linking it to the contemporaneous rise of the nation state. Deidre Lynch and William Warner, for example, referring to Anderson in *Cultural Institutions of the Novel*, argue that the genre's 'wide popularity has allowed [it] to assume a crucial role in the constitution of the nation as an imagined community'.[23] The tendency among literary historians to join 'nation' and 'novel' is so widespread that one critic, Srinivas Aravamudan, has coined the term 'national realism' for the resulting generic definition.[24] Given its frequent divergence from this paradigm, it is not surprising that the Romantic-era novel has fallen outside the mainstream of novel studies.

Nor is it surprising that more subtle kinds of experimentation have been missed. Michael Gamer, for example, has shown how Edgeworth invented and experimented with the 'Romance of Real Life', a merging of romance (typically seen as an anti-realist mode) with the gritty and splendid minutiae of quotidian existence.[25] One of the primary generic innovations of the Romantic novel was this overlapping of fantasy and realism, an especially vexed and complicated issue during this era because it creates a 'mixed' genre that instigated debate (both in its own time and in our own) about whether such works are aesthetically successful. Maria Edgeworth's novels have been at the forefront of this discussion. Mitzi Myers, commenting on this phenomenon, says that Edgeworth created 'stories which refuse to behave like well-bred realistic and rational fictions ought to'.[26] In other words, when Romantic-era novelists gesture realistically to the physical and historical world outside the text, they free themselves from the confinement of any particular set of literary protocols. Consequently, part of the Romantic novel's realism lies, paradoxically, in its ability to move beyond the conventions of realism set by its eighteenth-century counterpart, and thus present 'realities' – say, political situations, scientific advances, extreme states – not available in other instances of this genre.[27] In doing so, Romantic authors may have taken their cue from the already flexible genre of the novel, but their innovations certainly helped make realism the flexible genre that it is.

Thus the Romantic-era novel often departs from both topicality and conventional realism in surprising and innovative ways: the foreign, often historically distant, castles of the gothic, with their supernatural events (whether explained or not); the chronologically and geographically 'exotic' settings of the historical novel, the national tale and the oriental tale; and the nascent science fiction of Shelley's *Frankenstein* and *The Last Man*, to name just a few. In many more Romantic-era novels – including *Caleb Williams, Maria,* and *Confessions of a Justified Sinner* – the struggle over defining 'reality' (what Godwin called 'things as they are' in the subtitle to *Caleb Williams*) takes centre stage. Indeed, many have read these novels as explorations of madness, another aspect of the 'unreal'.

What is at stake in all this experimentation? The essays included in this volume suggest a number of compelling answers to this question. In this introductory essay, we would also like to propose two ideas. First, what unites Romantic-era fiction is not a fracturing of the genre into multiple, often failed, forms, but instead a drive to investigate the relationship between the 'real' and the 'topical'. In this, again, the fiction resembles the imaginative poetry of the age. It is true that some of the major novelists of the day, including Austen and sometimes Edgeworth (for example, in a novel such as *Belinda*), seem to perfect a realist style. But unlike Miles, who sees such novelists as the forces who destroyed the possibility of the Romantic novel, or 'philosophical romance',[28] we hope that reinserting them back into the milieu of experimentation from which they emerged will highlight both their formal innovations and their ideological engagement. Second, in the heterogeneity of its approaches to the 'real', the Romantic-era novel forces us to understand different kinds of communal imagining. This was an age when the constitution of the nation was being thoroughly *re*-imagined – indeed revolutionized – and consequently the kinds of 'imagined community' proffered by Romantic-era fiction vary widely.

We can see the reverberations of this re-imagining in the Romantic treatment of that microcosmic community of marriage. In *Desire and Domestic Fiction: A Political History of the Novel* (1987), Nancy Armstrong charts the cultural efficacy of the marriage plot in novels from Samuel Richardson to

Charlotte Brontë. Influentially, Armstrong puts 'domestic fiction' – fiction that focuses on achieved female happiness (and the capacity of women to make others happy) – at the centre of histories of the novel:

> The good marriage concluding fiction of this kind, where characters achieve prosperity without compromising their domestic virtue, could be used to resolve another order of conflict, the conflict between an agrarian gentry and urban industrialists, for one, or between labour and capital, for another. By enclosing such conflict within a domestic sphere, certain novels demonstrated that despite the vast inequities of the age virtually anyone could find gratification within this private framework.[29]

Thus Armstrong proposes that novels use the union between man and woman to 'solve' – or at least contain – the socio-cultural instabilities that roiled eighteenth- and nineteenth-century England. Yet this focus on exposing the ideological ramifications of the 'good marriage', fruitful as it has been, has also tended to push the Romantic-era novel to the margins of novel studies. Of course, some novels of this era do offer marriages that affirm a utopian ideal of personal and political fulfilment – such as the unions of Ivanhoe and Rowena and Emma and Knightley. Yet, in many others, the marriage plot is another generic characteristic of 'the novel' that comes in for blistering criticism during this period. Overall, the novels of this time boast many more unhappy and/or unfruitful marriages than were ever seen in the eighteenth-century novel, and often eschew the convention of a concluding marriage altogether. As Laura Mandell shows in this volume, critics and readers alike have often assumed that a novel that does not end in marriage cannot be a 'good' novel. But if the novel is understood only as succeeding when it ends 'happily' (that is, by supporting bourgeois culture) how do we assess those, like Mary Hays's *Memoirs of Emma Courtney*, that end, to use the word Mandell employs, in a 'queer' way – that is, in a way that encompasses a radical rethinking of love and intimacy?

Even more radically, the Romantic novel often ignores the plotting of heterosexual union altogether, and turns its attention to alternative social bonds, particularly to the vagaries of fraternity and sorority. The most iconic novels of the era – including *Caleb Williams* and *Frankenstein* – unroll a dystopian plot of violent doubling and fraternal or filial pursuit. In this category of stories that revolve around the uneasy bonds between siblings or friends of the same sex, we might place some of Austen's novels, highlighting the fraught sisterhood of *Sense and Sensibility*, and the tangled, even erotic, ties of female friendship in *Emma*. In his essay for this volume, Ian

Duncan demonstrates that attention to such plotlines reveals a striking similarity between novels as different as *Confessions of a Justified Sinner* and *Redgauntlet*. Just as the surrounding culture explored new kinds of social organization, Duncan argues, these novels examine the 'queerness' of brotherhood and reveal the way that 'ideology, or the imaginary relation of belief, constitutes the new bond'. This interest in non-conjugal social bonds cuts across many of the 'sub-genres' of Romantic fiction – from the Jacobin novel to the gothic to the 'realism' of Austen and Scott. In highlighting this commonality we draw attention to the way the Romantic novel can help us expand our generic definitions.

Along with challenging the structure of the marriage plot, the Romantic-era novel questions the structure and value of another conventional narrative form: the bildungsroman, or the story of individual growth and progress. The 'rise of the novel' has always been tied firmly to the 'rise of the individual'. Watt again:

> The novel's serious concern with the daily lives of ordinary people [i.e., its 'formal realism'] seems to depend upon two important general conditions: the society must value every individual highly enough to consider him the proper subject of its serious literature; and there must be enough variety of belief and action among ordinary people for a detailed account of them to be of interest to other ordinary people, the readers of novels.[30]

And indeed, the value of such narratives, what Michael McKeon designates 'histories of the individual',[31] is everywhere proclaimed in canonical eighteenth-century novels. *Pamela*, for instance, concludes with a long list of the 'many applications, of its most material Incidents, to the Minds of the Youth of both Sexes'. Most eighteenth-century novels, like *Pamela*, follow a narrative of progress: from rags to riches; from captivity to freedom; from illegitimacy to legitimacy; from wandering to homecoming. And even those that end unhappily, like *Clarissa*, do not question the value of the story being told, or their own capacity to transmit it. To generalize, for the eighteenth-century novel, stories of individual lives have a pedagogical value for their readers, and the novel, as a genre, has the capacity to transmit that value.

In the Romantic-era novel, however, the confident didacticism of the eighteenth-century novel tends to dissipate under the pressure of a thoroughgoing critique of both the form and the value of individual life stories, as well as an interrogation of the novel's own generic capacity to transmit them. Indeed, novels such as Burney's *The Wanderer* show that the cultural desire for feminine stories, in particular, reveals itself to be something more coercive than liberating – 'compulsory narration' as Suzie Asha Park describes it in her essay for this volume. Furthermore, Romantic fiction is persistently drawn to lives that end not in redemption or transcendence, but in ruin and failure. Foregrounding the end over the beginning, Romantic novels tend to start not with their protagonist's birth, but with an announcement of the devastation wrought by his or her life's disaster. Caleb Williams initiates his story by announcing, 'My life for several years has been a theatre of calamity. I have been a mark for the vigilance of tyranny, and I could not escape. My fairest prospects have been blasted'; and Hogg's justified sinner begins his 'private memoirs and confessions' by explaining, 'My life has been a life of trouble and turmoil; of change and vicissitude; of anger and exultation; of sorrow and vengeance'.[32] These retrospective narrations emphasize not the protagonist's progress through life, but the catastrophe that awaits him at the end. Even Austen plays with such a narrative of ruin in *Persuasion*. This narrative strategy critiques not only the form of the eighteenth-century novel but also the ideological structures – salvation, justice – on which that form is based.[33] In this, the Romantic-era novel evinces a thoroughgoing scepticism of Enlightenment ideals.

That critique extends to the possibility that some stories of individuals might be more destructive than they are edifying. The Romantic novel frequently meditates on the idea of a story that – because it is too singular, too scary, or simply too evil – should not be passed on. Such stories have the potential to eviscerate community rather than construct it. This trope is perhaps most recognizable as a gothic 'hook' – the tantalizing lure of transgressive reading. In *Melmoth the Wanderer*, for instance, John Melmoth is 'enjoin[ed]' by his uncle's will

> to search for a manuscript, which I think he will find in the third and lowest left-hand drawer of the mahogany chest standing under that portrait [of Melmoth the Wanderer], – it is among some papers of no value, such as manuscript sermons, and pamphlets on the improvement of Ireland, and such stuff; he will distinguish it by its being tied round with a black tape, and the paper being very mouldy and discouloured. He may read it if he will – I think he had better not. At all events, I adjure him, if there be any power in the adjuration of a dying man, to burn it.[34]

Of course he reads it. In this late, semi-parodic replay of the disintegrating manuscript trope deployed as early as Walpole's *Castle of Otranto*, the instructions seem too precise for him not to disobey. Yet Romantic novelists employed the idea of a story that cannot be told to explore seriously aberrant psychological states. Matilda, for example, muses, 'Perhaps a history such as mine had better die with me, but a feeling that I cannot define leads me on and I am too weak in both in body and mind to resist the slightest impulse. While life was strong within me I thought indeed that there was a sacred horror in my tale that rendered it unfit for utterance, and now about to die I pollute its mystic terrors'.[35] Here, Matilda's experience of incestuous love has cast her permanently outside human community, and her story can only be passed on under the aegis of her death.

And even as it explores these themes, the very structure of many Romantic-era narratives questions the capacity of novels to transmit the 'histories of individuals' across space and time. In Mary Wollstonecraft's posthumously published *Maria, or the Wrongs of Woman*, the heroine, while confined to a madhouse by her brutal husband, writes her life story with the hope that it 'might perhaps instruct her daughter, and shield her from the misery, the tyranny, her mother knew not how to avoid'.[36] Yet the narrative subsequently reveals that Maria's infant daughter has died before her mother even began her autobiography; the narrative's only reader is Maria's lover Darnford, who, the fragmented narrative hints, will be unfaithful. What good are 'instructive' life stories if their readers do not exist? Mary Shelley puts the question in even starker terms in *The Last Man* (1826). Since the world's population has been destroyed by a global plague, the life story of the only man to survive literally has no readers. The chronological gymnastics of the novel's frame – which see it transmitted back in time to readers via the Sybil's cave in Naples – only serve to underline the narratological *mise-en-abyme* of this structure. Moreover, Helen Thompson's essay for this volume suggests that even if such stories were to reach their intended audience the Romantic era had grave doubts about whether they would have any force; novels such as Burney's *Cecilia*, she argues, reveal the failure of Richardson's idealized account of the novel as a medium that could reform culture. Burney instead depicts an 'impolite public sphere' from which reading cannot save the virtuous subject.

Paradoxically, the Romantic-era critique of what has been seen as one of the defining characteristics of the novel – the value, legibility and transmissibility through narrative of 'histories of individuals' – has rendered the Romantic novel less accessible to later critics than it should be. We contend, however, that this critique not only unites the many 'sub-genres' of Romantic-era fiction but also offers important ways to expand our understanding of narrative. Below, we briefly illustrate our arguments for the particularly probing and experimental nature of the Romantic-era novel through analyses of two examples of the genre: Charlotte Smith's *The Banished Man* (1794) and Maria Edgeworth's *The Absentee* (1812).

The Benefits of Exile in *The Banished Man*

We can see the degree to which the Romantic-era novel was engaged with rewriting the narrative conventions inherited from previous generations in a work such as Charlotte Smith's *The Banished Man* (1794). This novel of the aftermath of the French Revolution takes up the limits of both the marriage plot and the plot of national identity. Moving back and forth between war-torn Europe and provincial England over the course of its four volumes, *The Banished Man* challenges the exemplary quality of 'stories of individuals' even as it experiments with narrating new forms of 'imagined community.' Smith pointedly explains that the times demand this kind of narrative experiment: when her hero considers his recent past, it seems 'an uneasy and distressing dream [...] but with this melancholy difference, that all these events, which a little time before would, if they could have been prophesied, have appeared more improbable than the wildest fiction of a disordered imagination, were now too real'.[37] Moreover, the novel's concerns with human interactions that cross national boundaries disclose the kinds of themes that traversed multiple genres during the Romantic era, and align the novel with other forms of writing from the period.

In order to explore new forms of imagined community, *The Banished Man*, like so many texts of the 1790s, begins by delineating the collapse of traditional social structures. To this end, the novel's first volume is book-ended by critiques of epic tropes of displacement and re-foundation. In its opening scenes, the Royalist hero, D'Alonville, appears at a castle in the war-torn borderland of France and Prussia bearing his dying father on his back: 'This young Frenchman, it seems, is quite a modern Eneas [sic]', an unsympathetic character sneers, underlining the allusion.[38] As the volume closes, D'Alonville, sitting in the midst of a ruined family estate, defers his quest to return to France. '*The world was all before him where to chuse*', he thinks, paraphrasing the closing lines of *Paradise Lost*, 'but no part of it offered to him "*a place of rest*"'.[39] As we discussed earlier, the Romantic-era novel is characterized by its reliance on allusions. This formal characteristic seems to evidence the novel's hyper-awareness of its debt to literary history, its engagement with revising the narrative conventions through which experience can be described, and the porous boundary between individual experience and the broader culture. In this instance, Smith uses allusions to interrogate the applicability of such epic conventions to her own world.

The image of Aeneas carrying his father Anchises out of conquered Troy has been an enduring trope of both filial piety and *translatio imperii* – the transference of glory from an old empire to a new one. As Suvir Kaul has shown, the idea of the westward movement of imperial splendour was important to English national identity from the Augustan Age to the early nineteenth century.[40] By embedding this trope in the war-torn landscape of Europe in the 1790s, however, *The Banished Man* seems to set itself against the epic narrative of nation-founding. Carrying his wounded father, D'Alonville arrives at a family estate on the Franco-Prussian border just as it is about to be overrun by the forces of Revolutionary France. But the Castle of Rosenheim offers no possibility for resettlement or the resuscitation of the values of the *ancien régime* in a foreign land. Instead, the Viscount de Fayolles soon dies, blaming his nation's downfall for his demise: 'I perish under the ruins of France', he sighs.[41] After D'Alonville buries his father, the family abandons the castle, and it is quickly burned by the advancing army. When D'Alonville returns to the Castle Rosenheim a short time later to retrieve some family documents, he finds the estate 'an almost shapeless mass of ruin'.[42] Smith thus rewrites the Virgilian trope of nation-founding for a world in which displacement and deracination seem permanent and inconsolable conditions. Driving home the point that national territories can no longer foster or maintain the communities they once sustained, she prefaces the third volume of *The Banished Man* – which features D'Alonville's brief, nightmarish return to France – with a passage from *Macbeth*: 'Alas! Poor country! / Almost afraid to know itself! – It cannot / be call'd our mother, but our grave' – lines that make a similarly vivid appearance in Shelley's *The Last Man*, a novel of global plague that also examines the fragile bond between national territory and human community.[43]

Thus *The Banished Man* rejects the kind of exile figured by Aeneas – in which expulsion from one country precipitates a new start in a new territory – in its opening pages. The first volume's closing pages reject a second trope of exilic redemption: that offered by Milton at the end of *Paradise Lost*, where he writes that 'The World was all before them, where to choose / Their place of rest'. Milton's is a more ambivalent account of exile than Virgil's. The verb 'to choose' hangs on the end of the line, suggesting the free will involved in exilic wandering. Furthermore, Adam and Eve go forth to choose a place 'to rest' – implying that their wandering will end.

D'Alonville reiterates the element of choice, but asserts that his own fate involves perpetual mobility. Tellingly he does not recall the final two and a half lines of the poem: 'Providence their guide. / They hand in hand with wand'ring steps and slow / Through Eden took their solitary way'.[44] Milton asserts that the conjugal happiness will assuage the anguish of exile, but *The Banished Man* rejects the idea that the community of marriage will be a consolation for the sorrow of statelessness. D'Alonville is both poignantly alone during most of the novel – having lost his entire family to death or political differences – and consistently positioned as just one among a crowd of sufferers. As we have argued is characteristic of the Romantic-era novel, *The Banished Man* illuminates experiences that lie outside the marriage plot.

Indeed, one of the most striking aspects of the novel is the way it focuses our attention on the mass dislocations of war, particularly the physical and emotional damage done to women and children. As they try to flee the battlefield, D'Alonville and his father fall in with 'several unhappy beings, who were quitting their homes to wander they knew not whither. Mothers with their infant children! Daughters with infirm parents!'[45] Characteristically, the novel foregrounds parent–child pairings anchored by women (it later emphasizes that all the men are away fighting), merging these fragmented and displaced families into an aggregate of refugees. D'Alonville's gender role may be unusual, but his enforced mobility is commonplace. Although its title suggests that it will tell the story of a single 'banished man', Smith's narrative might be more accurately described as a novel of mass experience. D'Alonville is highly conscious, in a way that could never be true of Milton's exiles, that he shares his fate 'in common with thousands'.[46] In this way, Smith challenges the convention that novels tell the story of individuals.[47]

Georg Lukács famously argued that the emergence of the historical novel in the Romantic era resulted from the upheavals of the Revolution and the Napoleonic wars. The mass movements of persons occasioned by these wars – tellingly, Lukács focuses on soldiers, rather than refugees – created 'the concrete possibilities for men to comprehend their own existence as something historically conditioned'.[48] For Lukács, this new historical consciousness was bound up with a kind of nationalism rooted in history. Although it is not a historical novel, *The Banished Man* certainly engages in this 'mass experience of history' in which 'more and more people become aware of the connection between national and world history'.[49] Yet Smith's characters understand national identity not as something to be treasured or defended, but rather, on the whole, as something pernicious, something destructive of other kinds of bonds. Most of them hope, like Mrs Denzil, to be 'cur[ed] of national prejudice'. Indeed, for the Royalist D'Alonville, patriotism is the worst aspect of revolutionary radicalism, since it places an abstract love of nation above all other ties: 'to a patriot burning with the sacred love of immortal liberty; – what are the ties of blood? – what are all the charities between man and man? Is it not part of your creed, that the holy flame of freedom bursts all these asunder, as flax is dissevered by the fire?'[50] In this formulation, the nation is not just a grave, but a funeral pyre.[51]

But despite the power of these scenes of national conflagration, *The Banished Man* represents the experience of exile as something other than a story of lost national identity and the consequent pathos and nostalgia; rather, exile enables a kind of mobility that paves the way for human connections not based on territorial origin. Throughout her work, Smith is interested in tracing the transnational, trans-class connections between different forms of disenfranchisement. For instance, in *The Emigrants*, her long poem on the Royalist exodus, Smith imagines an odd moment of sympathy between England's homeless, rural poor, and the French 'exil'd nobles' who landed along England's pastoral southern coast in 1791–92.[52]

> Poor vagrant wretches! Outcasts of the world!
> Whom no abode receives, no parish owns;
> Roving, like Nature's commoners, the land
> That boasts such general plenty: if the sight
> Of wide-extended misery softens yours
> Awhile, suspend your murmurs![53]

The poem invokes the dynamics of sight to generate mutual sympathy. The myriad forms of displacement encompassed by that sympathy – from political exile to brutal poverty – suggest that such mobility might be more common in the modern world than a settled existence. The poet herself joins this vista of 'wide-extended misery'; 'I mourn your sorrows', she states, gazing at the emigrants, 'for I too have known / Involuntary exile'.[54] *The Banished Man* reiterates this connection between the plight of the French exile and the internal exile of the female author, in this case Mrs Denzil, a nearly indigent writer whose story mirrors Smith's own, who asserts that she is 'in [her] own country, reduced to a situation as distressing as that which [the emigrants] are thrown into by being driven from their's [sic]'.[55] Yet, while *The Emigrants* keeps these connections on the level of the passive, if sympathetic, gaze, *The Banished Man* turns that sympathy into creative action; Mrs Denzil, despite her own straitened circumstances, opens her home to French exiles, and the novel's characters find a way to actualize their sympathetic connections.

What possibilities are there for human community, the novel seems to ask, if the nation can no longer be a home? As Laura Mandell discusses in this volume, writers of the 1790s were interested in imagining communities that diverged, in 'queer' ways, from the norms of family and narrative. April Alliston has dubbed such configurations 'sympathetic communities', since they cohere around emotional connections rather than blood ties, national allegiances or ideological commitments. Indeed, Alliston argues, in the narratives describing such communities, 'sympathy [...] [works] to establish bonds that *specifically transgress and replace those of kinship and nation*'.[56] And this quite accurately describes the aggregates of *The Banished Man*. The Rosenheims quickly replace D'Alonville's lost family. His friendship with the Englishman Ned Ellesmere provides the backbone of the novel's four volumes. The purest form of such sympathy is illustrated by D'Alonville's encounter with one of those 'daughters of infirm parents' in a German inn:

> [He] was struck by the sight of a woman kneeling by the side of a wretched bed, where lay a human figure, on which her eyes were fixed with a look of hopeless despair [...] almost without reflection he stepped towards her; she turned toward him a countenance pale and emaciated, but still lovely, and looking surprised to behold a stranger, spoke to him in a very soft and affecting voice, but in a language of which he did not understand a syllable. The expressive tones of distress, however, needed not words to make vibrate a heart which, like D'Alonville's, had been accustomed to suffer.[57]

The daughter, Alexina, and her father, Carlowitz, are radical Republicans, exiled from their native Poland. Thus the sympathy between the Royalist D'Alonville and the Republican Alexina traverses at least four barriers: national, linguistic, political and gender difference. Nor does Smith absorb this moment into romantic love – D'Alonville remains Alexina's friend, though Ellesmere becomes, after many pages, her lover. Again, this is an active sympathy; D'Alonville and Ellesmere defer their journey to help 'an exile too like them'.[58]

Alliston argues that narratives of sympathetic communities evolved from the all-female households found in mid-eighteenth-century novels such as Sarah Scott's *Millennium Hall* to the transnational, and decidedly unconventional, love relationships found in novels such as Madame de Staël's *Corinne*. In this context, *The Banished Man* is somewhat unusual in the way it de-emphasizes the heterosexual pairing and celebrates heterosocial community. Indeed, for almost the first half of the novel, Smith refuses the love plot altogether, not introducing a romantic attachment for D'Alonville until the end of the second volume, when Angelina Denzil appears. When D'Alonville reflects, in the middle of the second volume, that he still has 'the whole world before him', he finds no Eve to accompany him; on the contrary, '[his] English friend, Ellesmere, was the only person who now seemed interested for his fate' – they are what Mandell would term a queer re-imagining of Milton's exiled pair.[59] Only at the end of the fourth volume is D'Alonville able to tell his future mother-in-law, like Milton's Eve, 'Wherever Angelina is – where you are, is now my country; (alas! What other have I?)'; though, as is characteristic of the novel, the married pair is not alone, but includes at least one parent.[60] Aware of the unconventional structure of her narrative, Smith invents an interlocutor for the preface to Volume II, who asks 'if you are going to make in [*The Banished Man*] the experiment that has often been talked of, but has never yet been hazarded; do you propose to make a novel without love in it?'[61] The author defends herself by referring to the repeated criticism of her novels while articulating her desire to go beyond the conventional limitations of the genre: 'I have been assailed with remonstrances on the evil tendency of having too much of love – too much of violent attachments in my novels; and as I thought in the present instance, the situation of my hero was of itself interesting enough to enable me to carry him on for some time without making him violently in love, I was determined to try the experiment'.[62] Showing her awareness of the innovative fiction of her day, Smith footnotes her assertion that a novel without love 'has never yet been hazarded', admitting that she 'had not then heard of or seen, a work called, "Things as They Are"'.

Unlike Godwin, Smith does not maintain the experiment over all four volumes. She does introduce a love interest for D'Alonville, and allows two happy transnational marriages that Anne Mellor cites as examples of 'embodied cosmopolitanism'.[63] But the novel does not come to rest, as so many do, by embedding its hero in a 'native' domestic idyll. Rather, the main characters of the novel, united by sympathy across lines of politics, nation, gender and age, arrange a community in Verona. Here, D'Alonville, Angelina, her mother Mrs Denzil, Ellesmere, his new bride Alexina and Carlowitz reunite with D'Alonville's surrogate family of the first volume, the Rosenheims. Enfolded in this sympathetic community, D'Alonville's last words celebrate his escape from all inherited ties and allegiances. Writing to Ellesmere, he praises the experience of exile:

For it has given me fortitude and resolution: instructed me to conquer prejudice, and to feel for the sufferings of others. In losing everything but my
honour and integrity, I have learned, that he who retains those qualities can
never be degraded, however humble may be his fortune. If my calamities have
deprived me of my natural friends, they have been the means of creating for
me others, who in the unruffled bosom of prosperity I should never have
found.[64]

Although the narrative does not say much about the choice of Verona for
this new kind of imagined community, we might speculate that Smith made
it because the city, as part of Venice's empire during the eighteenth century,
represented a governmental alternative to nation-states.

Although Verona, along with Venice, fell to Napoleon in 1797, these
semi-autonomous cities retained their allure for later generations of
Romantics who, like Smith, were interested in jettisoning national identity.
Almost two decades later, Byron, like D'Alonville, invoked Milton when
he set forth on the journey that was to produce the first two cantos of *Childe
Harold's Pilgrimage*. 'The world is all before me', he wrote to his mother in
the summer of 1809, 'and I leave England without regret'.[65] Eventually
Byron, like the exiles of *The Banished Man*, found a home in exile in the (now
former) Venetian empire, claiming to have 'lost all *local* feeling for England
without having acquired any *local* attachment for any other spot'.[66] We can
see, then, that Charlotte Smith's interest in re-imagining the self outside
the nation cuts across the genres and decades of Romantic literature. Yet
it's worth pausing for a moment over the question of genre. Though it may
be an unfair comparison, we might ask whether the novel form allows a
different set of insights into the issue than Byron's (mock) epic. In *Childe
Harold*, Harold too leaves a ruined family estate behind, and meditates on
the devastation of war. But Harold 'soon [...] knew himself the most unfit
/ of men to herd with Man / [...] / Proud though in desolation; which
could find / A life within itself, to breathe without mankind'.[67] In relation
to *The Banished Man*, Byron's vision of 'self-exile' seems strikingly individualized and solitary. The multiple characters and storylines of *The Banished
Man*, its inset voices and narratives, allow Smith to explore the mass dislocations that engulfed Europe during the Romantic era, and re-imagine
community.

Interiority and Didacticism in *The Absentee*

We have argued that the Romantic novel breaks down the narrative conventions of realism. In doing so, it emphasizes the uncanny, the foreign, and the very mystery of what constitutes reality by exploring what the novel as a genre might mean and what it could do. In *The Absentee*, Maria Edgeworth experiments with definitions of realism by committing herself to the veracity associated with interiority and simultaneously to the schematicism associated with didacticism, an alliance some would find improbable.[68] Watt and others have convinced us that a key aspect of the reality effect is the presentation of interiority in depth and in such a schema, didacticism has no place. Yet, surprisingly, to further her didactic purposes in *The Absentee*, Edgeworth creates interiority and does so through literary allusions, which provide an unexpected view into her heroine's private life. In doing so Edgeworth offers both a feminist commentary on female education and a dramatization of history subjectified through personal experience. This unexpected glimpse into Grace Nugent's interiority grants some emotional power to what might otherwise be a wholly abstract characterization or unsophisticated instruction. Apropos, here is a passage from *Belinda*, where Lady Delacour resists primitive didacticism when she says of a letter she has just received that 'Every word of it is a lesson to me, and evidently was so intended. But I take it all in good part, because, to do Clarence justice, he describes the joys of domestic Paradise in such elegant language, that he does not make me sick'.[69] In contrast to other authors, however, particularly Austen, Edgeworth's use of quotations to explore interiority has its limits, functioning more prominently as a rhetorical strategy than as an exercise important in and of itself in illustrating the workings of the human mind.[70]

As we discussed earlier, Romantic novelists' tendency to quote verse breaks down the era's division between Romantic poetry and prose and acknowledges the paradoxical relation between originality, which apparently comes from nowhere, and literariness, which comes from everywhere. Mary Jacobus argues psychoanalytically in this volume that poetic allusions give us access to Anne Elliot's private thoughts and either 'signal a kind of addiction to melancholy on Anne's part' or, in contrast, function as signs of a determined and active seeking of self-knowledge.[71] As opposed to Austen's lavish fascination with Anne's internal existence, Edgeworth rarely allows Grace's inner life to emerge, yet when it does, it stems from such a barricaded place that insight into her interiority seems to have been provided almost reluctantly, as if too much of this kind of interest would upset the balance Edgeworth wishes to establish. And rather than positing a sense that an allusion is exponentially enriching, since it reveals the mutual depth of the one who alludes and the thing alluded to, she suggests that this particular kind of culturally enhanced interiority paradoxically reminds us that one's 'inside' thoughts result in some degree from something profoundly outside.[72]

Readers largely agree that Grace Nugent is a 'non-naturalistic'[73] character and that the associations between her and the historical Nugent family, subversive Irish Catholics, offer possibilities for rich surmisings about her emblematical role in the novel. The lack of a clear trajectory of associations between the historical figure and the fictional character, however, has led to two general critical assumptions – that one can neither construct a firm allegorical reading of Grace in relationship to Irish history or to the Union, nor can one read her as a complex, psychologically real or well developed fictional character. For W. J. McCormack and Kim Walker she remains a 'shadowy ideal', 'an enigmatic figure, promising union and redemptive grace, but never stepping forth from the sidelines to actualize that promise';[74] and for Julia Anne Miller, Grace signifies the 'radically unstable [...] ground upon which the Union is built'.[75] Part of what has led to deconstructive readings of the novel, such as these, is Edgeworth's own literal 'deconstruction' of Grace: she schematized this character by cutting out many of her speeches, rendering her, according to Miller, 'a mute and paralyzed figure [...] who rarely speaks, except to voice the unvoiced opinions of her [...] cousin, Colambre'.[76] No doubt, the heroine *is* a paragon who attends selflessly to her immature aunt and has allegedly never had, let alone expressed, a desire of her own. And from this vantage of disinterest, she is able to remain 'quite above all double dealing; she had no mental reservation – no metaphysical subtleties – but, with plain, unsophisticated morality, in good faith and simple truth, acted as she professed, thought what she said, and was that which she seemed to be'.[77]

The Absentee presents a good example of the way in which Romantic novels used allusion to render more subtle characterizations (and thereby engage readers hungry for psychological identification with fictional characters); at the same time Edgeworth does not appear to be superadding this private consciousness for aesthetic reasons, but for moral ones. This is not the author 'momentarily' achieving a 'transcendent synthesis'[78] of two generic modes, but Edgeworth pursuing a technique that incorporates two modes – didacticism and interiority – so as to make history live in the minds of readers. Thus, we want to show how Edgeworth uses literary allusion to emphasize Grace's dual position as truth-teller and as an inert figure whose lack of 'say' in the novel (both because her speeches were cut and because she lives as a dependent companion) represents a double subjectivity. This double subjectivity occurs when a character, at one level, represents a country or some kind of abstract ideal but also, at another level, represents the personal reactions of an individual who, rendered passive by historical events and living in the murky mess of a particular moment, tries also to uncover the truth of what that moment means.

Edgeworth effects this dual subjectivity when Grace, departing from her usual reticence, quotes from Anna Laetitia Barbauld's 'The Invitation' (1773),[79] a poem which takes up themes similar to those of Edgeworth's novel: friendship, nature, civic duty, education, and women's choices. In it, Barbauld invites her friend Elizabeth Belsham Kenrick (as Colambre does his parents) to 'fly' from the 'mimic grandeur and illusive light' of London society, 'from hollow friendships, and from sickly joys' to 'the pure pleasures rural scenes inspire'.[80] The poem addresses the ways in which the students of Warrington Academy (like Colambre) could 'fix [the nation's] laws', 'sustain [...] her spirit', and 'light up glory thro' her wide domain!'.[81] Thus the allusion signals another conversation buried beneath the explicit exchange between Grace and Colambre, for they both know that the poem addresses their mutual, though not secret, desire to remove his parents from England to Ireland. In addition to its general thematic significance for the novel, however, the poem has specific relevancy for understanding Grace, since her allusion illuminates how this apparently selfless heroine regrets her lack of education, longs for female companionship, freedom, and pleasure, and enjoys asserting her independence.

The actual quotation from Barbauld's poem occurs in an episode wherein Colambre, scandalized by the (as it later turns out, false) evidence of Grace's illegitimacy, decides he cannot marry her, and so to rid himself of his feelings for her, urges her to marry a Mr Salisbury, another suitor. She refuses to do so.

'I was aware that [Mr. Salisbury] would be so much better off after I refused him – so much happier with one suited to him in age, talents, fortune, and love – "What bliss, did he but know his bliss", were *his*!'

'"Did he but know his bliss!"' replied lord Colambre; 'but is not he the best judge of his own bliss?'

'And am not I the best judge of mine?' said miss Nugent: 'I go no farther.'[82]

Grace's repetition of Barbauld's line – '"What bliss, did he but know his bliss", were his!' – illuminates the power the heroine holds even in a dynamic where she seems powerless.[83] She clearly states that she will guide those who have no awareness of their own desires, and when she declares herself to be the 'best judge of [her own bliss] [...] I go no farther',[84] she authoritatively proclaims her capacity for following her own affinities and foils Colambre's attempts to obtain from her what Suzie Asha Park in her chapter in this book calls 'a compulsory narration' that 'shows that the demand for disclosure elicits narratives that merely reinforce prior assumptions'. For if Colambre expects Grace to help him out of his difficulty here by quietly marrying another, and thus 'reinforc[ing] prior assumptions', she surprises him by choosing a single life; and if he expects to hide his motives from her because she has been profoundly 'feminine' in a self-effacing and passive way throughout the novel, she surprises him by demanding the truth.

Her demand, not just for happiness, but for bliss – for transport, for rapture – triggers revelation after revelation in this scene, until Colambre finally and inadvertently declares his love. Thus what makes her an idealized figure of instruction – that she was 'quite above all double dealing' – here, through the confession of interiority that the allusion carries, also makes her a psychologically believable force in the novel, one who challenges Colambre twice in this episode and engages in what can be called 'sublime' truth-telling. By enriching a virtually allegorical female character of truth with affective reactions, Edgeworth renders domesticity a species of sublime worth. As we argued earlier in this essay, this is an instance of a larger pattern in the Romantic novel wherein those concepts of the sublime that we expect to find in poetry – spiritual transcendence, noble and elevated formulations of morality, and Enlightenment theories of subject–object relations – appear in as lofty a way in the genre of the novel, except that they are invoked to conceptualize courtship, marriage, and domestic life.[85] Without falling into a Burkean conservatism, Edgeworth suggests that if the nation *and* domesticity are to survive, it is crucial that Grace be the truth-teller, and that in order to do so, she must have some awareness of her own subjectivity and of her own subjective place in history.[86]

In her poem, Barbauld addresses both the poignancy of what women were denied – pure pleasure and formal education – as well as the specific limitations placed on her community of dissenters. 'The Invitation' envisions the poet and her friend following the 'smiling goddess' of 'Pleasure'; together they will 'haste away, / And [...] sweetly waste the careless day'.[87]

Further, in praising the superb education Warrington Academy offered to its students, the sons of Dissenters, the poem also criticizes those very pupils:

> Ye generous youth who love this studious shade,
> How rich a field is to your hopes display'd!
> Knowledge to you unlocks the classic page;
> And virtue blossoms for a better age.
> Oh golden days! Oh bright unvalued hours!
> What bliss (did ye but know that bliss) were yours?[88]

Here Barbauld, in her emphasis on '*your* hopes' and 'knowledge to *you*', underscores that these opportunities for education are available to men, not women, and that these 'generous youth' (like Salisbury or Colambre) cannot value their 'golden days', because they do not know 'what bliss' is theirs.

Grace's invocation of a poem that asks for pleasure and protests exclusion suggests different fantasies than we would normally associate with this ever-diligent heroine, who most certainly earns her keep by caring tirelessly for Lady Clonbrony.[89] Her allusion seems especially charged given her own lack of opportunities:

> in the life she had been compelled to lead she had acquired accomplishments [...] but [...] the ample page of knowledge had never been unrolled to her eyes. She had never had opportunities of acquiring literature herself, but she admired it in others, particularly in her friend miss Broadhurst. [...] Miss Nugent, perhaps overvaluing the information that she did not possess, and free from all idea of envy, looked up to her friend as to a superior being, with a sort of enthusiastic admiration.[90]

The word 'compelled' shows that she had no choice (any more than Barbauld did to attend the academy) in her education. The quotation from Barbauld (which comes later in the novel) and the one from Thomas Gray in this passage undercuts the qualifying 'perhaps' in the ambiguous phrase 'perhaps overvaluing the information that she did not possess', emphasizing even more thoroughly the value of 'acquiring literature'. The line 'the ample page of knowledge had never been unrolled to her eyes', a quotation from 'Elegy Written in a Country Churchyard', connects Grace's situation to the dead whom Gray honours, those whose 'noble rage' was repressed and whose 'genial current of the soul' was frozen.[91] Like the 'youth' for whom Gray writes the Epitaph, Grace's 'lot forbad' her education and her self-expression.[92] The narrator confidently states that Miss

Nugent was 'free from all idea of envy', but the passage complicates the idealization of her character both by undermining it and by reinforcing the importance Grace places on friendship with Miss Broadhurst. By super-adding intense longing and hero worship, Grace recalls Barbauld's desire to be partners in pleasure and education with Elizabeth. This in turn reminds us of another of the tendencies in the Romantic novel – the emphasis on the power of intense, non-marital attachments. These contra-dictions between the earlier statements in free indirect discourse and Grace's own disclosures through allusion suggest not so much the new historicist argument that Edgeworth is veiling her own or Grace's powers and desires, but rather that Edgeworth herself reveals some writerly conflict about how much interiority or 'portable psychology'[93] she will allow this character.[94] Though buried in poetic allusion and expressing a subjectivity only through an external vector – the poetry of Barbauld and Gray – the heroine, nevertheless, exposes feelings that the text is reluctant to elicit directly.[95]

In contrast to this conversation with Colambre in which she voices her will through literary allusion, most of what we could call Grace's interiority results from her silences and other characters' disclosure of her impeccable behaviour. As noted above, Edgeworth, much to the consternation of contemporary critics, cut many of Grace's speeches, especially those that assert a spunky side to her personality. At least in the following instance, from the 1812 edition, it seems unlikely, however, that Edgeworth's revi-sions diminish Grace's power either as a subjective presence or as a sublime truth-teller, but rather that the allusion to Barbauld's poem pres-ents a far more vital sense of her interiority than what was excised (the deleted lines are italicized):

> 'But really and truly I do not wish to marry. This is not a mere commonplace speech; but I have not yet seen any man I could love. *I like you, Cousin Colambre, better than Mr. Salisbury, I would rather live with you than with him; you know that is a certain proof that I am not likely to be in love with him.* I am happy as I am, especially now we are all going to dear Ireland, home, to live together: you cannot conceive with what pleasure I look forward to that.'[96]

The 'edited' Grace, speaking less directly and perhaps with more decorum, is less threatening as a woman, but still projects acute emotional intensity.[97] In other words, our identification with her as a symbol is not so strong that we cannot identify with her as a woman, yet, simultaneously, our identifi-cation with her as an individual is not so strong that we cannot also still think of her as a symbol of Ireland, and thus as a force of political power that declares that the country can and does know what causes its own 'bliss'.

Her demand – as a woman and as a country – to know why Colambre is rejecting her makes him lie twice in this episode: once when he says he wants her to marry another and second when, to avoid confessing his affection and admit his fears about her illegitimacy, he declares that instead of returning to Ireland with her he feels it is his duty to 'serve a campaign or two abroad':

> 'Good Heavens! What does this mean? What can you mean?' cried she, fixing her eyes upon his, as if she would read his very soul. 'Why? what reason? – O, tell me the truth – and at once.'
>
> His change of colour – his hand that trembled, and withdrew from hers – the expression of his eyes as they met hers – revealed the truth to her at once. As it flashed across her mind, she started back; her face grew crimson, and, in the same instant, pale as death.
>
> 'Yes – you see, you *feel the truth* now,' said lord Colambre. 'You see, you feel, that I love you – passionately.'
>
> 'O, let me not hear it!' said she; 'I must not – ought not. Never till this moment did such a thought cross my mind – I thought it impossible […].'[98]

The allegorical teller of truth now cannot bear 'to hear it!'. Further, the contradiction explicit in Grace's last sentence does more than the excised lines would have done to incarnate her ideal nature: her statement 'I thought it impossible' contradicts her claim that she has never thought about this event, since if she thought it impossible, she must have pondered it first as a possibility. When he tells her he loves her, Lord Colambre says 'you see, you *feel* the truth now'. In other words, if truth is to be known, it must be felt. The question, however, is what precise truth is *The Absentee* trying to make us feel?

As we pointed out earlier, the confident didacticism of the eighteenth century becomes more ambivalent as Romantic novelists experiment with the genre and emphasize their cultural analyses. This plays out in *The Absentee*, for if in this novel interiority serves instruction, it is paradoxically true that subjectivity does not, at least in this text, always clarify what that *specific* lesson about history might be, given that readers cannot agree on what Grace stands for: Ireland? Idealized femininity? Grace's silences produce what Deidre Lynch calls a 'retiring, deep femininity'.[99] However, the kind of psychological realism we see Edgeworth effecting through allusion in *The Absentee* differs from that produced by free indirect discourse, say in Austen or Burney, since Edgeworth is going out of her way to show that Grace is valued for her openness and describability, not her 'polyva-lence', 'hidden motivations', or 'unplumbed depths'.[100] Neither does Edgeworth appear to be interested in using reserve to 'questio[n] and chal-leng[e] the very pressure to disclose depths that an increasingly Romantic culture both exerts and manages to veil as a gentle invitation to express the self freely', as Suzie Park argues in her essay here on *The Wanderer*. Edge-worth's goal seems less to try to create the illusion of deep subjectivity in Grace or to suggest that interiority is compulsory but rather herself to limit Grace's interiority, so that even when we see the heroine expressing inner depths, she does so obliquely through literary allusion. This limitation occurs presumably because Edgeworth is primarily interested not in the presence of subjectivity for its own sake, but as a means of exploring the connection of interior experience to history and women's role in it. Instead of asserting that Edgeworth has slipped up, either as a moralist or a realist, we would like to make two points.

First, to return to the observation made earlier: in the Romantic novel, politics cannot be schematically divided up into clear camps (for example, Jacobin or anti-Jacobin or anti-Union or pro-Union), and neither do these individual texts offer themselves as conveying transparent party lines. Edgeworth, in particular, offered rather cryptic representations of her political positions, partly for her own safety.[101] Second, one lesson we could propose that *The Absentee* suggests is this: like most Romantic novels, it turns simultaneously towards history and towards an interrogation of selfhood *in order to analyse* the impact of political systems on individual development. To paraphrase Colambre's line earlier, we '*feel*' the impact of the accusations of Grace's illegitimacy and his rejection of her, and '*feel*' that Colambre is wrong to reject Grace as his wife if she is illegitimate, but also that a Union between Ireland and England is illegitimate, at least under the terms by which it was constituted. And we '*feel*' the truth that to render that union legitimate, many sacrifices must be made: thus, to maintain her propriety, parts of Grace's subjectivity must be cut; and for the two of them to marry, Colambre's propriety demands the condition that her Irish inheritance must be 'cut' so that she can be reinvented as British. This in itself suggests in rather radical terms that the only way a union between the two nations would be legitimate is if Ireland were already English. Grace's role as truth-teller, then, at both the emotional and symbolic levels, leads a reader to ask what is the truth – the true motives – behind a union between the two countries and on what conditions are those being accepted or rejected.

The Absentee is not a sustained investigation into personal, private consciousness, such as we would find in Henry James; but when those moments do occur, they also do not, to quote Fredric Jameson, 'furnish a powerful ideological instrument in the perpetuation of an increasingly subjectivized and psychologized world',[102] for in Edgeworth, the balance between the individual and the social is tipped towards the social, towards a vision that wants to engage the individual in a political world, in the active process of living in and assessing history. If Edgeworth is using private consciousness to help us understand the impact of political systems on individual development, the end result is that if we are fully absorbed into any kind of subjectivity, it is the subjectivity of history itself. Thus, though one can easily discern how Edgeworth feels about hard work, sobriety, frugality, and women's decorous behaviour, it is much more difficult to discern precisely what lesson we are expected to learn about the political union between Ireland and England in *The Absentee*, even though its style and tone are overtly didactic. What does make sense is that whatever moral she may have intended, her combination of the instructional and the subjective succeeds in dramatizing the complexities of being a historical subject in a time of revolution, rather than providing a sure-fire instance of political allegory which a reader will spontaneously recognize and respond to.

Conclusion

We have been suggesting that Romantic fiction interrogates the conventions that have often been used to define the English novel and, then, often enough, departs from those conventions completely. This criticism and rejection of such hallmarks of 'the novel' as its topicality, its focus on the individual, and its faith in the curative powers of marriage have often made the Romantic-era novel seem like a collection of failed forms. Those authors who have been granted a place in the mainstream history of the novel – Austen, and to a lesser degree, Scott – have been accorded it on the basis of their seeming interest in realism and successful unions (conjugal, in Austen's case, national, in Scott's). The essays in this volume, however, view the critique of Enlightenment values so forcefully launched by the Romantic novel as evidence not of the fissuring of the genre, but of its common pursuit of new modes of representing both individual consciousness and imagined communities. Our authors are concerned to show that such experimentation was never simply aesthetic, but the result of the way Romantic fiction, like Romantic poetry, struggled to find innovative strategies for representing the social and intellectual upheaval of its times.

In 1795, William Godwin declared that his goal in *Caleb Williams* was 'to disengage the minds of men from prepossession, and launch them upon the sea of moral and political inquiry'.[103] This phrase could serve as the motto of the Romantic-era novel, in all its myriad forms. When Austen begins *Pride and Prejudice* with 'a truth universally acknowledged', she very quickly reveals that her project is to ironize such 'universal' truths by revealing their situatedness and self-interest. From Godwin's gothic political melodrama to Austen's domestic comedy of manners, the Romantic-era novel seeks to pry its readers away from their assumptions about reality, and urge them to understand the processes of their own cognition. Thus the critique of Enlightenment values in the Romantic novel is not one with negative ends. On the contrary, we begin this volume with the assertion that, like all Romantic literature, the novel bodied forth utopian impulses, imagining a more perfect future in terms of the role of women, politics, literary experimentation, and social structures.

Notes

1   Peter Garside, 'The English Novel in the Romantic Era: Consolidation and Dispersal', in Peter Garside, James Raven and Rainer Schöwerling, general eds., *The English Novel 1770–1829: A Bibliographical Survey of Prose Fiction Published in the British Isles* (Oxford: Oxford University Press, 2 vols., 2000), Vol. 2, p. 15.
2   Raven, *The English Novel 1770–1829* ,Vol. 1, p. 72, and Garside, Vol. 2, p. 36.
3   Clifford Siskin, *The Work of Writing: Literature and Social Change in Britain 1700–1830* (Baltimore: Johns Hopkins University Press, 1998), p. 155.
4   Alexander Pope, *The Dunciad,* in David Fairer and Christine Gerrard, eds., *Eighteenth-Century Poetry* (Oxford: Blackwell Publishing, 2 nd edn, 2004), Canto I, ll. 123-24.
5   Robert Kiely, *The Romantic Novel in England* (Cambridge, MA: Harvard University Press, 1972), p. vii.
6   Amanda Gilroy and Wil Verhoeven, Introduction, 'The Romantic-Era Novel: A Special Issue', *Novel: A Forum on Fiction* 34.2 (Spring 2001), p. 155.
7   Kiely, *The Romantic Novel in England,* p. 1.
8   Claudia Johnson, '"Let Me Make the Novels of a Country": Barbauld's *The British Novelists* (1810/1820)', *Novel: A Forum on Fiction* 34 (Spring 2001), p. 166.
9   See Kiely, who, though not specifically mentioning Wollstonecraft or Shelley, makes the larger point that Romantic writers, wanting to '*see* with the eyes' of earlier

authors, 'echoe[d]' their 'lines' and 'imitate[d]' their 'characters'. *The Romantic Novel in England*, p. 7.

10 Charles Maturin, *Melmoth the Wanderer* (Oxford: Oxford University Press, 1968).

11 Jacobus has argued that the excessive allusiveness of Mary Shelley's novella *Matilda* 'suggests that literary transmission is complicit in the defacement and consumption of "little bits" of prior texts'. See Mary Jacobus, *Psychoanalysis and the Scene of Reading* (Oxford: Oxford University Press, 1999), p. 199.

12 Katie Trumpener, *Bardic Nationalism: The Romantic Novel and the British Empire* (Princeton: Princeton University Press, 1997), p. 147.

13 Here Dorothy Wordsworth is quoting John Logan's *The Braes of Yarrow*. Dorothy Wordsworth, *The Journals of Dorothy Wordsworth*, ed. Mary Moorman (Oxford: Oxford University Press, 1971), Thursday 3 June 1802, p. 131.

14 The quotation is from Ellis, chapter 3, below.

15 Walter Scott, *Ivanhoe*, Dedicatory Epistle (Oxford: Oxford University Press, 1996, p. 15.

16 William Godwin, *Caleb Williams*, ed. Gary Handwerk and A. A. Markley (Peterborough, Ontario: Broadview Press, 2000), p. 55.

17 Walter Scott, *Waverley* (Harmondsworth: Penguin, 1972), p. 176.

18 Mary Shelley, *Matilda*, in *Mary and Maria / Matilda*, ed. Janet Todd (London: Penguin Books, 1992), pp. 178, 162.

19 Kiely, *The Romantic Novel in England*, p. 2.

20 Robert Miles, 'What is a Romantic Novel?', in Gilroy and Verhoeven, eds., *Novel: A Forum on Fiction* 34.2 (Spring 2001), p. 181.

21 Benedict Anderson, *Imagined Communities: Reflections on the Origins and Spread of Nationalism* (London: Verso, rev. edn, 1991) and Jürgen Habermas, *The Structural Transformation of the Public Sphere: An Inquiry into a Category of Bourgeois Society*, trans. Thomas Burger (Cambridge, MA: The MIT Press, 1989).

22 Habermas, *The Structural Transformation of the Public Sphere*, pp. 50–51.

23 Deidre Lynch and William Warner, *Cultural Institutions of the Novel* (Durham, NC: Duke University Press, 1996), p. 4.

24 Srinivas Aravamudan proposes that 'if countries didn't exist, novels of national realism would need to invent them, or perhaps, as some accounts have it, they actually imagined them into existence'. The 'vertical and genealogical "history" or the national model', he argues, 'was itself a product of later eighteenth-century and Romantic models of national culture that retroactively synthesized "the novel" as a particularity arising from a range of disparate genres and modes. In this respect, the agency ascribed to "the novel" is a displaced function of the teleological project of constructing national culture'. Srinivas Aravamudan, 'Fiction/Translation/Transnation: The Secret History of the Eighteenth-Century Novel', in Paula R. Backscheider and Catherine Ingrassia, eds., *A Companion to The Eighteenth-Century English Novel and Culture* (Oxford: Blackwell, 2005), pp. 48, 71.

25 Michael Gamer, 'Maria Edgeworth and the Romance of Real Life', in Gilroy and Verhoeven, eds., *Novel: A Forum on Fiction* 34 (Spring 2001), pp. 232–66. In this excellent article, Gamer argues that Edgeworth's fiction is 'realist neither in its technique nor in its aims', he lays out contemporary reviewers' criticisms of Edgeworth's generic innovations, and he demonstrates the astounding impact her

tectonic modernizations had on later authors who strove to write in this mode, which he calls the 'romance of real life' (p. 235).

26 See Myers' '"We Must Grant a Romance Writer a Few Responsibilities": "Unnatural Incident" and Narrative Motherhood in Maria Edgeworth's *Emilie de Coulanges*', *The Wordsworth Circle* XXVII.3 (1996), p. 152.

27 See Peter Brooks, for example, who comments that the early novel is valuable for the way it reminds us both of the genre's strong connection to ordinary human experience and its essential freedom: '[r]ealism [...] belongs to the rise of the novel as a relatively rule-free genre that both appealed to and represented the private lives of the unexceptional – or rather, found and dramatized the exceptional within the ordinary, creating the heroism of everyday life'. *Realist Vision* (New Haven: Yale University Press, 2005), p. 12.

28 Miles, 'What is a Romantic Novel?', pp. 195–97.

29 Nancy Armstrong, *Desire and Domestic Fiction: A Political History of the Novel* (Oxford: Oxford University Press, 1987), p. 48

30 Ian Watt, *The Rise of the Novel: Studies in Defoe, Richardson and Fielding* (Berkeley: University of California Press, 1957), p. 60.

31 Michael McKeon, *The Origins of the English Novel* (Baltimore: Johns Hopkins University Press, 1987), chapter 3.

32 *Caleb Williams*, p. 59. James Hogg, *The Private Memoirs and Confessions of a Justified Sinner*, ed. Peter Garside (Edinburgh: Edinburgh University Press, 2001), p. 117.

33 For a brilliant examination of the 'formal tension between [...] individual life and the overarching pattern' in the eighteenth-century novel see McKeon, *The Origins of the English Novel*, pp. 90–128.

34 Charles Maturin, *Melmoth the Wanderer*, p. 21.

35 Shelley, *Matilda*, p.151.

36 Mary Wollstonecraft, *Maria, or the Wrongs of Woman*, in *Mary and Maria / Matilda* (London: Penguin Books, 1992), p. 66.

37 Charlotte Smith, *The Banished Man* (London: printed for T. Cadell, Jun., and W. Davies, 1794), Vol. 2, p. 6.

38 Smith, *The Banished Man*, Vol. 1, p. 55.

39 Smith, *The Banished Man*, Vol. 1, p. 209.

40 Suvir Kaul, *Poems of Nation, Anthems of Empire: English Verse in the Long Eighteenth Century* (Charlottesville, VA: University of Virginia Press, 2000).

41 Smith, *The Banished Man*, Vol. 1, p. 64.

42 Smith, *The Banished Man*, Vol. 1, p. 144.

43 Smith, *The Banished Man*, Vol. 3, front cover.

44 John Milton, *Paradise Lost*, Book XII, ll. 647-49. Ed. Gordon Teskey (New York and London: W.W. Norton & Company, 2005).

45 Smith, *The Banished Man*, Vol. 1, p. 44.

46 Smith, *The Banished Man*, Vol. 1, p. 226.

47 In her excellent article on the novel, Toby Benis charts another way in which it challenges the narrative of individual identity through D'Alonville's heavy use of disguise and alibi. See '"A Likely Story": Charlotte Smith's Revolutionary Narratives', *European Romantic Review* 14.3 (2003), pp. 291–306.

48 Georg Lukács, *The Historical Novel* (Lincoln, NE: The University of Nebraska Press,

1962), p. 24.

49 Lukács, *The Historical Novel*, p. 25.

50 Smith, *The Banished Man*, Vol. 3, p. 213.

51 Elsewhere in the novel, Smith calls politics 'a subject which has too often divided the most sacred connections, by the warmth of the contention it raised'. Smith, *The Banished Man*, Vol. 2, p. 52.

52 Charlotte Smith, *The Emigrants*, Book I, l. 310. In *The Poems of Charlotte Smith*, ed. Stuart Curran (New York and Oxford: Oxford University Press, 1993), p. 146.

53 Smith, *The Emigrants*, Book I, ll. 303-308.

54 Smith, *The Emigrants*, Book I, ll. 155-56. Smith refers here to her flight to France with her husband in 1784–85, in an attempt to escape his creditors.

55 Smith, *The Banished Man*, Vol. 3, p. 180.

56 April Alliston, 'Transnational Sympathies, Imaginary Communities', in Margaret Cohen and Carolyn Dever, eds., *The Literary Channel: The Inter-National Invention of the Novel* (Princeton and Oxford: Princeton University Press, 2002), pp. 133–49: p. 134. Emphasis Alliston's.

57 Smith, *The Banished Man*, Vol. 2, p. 38.

58 Smith, *The Banished Man*, Vol. 2, p. 40.

59 Smith, *The Banished Man*, Vol. 2, p. 75.

60 Smith, *The Banished Man*, Vol. 4, p. 305.

61 Smith, *The Banished Man*, Vol. 2, p. vii.

62 Smith, *The Banished Man*, Vol. 2, p. viii.

63 Anne K. Mellor, 'Embodied Cosmopolitanism and the British Romantic Woman Writer', *European Romantic Review* 17.3 (July 2006), pp. 289–300: p. 293.

64 Smith, *The Banished Man*, Vol. 4, p. 340.

65 22 July 1809. Quoted in Fiona MacCarthy, *Byron: Life and Legend* (New York: Farrar, Straus, Giroux, 2002), p. 88.

66 Quoted in Celeste Langan, 'Venice', in James Chandler and Kevin Gilmartin, eds., *Romantic Metropolis: The Urban Scene of British Culture, 1780–1840* (Cambridge: Cambridge University Press, 2005), p. 270. See Langan's excellent article more generally for Byron's interest in post-national forms of community.

67 Lord Byron, *Childe Harold's Pilgrimage*, Canto III, ll. 12, 16, in *Lord Byron: The Major Works*, ed. Jerome McGann (Oxford: Oxford University Press, 1986), pp. 107–108.

68 In her discussion of *Mansfield Park*, Marilyn Butler, for example, suggests that didacticism and interiority are incompatible: 'Since Fanny is the representative of [...] orthodoxy, the individuality of consciousness must to a large extent be denied'. *Jane Austen and the War of Ideas* (Oxford: Clarendon Press, 1975), pp. 246–48.

69 Maria Edgeworth, *Belinda*, ed. Kathryn J. Kirkpatrick (Oxford: Oxford University Press, 1994, reissued as Oxford World's Classics, 1999), p. 272. Even in her own time, Edgeworth was accused of a crude didacticism: as Ina Ferris points out, critics came to feel that there was a 'dissonance between ethical intent and the representation of feeling' in her novels. Ferris quotes Francis Jeffrey, who 'by 1817 [...] finds Edgeworth too obsessively "a Moral Teacher", her every page making the reader feel that it was "intended to do good"'. *The Achievement of Literary Authority: Gender, History, and the Waverley Novels* (Ithaca and London: Cornell University Press, 1991), p. 65.

70 Alan Richardson argues that the Romantic novel could 'exercise didactic force through its unique capacity to delineate the formation of character and depict the struggle of reason and passion within the mind'. Our point, however, is how rarely we see in Grace's mind 'the struggle of reason and passion', and how when we do, it is buried in literary allusion. *Literature, Education, and Romanticism: Reading as Social Practice, 1780–1832* (Cambridge: Cambridge University Press, 1994), p. 188.

71 See also Greg Kucich's work. He has recently argued that Charlotte Smith includes vignettes of horror for rhetorical purpose in her educational works. 'Charlotte Smith and the Political Uses of Women's Educational History', a paper given at the BARS/NASSR Conference, 'Emancipation, Liberation, Freedom', Bristol, 26 July 2007.

72 Apropos of this, Adela Pinch reads Charlotte Smith's dependence on citation in her *Elegiac Sonnets* as an acknowledgment, new to the Romantic period, that 'writing always involves taking in, reproducing, other people's expressions of feelings'. *Strange Fits of Passion: Epistemologies of Emotion, Hume to Austen* (Stanford: Stanford University Press, 1996), p. 63.

73 For Marilyn Butler, Heidi Van de Veire, and Kim Walker, Grace is 'a non-naturalistic figure, standing for family love and the love of country'. 'Introductory Note', in *The Novels and Selected Works of Maria Edgeworth*, general eds. Marilyn Butler and Mitzi Myers, 12 vols. (London: Pickering & Chatto, 1999), Vol. 5 (ed. Van de Veire and Walker with Butler), p. xxiii.

74 W. J. McCormack and Kim Walker, eds., Appendix I, *The Absentee* (Oxford: Oxford University Press), p. 275.

75 Julia Anne Miller, '"Acts of Union": Family Violence and National Courtship in Maria Edgeworth's *The Absentee* and Sydney Owenson's *The Wild Irish Girl*', in Kathryn Kirkpatrick, ed., *Border Crossings: Irish Women Writers and National Identities* (Tuscaloosa and London: University of Alabama Press, 2000), p. 31.

76 '"Acts of Union"', p. 19.

77 Maria Edgeworth, *The Absentee*, ed. Heidi Thomson and Kim Walker (London: Penguin, 1999), p. 41. All quotations from the novel are from this volume.

78 Michael Gamer explains, 'for historians of the novel used to imagining realism as a dialectic practice – an author balancing the antithetical urges of romance and reality or didactic fable and verisimilar description to produce a transcendent synthesis – Edgeworth's technique will appear oddly quirky and only partially successful, her Romantic plot twists at odds with her frequent "facts", her "realistic proclivities" perplexing in a writer so frequently pedagogical'. 'The Romance of Real Life', p. 233.

79 *The Poems of Anna Letitia Barbauld*, ed. William McCarthy and Elizabeth Kraft (Athens and London: The University of Georgia Press, 1994), pp. 9–15.

80 Barbauld, 'The Invitation', ll. 15, 10, 12, 14.

81 Barbauld, 'The Invitation', ll. 137-38.

82 Edgeworth, *The Absentee*, p. 205.

83 In regard to Grace's power here, Julia Anne Miller's point is important: she argues that '[w]hile both Edgeworth's and Owenson's novels superficially voice a liberal message of reconciliation between opposing parties, their portrayal of their Irish heroines as unmanageable, revolutionary agents who are forcibly disarmed through

marriage exposes the founding violence beneath the proposed Union' between Ireland and England. "'Acts of Union'", p. 13.

84 Edgeworth, *The Absentee*, p. 205.

85 The use of the word 'sublime' here is deliberate, first to underscore what Burke would call 'masculine' nobility and the sense of justice that this female character evinces, and second to contrast it with Burke's own view of women as the 'Beautiful'. He sees women as 'the primary creators and maintainers of "family affections" and as the embodied and embodying agents of inheritance'. See Mary Jean Corbett, 'Affections and Familial Politics: Burke, Edgeworth, and the "Common Naturalization" of Great Britain', *ELH* 61.4 (1994), pp. 877–97: p. 880. As will become clearer, we are arguing against Corbett's excellent essay. There is no doubt that Grace maintains 'family affections' and that once cleared of illegitimacy she can become a safe 'agent of inheritance'. The point we are making is that Edgeworth's focus on Grace's subjective, rather than wholly disinterested, responses to her own needs expands the role of woman beyond Burke's conception of it.

86 See, in contrast, Corbett, who argues that Grace's purported illegitimacy and Colambre's reaction to it and therefore rejection of her as his future wife asserts, like Burke, that for the stability of the family and consequently the socio-political order, female sexuality must be restrained. Thus, Grace's inheritance must be known so as to 'insur[e] continuity' and 'projec[t] the metaphorical family / property / civil society nexus as indissoluble'. Once Grace is acquitted of illegitimacy, Corbett continues, Edgeworth can have a 'Burkean resolution to this strand of the double plot: the union of the happy and virtuous couple embodies the stable fixation of sexual and affective desires across generations'. 'Affections and Familial Politics', pp. 878, 886.

87 Barbauld, 'The Invitation', ll. 33, 21, 51-52. See William McCarthy, who highlights how Barbauld, herself, 'opposes the patriarchal ideology encoded in the word[s] wisdom […] care […] improvement […] [and] profit' with images of 'pleasure, […] careless[ness] […] waste […] [and] haste'. 'We Hoped the *Woman* Was Going to Appear', in Paula R. Feldman and Theresa M. Kelley, eds., *Romantic Women Writers: Voices and Countervoices* (Hanover and London: University Press of New England, 1995), p. 126.

88 Barbauld, 'The Invitation', ll. 111-16.

89 McCarthy ('We Hoped the *Woman* Was Going to Appear') has noted the wistful yearning for such an education in Barbauld's lines. See also Penny Bradshaw, who notes '[the] bitterness Barbauld feels about her exclusion as a woman from fields of learning in […] "The Invitation"'. 'Gendering the Enlightenment: Conflicting Images of Progress in the Poetry of Anna Laetitia Barbauld', *Women's Writing* 5.3 (October 1998), pp. 353–71: p. 357. Julia Saunders shows how 'Barbauld equates science with intellectual liberty in a dramatic struggle with the forces of repression', though she does not cast this in feminist terms. "'The Mouse's Petition": Anna Laetitia Barbauld and the Scientific Revolution', *The Review of English Studies* 53 (2002), pp. 500–16: p. 506.

90 *The Absentee*, p. 44.

91 Thomas Gray, 'Elegy Written in a Country Churchyard', in David Fairer and Chris-

tine Gerrard, eds., *Eighteenth-Century Poetry: An Annotated Anthology* Oxford: Black-well Publishing Ltd, 2nd edn, 2004), pp. 354–58, ll. 49-50, 51, 52. Barbauld is also referring to Gray in 'The Invitation' when she writes, 'How rich a field is to your hopes display'd! / *Knowledge to you unlocks the classic page*; / And virtue blossoms for a better age', ll. 12-14. Emphasis added.

92 Gray, 'Elegy', l. 65. See John Guillory, who discusses Gray's 'Elegy' in relation to Barbauld's 'The Invitation' (he works with a version called 'Warrington Academy'). *Cultural Capital: The Problem of Literary Canon Formation* (Chicago: The University of Chicago Press, 1993), pp. 103–107.

93 John Plotz uses the term 'portable psychology' to describe the moment when a character 'offers the reader the ability to identify with her'. In relation to Edge-worth, Plotz uses this term to argue the opposite point: that the two lovers in *The Absentee* lack 'romantic intensity'. John Plotz, *The Crowd: British Literature and Public Politics* (Berkeley: University of California Press, 2000), pp. 49, 50.

94 Contrast Julia Anne Miller's point that Grace 'is a mute and paralyzed figure in the narrative, [who] rarely speaks, except to voice the unvoiced opinions of her beloved cousin, Colambre'. '"Acts of Union"', p. 19.

95 Here Mitzi Myers' point is relevant: 'Edgeworth's gradual and realistically depicted psychological changes are a far cry from the instantaneous conversions in many of the period's moral tales'. 'De-Romanticizing the Subject: Maria Edgeworth's "The Bracelets", Mythologies of Origin, and the Daughter's Coming to Writing', in Paula R. Feldman and Theresa M. Kelley, eds., *Romantic Women Writers: Voices and Coun-tervoices* (Hanover and London: University Press of New England, 1995), p. 288, n. 40. Myers' essay focuses not on the relationship between the didactic and the psychological, but instead on 'the relation between the child's "I" and the adult's voice, between women's subjectivity and the masculine Romantic subject, the strong psyche of poetic self-assertion' (p. 90).

96 Edgeworth, *The Absentee*, p. 206. For the deleted lines, see Van de Veire, Walker and Butler, eds., *The Novels and Selected Works of Maria Edgeworth*, Vol. 5, p. 351.

97 Julia Ann Miller Miller contends that this 'binding and gagging of her heroine results in […] a figure of contained rebellion […] reveal[ing] […] the connection between sexual and political impropriety'. '"Acts of Union"', p. 20.

98 Edgeworth, *The Absentee*, pp. 206–07; emphasis added.

99 Deidre Lynch, *The Economy of Character: Novels, Market Culture, and the Business of Inner Meaning* (Chicago: The University of Chicago Press, 1998), p. 155.

100 See Lynch, *The Economy of Character*, pp. 76, 213.

101 Butler, *Jane Austen and the War of Ideas*, p. 126.

102 Fredric Jameson, *The Political Unconscious: Narrative as a Socially Symbolic Act* (Ithaca: Cornell University Press, 1981), p. 221.

103 William Godwin, *The British Critic*, July 1795, p. 94.

CHAPTER TWO

Bad Marriages, Bad Novels:
The 'Philosophical Romance'

LAURA MANDELL

Mr S[elby]. [...] Adsheart! we shall have a double marriage, as sure as two and two make four. [...]

The Curtain Falls

– Jane Austen, *Sir Charles Grandison or The Happy Man: A Comedy in Five Acts* (written 1799)[1]

Written just after Austen had completed her first draft of *Pride and Prejudice*,[2] this sentence attests to what remains the same in the novel genre as it is transformed towards the end of the eighteenth century into a vehicle for psychological realism. Clearly, Austen had figured out by the time she co-authored this dramatic adaptation of Richardson's novel that good marriages make good novels, just as they end comic plays.[3] The satisfaction is not simply aesthetic. An ending via double marriage ensures that two and two make four; it conserves or perhaps even creates cultural rationality, the kinds of reasoning that a particular social order recognizes as indisputable. John Stevenson reminds us that, in Northrop Frye's generic theory, the distinctive feature of 'comedy' in the broadest sense of the term is 'that a concluding marriage offers its audience an image of restored social order', containing the anarchic sexual energies that had threatened its dissolution.[4]

Austen's contemporaries, the 'female Jacobin' authors Mary Hays and Mary Wollstonecraft, of course much lamented the social order.[5] If marriage is a way of rejoining and reaffirming the world as currently constituted, it offers no solution to their demand for change. The character Mary ends Wollstonecraft's novel of the same name by preparing and wishing to die, reassured that 'she was hastening to that world where there is neither marrying, nor giving in marriage'.[6] And Maria in Wollstonecraft's posthumously published *The Wrongs of Woman* connects marriage to social order and the question of its renewal when she says, 'Marriage had bastilled me for life'.[7] The 'revolution in female manners' for which Wollstonecraft calls, repeatedly, in her *Vindication of the Rights of Women* (1792) will require overturning marriage as constituted at the end of the eighteenth century.[8]

Of course, the novel form is revolutionary in the sense that, from its inception, it participates in the bourgeois 'revolution' by creating and disciplining the emerging middle class.[9] But in the sense of 'revolution' as overturning society to institute radical justice, a simultaneously classic, realistic and radically revolutionary novel is a contradiction in terms. One could argue that, as a novelist, William Godwin did not try to create a revolutionary, realistic novel, but that he strove instead to bring about a revolution in the feelings of his readers by depicting the corruption of 'things as they are'. Of course, utopianism is possible in the novel, but such imaginings alter the genre from the novel of classic realism to something else: the gothic, science fiction, allegory, fantasy literature. 'The comedy of romance', as Samuel Johnson calls the realistic novel,[10] romantically opens up the possibility of discord between an individual and social mores, but then comedically, in Dante's sense of the word, closes it down. Realism and revolution thus cannot co-exist generically – except to the extent that the classic realist novel's ending fails. 'It is just possible,' D. A. Miller says, 'that Edward Ferrars will marry Lucy Steele, or that Captain Wentworth will go away again.' Those endings would leave Austen's heroines unfulfilled within the given social structure. However, Miller continues, '[if] these possibilities were realized, [...] they would have the status of sheer and utter mistakes'.[11] A radically revolutionary novel written at the beginning of the nineteenth century would by definition be an artistic blunder.

The incompatibility of good art with progressive politics is a story we've heard repeatedly, beginning with attacks on socialist realism up to more recent attacks on aesthetic ideology. What is ideological about aesthetically pleasing totalities is the way that they seem to paper over social, political, and economic problems visible as textual contradictions, aporia, and gaps.[12] And yet in this case what is ideological is aesthetic displeasure insofar as it forecloses upon further literary analysis of so-called Jacobin novels which seem to present only an unambiguous political platform.

Wollstonecraft reports in a private letter a dinner conversation in which she and Mary Robinson debated over where, at what precise event, her novel *Mary* should have ended because the readers' sympathies were no longer engaged.[13] As a result of similar revolutionary sympathies, Hays also wrote novels contesting marriage, despite exhortations not to do so: Godwin tells her that her novel *Memoirs of Emma Courtney* (1796) has 'little story',[14] and that it would have been 'more interesting had [her] heroine been beloved'.[15] Required for readerly interest and sympathy as well as for plot ('story') is romance, a plot form that is fundamentally inimical to the Enlightenment feminist writer's desire to set her heroine on a quest for radical justice, according to Rachel Blau DuPlessis:

> [A] contradiction between love and quest in plots dealing with women as a narrated group, acutely visible in nineteenth-century fiction, has, in my view, one main mode of resolution: an ending in which one part of that contradiction, usually quest or *Bildung*, is set aside or repressed, whether by marriage or by death.[16]

Hays refuses, however, to believe that she cannot portray heroines on a quest for justice and still have romance too. Hays balked at Godwin's injunction that she make her novel 'more interesting' by making the plot conform to the rules of courtship and romance as instituted in her own imperfect world. She demurs, and responds, 'may there not be philosophical romance?'[17]

The word 'philosophical' has, of course, a long and varied history.[18] But by 'philosophical', Wollstonecraft and Hays meant 'not prejudiced', 'unsophisticated' to use another of their favourite terms which only later became a slur. At this moment, to be philosophical is to steer a course through society's sophistical reasoning, employed to justify its own corrupt practices, by refusing to grant any prejudged notion about the quality or value of things as they are. To be philosophical is to be able to stand apart from one's own historical moment and social mores in order to judge their validity. It is to be critical – not in the Kantian sense of the word – but rather by using Lockean/Hartleyian analytical method: one analyses one's associations, determining whether they have become associated in one's own mind by prejudice, culture, or personal experience, and then decides whether the association is 'rational' or 'just'.

This chapter attempts to overturn prejudices instilled by taste, arguing that novels written in the genre of philosophical romance[19] by Wollstonecraft, Hays, Mary Shelley, and Amelia Opie are in fact 'good' novels, not despite but because of their endings. In her *Vindication of the Rights of Men* (1790), Wollstonecraft insists that taste will change once radical equality is seen for what it is – once 'domination' no longer 'blasts all [our] prospects';[20] clearly she and Hays write 'philosophical romance' to an audience not yet in existence, one that will find their work beautiful because situated differently in relation to the prospect of radical democracy. Though burdened with considerably more complicated political views, Shelley and Opie too write in the genre, showing us that the term 'philosophical romance' is not at all equivalent to 'Jacobin novels', and moreover show us the value of considering these works to be interventions in form as well as politics. Beyond defending these novels by showing that their aesthetic failure comes out of adherence to an epistemological system underlying Godwin's radical vision of a just society, I show that Wollstonecraft, Hays, and Shelley deploy the novel form as a way of interpreting and revising Godwin's system, while Opie mourns its impracticality. In the process, these authors develop a new aesthetic, one that need not be considered a failure – not yet.

Godwin's radical philosophy, the one that Hays and Wollstonecraft attempted to embody in novels, had a problem insofar as rationalism can form the basis of individual but not social virtue. Looking for a way to import feeling into rationalist calculations, Hays and Wollstonecraft turned to the novel.[21] Marriage is both a metaphor for and instance of social values; the novel with its marriage plot therefore provides a space for experimentation, for trying to render 'interesting' – i.e., emotionally binding – that rationalist, equalizing virtue that according to Godwin would rule a radically egalitarian, just society. Hays, Wollstonecraft, and Shelley romanced philosophy in order to render it sociable. Their efforts should be especially interesting to scholars of British and American Romanticism insofar as they deliberately desynonymize 'Romantic' and 'individual'.[22] I argue below that the philosophical romance queers Romanticism, rendering it communal.

The Problem of Radical, Rational Philosophy

In the 1793 edition of *An Enquiry Concerning Political Justice*, William Godwin argues that human beings can achieve consensus about what should be done in any given situation ('justice') through the proper use of reason if the mind has not been imbued with 'false principles engendered by an imperfect system of society'.[23] Based on reason, civic action is voluntary. From this perspective, 'all government', from absolute monarchy ruled to a Republic regulated by laws, 'corresponds in a certain degree to what the Greeks denominated a tyranny'.[24] He then articulates the anti-authoritarian and anarchical basis of what Kant had called, nine years earlier, 'the motto of the Enlightenment':[25]

> Natural independence, a freedom from all constraint except that of reason and argument presented to the understanding, is of the utmost importance to the welfare and improvement of mind. [...] Beware of reducing men to the state of machines. Govern them through no medium but that of inclination and conviction. [...] The proper method for hastening the decay of error, is not, by brute force, or by regulation which is one of the classes of force, to endeavour to reduce men to intellectual uniformity; but on the contrary by teaching every man to think for himself.[26]

But if it is true for Godwin that 'government [...] is nothing more than a scheme for enforcing by brute violence the sense of one man or set of men upon another',[27] how can all these individuals thinking for themselves ever cohere for Godwin into a society? As he admits in the sentence following the motto 'think for yourself', 'From these principles it appears that every thing that is usually understood by the term cooperation is in some degree an evil'.[28] How will a rational society work in practice?

In Godwin's scheme, reason ensures social existence in two ways. First, as a rational creature, one realizes that promoting mutual benefit is the best way of securing one's own happiness. 'Vice' is nothing more than 'error'.[29] Second, in thinking for himself or herself, each individual will come to 'the truth': that is, consensus is possible because there is a 'single and uniform' truth.[30] The force of conviction is, for Godwin, an internal force, that, in an ideal society, would take the place of any usurping and illegitimate external force – that is, of government and rule by law. But Godwin recognizes that 'there are subjects about which we shall continually differ, and ought to differ': in those cases, what will hold us together as a group?[31]

I have just summarized part of the chapter of *Political Justice* dealing with the problem as to how 'the endless variety of mind' affects the project of regulating society rationally rather than by government. It in part attempts to answer Edmund Burke's contention that 'this new conquering empire of light and reason' won't hold together:

> On the scheme of this barbarous philosophy, which is the offspring of cold hearts and muddy understandings, [...] laws are to be supported only [...] by the concern which each individual may find in them from his own private speculations [...]. On the principles of this mechanic philosophy, our institutions can never be embodied [...] in persons [i.e., authorities]; so as to create in us love, veneration, admiration, or attachment. But that sort of reason which banishes the affections is incapable of filling their place.[32]

Burke does not see how 'bare' or 'naked' reasoning can commit people to honourable social interaction.

Whereas for conservative ideology, the law that operates in the political realm might serve as a metaphor for laws that act in the sphere of the domestic,[33] for Godwin, imagining a lawless political realm in which each individual operates rationally and responds to another individual's rational thought ('justice', he calls this[34]), the political and the domestic cannot be in any real sense separate. 'The true reason why the mass of mankind has so often been made the dupe of knaves, has been the mysterious and complicated nature of the social system' played out in everyday arrangements.[35] Hence the easy movement in this chapter from a discussion of governmental power to a discussion of when to have dinner. Because 'cooperation' with others names for Godwin all public and private action in his 'empire of reason',[36] this chapter defending rational rule contains in it Godwin's discussion of 'cohabitation' and 'marriage', though later, in the 1798 edition, it became an Appendix.

One paragraph of that appendix completely new to the 1798 edition – and written, therefore, after Godwin had met, fallen in love with, and married Mary Wollstonecraft, after the birth of their daughter Mary and after Wollstonecraft's death – adds this idea to the question of social cement in a rational society:

> It is a curious subject, to enquire into the due medium between individuality and [acting in] concert. […] [H]uman beings are formed for society. Without society, we shall probably be deprived of the most eminent enjoyments of which our nature is susceptible. In society, no man, possessing the genuine marks of a man can stand alone. Our opinions, our tempers and our habits are modified by those of each other. This is by no means the mere operation of arguments and persuasives[.][37]

Hays and Wollstonecraft take up this 'curious subject', assuming with Godwin that personal relationships are not merely a metaphor for, nor merely on a continuum with, but in fact constitutive of the political scene.[38] And of course the novel, generically tied to marriage, provides the perfect laboratory for trying the experiment of whether there can be such a thing as rational society held together through a sense of connectedness to them, i.e., through love. Needless to say, there is a great deal at stake in the success of 'philosophical romance.'

Marriage and Politics

Coleridge ends his 'Rime of the Ancyent Marinere' of 1798 by telling the 'Wedding-guest' whom he has detained to tell his tale that 'sweeter than the Marriage-feast, / 'Tis sweeter far [...] / To walk together to the Kirk / And altogether pray'.[39] The Wedding-guest leaves, 'stunn'd', having been successfully by the Marinere 'Turn'd [away] from the bridegroom's door'.[40] Relying upon these passages, Stanley Cavell argues that the poem offers prayer as a necessary substitute for marriage as a way of rendering humans social:

> [Coleridge's] Mariner teaches [his moral] by buttonholing Wedding-Guests, preferably next of kin, and leaving them stunned, so that they too '[turn away] from the bridegroom's door.' Why? Even if [the] ceremony [of all praying together] is 'sweeter than the marriage-feast,' it does not yet follow that they are incompatible, that we must choose between them. Why is the marriage deserted [...]?

Cavell ends his reading with a question that echoes *Hamlet*: '[S]hall there be no more marriages?'[41] Cavell's reading of Coleridge's 'Rime' shows that it is concerned with the problem of witnessing: the Marinere prevents the Wedding-guest from witnessing a marriage.

The question as to how witnesses might determine the authority of any performative act – its binding sacrality – is an especially pressing one during the 1790s. Questions as to the legality of performances made in front of social bodies that may not be, or not *yet* be, legitimate enforcers of legal authority, are paramount. When exactly the Third Estate actually became the National Assembly in France, when exactly its edicts began to have the force of 'state' authority, has to do with the problem of witness, of when French citizens began to react to Third Estate edicts as laws. Many such extra-legal bodies sprang up in England and Scotland, prompting the Two Acts: as can be seen in the treason trials over what was said at these conventions, the fear is that one body could or would suddenly *become* the state because witnessed as such. At such a political moment, anxieties run high about the power of performatives such as 'we declare' or 'I will'. The convening of assemblies is outlawed in 1795 by the Two Acts, also called the Gagging Acts, out of fear of the spontaneous creation of social bodies that might be taken by witnesses to have political efficacy, just as 'clandestine marriage' – the marrying of two people without parental consent and published church banns – is declared ineffective in creating a legal body, the married couple, by Lord Hardwicke's Act. Lord

Hardwicke's Act remained in effect from 1753 to 1835/6. This law insisted that marriages were not only illegal without the proper witnesses of parish and parents (they had always been that), but also – and this is new – that they were invalid.[42] The government enacts laws to prohibit private enactment of public meaning, both at the macro-level of politics and at the micro-level of marriage. Expecting people to violate the prohibition, the law declares secret acts to be null and void, meaningless. The problem is that, as the novels examined here show, secret acts are at this historical moment seen to be utterly possible.

Marriage and Meaning

Over the course of a lifetime of work on how God becomes present in the bread and wine during holy communion, Luther transfers the agent which makes possible the effect of eating the bread, God's forgiveness, from the priest to inner faith, from worldly convention witnessed by authority to interior mental act, potentially witnessed by no one.[43] The consequences of this anti-authoritarian theology were rendered practical in marriage: 'Ecclesiastical rites were prescribed by the authority of the state [in Germany] as the best means of securing publicity [for marriage], but neither Luther nor the other Protestant leaders insisted upon them as necessary to a binding marriage'.[44] Spousals, the betrothal or engagement that could be public or secret, preceded nuptials or a public marriage ceremony, but '[as] a rule, the [ecclesiastical] courts tended to treat all secret betrothals followed by actual connubial life as binding marriages. Until far down into the eighteenth century the engaged lovers before the nuptials were held to be legally husband and wife'.[45] Two people would only need to consent to marry each other for a marriage to have effectively taken place. Once verbal consent between two people who are alone is accepted as the necessary and sufficient condition for performing an act of marriage, it is a short step to imagining marriages made through a wordless mental act of internal consent on the part of both parties, along the lines of Luther's communion.

In 1685, the English legal thinker Henry Swinburne describes marriage as quite possibly even a silent act of consent when discussing the grammatical difference between promises to marry in the future and actual performances of the act:

> [The] Vulgar sort [sometimes] intend to tye such a Knot as can never be loosed, and make the [marriage] Contract so sure as it may never be dissolved; yet such

is their unskilfulness and ignorance herein, that they cannot frame their words to their minds [...] And therefore, since it is the very Consent of Mind only which maketh Matrimony, we are to regard not their Words, but their Intents, not the formality of the Phrase, but the drift of their Determination, not the outward sound of their Lips, which cannot speak more cunningly, but the inward Harmony or Agreement of their Hearts, which mean uprightly [...].[46]

Though perhaps not advocating private ceremonies, Swinburne in effect indicates that it is possible to marry through an inward aligning of hearts: it is possible to marry someone without uttering a word.

Mary Wollstonecraft's posthumously published and unfinished novel *The Wrongs of Woman, or Maria* describes how Maria's husband, Mr Venables, adds to his own infidelities by attempting to barter Maria's sexual favours for a loan; he then incarcerates her in a madhouse for the sake of obtaining control over an inheritance left to their daughter under her guardianship. While imprisoned, Maria meets and befriends an at first cruel keeper named Jemima, and then Henry Darnford, a dandy whose dissipating habits were cured by living in America. He is imprisoned in the madhouse against his will upon returning to Europe by someone who wished to defraud him of an inheritance. In *The Wrongs of Woman*, Maria and Darnford fall in love while imprisoned. Early in the novel, they marry each other through gestures: 'They were silent – yet discoursed, how eloquently?'[47] It is not till much later that they consummate their spousals, rendering them, as Darnford says, irrevocable; she then in a letter to him 'call[s] him by the sacred name of "husband"'.[48]

Mary Shelley's *Lodore*, written 40 years later, is still arguably part of this genre. Ethel is the daughter of an impetuous Byronic hero, the title character Lord Lodore. Lodore had taken her to America when she was only an infant, raised her to be virtuous in the isolated wilds of Illinois, and then died fighting in a duel when they were both on their way to return to England. Ethel falls in love with a deserving man, Villiers, who fails in subscribing too entirely to social judgements of his own worth. *Lodore* provides a dramatic instance of the wordless ceremony:

Villiers took [Ethel's] hand and held it in his [...] He felt that he was loved, and that he was about to part from her for ever. The pain and pleasure of these thoughts mingled strangely – he had no words to express them, he felt that it would be easier to die than to give her up. [...] [O]ne kindred emotion of perfect affection had, as it were, married their souls one to the other.[49]

Villiers thinks he must leave Ethel forever because he is too poor to marry her – worse, he is in debt. Ethel prefers (as she later actually demonstrates) to live in debtors' prison with him than without him. Though the 'kindred emotion' described in the above passage causes marriage for Villiers only metaphorically ('as it were'), it does so literally for Ethel, which is why she is so stunned and betrayed by his initial decision to leave her: she takes this private ceremony to mean that he is coming back; he takes it to mean that she accepts his inability to marry her but knows that he is married to her in soul, 'as it were', not in reality. Villiers's problem is his inability to prevent his life and his words from betraying each other. Even much later in the novel, even after and despite their public wedding ceremony, Villiers does not really marry Ethel until he can, as she does, see riches and social station as ancillary to a marriage rather than constitutive of it: his education as to the unreality of social appearances causes a change in his soul that renders his outlook on the value of riches the same as Ethel's, and it is only this change that allows him to truly consent to his marriage.[50] Long after their formal marriage ceremony and its consummation, the couple achieve marriage: 'the intimate union of their thoughts' allows them to 'dr[i]nk life from one another's gaze'.[51]

In Hays's *The Victim of Prejudice*, an orphan named Mary is virtually adopted by one Mr Raymond who had loved but failed to act on his love for her mother. Mr Raymond adopts and raises Mary because he feels partly responsible for – in his own self-distrusting timidity – having abandoned her mother to her seducer and father of Mary, an illegitimate child. Mr Raymond takes in two boys, sons of a gentleman, in order to raise them as well. Mary and William, the eldest of the boys, grow up living as brother and sister in Mr Raymond's house. At a crucial moment, Mr Raymond realizes that they have become too attached – William's father would never let him marry an illegitimate child. Yet by the time Mr Raymond realizes this, it is too late. Mary and William have married each other insensibly, simply in growing up together. When Mr Raymond tries to separate them, they realize that they are indeed wedded together. Again, in this case, the moment of realization happens wordlessly. Mary responds physically to the injunction of her beloved guardian not to marry William as it is contradicted by her knowledge that she is in fact already bound to him in her soul:

> my heart was rent by contending passions; confused notions of danger and impropriety, of respect for the judgement of my guardian, struggled with my native sincerity: I trembled; I felt the blood alternately forsake and rush back to my heart, which a faint sickness overspread. I sunk into a chair, and remained silent.

'I understand you,' said William [...].[52]

Mary refuses to have a minister preside over their 'nuptial-ceremony',[53] in true Godwinian form refusing to take an oath made unnecessary by the firmness of her heart:[54]

> 'If your knowledge of my heart,' [she says to William,] 'afford you not a security for my faith, weak indeed were the sanction of oaths, and unworthy the sacred flame that animates us [...].'[55]

The 'sacred flame' is the intent behind any words, its existence, these novels seem to insist, being either unnecessary to articulate or even potentially falsified in the articulation.[56]

And here we get back to why the wedding guests cannot adequately witness the wedding in Coleridge's 'Rime'. Social forms have become so corrupt that social ceremonies or rituals mean the opposite of what they pretend, marriage in fact licensing infidelity, oaths hypocrisy. As Wollstonecraft's Maria realizes, 'Had she remained with her husband, practicing insincerity, and neglecting her child to manage an intrigue, she would still have been visited and respected'.[57] Eliza Fenwick's *Secresy* makes plain that marrying legally, publicly, actually falsifies one's vows to monogamy insofar as the social form of marriage bespeaks its incipient violation.[58] 'Marriage, as at present constituted,' Wollstonecraft says in *Maria*, 'lead[s] to immorality.'[59] And the young Mary Wollstonecraft describes the insidious emptiness of public ritual in her earliest novel *Mary*.

Because it is her mother's dying wish, the heroine Mary marries one 'Charles' in order settle a suit of contested inheritance:

> The clergyman came in to read the service for the sick, and afterwards the marriage ceremony was performed. Mary stood like a statue of Despair, and pronounced the awful vow without thinking of it, and then ran to support her mother who expired the same night in her arms. Her husband set off for the continent the same day [...].[60]

It is the corruption of social institutions that forces the uttering of empty vows in marriage as well as civic engagement. Godwin describes living under a government: 'I am bound to co-operate with government, as far as it appears to me to coincide with [the] principles [of justice and truth]. But I submit to government when I think it erroneous, merely because I have no remedy.'[61] Yet both agreement and submission despite disagreement will appear the same to 'outside' observers. Godwin's predicament also obtains for participants in public marriage: vows can be said and meant or said and not meant, but what witness will be able to tell the difference? The wedding guests are detained by the Marinere: they cannot uphold the meaning of the marriage performed at a public marriage ceremony because what is performed there is undecidably marriage or its failure.

But more is rotten in Denmark than the corruption of the social ceremony's meaning. In Wollstonecraft's later novel, Maria is shunned by society for having privately married her lover, though she did so after she publicly divorced her husband for offering her sexual services for money. 'We part for ever,' she utters, a performative that has for her the efficacy of divorce:

> Then, turning to Mr. S—, I added, 'I call on you, Sir, to witness,' and I lifted my hands and eyes to heaven, 'that, as solemnly as I took his name, I now abjure it,' I pulled off my ring, and put it on the table; 'and that I mean immediately to quit his house, never to enter it more. I will provide for myself and child. I leave him as free as I am determined to be myself – he shall be answerable for no debts of mine.'[62]

Maria adheres to her vow of divorce to the bitter end, even refusing to go back to her husband in exchange for release from the madhouse. But she is not allowed by society to keep her freedom or her child. The problem is Mr S—: he is the man who attempted to purchase her sexual favours from her husband, reminding her of Mr Venables' blatant infidelities in the process. This witness is not himself virtuous enough to help her uphold her meaning. Until Society is no longer as vicious as S—, until people's intentions stand behind the meaning of their public pronouncements, marriages, Cavell takes Coleridge to be saying, cannot take place.

In Wollstonecraft's *The Wrongs of Woman*, Mr Venables' last ploy to get money out of his wife is to sue Darnforth for seduction and adultery.[63] The judge in the civil court in which Maria defends Darnforth becomes the voice of injustice whose edict almost ends the novel. In response to Maria's claim that she never committed adultery in her feelings, the judge responds:

> What virtuous woman [ever] thought of her feelings? – It was her duty to love and obey the man chosen for her by her parents and relations, who were qualified by their experience to judge better for her, than she could for herself.[64]

This unjust judge articulates the aristocratic code of honour, duty to parents in choice of a marriage partner, but then adds a bourgeois twist to the plot: she must be virtuous as well.[65]

The realistic or good novel similarly attacks aristocratic 'honour' for its corruption, participating as it does in bourgeois revolution. Both *Clarissa*[66] and *Sense and Sensibility* test out the validity of the judge's proposition, the latter demonstrating through Marianne's tragedy the inadvisability of working outside kinship networks – an affirmation of things as they are that is later more directly modified by *Persuasion*. Richardson finds greater corruption in things as they are than does Austen, showing how much 'experienced' parents and relations might operate selfishly, out of a concern for their own profit, and revealing the corruption and meaninglessness of aristocratic forms: 'If you yourself think your Word insufficient, what reliance can I have on your Oath!'[67] Like hypocritical words, the oath too often signifies the withdrawal of the very consent it is meant to mark.[68] Clarissa ultimately succeeds in reforming her parents and Lovelace, though it requires her death to do so, ensuring that the judge's ruling in *The Wrongs of Woman* could actually dispense justice (social order preserved) and simultaneously creating an ideological space of virtue that will be inhabited by the middle class (that is, by overturning aristocratic hegemony).[69] How do the novels of philosophical romance differ from 'THE novel'?

Virtue

Typically, 'virtue', like the novel itself, is seen as a fundamentally 'bourgeois' ideal.[70] Fairly certain that the French Revolution was a convulsion staged not for the sake of instituting radical democracy but rather for bringing into being the middle class, critics of Jacobin literature such as Gary Kelly have seen the Jacobin novel as an artistic 'variant' of the artefacts produced for and by 'the professional middle-class cultural revolution'.[71] As Lisa Moore puts it, 'Wollstonecraft's ideas exemplified rather than resisted the new bourgeois consensus about the virtuous self'; '[the] rational heroines of Austen and Edgeworth were much closer to Wollstonecraft's ideal [of virtue] than their political investments would seem to indicate'.[72] But is the virtue of the heroine of philosophical romance simply bourgeois?

Hays's later novel *The Victim of Prejudice* (1799) contains a moment when a Lord asks a woman to be his mistress:

[William Pelham:] 'Hear me, Mary! Drive me not to despair! – Distinguish, I pray you, between the dictates of nature and virtue and the factitious relations of society. By the former, infinitely more dear and sacred, my soul is bound to you, the first and only object of its tenderest sympathy [...]. [By the latter], in my nuptials [with another woman], mutual convenience was the bond of union; affection was, on neither side, either felt or pretended. [...]'

[Mary:] 'Think not by this sophistry, to seduce my judgement: [...] *it is virtue only that I love better than William Pelham* [...].'[73]

'What man of taste marries a woman after an affair with her?' is a line uttered by a worldly wise woman at the end of another philosophical romance, Eliza Fenwick's *Secresy* (1795),[74] and novels of taste don't marry the fallen woman either. How would someone who knows good novels from bad construct the novel's denouement from here? If Mary means by 'virtue' what Pamela means, then Pelham's wife of convenience will die suddenly and, because Mary has refused his offer to be his mistress, he will be able to convince his father that her virtue outshines her lineage and legally marry her. Or if the main character's virtue is Clarissa's, then Pelham, swept away by uncontainable desire, will rape her, and, despite the fact that his wife subsequently dies and he is free to marry her legally to repair the fault, despite her love for him, she will waste away Clarissa-like and die. *Victim of Prejudice* ends neither way. What kind of virtue is this?

Queer Families

In Hays's *Memoirs of Emma Courtney*, Emma continuously veers away from the traditional romantic quest of trying to win Augustus in marriage, ostensibly the novel's central plot. When Augustus is finally able to declare his love for Emma, after his wife's death and the end of his clandestine marriage, he is in a delirium. Coming to find her, he has fallen from his horse and lies dying, slipping in and out of consciousness: they are unable to engage together in the mental act of marriage. When he regains consciousness, it is only long enough to communicate through broken words. What Emma consents to in this disjointed conversation is not marriage but adoption of Augustus's son: 'I comprehend you – say no more – *he is mine*.'[75] This is marriage to a child, perhaps desexualized (although sometimes Emma sounds like the boy's lover), and definitely maternal: it is the performance of a promise to be his devoted mother. There is also a marriage scene in the novel resembling the marriage scenes described above: 'a strong sympathy united us, and we became almost inseparable'.[76] This scene is enacted with Augustus's mother, whom Emma calls 'more than mother', which undecidably suggests something sexual and something familial.[77] It is quite clear that Emma has fallen in love with Augustus via her love for his mother.[78] In this romance Emma falls for a family. That the goal of this romance is to establish a queer family is amply demonstrated by its ending: after the suicide of her husband Montague out of remorse for the abortion he induced in his mistress (Emma's maid) Rachel, Emma sets up a household comprising herself, her daughter, the victim Rachel, and Augustus's son whom she loves with 'more than a mother's fondness'.[79]

Like the clandestine marriage between Emma and Mrs Hartley, there is another such marriage between Maria and Jemima: Maria promises Jemima that she will teach her daughter 'to consider you as her second mother, and herself as the prop of your age. Yes, Jemima, look at me – observe me closely, and read my very soul; you merit a better fate'.[80] Jemima later asks Maria to enact 'the performance of her promise' and flee the insane asylum with her – which Maria does, despite her commitment to Darnford and the presumed death of the child, for whose sake she had offered Jemima her promise in the first place.[81] The promise to Jemima is made in the mode of marriage. Immediately before it, Maria has become married to Darnford by similarly looking into his eyes, letting him read her intentions in them as she insists that Jemima do.[82] The novel will end, Wollstonecraft's notes suggest, with Darnford's desertion and Maria, after a thwarted suicide attempt, living with Jemima and her daughter, discovered to be alive. I would call the household that ends Hays's *Victim of Prejudice* (although all the members of it die) a queer family as well, though Mary lives with her 'second father', the deceased Mr Raymond's ex-servant, then later with a family that she saved from destitution.

What's queer about these endings is that they wed together people by transgressing class and gender lines with a social glue that is paternalistic except for two things. First, the charity comes from the servants rather than the masters, who are 'more than' parental or filial, and undecidably erotic or platonic figures. This glue is based upon the capacity of its primary characters to witness each other's virtue or true intent in a society that mislabels them adultress, prostitute, or immoral indigent – in short, vicious in feeling. But that does not obviate the paternalism here: charity flows upward when recognition – what Cavell calls 'acknowledgement' of the other – flows downward.

When Jemima calls upon Maria to adhere to her promise to make her a 'second mother' to Maria's child, she says, 'on you it depends to reconcile me with the human race'.[83] Jemima, as her story shows, has been duped by everyone, even the libertine 'friends of freedom' who educated her.[84] This treachery mis-educates her, which is to say, seeing oaths uninhabited by intentions teaches her to tell lies and to mistrust any pretence of virtue. For Godwin, insincerity injures the capacity to think:[85] 'Human beings will never be so virtuous as they might easily be made, till justice be the spectacle perpetually presented to their view, and injustice wondered at as a prodigy.'[86] At stake in speaking sincerely is creating an audience of virtuous witnesses, and hence a society of virtuous people, though what most often happens is that meaning fails. For Jemima to reform into a virtuous person, someone must mean what they say to her. Maria inhabits her promise to make Jemima her child's second mother completely by the novel's end: the girl and two women live as a queer family happily ever after. Though sometimes the heroines die in the end, even those who die leave behind a primarily female family devoted to each other's future happiness. Here 'virtue' names the force ensuring social bonds that are not oppressive: these bonds are woman-to-woman.

And so this brings us to the second difference between the love found in philosophical romance and the older, feudal system of paternalistic benevolence: this glue is not paternalistic insofar as all those who are capable of performing acts of acknowledgement that involve continuously ratifying their promises, continuously inhabiting them with intention, are women.

Acknowledgement

In 'The Avoidance of Love', Stanley Cavell defines 'acknowledgement' as recognition of our helplessness before the suffering of another, as if watching a tragedy, all the while recognizing our own implication in his or her suffering.[87] While 'helplessness' suggests that Cavell's formula is a recipe for political quietism, 'implication' does not. Cavell's idea is that the pain of watching someone whom one loves suffer becomes excruciating insofar as the spectator knows himself or herself to be the cause. One avoids love, according to Cavell, insofar as to avoid one's own implication in another's pain. This formula explains the Enlightened understanding of the 'social affections'[88] at work in these novels. One member of Emma Courtney's queer family, Rachel, was at the age of 18 seduced and impregnated by Emma's husband, his jealous reaction to her '*fatal attachment* to Augustus Harley.[89] Emma's husband murders Rachel's infant after failing to abort it, then commits suicide. Emma recognizes her personal guiltlessness on the one hand: she did not commit adultery with Harley, and she told Montague of her undying love for him before they were married. Of Montague's suicide and murder, she says, 'These are the consequences of a confused system of morals' that would brand the servant Rachel a whore and unemployable were she to publicly bear and care for an illegitimate child.[90] Had she said 'These are the wages of sin', and condemned Rachel, she would be upholding that confused system of morals, putting Rachel in the position that the heroine Mary finds herself in *Victim of Prejudice*. But Emma backs up her recognition of Rachel's innocence, filling the words 'These are the consequences of a confused system of morals' with effective intentionality, by participating in and thereby creating a society that does not have such a confused system: 'I proposed to the poor girl to take her again into my family, to which she acceded with rapture'.[91] Though of course 'take her into my family' means to rehire her, the language here ('proposed', 'rapture') suggests a marriage proposal, in any case insisting that Emma's reaction to the woman's victimization by her husband is an act of love. Conversely, then, 'These are the wages of sin' is an act of hate: according to Cavell, such a refusal of acknowledgement is a way of taking revenge on the other for his or her suffering, for the demand to recognize one's own implication.

No matter how humanitarian, this love seems cold-blooded, rational, detached: what if Emma and Rachel don't really get along in personality – what if they don't *really* love each other, and so Emma acknowledges Rachel only out of a sense of duty?

Female versus Male Sentiment

In Godwin's *Memoirs* of Mary Wollstonecraft, he justifies their initial refusal to marry: 'certainly nothing can be so ridiculous upon the face of it, or so contrary to the genuine march of sentiment, as to require the overflowing of soul to wait upon a ceremony'.[92] This declaration seems so quintessentially Romantic: the spontaneous overflow of powerful feelings will brook no form, convention, or ceremony. But while it may seem that Godwin romantically focuses on the inability for lovers to wait to consummate their love, the sentence really insists that a sacred bond is forged when 'the genuine march of sentiment' meets 'the genuine march of sentiment', whether with or without words. Because the intentions must be there for both parties, it is unlikely that one could plan a ceremony and then, at the moment of publicly saying 'I will', feel, think, and intend together, as if by rote. Sentiment is of course not mere emotion, but derives from 'sententiousness', an amalgam of thought and emotion. Godwin's phrase 'genuine march of sentiment' emphasizes that genuine feeling is militaristic in some way, revolutionary, since current cultural forms require its absence.[93]

Maria and Darnforth are privately married before they can publicly announce their marriage. Though wanting the public ceremony so as 'not to be confounded with women who act from very different motives', Maria's 'conduct would be just the same without the [public] ceremony as with it'.[94] In Wollstonecraft's notes to the unfinished novel, we discover that Darnforth's unspoken oath was not as 'firm' as Maria's:[95] 'Her lover unfaithful – Pregnancy – Miscarriage – Suicide'.[96] In another ending to the novel, perhaps contradicting the first outlined ending, or perhaps adding to it, Jemima rushes in upon Maria just after she has taken an overdose of laudanum, bringing with her Maria's daughter, whose death had been faked to prevent her mother from seeking her. Maria vomits up her poison and is saved.

Whether the male characters be the worst of men (Mr Venables and Mr S— in Wollstonecraft's *Wrongs of Woman*) or the best (Darnforth in *Wrongs*, Villiers in *Lodore*, and William in Hays's *Victim of Prejudice*) it is only the women who can keep their word. Even in the latter novel, which uniquely contains some 'more than fathers', the one to live and die by her word is Mary. Wollstonecraft explains gender differences in performative power: 'A fondness for the [female] sex often gives an appearance of humanity to the behaviour of men, who have small pretensions to the reality; and they seem to love others, when they are only pursuing their own gratification'.[97] This seems like a sexist attack on Wollstonecraft's part, and yet, if one understands what's going on in this genre of novels, one can see that the crime is really impersonal, structural.

Women keep their promises because the only power they have is the personal power over their own virtue, whereas men, granted too much power in an unequal society, love other kinds of power. Women don't love the Rachels and the Darnfords, the Augustuses and the Williams, as people, but love their own power to create a permanent bond with them through virtue, the genuine march of sentiment, the strength of meaningfulness that stands outside any of society's rituals. '*[It] is virtue only that I love better than William Pelham*', Mary says.[98] As the case histories of Lodore, Villiers, Darnford, and Harley tell us, men are seduced away from the love of the power that is virtue into love of other kinds of power. As the case histories of all these Marys, Jemima, Maria, and Ethel show, women are either subjected to 'the tyranny of passions' – the feelings that arise from being victim to an unjust social system – or insist upon their capacity to act rightly independently of that system. In this case, they exercise freedom, but they still feel love. It is simply not love of a particular person, but love of their own virtue or performative power. Thus, in being 'more anxious not to deceive, than to guard against deception' in expressing her love to Darnford, Maria enacts 'true sensibility'.[99] Because women are not given the power to effect what they mean, to really mean what they mean, they must sustain their own meaningfulness with ardour. Like the word in a private language, the intention of which is insecure, their loves must be checked and rechecked. It is really this extra layer of consciousness, this critiquing of one's own feelings to make sure that one's own humanity is present to others, that allows women to partake of 'the sensibility which is the auxiliary of virtue, and the soul of genius; [the woman is] in society so occupied with the feelings of others, as scarcely to regard her own sensations'.[100] Concerned with their own virtue, their own performative power to mean what they say, the heroines of philosophical romance stand beside themselves in a sane sense, questioning their own reactions, stemming the passionate desire to take vengeance on others for their sufferings because occupied with acknowledging the feelings that arise out of unjust social circumstances and meeting those feelings with justice.

When the judge exclaims to Maria, 'What woman of virtue ever thought of her own feelings?' he is using 'feelings' to mean sensations, with a sexual innuendo. She on the other hand in insisting that she never violated any of her own vows, 'pleads her feelings', in the judge's phrase: there, feelings mean the sentiment marshalled to shore up a meaning not granted by society, and her investment in that personal virtue or strength just is the love, a love that substitutes for object love. Is it cold to love a principle rather than a person? Well, maybe. But maybe it is colder to love a person for gratification than to love a principle defining subjective power for both oneself and the loved one: these heroines don't simply uphold their own meanings but mutual meanings.

Maria divorces her husband and marries Darnford by her own performative act, and she loves her own power to do that, but it is a divorce he calls for by prostituting her: she enacts their mutual and deeply felt intentions. Making her performance of the act of marrying the treacherous Darnford into an efficacious act means allotting to herself historical and subjective performative power. Maria can only choose suicide, as Mary Wollstonecraft had once done, to enforce the meaning of the word 'husband' upon a man who has deserted her for another; only suicide allows her to preserve the power of her own utterance: I am his wife, as I said and meant, or I am non-existent. But, and this is why the novel requires two endings, suicide violates her marriage contract with Jemima and her maternal contract with her daughter. She must both die and live to be a powerful historical agent and thereby not subject to the 'tyranny of the passions' that comes from victimhood.[101]

Anti-Anti-Jacobin: Adeline Mowbray

Within the literary history of the Jacobin novel, Amelia Opie's *Adeline Mowbray* has been seen as an anti-Jacobin novel, directly attacking Godwin and his ideals about marriage in the ill-fated and destructive character of Glenmurray who quite literally wrecks Adeline's life by living with her without marrying her.[102] But Miriam Wallace has rightly argued that it is reductive to see Opie's novel as simply anti-Jacobin.[103] For one thing, Opie never withdraws sympathy from her heroine, nor prompts us to do so, even though Adeline has been misguided by Godwin's system.

Early in the novel, Adeline utters a speech that expresses and affirms Godwin's ideas about marriage, wishing to communicate her views to Glenmurray who, in the novel's world, had written and published about them. Adeline has met this radical philosopher at Bath, and has been taught by her similarly 'philosophical' mother to think freely. For Opie, though, Adeline's mother puts on radical philosophy for the sake of being fashionable in an avant-garde way, and, when it comes to her daughter's and her own romances, she reveals herself underneath it all to be truly conventional. Glenmurray is treated less cynically, but he too abandons his principles when their social consequences become completely clear to him. At Bath, Adeline's speech reiterating Glenmurray's unorthodox views of marriage precipitates unwanted advances from her widowed mother's gold-digging new young paramour, who happened also to be in the room when she spoke. In protesting against this rake's definition of 'honour' – in the phrase 'man of honour' – as promiscuity, Adeline proclaims that it is not marriage but 'the individuality of an attachment that constitutes its chastity', echoing a statement made by Emma in Hays's novel published eight years earlier:[104]

> I loved you, not only rationally and tenderly – *but passionately* – it became a pervading and a devouring fire! And yet, I do not blush – my affection was modest, if intemperate, *for it was individual* – it annihilated in my eyes every other man in the creation.[105]

Adeline comes to regret that she placed her faith in her own understanding of chastity rather than in traditional marriage or 'a continuance in those paths of virtue and decorum which the wisdom of ages has pointed out to the steps of every one'.[106] And yet, we have in this novel as well two scenes showing the main characters making sometimes secret[107] and sometimes private vows[108] that both Glenmurray and Adeline Mowbray hold sacred and binding throughout the novel: Adeline is tempted to lie about her past, but never does.[109] And this novel, too, ends with a community of women all of whom are committed to either living together or supporting each other financially: Adeline's mother; Mrs Pemberton the Quaker; two women who have hastened Adeline's ruin (her greedy and lying cousin Miss Woodville, and her one-time servant Mary Warner, a woman who had an illegitimate child); Savanna (Adeline's devoted 'mulatto' servant who often works for her without food and pay); and Editha, Adeline's legitimate daughter. Only one male character remains at the end within this circle of women, Dr Norberry, who several times identifies himself as 'an old woman'.[110]

As the subtitle suggests, the novel is really about the star-crossed but pure and passionate love between mother and daughter. As she is dying, Adeline asks her mother if she 'loves [her] still':

> 'Love you still!' replied Mrs. Mowbray wth passionate fondness: – 'never, never were you so dear to me as now!'

Adeline does die in the end, but she does so grasping her mother's hand in passionate joy and with 'her head on Savanna's bosom'.[111] She has adored these women and has been adored by them precisely because of her difference from all the men in the novel: 'Do you tink, if she be one selfish beast like her husband, Savanna lover her so dear?' exclaims her mulatto servant.[112] When Adeline dies, she leaves a strong community of worshippers dedicated to following her unselfish principles in dealings with each other – a utopian and completely female community. This novel, I would suggest, is classifiable as philosophical romance as well. That

Adeline Mowbray articulates ideas opposed to *Emma Courtney* does not disqualify it from the genre of philosophical romance. Like *Emma*, it threatens to seem aesthetically inferior because its ending is so queer.

Conclusion

In *The Trouble with Normal*, Michael Warner implicates the novel genre as inspiring the push among some gay and lesbian groups for state-sanctioned same-sex marriage.[113] Opposing that desire, Warner says that advocating same-sex marriage by adopting (novelistic) discourses of chastity and virtue requires 'a massive repudiation of queer culture's best insights on intimate relations':

> The impoverished vocabulary of straight culture tells us that people should be either husbands and wives or (nonsexual) friends. Marriage marks that line. It is not the way many queers live. If there is such a thing as a gay way of life, it consists in these relations, a welter of intimacies outside the framework of professions and institutions and ordinary social obligations. Straight culture has much to learn from it [...].[114]

In her life, Wollstonecraft showed herself to be less impoverished, in her romantic friendship with Fanny Blood as well as in the famous escapade in which she asked Henry Fuseli to allow her to live with him and his wife. In one of her letters to Imlay, Wollstonecraft offers rather queerly to establish a home consisting of Imlay, Wollstonecraft, their daughter Fanny, and Imlay's current mistress. Imlay refuses. Could Wollstonecraft's proposal really have been indecorous to such a hardened and public philanderer as Imlay? This was an arrangement that Imlay was certainly not too *sexually* but too *politically* prudish to accept. Godwin calls the proposal 'injudicious', his word for 'queer'.[115] Insofar as he (consciously, at least) uses the word 'injudicious' as a term of disapprobation for Wollstonecraft's attempt to live with Imlay and his mistress, Godwin points to his own inability to imagine the most radical consequences of fully lived political justice.

Yes, these novels can be read as only revolutionary in the sense of bourgeois. But then of course they will have to be condemned aesthetically as bad novels because they do not effectively imagine the heterosexual *domos*. They portray families neither nuclear nor 'extended' with kin, but queer, bound together by the continuous performance of personal justice. One can see the achievement of these novels when one looks at them as explorations of what fails in Godwin's revolutionary epistemology once it is put into action in the real world, which Hays and Wollstonecraft at least were trying to do in their lives. The endings of these novels, and the domestic arrangements that they idealize, are queer as Warner defines it, naming 'relations of durability and care' and involving 'an astonishing range of intimacies' that are sexually charged but also very complex because 'the rules [for these relationships] have to be invented as we go along'.[115] We do not have to read philosophical romance through the lens of compulsory heterosexuality. If the political and aesthetic power of the philosophical romance depends upon the virtue of witnesses, then let's witness better and call it 'good'.

Notes

1 Jane Austen, *Sir Charles Grandison*, ed. Brian Southam (Oxford: Clarendon Press, 1980), p. 57.

2 Austen, *Sir Charles Grandison*, p. 6.

3 Such is the assumption of all the essays gathered together by Robert Clark about two of Austen's novels. Written by major literary critics, these essays ruminate on the extent to which, given the aesthetic satisfaction of the endings, Austen's novels actually close down or open up the possibility for critiquing the patriarchal ideology that would like to see women objectified and legally restrained. See articles by Butler, Armstrong, and Newman, in Robert Clark, ed., *New Casebooks: Sense and Sensibility and Pride and Prejudice* (London: St Martin's Press, 1994).

4 John Allen Stevenson, '"A Geometry of His Own": Richardson and the Marriage-Ending', *Studies in English Literature, 1500–1700* 26.3 (Summer 1986), pp. 469–83, p. 471.

5 Miriam Wallace discusses the differences between them that tend to be erased by this rubric, Hays's valuation of feeling as an element of philosophy versus Wollstonecraft's privileging of reason ('Mary Hays's "Female Philosopher": Constructing Revolutionary Subjects', in Adriana Craciun and Kari Lokke, eds., *Rebellious Hearts: British Women Writers and the French Revolution* [Albany, NY: SUNY Press, 2001], pp. 233–60).

6 Mary Wollstonecraft, *Mary and The Wrongs of Woman*, ed. Gary Kelly (New York: Oxford University Press, 1976, 1980), p. 68.

7 Wollstonecraft, *Wrongs*, pp. 154–55.

8 Mary Wollstonecraft, *A Vindication of the Rights of Woman* (1792, 2nd edn), ed. Carol Poston (New York: Norton, 1988, 1975), pp. 45, 192.

9 Nancy Armstrong, 'Writing Women and the Making of the Modern Middle Class', in Amanda Gilroy and W. M. Verhoeven, eds., *Epistolary Histories: Letters, Fiction, Culture* (Charlottesville: University Press of Virginia, 2000), pp. 29–50, 35, 42–44; Mary Poovey, 'Ideological Contradictions and the Consolations of Form', from *The Proper Lady and the Woman Writer: Ideology as Style in the Works of Mary Wollstonecraft,*

Mary Shelley, and Jane Austen (Chicago: University of Chicago Press, 1984), reprinted in Clark, ed., *New Casebooks*, pp. 83–118, 85.

10 Samuel Johnson, *Rambler* No. 4 (Saturday, 31 March 1750), in Samuel Johnson, *Selected Poetry and Prose*, ed. Frank Brady and W. K. Wimsatt (Berkeley: University of California Press, 1977), p. 155.

11 D. A. Miller, 'Closure and Narrative Danger', in Clark, ed., *New Casebooks*, pp. 67–82, 72.

12 The locus classicus of this argument in British Romantic Studies is Jerome McGann, *The Romantic Ideology* (Chicago: University of Chicago Press, 1983); see also Marjorie Levinson, *Wordsworth's Great Period Poems* (Cambridge: Cambridge University Press, 1986). The best rebuttal I have seen to date is Susan Wolfson, 'The Speaker as Questioner in *Lyrical Ballads*', *Journal of English and Germanic Philology* 77 (1978), pp. 546–68, a polemic that she continues in *Formal Charges* (Stanford: Stanford University Press, 1997).

13 Mary Wollstonecraft to Mary Hays, unpublished letter, postmarked November 1796 (Carl Pforzheimer Collection, New York Public Library, MW 43).

14 I am distilling comments made by Godwin in his letter to Hays dated 9 March 1796 (reprinted in Mary Hays, *Memoirs of Emma Courtney* [1796], ed. Marilyn Brooks [Peterborough, Ontario: Broadview Press, 2000], p. 250) and in a very psychologically distressed undated, unpublished letter (MH 18 in the Carl Pforzheimer Collection) that clearly responds to Godwin's critique of her novel, and in my view responds specifically to his letter of 9 March. I will cite Hays's letters from Brooks edition, unless I quote from letters such as MH 18 that Brooks did not include. I am grateful to the Pforzheimer Collection of the New York Public Library for giving me access to these manuscripts.

15 Hays, *Memoirs*, p. 256.

16 Rachel Blau DuPlessis, *Writing Beyond the Ending: Narrative Strategies of Twentieth-Century Women Writers* (Bloomington: Indiana University Press, 1985), pp. 3–4.

17 Mary Hays to William Godwin, handwritten date 10 January 1796; postmark 9 February 96 (MH 13, Pforzheimer).

18 John Vladimir Price, 'The Reading of Philosophical Literature', in Isabel Rivers, ed., *Books and their Readers in Eighteenth-Century England* (New York: St Martin's Press, 1982), pp. 165–96.

19 Though I won't discuss it here, Eliza Fenwick's *Secresy* fits into this category. It has been analysed in relation to the politics of marriage by Sarah Emsley, 'Radical Marriage', *Eighteenth-Century Fiction* 11.4 (July 1999), pp. 477–98.

20 Mary Wollstonecraft, *Vindication of the Rights of Men*, in *A Wollstonecraft Anthology*, ed. Janet Todd (New York: Columbia University Press, 1989), pp. 80–81.

21 Wallace, 'Mary Hays's "Female Philosopher"'.

22 Though often seen as originating in Descartes's cogito and Locke's notion of identity, 'individualism' can often be glossed 'Romantic individualism', especially during the 1790s. The word 'individual' means 'singular, not plural', and 'romantic' often means 'singular, peculiar' – or 'wild, uncivilized', a singularity and wildness that, from Charlotte Lennox's *The Female Quixote* to Wollstonecraft's *Mary*, comes into existence out of a person's isolation. 'Desynonymy' is Coleridge's term for an analysis that distinguishes two ideas confused under one word, and his own act of

desynonymizing distinguishes, famously, imagination from fancy. (*Biographia Literaria*, 1817, 2 vols., ed. James Engell and Walter Jackson Bate [Princeton: Princeton University Press], Vol. 1, pp. 82–84. The best explication of 'desynonymy' that I have seen can be found in Barrett Watten, *The Constructivist Moment: From Material Text to Cultural Poetics* (Middletown, CT: Wesleyan University Press, 2003), pp. 16–25.

23 William Godwin, *Enquiry Concerning Political Justice*, 1793, 1796, 1798, Vols. 3 and 4 of *Political and Philosophical Writings of William Godwin*, ed. Mark Philp (London: William Pickering, 1993), Vol. 3, p. 19.

24 Godwin, *Political and Philosophical Writings*, Vol. 3, p. 308.

25 Immanuel Kant, 'An Answer to the Question: What is Enlightenment?' (1784), in *On History*, trans. Lewis White Beck et al. (New York: Macmillan, 1963), p. 3.

26 Godwin, *Political and Philosophical Writings*, Vol. 3, pp. 448–50.

27 Godwin, *Political and Philosophical Writings*, Vol. 3, p. 110.

28 Godwin, *Political and Philosophical Writings*, Vol. 3, p. 450.

29 Godwin, *Political and Philosophical Writings*, Vol. 3, p. 20.

30 Godwin, *Political and Philosophical Writings*, Vol. 3, p. 131; Vol. 3, p. 104.

31 Godwin, *Political and Philosophical Writings*, Vol. 3, p. 450.

32 Edmund Burke, *Reflections on the Revolution in France* (1790), ed. Conor Cruise O'Brien (New York: Penguin, 1968, 1987), pp. 171–72.

33 David Kaufmann, 'Law and Propriety, Sense and Sensibility: Austen on the Cusp of Modernity', *ELH* 59.2 (1993), pp. 385–408, 396.

34 'Justice is a rule of conduct originating in the connection of one percipient being with another' (Godwin, *Political and Philosophical Writings*, Vol. 3, p. 49).

35 Godwin, *Political and Philosophical Writings*, Vol. 3, p. 309.

36 Godwin, *Political and Philosophical Writings*, Vol. 3, p. 311.

37 Godwin, *Political and Philosophical Writings*, Vol. 4, p. 335.

38 Evidence of just how indebted the feminist movement is to Enlightenment thinking, should we need any more, is that Godwin's notion of political justice entails the idea that the personal is the political.

39 Samuel Taylor Coleridge, 'Rime of the Ancyent Marinere', in William Wordsworth and Samuel Taylor Coleridge, *Lyrical Ballads* (1798), ed. W. J. B. Owen (New York: Oxford University Press, 2nd edn, 1969), pp. 7–32, 31, ll. 630, 634–35, 638–39.

40 Coleridge, 'Rime', ll. 654–55.

41 Stanley Cavell, 'In Quest of the Ordinary', in Morris Eaves and Michael Fischer, eds., *Romanticism and Contemporary Criticism* (Ithaca: Cornell University Press, 1986), pp. 183–213, 201.

42 Emsley, 'Radical Marriage', p. 481.

43 Ralph W. Quere, 'Changes and Constants: Structure in Luther's Understanding of the Real Presence in the 1520s', *Sixteenth Century Journal* 16.1 (1985), pp. 45–78, 72.

44 George Elliott Howard, *A History of Matrimonial Institutions*, 2 vols. (Chicago: University of Chicago Press, 1904), Vol. 1, p. 370.

45 Howard, *History*, Vol. 1, p. 374.

46 Henry Swinburne, *A Treatise of Spousals, or Matrimonial Contracts wherein all the questions relating to that subject are ingeniously debated and resolved* (London: Robert Clavell, 1st edn, 1686), p. 62. On the difference between spousals in the future and spousals in

the present, see Emsley, 'Radical Marriage', pp. 478–79.

47 Wollstonecraft, *Wrongs*, p. 100.

48 Wollstonecraft, *Wrongs*, pp. 188, 190.

49 Mary Shelley, *Lodore* (1835) (Peterborough, Ontario: Broadview Press, 1997), p. 238.

50 Shelley, *Lodore*, pp. 338, 338–39.

51 Shelley, *Lodore*, p. 339.

52 Mary Hays, *The Victim of Prejudice* (1799, 2nd edn), ed. Eleanor Ty (Peterborough, Ontario: Broadview Press, 1998), p. 52.

53 Hays, *Victim*, p. 84.

54 Godwin, *Political and Philosophical Writings*, Vol. 3, pp. 339–41.

55 Hays, *Victim*, p. 85.

56 On falsification of wedding vows through publicly uttering them, see Laura Mandell, 'Sacred Secrets: Romantic Biography, Romantic Reform', *Nineteenth-Century Prose* 28.2 (2001), pp. 28–54.

57 Wollstonecraft, *Wrongs*, p. 192.

58 For a detailed discussion of Fenwick's novel, see Mandell, 'Sacred Secrets'.

59 Wollstonecraft, *Wrongs*, p. 193.

60 Wollstonecraft, *Mary*, p. 15.

61 Godwin, *Political and Philosophical Writings*, Vol. 3, p. 97.

62 Wollstonecraft, *Wrongs*, p. 162.

63 Wollstonecraft, *Wrongs*, p. 192; see also Lawrence Stone on the law of 'criminal conversation', *Broken Lives: Separation and Divorce in England 1660–1857* (New York: Oxford University Press, 1993), pp. 22–25.

64 Wollstonecraft, *Wrongs*, p. 199.

65 Michael McKeon articulates the novel's attempt to elevate bourgeois over aristocratic ideology in *The Origins of the English Novel 1600–1740* (Baltimore: Johns Hopkins University Press, 1987), pp. 131–33.

66 I'm grateful to Sarah Pittock for alerting me to continuities between Richardson's work and the revolutionary writings I wish to explore.

67 Samuel Richardson, *Clarissa or the History of a Young Lady*, ed. Angus Ross (New York: Penguin, 1985), p. 1071.

68 Richardson, *Clarissa*, pp. 73, 376, 1280, 1283, 1433. Frances Ferguson, 'Rape and the Rise of the Novel', in R. Howard Bloch and Frances Ferguson, eds., *Misogyny, Misandry, and Misanthropy* (Berkeley: University of California Press, 1989), pp. 88–112. Though in Ferguson's view the problem of being unable to mean what one wishes in social forms has to do with 'symbolic systems themselves' (pp. 108–109), one can argue that it is historically locatable.

69 Armstrong, 'Writing Women', p. 42.

70 McKeon, *Origins*, pp. 131–33, 212.

71 Gary Kelly, *Women, Writing, and Revolution, 1790–1827* (New York: Oxford University Press, 1993), p. 81.

72 Lisa Moore, *Dangerous Intimacies: Toward a Sapphic History of the Novel* (Durham, NC: Duke University Press, 1997), p. 152. It is possible to conclude (though Moore doesn't) that the difference between Wollstonecraft's and Austen's novels has to do with artistic skill. Insofar as it is true that, in the verbal battle between English

Jacobins and anti-Jacobins, 'both sides were really on the same side', the side 'of bourgeois culture' (Moore, pp. 151–52), the difference between Hays's and Austen's *Emmas* is really uninteresting – and perhaps even embarrassing to feminists. Hays's works could be seen as revealing a Romantic enthusiasm inimical to the artistry required for novel writing that provides a sad contrast to Austen's realistic and ironic wit.

73 Hays, *Victim*, p. 127.

74 Eliza Fenwick, *Secresy; or, The Ruin on the Rock* (1795), ed. Isobel Grundy (Peterborough, Ontario: Broadview Press, 1994), p. 345.

75 Hays, *Memoirs*, p. 205.

76 Hays, *Memoirs*, p. 91.

77 Hays, *Memoirs*, pp. 101, 183.

78 Hays, *Memoirs*, p. 91.

79 Hays, *Memoirs*, p. 219.

80 Wollstonecraft, *Wrongs*, p. 121.

81 Wollstonecraft, *Wrongs*, p. 189.

82 Wollstonecraft, *Wrongs*, p. 100.

83 Wollstonecraft, *Wrongs*, p. 189.

84 Wollstonecraft, *Wrongs*, p. 119.

85 Godwin, *Political and Philosophical Writings*, Vol. 3, p. 135.

86 Godwin, *Political and Philosophical Writings*, Vol. 3, p. 254.

87 Stanley Cavell, 'The Avoidance of Love: A Reading of *King Lear*', in Stanley Cavell, *Must We Mean What We Say?* (New York: Cambridge University Press, 1976), pp. 267–356.

88 Hays, *Memoirs*, p. 220.

89 Hays, *Memoirs*, p. 211.

90 Hays, *Memoirs*, p. 217.

91 Hays, *Memoirs*, p. 218.

92 They did marry later, after Wollstonecraft became pregnant. Mary Wollstonecraft and William Godwin, *A Short Residence in Sweden [1796] and Memoirs of the Author of 'The Rights of Woman' [1798]*, ed. Richard Holmes (New York: Penguin, 1987), p. 258.

93 The first book about the revolutionary potential of sensibility is C. B. Jones, *Radical Sensibility: Literature and Ideas in the 1790s* (New York: Routledge, 1993); on Hays's and Wollstonecraft's understanding of sentiment and feeling, see Wallace, 'Mary Hays's "Female Philosopher"'; Claudia Johnson, *Equivocal Beings: Politics, Gender, and Sentimentality in the 1790s* (Chicago: University of Chicago Press, 1995).

94 Wollstonecraft, *Wrongs*, p. 194.

95 Wollstonecraft, *Wrongs*, p. 194.

96 Notes to the as yet unwritten Vol. III, ch. IV; Wollstonecraft, *Wrongs*, p. 202.

97 Wollstonecraft, *Wrongs*, p. 192.

98 Hays, *Victim*, p. 127.

99 Wollstonecraft, *Wrongs*, p. 188.

100 Wollstonecraft, *Wrongs*, p. 176.

101 Hays, *Memoirs*, p. 221.

102 I'm grateful to Anne Mellor for insisting that I compare this novel to the others

insofar as doing so helped me to see the generic features of philosophical romance and distinguish it from the Jacobin political platform. The best edition for conducting such a comparison is Miriam L. Wallace, ed., Mary Hays, *Memoirs of Emma Courtney*, and Amelia Alderson Opie, *Adeline Mowbray; or, the Mother and the Daughter* (Glen Allen, VA: College Publishing, 2004).

103 Miriam L. Wallace, 'Introduction', in Wallace, ed., *Memoirs and Adeline Mowbray*, pp. 1–41, 4.

104 Opie, *Adeline Mowbray*, p. 317.

104 Opie, *Adeline Mowbray*, p. 159. Wallace quotes Roxanne Eberle: that 'the individuality of an affection constitutes its chastity' is Wollstonecraft's ideal (see Roxanne Eberle, 'Amelia Opie's Adeline Mowbray: Diverting the Libertine Gaze; or, the Vindication of a Fallen Woman', *Studies in the Novel* 26.2 (1994), pp. 121–54, quoted in Wallace, 'Introduction', p. 11).

106 Opie, *Adeline Mowbray*, p. 506.

107 Opie, *Adeline Mowbray*, p. 318.

108 Opie, *Adeline Mowbray*, p. 330.

109 Opie, *Adeline Mowbray*, pp. 504–505.

110 Opie, *Adeline Mowbray*, p. 621. As Anne Mellor puts it in discussing the utopianism of women's political writing, 'One might also look to Amelia Opie's novel *Adeline Mowbray* (1802), which sites the future salvation of the British body politic in a reconstituted family of choice, one composed of an upper-class British woman, a middle-class Quaker woman, a working-class freed African slave woman' (*Mothers of the Nation: Women's Political Writing in England, 1780–1830* [Bloomington: Indiana University Press, 2000], p. 145). For me what is most striking about this community is that it includes two women who tried to destroy and succeeded in killing the heroine: their crimes are seen as structural and their corruption thus curable by relocating them in a community with equitable power distribution.

111 Opie, *Adeline Mowbray*, p. 625.

112 Opie, *Adeline Mowbray*, p. 561.

113 Michael Warner, *The Trouble with Normal: Sex, Politics, and the Ethics of Queer Life* (New York: Free Press, 1999), p. 100. Warner does so directly, but also implicitly: he accuses proponents of same-sex marriage as attempting 'to woo marriage' and therefore of participating in the romance plot as they construct a 'revisionist and powerfully homophobic narrative' (p. 95).

114 Warner, *Trouble*, pp. 91, 116.

115 Godwin, in Wollstonecraft and Godwin, *Short Residence and Memoirs*, p. 252.

116 Warner, *Trouble*, p. 116.

CHAPTER THREE

Enlightenment or Illumination: The Spectre of Conspiracy in Gothic Fictions of the 1790s

MARKMAN ELLIS

What is enlightenment? In the twentieth century, scholars have found the term 'the Enlightenment' a convenient designation for the intellectual history of the eighteenth century, although there has been little agreement between different scholars, disciplines and national traditions about what the term might mean. In his landmark study *The Philosophy of the Enlightenment*, first published in German in 1932, and belatedly translated into English in 1951, Ernst Cassirer (1874–1945) defined the Enlightenment as 'a value-system rooted in rationality', whose history was bounded by the lives of two philosophers, Gottfried Wilhelm Leibniz (1646–1716) and Immanuel Kant (1724–1804).[1] In Cassirer's intellectual history, the term 'Enlightenment' denotes the major movement in the history of ideas in eighteenth-century Europe, defining the modernity of the period, championing rationality over faith and superstition, reason and liberty over custom and tyranny, science over religion. Yet in the period itself, the term 'Enlightenment' was almost unknown: the *Oxford English Dictionary* suggests the term was not used in English in the modern sense until the 1860s, when it was derived from a translation of the German *Aufklärung*.[2]

This essay explores the coincidence between three phenomena in the intellectual life of late 1790s' Britain. The first is the emergence of the sub-genre of Romantic fiction that later became known as the gothic novel, particularly that of Ann Radcliffe (1764–1823) and Matthew Lewis (1775–1818), but also in a group of minor novelists. The second is the first publication of English translations of Kantian philosophy, published in the late 1790s by a small group of English philosophers who had a reading knowledge of German, and an interest in German thought. The third is the media event of the Illuminati Conspiracy, a spectacular controversy that engulfed British and American political debate in 1797 and 1798, supposedly exposing a large-scale subversion of the church and the monarchy prosecuted by a trans-national secret society. Through the debate engendered by this coincidence, which was in no sense accidental, the Romantic period witnessed a new understanding of Enlightenment thought, both in its intellectual principles and in its characteristic methods of social organization.

The gothic novel, with its spectacular hunger for ghosts, revenants and the world of spirits, seems to propose an allegiance to supernatural forms of knowledge and, as such, it might be supposed to be part of the project of the counter-Enlightenment. Many critics of the mid-twentieth century have followed this line of analysis: in 1973 Peter Brooks identified the gothic novel's hostility to 'the pretensions of rationalism', invoking Devendra Varma's claim in 1957 that the works of Radcliffe and Lewis participate in a 'quest for the numinous' (suggesting the presence of a spirit or god).[3] Nonetheless, in recent years the gothic novel has been located as a participant in the rationalizing project of Enlightenment. Clara Tuite, for example, has argued that *The Monk* 'is not a reaction to the Enlightenment […] but a form of Enlightenment discourse', in which the novel's 'unmasking, revelation and rending the veil of church hypocrisy' has the effect of 'opening superstitious church institutions to the light of reason'.[4] In the gothic novel of Radcliffe and Lewis, the dynamics of the supernatural experience are explored and examined in a succession of spectral simulacra, defined here as the novelized simulation of supernatural phenomena, typically articulated through a complex grammar of narrative machinery and a repertoire of gothic tropes. In their imaginative speculations, this essay suggests, these gothic fictions of the 1790s make an important, yet overlooked, contribution to the Anglophone understanding of the 'the Enlightenment'.

A key moment in the modern understanding of 'the Enlightenment' occurred in 1783 in the columns of a Berlin newspaper, the *Berlinische Monatsschrift*, which challenged its readers to answer the question 'What is enlightenment?' (Was ist Aufklärung?). The essays it received in response from Kant and Moses Mendelssohn (1729–86) suggested that enlightenment was not a condition in itself, but a process guided by reason.[5] Kant's response, the much celebrated essay now known in English as 'An Answer to the Question: What is Enlightenment?' (1784), has subsequently gained great notice as a summary statement of the Enlightenment project in Germany and Europe. Kant's essay first appeared in English in 1798, as the introduction to a collection of Kant's writing translated by a little-known Scottish philosophical writer, John Richardson.[6] In his translation, the famous first paragraph answered the question 'What is Enlightening?' in this way:

> *Enlightening is, Man's quitting the nonage occasioned by himself. Nonage* or minority is the inability of making use of one's own understanding without the guidance of another. This nonage is *occasioned by one's self,* when the cause of it is not from want of understanding, but of resolution and courage to use one's own understanding without the guidance of another. *Sapere aude!* Have courage to make use of thy own understanding! is therefore the dictum of enlightening.[7]

Kant suggested that mankind could only be free from superstition and autocracy by trusting in mankind's own power of reasoning. 'If it is now enquired, do we live at present in an *enlightened* age?', Kant concluded, 'The answer is, No, but by all means in an age of *enlightening*.[8] In later translations, this final phrase becomes 'an age of *enlightenment*' – not in the sense used by Cassirer in the twentieth century of 'the Enlightenment', but rather, a process. As Kant suggests, enlightenment is not a state of being or a condition of the understanding, but a process or a methodology. In Richardson's translation, this methodological concern is reinforced by his use of the term 'enlightening'. Kant defends the questioning power of reason, urging mankind to resist the clergyman's exclamation, 'Don't reason, but believe!'[9] Richardson's translation of *Aufklärung*, however, did not take root. Throughout most of the nineteenth century, the dominant term used to translate it was 'illumination'; and only in the 1890s was 'enlightenment' adopted widely.[10] In its particular sense of 'the Enlightenment', then, the term is more a part of the history of philosophy's twentieth-century historiography than it is an integral part of the history of eighteenth-century or Romantic-period philosophy.

Enlightenment, in Kant's formulation, implies the liberation of mankind from superstition and irrational thinking. In Richardson's translation, the term is a binary, enlightening *from* something, the darkness of unreason. The metaphor of illumination is deeply embedded in the term: especially the action or process of shedding light upon something, to supply with intellectual light, to impart the light of knowledge. 'In the dark,' the German poet Christoph Martin Wieland (1733–1813) remarked in 1789, 'one either sees not at all or at least not so clearly.' But 'as soon as light is brought, things are cleared up, become visible, and can be distinguished from one another'.[11] Wieland's stolid unpacking of the metaphorics of illumination demonstrates how light brings with it clarity, resolution and closure, and by contrast, how darkness – so loved by the gothic novel – breeds superstition, spectral phenomena, and all the *diablerie* of the supernatural. The debate around 'the Enlightenment' is structured by a series of significant oppositions: light and dark, reason and superstition, liberty and tyranny, democracy and autocracy, public and secret. These oppositions are however mutually informative, entangled in the same debates and discourses. In the case of the gothic fiction, the form of the novel undertakes a rational inquiry into the nature of the rational and supernatural.

Secrecy and the Plot of Conspiracy

A central aspect of Enlightenment science was sociability, undertaken through learned institutions such as the Royal Society, scientific clubs and associations, and debating associations and assemblies in coffee-houses and taverns. Through their meetings, these sociable circles encouraged the dissemination of a learned and progressivist philosophy. Following Habermas, it has been customary to describe these public gatherings as part of a public sphere, but their meetings were also, in an important sense, private and exclusive, open only to members and adepts. Private and exclusive societies, as well as secret societies, were integral to the intellectual circles of the Romantic period.[12] The most extensive of these private fraternal societies was the Freemasons. After the movement's foundation in Britain in the early years of the eighteenth century, Freemasons following various different ritual practices became widespread across continental Europe. Their secret meetings, with arcane hierarchies, secret signs and cryptic tokens, exerted a profound attraction for a broad cross-section of men drawn from the nobility and the middle stations of life.[13] Unlike its British origins, German freemasonry took on a notably secret associational form, given to esoteric and mystical elaboration.[14]

An influential example of such secret societies was the League of Illuminati, supposed to have been founded in 1776 by Adam Weishaupt, a professor of canon law at the University of Ingolstadt in Bavaria. The nature of their influence, and most of the facts relating to their history, remain contested and obscure (secret societies, as their name suggests, tend to evade historical analysis). Their name, from the Italian *illuminati*, referred to their self-conception as the enlightened ones. The Illuminati were committed to an Enlightenment programme of utopian political social and educational reform derived from their study of progressivist philosophy, including Adam Smith, Lessing, Rousseau, Holbach, and Helvetius. To secure their reformist aims in the potentially hostile climate of the Bavarian court, they worked in secret, infiltrating the institutional structures of the state, aiming to resist the influence of the Jesuits. To protect their identity and their plan, they adopted secret names derived from classical and alchemical sources for themselves and their cities (Weishaupt was known as Spartacus, after the rebel Roman slave, for example, while Munich was known as Athens). Their moderate and reformist ideas gained some influence among intellectuals in Germany, including Goethe, Herder and possibly the poet Wieland. Nonetheless, the Elector of Bavaria, Karl Theodore (1777–99), came under the increasing influence of their enemies the Jesuits, and in 1784 and 1795, their anti-clerical agitation led to their exposure and suppression. The celebrity of the society was ensured by the publication (or fabrication) of hitherto secret documents seized after their suppression, detailing their plans, secret meetings and ritual practices.[15]

The exact nature of the Illuminati programme is now impossible to determine: their own secrecy, and their official suppression, have both rendered their intentions and influence obscure. While their direct influence is supposed to have faded quickly, in the following decades their legacy took on new force as spectres of revolutionary subversion. An early notice was given of them in Edmund Burke's *Reflections on the Revolution in France* (1790), where he noted their influence on the principles and events of the Revolution.[16] In Britain in the 1790s, their memory was kept alive, or perhaps invented, by the publication of texts purporting to give evidence of their thought and philosophy. The Freemason, and supposed Illuminatus, Baron Adolph von Knigge (1752–96) commented on this in his *Practical Philosophy of Social Life* (1799), translated by Peter Will, a Grub Street hack.

> Amongst the great variety of dangerous and harmless amusements with which our philosophical age abounds, none is more prevailing than the rage for Secret Societies. There are few people possessing an eminent degree of ability and activity [...] who being actuated by a desire for knowledge, or sociability, curiosity, or restlessness of temper, have not been for some time at least members of secret associations.[17]

Obeying Kant's command 'dare to know', von Knigge argues that the seeker of philosophical enlightenment is inexorably drawn towards secret societies. The publication of Illuminati texts not only advertised their secret status, but also their esoteric structures of intellectual hierarchy.

Georg Simmel has suggested that reformist groups have a structural relation with secrecy: both reformers and secret societies propose an alternative version of the truth of social conditions. 'Secrecy secures [...] the possibility of a second world alongside the obvious world, and the latter is most strenuously affected by the former'. As such, secret societies enter into combination with treason and subversion: 'the secret society, purely on the ground of its secrecy, appears dangerously related to conspiracy against existing powers'.[18] Furthermore, in the late eighteenth century, the practices of secret association overlapped with the practices of secret interpretation, especially with esoteric forms of arcane knowledge. Mystical, cabbalistical, and alchemical forms of knowledge could only ever be secret, because they could only be understood by adepts and initiates. The Illuminati were the paradigmatic example of the fertilization of radical politics by the alchemical culture of secrecy.[19]

The politics of the secret society in Britain were transformed in the 1790s when conservative analysts identified the Illuminati, and other secret societies, as the central cause of the French Revolution. According to the proponents of this hypothesis, their intellectual subversion had weakened the *ancien régime* in France to the extent that it fell prey to opportunistic and self-interested rebellion; furthermore, a similar chain of events pertained in Britain and America. The first significant statement of the Illuminati conspiracy, as it came to be called, was published by the Scottish scientific writer and science lecturer John Robison (1739–1805) in September 1798, called *Proofs of a Conspiracy Against all the religions and governments of Europe, carried on in the secret meetings of Free Masons, Illuminati, and Reading Societies.* A professor at Edinburgh University, Robison lectured on the science of mechanics, hydrodynamics, astronomy, optics, electricity and magnetism – he wrote entries on the last two for the influential third edition of the *Encyclopaedia Britannica* in 1797. As this suggests, his intellectual allegiance was with empirical enlightenment science and the archive. The serious purpose of Robison's *Proofs of a Conspiracy* was underlined by its dedication to William Wyndham, Secretary at War, the minister responsible for domestic counter-subversion measures. In Robison's research, undertaken over many years, he claimed to have detected a group acting under 'the covert of a Mason Lodge' for the purpose of 'venting and propagating sentiments in religion and politics' that were contrary to the public good.

> I found, that this impunity had gradually encouraged men of licentious princi-
> ples to become more bold, and to teach doctrines subversive of all notions of
> morality – of all our confidence in the moral government of the universe – of
> all our hopes of improvement in a future state of existence – and of all satis-
> faction and contentment with our present life, so long as we live in a state of
> civil subordination. I have been able to trace these attempts, under the specious
> pretext of enlightening the world by the torch of philosophy, and of dispelling
> the clouds of civil and religious superstition which keep the nations of Europe
> in darkness and slavery. I have observed these doctrines gradually diffusing and
> mixing with all the different systems of Free Masonry; till, at last, AN ASSOCIA-
> TION HAS BEEN FORMED FOR THE EXPRESS PURPOSE OF ROOTING OUT ALL THE
> RELIGIOUS ESTABLISHMENTS, AND OVERTURNING ALL THE EXISTING GOVERN-
> MENTS OF EUROPE.

Robison detects the conspiracy in a subversive cabal of libertines, enlightenment philosophes and Freemasons, among whom he has been able to
identify 'the most active leaders in the French Revolution'. The book is
thus intended as a memorandum to authority and a warning, for as
Robison declares, 'I have seen that this Association still exists, still works
in secret, and that not only several appearances among ourselves show that
its emissaries are endeavouring to propagate their detestable doctrines
among us'.[20]

The four volumes of Abbé Augustin Barruel's *Memoirs, Illustrating the
History of Jacobinism* were conceived with the same prophylactic intention
as Robison's, but with a wider range of villains. Barruel (1741–1820)
explains the emergence 'at an early period of the French Revolution' of 'a
Sect calling itself Jacobin, and teaching *that all men were equal and free!*' Under
the 'auspices of this Sect, and by their intrigue, influence, and impulse', the
Jacobins had destroyed church, monarchy and had unloosed terror over
all Europe. The Jacobin plot, Barruel continues, even 'to the most horrid
deeds', 'was foreseen and resolved on, was premeditated and combined' as
'the offspring of deep-thought villainy'. The seemingly inchoate incidents
of revolution had a plot: 'Though the events of each day may not appear
to have been combined, there nevertheless existed a secret agent and a
secret cause, giving rise to each event, and turning each circumstance to
the long-desired end'. The plotters, Barruel revealed, were 'men who styled
themselves Philosophers', specifically Voltaire, Diderot and D'Alembert.

The '*Antichristian conspiracy*' of these '*Sophisters of Impiety*' coalesced with a 'conspiracy against kings' by the '*Sophisters of Rebellion*' associated with 'the *Occult Lodges* of Free-masonry'.[21]

Robison and Barruel derived their theories independently and published them almost simultaneously: a coincidence, both claimed, that lent weight to their hypothesis.[22] In the 'Postscript' added in to his second edition (1798), Robison stressed that the kinds of subversion he imputed to the Illuminati were at the level of ideas, rather than events:

> I meant to prove that the machinations of the Illuminati, whether associated under that denomination or not, had contributed to the revolution, by making a revolution, unfavourable to virtue and good order, in the public mind.

Nonetheless, the secret plots of the 'Enlighteners' (the equivalent, Robison remarks, of Barruel's '*Philosophists*') even if not 'not the *sole*, nor perhaps the *chief*, cause of that extraordinary event' the French Revolution, still posed a considerable threat to British society.[23] The popular success of the book, which sold its first impression in days, proved to him its timeliness, and justified, he thought, his claim that 'that *this detestable Association exists, and its emissaries are busy amongst ourselves*'.[24] American controversialists were quick to seize upon the British exposure of the Illuminati conspiracy, detecting a conspiracy against the public order of the republic. Jedidiah Morse, an influential Calvinist preacher and geographer in New York, unveiled evidence of Illuminati activity in American politics in 1798, detecting both the general intellectual influence of Illuminati philosophy and the presence of emigrant agents among the 'Jacobin clubs' established by the Republican faction in recent years.[25] All this was grist for the mill of conspiracy.

The conspiracy theories of Barruel and Robison had conflated huge quantities of intellectually disparate material, arguing that this diversity provided evidence for the theory. In their works, interested readers found bizarre comminglings of alchemical language, Rosicrucian and Masonic imagery, and neoclassical cyphers, all of which were coalesced around real, suppressed and imagined historical events. The conspiracy theory is a restructuring of the information order. As a piece of research it is not conducted at the level of policing, using the security services' repertoire of interrogation, torture and confession, but as a piece of archival research, using such tools as the card index, the library, and the armchair. Examining published reports and tracts, both by Illuminati such as von Knigge and by their intellectual opponents, Robison and Barruel reconfigure the archive, ordering and emplotting the discrete materials of their research: seventeenth-century necromancy, alchemical science, 'German' philosophy, 'French' political theory, newspaper narratives of historical events. As Gordon S. Wood has argued, as a narratological structure, the conspiracy by secret hands has a powerful historiographical force. Rather than being the result of 'social forces' or 'the stream of history', events are shown to be the result of 'the concerted designs of individuals'. As such, apparently meaningless acts can be understood as rational consequences of human will and agency.[26] The Illuminati conspiracy, then, makes sense of the dreadful confusions of revolutionary history by providing a single orchestrating villain, whose spectral presence can be detected behind the varied scene of declarations, insurrections and atrocities.

Gothic Illumination and the Novel of Spectral Simulacra

In the English school of gothic novel in the 1790s, the dominant mode was Ann Radcliffe's 'explained supernatural', which I will here call the novel of spectral simulacra. In the most extreme form of this mode, plot is made subservient to closure, and the weight of the narrative falls ever more heavily on the concluding teleology of clarification. In *The Mysteries of Udolpho* (1794), the main character Emily is continually beset by events that perplex her and test the parameters of her understanding. When she becomes concerned that her aunt has been murdered, for example, she finds herself carried away with fear: 'She blamed herself for suffering her romantic imagination to carry her so far beyond the bounds of probability, and determined to endeavour to check its rapid flights, lest they should sometimes extend into madness'.[27]

The novel's detailed examination of Emily's state of mind, both curious and fearful, contributes much to the signal texture of the novel. Emily's search of the Castle Udolpho allows Radcliffe to study her fearful condition, noting how it makes her suggestible, prey to further fears. In a chamber in the tower, when Emily hears a 'hollow voice' in the 'dusky and silent chamber', she questions whether it is a 'terrible apparition' even after she recognizes it as the voice of her aunt.[28] The novel awakens fears, even as it wants to dispel them with material causal explanations. At the conclusion of each of Radcliffe's novels, each and every suggestion of enchantment or supernaturalism is shown to have a natural or human cause, either in coincidence or in conspiracy. This narrative strategy – the revelation of the spectral as simulacra – was identified by contemporary critics as the major technical signature of Ann Radcliffe. Sir Walter Scott noted that '[a] principal characteristic of Mrs Radcliffe's romances is the rule which the author imposed on herself, that all the circumstances of her narrative, however mysterious, and apparently superhuman, were to be accounted for on natural principles, at the winding up of the story'.[29] Radcliffe's technique of 'the supernatural *explain'd*', as she termed it, is a novelizing procedure, including nothing that was outside the expectations of the audience. One of the most famous examples of Radcliffe's technique occurs when Emily reveals, behind a black veil in one chamber, what appears to be a rotting corpse. Hundreds of pages later, Emily (and the reader) discovers that she has caught a glimpse of a wax funerary model prepared for a church festival.[30] Without any inkling of this curious reversal, subjected to extended periods of misapprehension and speculative supernaturalism, the reader is underwhelmed by the cause. In Radcliffean narrative the moment of enlightenment is experienced as bathos, not the transcendence of explanation.

Radcliffe was the most popular but by no means the only exponent of this mode of gothic fiction. Translations of German novels offered the most extravagant examples of this explanatory tendency in the mid-1790s. As noted in the editors' introductory essay to this volume, the Romantic-period novel undertook numerous formal experiments akin to this, which now seem less than satisfying to the reader. Yet such fictions were compelling and popular. The vogue for fictions of spectral simulacra was satirized by Jane Austen in *Northanger Abbey* (published in 1818, but probably written in 1798). In the novel, Catherine Morland is excited when a new acquaintance at Bath, Isabella Thorpe, introduces her to gothic novels. Isabella's fashionable reading list includes Radcliffe's *The Mysteries of Udolpho* and *The Italian*, but also extends to a list of seven other less well-known gothic novels, including Eliza Parsons' *The Castle of Wolfenbach* (1793) and *Mysterious Warnings* (1796); Regina Maria Roche's *Clermont* (1798); Peter Teuthold's *Necromancer of the Black Forest* (1794); Francis Lathom's *Midnight Bell* (1798); Eleanor Sleath's *Orphan of the Rhine* (1798); and Peter Will's *Horrid Mysteries* (1796). In her enthusiasm, Catherine asks 'but are they all horrid? Are you sure they are all horrid?'[31] The novels were all published by William Lane's Minerva Press, and Austen suggests that, as a group, they represent a debased and irredeemably popular taste for gothic fiction.[32] Austen's list reflected the taste of the late 1790s, and when she was revising the novel for publication, she was worried that it would not be understood.

Among these horrid mysteries was *The Necromancer, or a Tale of the Black Forest* (1794), a translation by Peter Teuthold of Karl Friedrich Kahlert's gothic novel *Der Geisterbanner*, issued under the pseudonym of Lawrence Flammenberg.[33] *The Necromancer* deploys an extreme version of the explained supernatural. The novel's anti-hero, Volkert, entices people into witnessing terrifying scenes in which he apparently conjures up ghosts from the dead in extensively described necromantic rituals. Like the unwilling observer in the text, the reader encounters these experiences as if they are genuine (the novel does not signal any suggestion of trickery or deception). Nonetheless, in the end it is revealed that all the experiences were faked by Volkert as part of his elaborate plots to defraud his spectators of their fortunes. The supernatural is not only explained but revealed to be a fraudulent deception. *The Victim of Magical Delusion* (1795), Peter Will's loose translation of the German-language novel *Geschichte eines Geisterseher* (1795) by the Hungarian writer Cajetan Tschink (1763–1813), was premised on a similarly radical counter-supernatural scepticism. In this novel, a series of supernatural events, such as appearances of apparitions or demonstrations of immortality, are shown to be elaborately executed theatrical effects. These '*delusive miracles*' use a wide variety of stage effects, produced by trap-doors, hidden recesses, concealed mirrors, translucent veils, lantern slides, and various pyrotechnic effects of smoke and explosion. All these spectral simulacra use technology familiar to the theatrical stage and related visual spectacles of the 1790s, such as panorama, eidophusicon, and magic lantern shows. In Tschink's novel, these 'fictitious miracles' are wrought by an adept, the conspiratorial Alumbrado, exploiting the credulity of his victims.[34]

As Walter Scott argued, this kind of novel was based upon on Radcliffe's 'mode of expounding her mysteries', although unlike her prosaic explanations, they made recourse to an even more 'artificial' solution. In the 'mysterious obscurity' of these spectral simulacra, many incidents 'highly tinctured with romantic incident and feeling' were 'afterwards [...] explained by deception and confederacy'. Scott explicitly identified this strategy with the conspiratorial politics of the Illuminati: 'Such have been the impostures of superstition in all ages, and such delusions were also practised by the members of the Secret Tribunal, in the middle ages, and in more modern times by the Rosicrucians and Illuminati'. Nonetheless, Scott argued that the novel of spectral simulacra was a contribution to the Enlightenment project, a continuation of the attack on superstition and credulity. As Scott concluded, 'the reader feels tricked', likening the experience of disappointment at the explanatory conclusion to a child 'who has once seen the scenes of a theatre too nearly, the idea of pasteboard, cords, and pullies'.[35] Exploring the real disappointments engendered by this narrative strategy, the novel forces the reader to a self-reflexive examination of the delusive tendency.

In writing his novel *The Monk* (1796), Matthew Lewis claimed to have been inspired by the popular and imaginative success of Radcliffe's fictions.[36] Rather unusually for his time, Lewis also had a taste for contemporary German and French literature, including the more lurid novels of spectral simulacra, which he read in their original languages.[37] Co-opting these influences, *The Monk* adapted and subverted the characteristic effects of Radcliffe's fiction. *The Monk*'s representation of magic provides an interesting test case. After her seduction of Ambrosio, Matilda explains that she has knowledge of magic, and is capable of 'raising a dæmon' to secure his desire.[38] These powers are demonstrated in Matilda's magic mirror, a far-seeing device that allows Ambrosio to see Antonia naked in the bath.[39] Matilda's subsequent magic is related in a more conventional discourse of conjuring, sleight of hand and spectral simulacra. In these supernatural scenes, it appears that Lewis expresses a credulous attitude to witchcraft and demonology, supposedly distinct from Radcliffe's enlightenment scepticism. However, while the fictive world of Ambrosio inhabits the pre-scientific world-view of magic, the novel frames this within a materialist and empirical understanding of the world, closely associated with the realist technique of the novel itself.[40] There are here, then, two iterations of the archival: one at the level of character, as Matilda and Ambrosio go about acquiring and disseminating esoteric knowledge, and another at the level of the reader, as Lewis displays his own interest in forms of medieval and quasi-Catholic scholarship.

It is unlikely that Lewis's knowledge of witchcraft was deep, although he was probably aware of residual eighteenth-century research on the scientific status of demonology. He was certainly familiar with Joseph Glanvill's *Sadducismus trimphatus* (first published 1681, fourth edition 1726), one of the last substantial defences of the existence of witches, which he notes was his mother's favourite reading.[41] *The Monk*'s historical reconstruction of the world-view of magic suggests a seventeenth-century context. As the narrator explains, Matilda's knowledge of 'Magic', taught by her guardian, might equally be described as a kind of science, taught alongside other branches of 'natural philosophy' like mineralogy and pharmacopoeia:

My Guardian was a Man of uncommon knowledge: He took pains to instil that knowledge into my infant mind. Among the various sciences which curiosity had induced him to explore, He neglected not that, which by most is esteemed impious, and by many chimerical. I speak of those arts, which relate to the world of Spirits. His deep researches into causes and effects, his unwearied application to the study of natural philosophy, his profound and unlimited knowledge of the properties and virtues of every gem which enriches the deep, of every herb which the earth produces, at length procured him the distinction, which He had sought so long, so earnestly.[42]

The intellectual endeavour pursued by Matilda's mysterious teacher is as much science as it is magic: as Lewis suggests, the two kinds of knowledge cannot be discriminated. In *Sadducismus triumphatus,* Joseph Glanvill offered what he considered a conventional definition of the witch: '*A witch is one, who can do, or seems to do strange Things, beyond the known power of Art and ordinary Nature, by virtue of a Confederacy with evil Spirits*'.[43] He argues that research into witches and demonology, however, should be pursued by the kinds of experimental science recommended by the Royal Society, without contravening its materialist and empirical standards of enquiry.[44] The research of Matilda's teacher into the material causes of demonic effects locates 'natural philosophy' as the dominant account of the world: his is essentially an enlightenment understanding. The intellectual regime of Matilda's teacher can be identified with a key moment in the history of both science and witchcraft beliefs: a period in the late seventeenth and early eighteenth century when the one was allied with the other, when science announced, finally and permanently, the decline in belief in witchcraft in England.

Belief in diabolical witchcraft, invented in the Middle Ages and flourishing in the sixteenth and seventeenth centuries, was by the 1790s almost entirely devoid of intellectual substance, having declined in the eighteenth century to an antiquarian curiosity of history.[45] The late eighteenth century evinces a curiosity about magic only as a variety of entertainment: that is, as forms of sleight of hand or prestidigitation, and visual tricks such as magic lantern projection. Publications such as *The Conjurer Unmasked* (1785), which claimed to provide 'a clear and full explanation of all the surprising performances exhibited by the most eminent and dextrous professors of slight of hand', found a ready public.[46] One of the less well-known of Horace Walpole's gothic publications was a card trick: a cryptogrammic game comprising 10 cards and a set of instructions, printed at Strawberry Hill, by which an adept would be able to identify another person's apparently random choice of card.[47]

Lewis's depiction of satanic ceremony in *The Monk* belongs to the imaginative world of the novel of spectral simulacra where the supernatural is simulated. In the manner of *The Necromancer*, Lewis describes Matilda's invocation of Satan at some length, without actually explaining how it works. From this description, it is not an experiment that could be repeated by the reader. But Matilda's incantations and rituals are essentially comic, the narrator pompously describing only the appearance of her actions in the arcane ritual. Through Ambrosio's imperfect view of proceedings in the cellar, his sight-lines obstructed by pillars and smoke, the narrator can only offer a superficial description of Matilda's 'mysterious rites', reminiscent of the theatre. In a cavern (in which '[a] profound obscurity hovered'), illuminated by a mysterious cold blue flame, Matilda draws circles on the ground, and, while mumbling indistinctly, crumbles into the fire three desiccated human fingers and an Agnus Dei (a wax tablet blessed by the Pope). The result is spectacular: she shrieks and is possessed by delirium, she stabs herself in the arm, and sprinkles her blood about, while smoke, dark clouds and claps of thunder reverberate around. Finally, the 'Dæmon' appears to 'a full strain of melodious Music', and Ambrosio is astonished to find he is no ugly misshapen monster, but rather a beautiful youth – a 'fallen angel' who recalls the figure of Satan in Milton's *Paradise Lost*.[48] Despite the extravagant rhetoric, what is noticeable about these events is their banal theatricality: as in the novel of spectral simulacra, they might all have been achieved using the familiar stage machinery of late-eighteenth-century theatre. The narrator, in short, is not an adept who understands the esoteric magic he describes. The narrator's mode of description remains the kind of empirical eye-witness observation categorically associated with the formal realism of the novel as a genre. Lewis retains much more of Radcliffe's scepticism than is immediately apparent. Adopting the discourse of spectral simulacra, the novel is, quite literally, a sadducee, a materialist who denies the existence of angels and spirits.

This formal incredulity towards magic in *The Monk* is reinforced by the novel's ridicule of popular notions of the supernatural, and its pronounced anti-Catholicism and anti-clericalism. The prattle of the servant Flora and the house-keeper Dame Jacintha allows the novel to explore the folly of popular superstitions about ghosts and the supernatural. The anti-clerical posture of the novel, seen in such scenes as the crowd's destruction of the Convent of St Clare, was much noted even by contemporaries.[49] At the end of *The Monk*, however, Lewis famously leaves the supernatural unexplained. There is no rational explanation for the appearance of Satan and the Mephistophelean contract he makes with Ambrosio. Yet the novel's faith in these *diablerie* is underwhelming, to say the least: it would be a credulous reader who found Matilda's magical theatrics convincing, or who failed to detect the whiff of ironic insincerity in the final sublime pages. The consistent attitudinal pattern of *The Monk*, building on its credulous novelising form, suggests its allegiance to Enlightenment principles and politics: anti-clericalism, sceptical satire, and the simulacra of supernaturalism.

German Enlighteners and the Delusions of Conspiracy

The evidence accumulated in the Illuminati Conspiracy made sure that by the late 1790s, 'German philosophy' was understood in England to be shorthand for a conspiratorial mixture of secrecy, subversion and necromancy. Himself one of the Illuminati (code-named 'Philo'), Baron von Knigge pointed to the reason in his *Practical Philosophy of Social Life*. He observed that 'to people of a lively imagination' – by which he meant everyone not enlightened – 'ghost-seers, alchymists and mystic impostors' were extremely powerful.

> The belief in supernatural effects and apparitions is extremely catching. The many chasms which still are in our philosophical systems and theories, and the desire to soar above the terrestrial limits of our understanding, renders it very natural that man should be inclined to attempt explaining incomprehensible matters *a posteriori*, when the arguments a priori are insufficient; that is, to infer such results from collected facts as are pleasing to us, but cannot be theoretically deduced from them by regular conclusions.[50]

Knigge argued that by investing themselves with the power of magic and alchemy, secret societies could possess uncommon powers to influence the body politic.[51] As an American critic of Schiller's *The Ghost-Seer* (1789) opined when it was translated in 1795, 'the sect of the *Illuminated* [...] were accustomed to seduce the ignorant and the superstitious, by extravagant and incredible powers and appearances'.[52]

The meta-narrative of a conspiracy of the enlightened against the body politic is central to the plots of many gothic novels of the 1790s. Cajetan Tschink's novel *The Victim of Magical Delusion* explores such a conspiracy in some detail. The novel is subtitled '*a magico-political tale*', and the translator Peter Will explained that central aspects of the plot relied on the history of the revolution of 1640 in Portugal.[53] The source text was Réné Vertot's *The History of the Revolution in Portugal in the year 1640* (1700) which described the rebellion of the Portuguese against the Spanish under the Duke of Braganza.[54] In Tschink's version, however, the plotters are led by an enigmatic conspirator called Alumbrado, whose name means the Illuminated or Enlightened One. A man of uncommon abilities, Alumbrado is possessed of rare skills of persuasion and a chameleon-like quality of changing his appearance, ethnicity and religion. At the end, the novel explains how he has used his skill in '*delusive miracles*' and '*apparitions of ghosts*' to gain his purpose. His immortality is revealed to be based on his invulnerability to death, which is achieved using various tricks such as a specially prepared gunpowder which does not carry the ball of shot further than five feet, and a dagger with a sprung blade that disappears into its handle. These 'fictitious miracles' persuade his followers that 'God was working and speaking' through him.[55] Alumbrado's name further refers to a sect of Spanish mystics brutally suppressed by the Inquisition in the late sixteenth century. Conspiracy theorists made much of the sect's name, which was sometimes translated as the Illuminati, suggesting a longer history for Weishaupt's band of reformers. Adherents of the Alumbrado sect claimed to have direct contact with God, a heresy similar to the Protestant doctrine of justification by faith alone, in which external worship is unnecessary, the reception of the sacraments is useless, and as sin is impossible, carnal desire may be indulged, and other sinful actions committed without staining the soul.[56] Tschink's novel maps the historical discourse of the Alumbrado secret society onto the historical narrative of the Portuguese national liberation, phrasing it through the narrative technique of spectral simulacra.

In *Wieland* (1798), the first of four gothic fictions by the American writer Charles Brockden Brown (1771–1810), the mysterious Carwin is an adept of a para-scientific skill, that of biloquy or ventriloquism. Using his unearthly ability, Carwin is able to exert a preternatural influence over a family of young Americans who pride themselves on their rationality and intelligence. Brown had read Robison's *Proofs of a Conspiracy*, while residing with his close friend Elihu Hubbard Smith in New York in 1798.[57] In an unfinished prequel to *Wieland*, entitled *Memoirs of Carwin the Biloquist*, Brockden Brown explained that this particular case was evidence of a wider conspiracy against the American nation, perpetrated by foreign agents known as the Illuminati. The unfinished manuscript of *Carwin* was published in 1803 (in ten short instalments) in the *Literary Magazine and American Register*, edited by Brockden Brown himself. In it, Carwin is shown to be an agent of the Illuminati: a student of a wealthy, Machiavellian magician called Ludloe, initiated and illuminated into the higher orders of a secret society dedicated to radical and utopian political schemes.[58]

While Tschink and Brockden Brown are explicit about their use of the Illuminati conspiracy, a similar conspiratorial structure can also be discerned in Radcliffe and Lewis. In the case of Radcliffe's supernatural-explained, all events, even those wondrous and passing nature, are shown to be the result of human agency. Emily learns that she is not assailed by apparitions and spectres, but is rather the victim of a plot against her sexuality and her property, perpetrated by one man, her guardian Montoni, acting in concert with a confederacy of plotters. In Montoni, the novel conceals a realist material cause (rational and empirical), and thus perversely adopts the posture of the counter-Enlightenment. In Lewis's *The Monk* (1796), this conspiratorial structure is also evident. Read in the light of the Illuminati conspiracy, Matilda's seduction of Ambrosio is a kind of sedition: the supernatural subversion of reason brought about by a diabolical conspiracy. In the final sections of the novel Ambrosio sells his soul to the Devil in exchange for delivery from the prison of the Inquisition. The Devil is a conventionally depicted monster of blasted limbs, talons, sable wings and hair of living snakes.[59] Yet the transaction between the Devil and Ambrosio is oddly modern: the Devil has a contract which Ambrosio must sign (using a pen filled with his own blood, like Faustus in Marlowe's *Dr Faustus*). The Devil is a facile sophister: like those of a lawyer, his arguments are convincing, even as they are untrue. When Ambrosio eventually brings himself to sign the contract, written in small print in an unknown language, he finds it does not deliver all it seem to promise. The Devil laughs as he explains

> You have given up your claim to mercy, and nothing can restore to you the rights which you have foolishly resigned [...]. What more did I promise than to save you from your prison? Have I not done so? Are you not safe from the Inquisition – safe from all but me?[60]

The liberty the Devil promised is a trick, a conspiracy, brought about by his linguistic sleight of hand. The Devil does deliver Ambrosio's freedom from the Inquisition, but only to condemn him to death, cast from a great height onto the mountains to be consumed by insects and carrion eagles.

Through Matilda's instruction, Ambrosio has risen through the ranks of the sinful to achieve this final understanding. Ambrosio's progress is not enlightenment: perhaps a better metaphor would be illumination. In the novel, Lewis uses the language of monastic organization to mirror Matilda's initiation of Ambrosio in her esoteric Satanic knowledge. Both forms of hierarchical organization are also mimicked in Robison's description of the education of the Illuminati novice. Robison describes how a Mentor instructs the novice by bringing him through common knowledge to a realization that a higher knowledge awaits within himself. Later, this 'speculative' (or abstract) information is shown to have an 'active' quality, whereupon the novice can be initiated into the 'hidden science' of the unknown higher echelons, the Minervals and Illuminatus Minor.[61] Lewis's version ridicules the 'Unknown Superiors' of the knights of Illuminism, depicting them as Satan: but the target of his satire is neither illuminati minervals nor demonic spectres, but rather, those readers so credulous as to believe in them.

In the late eighteenth century, English thought had little time for the speculative abstractions of continental philosophy. In Bacon, Hobbes, Locke, Shaftesbury, Hutcheson, Berkeley, Hume, and Smith, an English tradition could be conceived as an almost self-sufficient chain, working without influence from abroad. British philosophy was insular and isolationist; it was mercantile, Atlanticist and imperial rather than continental; concerned with commerce, progress and liberty, not enlightenment. To such a view, British empiricism was uninterested in the philosophical speculations of Kant, or any other 'enlightened' philosophes, whose speculative explorations could be dismissed as airy metaphysics. Intellectual historians may have shown the notion of the exceptionalism of English philosophy to be unconvincing, but it was nevertheless a powerful idea in the 1790s. The startling innovation of the Illuminati conspiracy was the visionary and disturbing picture it cast of England, re-imagined as a central participant in European intellectual activity: integrated, not insular. Gothic novels of illumination – including those of Radcliffe and Lewis and the other novels of spectral simulacra – contribute to this imaginative vision of a European-wide intellectual ferment.

Through such imaginings, British thought participated in the European intellectual enterprise of the Enlightenment, even if only as the victim of conspiratorial sedition. It is in this sense that it is no accident that Kant's philosophy was first introduced into England in 1795.[62] Abbé Barruel, in fact, argued that Kant was a Jacobin: the Königsberg professor was, he said, the 'Magus of Weishaupt', professing 'hatred of revelation', a 'spirit of impiety' and a 'pretension to superior genius'.[63] In the years 1795–98, the phrase 'enlightened philosophy', and the notion of 'the Enlightenment', takes root in England for the first time, but only as a pejorative expression for the supposed treasonous hypocrisy of modern French political philosophy. In his examination of the 'Antichristian Conspiracy' Barruel observed the 'numerous tribe' of 'Philosopher' in every rank, age and sex. 'Like Voltaire', he said, this common philosopher will 'style this the Age of Reason, and of enlightened Philosophy'. Barruel's depiction of the enlightened philosopher reads like a description not only of Immanuel Kant, but also of Matthew Lewis: he will

> [h]arangue the vilest of the populace; tell them that the priests are imposing upon them, that hell is of their own invention, that the time is come to throw off the yoke of fanaticism and superstition, to assert the liberty of their reason; and in a few minutes, the ignorant plough-boy will rival, in Philosophic science, the most learned of the adepts.[64]

Notes

1 Ernst Cassirer, *The Philosophy of the Enlightenment*, trans. Fritz Koelln and James Pettegrove (Princeton: Princeton University Press, 1951).

2 James Schmidt, 'Inventing the Enlightenment: Anti-Jacobins, British Hegelians, and the *Oxford English Dictionary*', *Journal of the History of Ideas* 64.3 (2003), pp. 421–43.

3 Peter Brooks, 'Virtue and Terror: *The Monk*', *ELH* 40 (1973), pp. 249–63, 249–50; Devendra Varma, *The Gothic Flame. Being a History of the Gothic Novel in England: Its Origin, Efflorescence, Disintegration, and Residuary Influences* (1957; repr. New York: Russell & Russell, 1963).

4 Clara Tuite, 'Cloistered Closets: Enlightenment Pornography, The Confessional State, Homosexual Persecution and *The Monk*', *Romanticism on the Net* 8 (November 1997), n. p. (http://users.ox.ac.uk/~scato385/closet.html, accessed 2 August 1998).

5 James Schmidt, 'The Question of Enlightenment: Kant, Mendelssohn, and the Mittwochsgesellschaft', *Journal of the History of Ideas* 50.2 (1989), pp. 269–91.

6 René Wellek, *Immanuel Kant in England, 1793–1838* (Princeton: Princeton University Press, 1931), pp. 1–21.

7 Emanuel [sic] Kant, 'An Answer to the Question, What is Enlightening?', in *Essays and Treatises on Moral Political and Various Philosophical Subjects*, trans. William Richardson, 2 vols. (London: published for the translator by William Richardson, 1798), Vol. 1, pp. 1–14, 5. Compare with the most frequently cited recent translation: '*Enlightenment is man's emergence from his self-incurred immaturity*'. Immanuel

Kant, 'An Answer to the Question: What is Enlightenment?', in *Political Writings*, trans. Hans. S. Reiss (Cambridge: Cambridge University Press, 1996), pp. 54, 58.

8 Kant, 'What is Enlightening?', p. 11.

9 Kant, 'What is Enlightening?', p. 5.

10 Schmidt, 'Inventing the Enlightenment', pp. 428–29. An early adopter was Susan Austin in *Fragments from German Prose Writers* (London: John Murray, 1841), who translated Kant's essay as 'What is Enlightenment?', but noted that the term 'enlightenment' was inadequate, though exact. She argues 'a more significant title would be, "a plea for the liberty of philosophizing"' (p. 228n).

11 Christoph Martin Wieland, 'A Couple of Gold Nuggets' (1789), in James Schmidt, ed., *What is Enlightenment? Eighteenth-Century Answers and Twentieth-Century Questions* (Berkeley: University of California Press, 1996), pp. 78–83, 79.

12 Jürgen Habermas, *The Structural Transformation of the Public Sphere: An Inquiry into a Category of Bourgeois Society*, trans. Thomas Burger (Cambridge, MA: The MIT Press, 1989). See also Hans Speier, 'Historical Development of Public Opinion', *American Journal of Sociology* 55.4 (January 1950), pp. 376–88. Speier's account, an important source for Habermas's public sphere argument, argues that secret societies were an important impediment to the development of public opinion in Germany.

13 Margaret Jacob, *The Radical Enlightenment: Pantheists, Freemasons and Republicans* (London: George Allen & Unwin, 1981), p. 246.

14 Richard van Dülmen, *The Society of the Enlightenment: The Rise of the Middle Class and Enlightenment Culture in Germany*, trans. Anthony Williams (Cambridge: Polity Press, 1992), pp. 52–65.

15 *Einige Originalschriften des Illuminatensordens* (Munich: Johann Baptist Strobl, 1787).

16 Edmund Burke, *Reflections on the Revolution in France*, ed. Conor Cruise O'Brien (Harmonsworth: Penguin, 1986), p. 265.

17 Adolph Freiherr von Knigge, *Practical Philosophy of Social Life; or the Art of Conversing with Men*, trans. Peter Will, 2 vols. (London: T. Cadell, Jun. and W. Davies, 1799), Vol. 2, p. 255. This is a translation of *Über den Umgang mit Menschen*, first published in German in 1788.

18 Georg Simmel, 'The Sociology of Secrecy and of Secret Societies', trans. Albion Small, *The American Journal of Sociology* XI, 4 (1906), pp. 441–98, 462, 498.

19 Amos Hofman, 'Opinion, Illusion and the Illusion of Opinion: Barruel's Theory of Conspiracy', *Eighteenth-Century Studies* 27.1 (1993), pp. 27–60.

20 John Robison, *Proofs of a Conspiracy Against all the religions and governments of Europe, carried on in the secret meetings of Free Masons, Illuminati, and Reading Societies* (London: T. Cadell and W. Davies, 1797), pp. 10–12.

21 Augustin Barruel, *Memoirs, Illustrating the History of Jacobinism*, trans. Robert Clifford, 4 vols., 2nd edn revised and corrected (London: published for the translator by T. Burton, 1798), Vol. 2, pp. i, vi, xiv.

22 Barruel, *Memoirs*, Vol. 3, p. xiv. Barruel relates his first encounter with Robison's volume: Robison's first volume was published as Barruel's third volume was in press. The first two volumes of Barruel have no knowledge of Robison, although Barruel is mentioned in Robison's second edition.

23 Robison, *Proofs of a Conspiracy*, pp. 501, 535.

24 Robison, *Proofs of a Conspiracy*, p. 14.

25 Jedidiah Morse, *A Sermon, Delivered... May 9, 1798* (Boston, 1798). See Vernon

Stauffer, *New England and the Bavarian Illuminati* (New York: Faculty of Political Science, Columbia University, 1918), pp. 142–228; and Seth Payson, *Proofs of the Real Existence and Dangerous Tendency of Illuminism* (Charlestown: Samuel Etheridge, 1802).

26 Gordon S. Wood, 'Conspiracy and the Paranoid Style: Causality and Deceit in the Eighteenth Century', *William & Mary Quarterly*, 3rd ser., 39 (1982), pp. 401–44, 407–408. See also Ina Ferris, 'Scholarly Revivals', in this volume.

27 Ann Radcliffe, *The Mysteries of Udolpho*, ed. Bonamy Dobrée (Oxford: Oxford University Press, 1998), p. 342.

28 Radcliffe, *Mysteries*, p. 364.

29 Walter Scott, 'Mrs Radcliffe', in *Lives of the Novelists*, 2 vols. (Paris: A. and W. Galignani, 1825), Vol. 2, p. 245.

30 Radcliffe, *Mysteries*, pp. 248–49, 662. Compare also the corpse glimpsed behind another curtain (p. 348), explained later as the body of a soldier killed in a skirmish (p. 365).

31 Jane Austen, *Northanger Abbey, Lady Susan, The Watsons, Sanditon*, ed. John Davie (Oxford: Oxford University Press, 1990), p. 24.

32 Dorothy Brokey, *The Minerva Press, 1790–1820* (London: The Bibliographical Society at the University Press, Oxford, 1939).

33 Lawrence Flammenberg [pseudonym of Karl Friedrich Kahlert], *Der Geisterbanner, eine Wundergeschichte aus mündlichen und schriftlichen Traditionen gesammelt* (1792), trans. Peter Teuthold, *The Necromancer: or, The Tale of the Black Forest* (London: Minerva Press, 1794). There is a modern edition: London: Skoob Books, 1992.

34 Cajetan Tschink, *The Victim of Magical Delusion; or, The Mystery of the Revolution of P——L: a magico-political tale. Founded on historical facts*, trans. Peter Will, 3 vols. (London: G. G. and J. Robinson, 1795), Vol. 3, pp. 299, 314–19.

35 Scott, 'Radcliffe', pp. 248–50.

36 Lewis to his mother, The Hague, 18 May 1794, in Louis F. Peck, *A Life of Matthew G. Lewis* (Cambridge, MA: Harvard University Press, 1961), pp. 208–209.

37 Lewis's sources are briefly assessed in Peck, *Lewis*, pp. 21–23. On Lewis's German sources see Karl S. Guthke, 'C. M. Wieland and M. G. Lewis', *Neophilologus* 40 (1956), pp. 231–33; Helga Hushahn, 'Sturm und Drang in Radcliffe and Lewis', in Valeria Tinkler-Villani, Peter Davidson, and Jane Stevenson, eds., *Exhibited by Candlelight: Sources and Developments in the Gothic Tradition* (Amsterdam: Rodopi, 1995), pp. 89–98.

38 Matthew Lewis, *The Monk*, ed. Emma McEvoy (Oxford: Oxford University Press, 1995), pp. 267–68.

39 Lewis, *Monk*, pp. 270–71.

40 See for example J. Paul Hunter, *Before Novels: The Cultural Contexts of Eighteenth-Century English Fiction* (New York and London: W. W. Norton and Company, 1990) and Michael McKeon, *The Origins of the English Novel, 1600–1740* (Baltimore: Johns Hopkins University Press, 1987).

41 Peck, *Lewis*, p. 4.

42 Lewis, *Monk*, p. 267.

43 Joseph Glanvill, *Sadducismus triumphatus: Or, A full and plain Evidence, Concerning Witches and Apparitions*, 4th edn with additions (London: A. Bettesworth and J. Batley, 1726), p. 225.

44 Stuart Clark, 'Scientific Status of Demonology', in Brian Vickers, ed., *Occult and Scientific Mentalities in the Renaissance* (Cambridge: Cambridge University Press, 1984), pp. 351–74. See also Irving Kirsch, 'Demonology and Science during the Scientific Revolution', *Journal of the History of the Behavioural Sciences* 16 (1980), pp. 359–68 and Keith Thomas, *Religion and the Decline of Magic* (London and New York, 1968).

45 Jeffrey B. Russell, *A History of Witchcraft: Sorcerers, Heretics, and Pagans* (London: Thames and Hudson, 1980), p. 123.

46 *The Conjurer Unmasked; or, La Magie Blanche Dévoilée: being a clear and full explanation of all the surprising performances exhibited by the most eminent and dextrous professors of slight of hand*, trans from M. Decremps (London: T. Denton, 1785).

47 Horace Walpole, *The Impenetrable Secret* (London: Strawberry Hill, n.d.). BL: C.31.b.32.

48 Lewis, *Monk*, pp. 276–77.

49 Lewis, *Monk*, pp. 321–24, 356.

50 Knigge, *Practical Philosophy*, Vol. 2, p. 250.

51 Knigge, *Practical Philosophy*, Vol. 2, pp. 255–63.

52 *New York Weekly Magazine*, I: 20 (18 November 1795), p. 157. Friedrich Schiller, *Der Geisterseher* (1789), trans. as *The Ghost-Seer; or Apparitionist* by Daniel Boileau (London: Vernor & Hood, 1795). A second translation was offered by William Render, *The Armenian; or, The Ghost-Seer* (London: C. Whittingham for H. D. Symonds, 1800). In his preface, the translator noted that 'It has been supposed [...] that it was intended to expose the impostures of the sect of the *Illuminati*, which was then beginning to extend itself in Germany' (p. iii).

53 Tschink, *Magical Delusion*, 'Translator's appendix', Vol. 3, p. 318.

54 Réné Aubert de Vertot D'Auberf, *The History of the Revolution in Portugal in the year 1640* (London: Matt. Gilliflower, Tim. Goodwin, Mat. Wotton, Rich. Parker, and Benj. Tooke, 1700).

55 Tschink, *Magical Delusion*, Vol. 3, pp. 286–93, 299, 306–307.

56 Alastair Hamilton, *Heresy and Mysticism in Sixteenth Century Spain: The Alumbrados* (Cambridge: James Clarke & Co., 1992). See also Marie Mulvey Roberts and Hugh Ormsby-Lennon, *Secret Texts: the Literature of Secret Societies* (New York: AMS Press, 1995).

57 *The Diary of Elihu Hubbard Smith*, ed. James E. Cronin (Philadelphia: American Philosophical Society, 1973), pp. 454–59. Brown discusses Barruel's *Memoirs* in the July 1799 edition of his *Monthly Magazine and American Review*.

58 Charles Brockden Brown, *Carwin the Biloquist*, in *Wieland or The Transformation. An American Tale*, ed. Jay Fliegelman (1798; New York: Penguin Books, 1991), pp. 315–16. See Markman Ellis, *The History of Gothic Fiction* (Edinburgh: Edinburgh University Press, 2000), ch. 4; Robert S. Levine, *Conspiracy and Romance: Studies in Brockden Brown, Cooper, Hawthorne, and Melville* (Cambridge: Cambridge University Press, 1989).

59 Lewis, *Monk*, p. 433.

60 Lewis, *Monk*, pp. 440–41.

61 Robison, *Proofs of a Conspiracy*, pp. 119, 121.

62 Wellek, *Kant in England*, pp. 1–21.

63 Barruel, *Memoirs*, Vol. 4, pp. 541–46.

64 Barruel, *Memoirs*, Vol. 1, pp. 375–76.

CHAPTER FOUR

Burney's Conservatism: Masculine Value and 'the Ingenuous Cecilia'

HELEN THOMPSON

Somebody in the horde of fops and merchants populating Frances Burney's second novel, *Cecilia, or Memoirs of an Heiress* (1782), names Vauxhall Gardens one of London's 'semi-barbarous places'.[1] This testimony neatly refutes the historian of manners Norbert Elias, who designates such sites of eighteenth-century leisure 'pacified social spaces'.[2] Indeed, Burney's London is not only not pacified, as Cecilia's guardian, who extorts his ward's property and then shoots himself in the head while rioting at Vauxhall, spectacularly demonstrates; Burney's London is also imbecilic. In a late draft of the novel, Burney blotted out the still-legible commentary of another one of *Cecilia*'s onlookers, who remarks that urban 'Conversation' fails to elicit from adults even the 'little skill' required by 'Children's Games': 'Thread the Needle may teach them grace, Hunt the Slipper dexterity, Move-all agility, & Blind Man's Buff penetration, while Hide & Seek calls for more address, perseverance & ingenuity than will be either displayed or required in such an assembly as this for a year & an half'.[3] Burney's deleted censure offers this failure of even rudimentary cultivation as the source of *Cecilia*'s preponderance of 'characters, incapable of animating from wit or from reason [...] [who,] void of all internal sources of entertainment, require the stimulation of shew, glare, noise and bustle to interest or awaken them'.[4] Her list of games shows how readily Burney could gloss the sources of these characters' inner failings.

By suggesting that the lapse of internalizing pedagogy produces persons responsive to no subtler medium of sociability than 'shew', Burney recalls the definition of bourgeois ideology proposed by Jürgen Habermas in *The Structural Transformation of the Public Sphere*. According to Habermas, an eighteenth-century domestic sphere whose sentimental intersubjectivity is refined by novels takes on the function of humanizing public men. A domestic sphere where feelings have been pacified by books facilitates the equation that, for Habermas, marks the historical origin of ideology as such: '*the fictitious identity of the two roles assumed by the privatized individuals who came together to form a public*', the identity of owners of private property and of '*human beings pure and simple*' (emphasis Habermas's).[5] Because domestic literature helps transmute economic coercion into spontaneous sentiment, Habermas argues, it assists the '*fictitious*' collapse of property owners and human beings, a claim whose support Habermas locates in the first two volumes of Samuel Richardson's novel *Pamela; or, Virtue Rewarded* (1740). In what follows, I depart from Habermas's insistence upon the congruity of ideology and eighteenth-century literary history, a congruity which even *Pamela*'s sequel cannot sustain. Rather than granting novels the ability to dissimulate economic privilege under the aegis of human feeling – that is, for Habermas, the ability to 'humanize' – Burney portrays a public sphere whose pervasive semi-barbarity isolates masculine virtue in one resolutely unrepresentative man, a man whose value inheres not in the communicative promise of literary cultivation but rather in the inimitable virtue of his name and blood.

What I call Burney's conservatism is expressed in *Cecilia*'s refusal to attribute humanizing or pacifying power to *itself*, for characters 'void of internal sources of entertainment' do not testify to the achievements of the literary-domestic sphere. Indeed, it is through the medium of her novel or, more particularly, through the medium of its marriage plot that Burney most emphatically denies the humanizing influence of both books and, as is the case in *Pamela*, women. Elsewhere, I coin the phrase 'transitively modernizing agency' to define the capacity of wives to obey their husbands in ways that defuse these men's domestic authority. Wives and future wives like Pamela would humanize men by reflecting back at them a practice of assent whose unforced spontaneity masks the still arbitrary – that is, sex-based – ground of masculine conjugal power.[6] Burney does not involve Cecilia in the transitively assisted apparition of softened or modernized men. Instead, she locates masculine virtue in the unmistakably regressive figure of Cecilia's one (in)eligible suitor Mortimer Delvile, an aristocrat whose value is not enhanced by his love. Unlike every other man in Cecilia's London, the noble Delvile cannot want to marry her, because entailed with Cecilia's independent fortune is the condition that her husband relinquish his name and assume her ungentle patronymic.

Burney's insistence upon the singular value of her hero is intermittently self-parodying, but she nonetheless rejects a long, increasingly Whiggish genealogy of nobility as the practice of cultivation. Rather than advancing a retrograde or nostalgic wish, however, Delvile's incommunicable virtue leverages this novel's refusal to credit the humanizing influence of domestic fiction; Burney's refusal of the ideological power of novels cannot be dissociated from her imagined retrenchment of masculine value. To make this suggestion is not to defer the question of whether Burney is really 'conservative' or 'progressive' but rather to gesture towards the inadequacy of the opposition. Unlike *Pamela*'s Mr B, Delvile does not pass through a private sphere where his economic and conjugal privilege is transmuted into classless human sentiment. Burney refuses to endorse the fictitious identity of property owners and representative human beings; books and wives do not convert *Cecilia*'s property owners into sentimental avatars of representative humanity. Yet Cecilia does assist in shoring up Delvile's worth. For by opposing him to the pretences of every other man in London, Burney sets in motion the paradox that defines her effort to isolate an intransitive form of masculine value: rather than divesting Cecilia's love of the taint of money, Cecilia's fortune serves to measure the value of the one man in the novel whose worth her money would lessen.

The Intransitivity of Masculine Value; or, After Orville

In her first novel, *Evelina, or, A Young Lady's Entrance into the World* (1778), Burney describes its hero Lord Orville as a gentleman 'undoubtedly, designed for the last age; for he is really polite!'[7] Here a witness remarks upon *Evelina*'s most economical and amusing proof of Orville's anachronism, his 'slow' and 'cautious' handling of a phaeton that every other 'young man' in this novel would drive recklessly.[8] But what really qualifies Orville as an artefact of the last age is his ability to recognize that the novel's possibly illegitimate protagonist Evelina, 'a young woman of obscure birth, but conspicuous beauty', nonetheless possesses 'a mind that might adorn *any* station, however exalted'.[9] Instead of dwelling on the more-than-Richardsonian acuity with which Orville perceives the purity of Evelina's mind (for he never reads her letters), I will take him as an exemplar of politeness whose schematics *Evelina* provides when, on the evening of her arrival in London from the country, Evelina writes to her guardian of David Garrick's performance in Benjamin Hoadly's play *The Suspicious Husband* (1747):[10]

> I had not any idea of so great a performer.

Such ease! such vivacity in his manner! such grace in his motions! such fire and meaning in his eyes! I could hardly believe he had studied a written part, for every word seemed to be uttered from the impulse of the moment.

His action – at once so graceful and so free! – his voice – so clear, so melodious, yet so wonderfully various in its tones – such animation! – every look *speaks*![11]

Evelina's breathless delivery recalls the immediacy of Garrick's acting. Yet Garrick's apparently spontaneous embodiment of impulse does not de-theatricalize his performance to such an extent that Evelina forgets he acts at all.[12] Rather than being wholly absorbed by the part Garrick plays, in this passage Evelina theorizes how such absorption would be sustained – through Garrick's confusion of the 'studied' and the 'free'.

In praising 'action' that masks the anterior discipline of studying 'a written part', Evelina articulates what can be called an anti-performative ideal of performance, one of whose most influential expressions is found in John Locke's *Some Thoughts Concerning Education* (1693), a pedagogical treatise written for gentlemen's sons.[13] In *Some Thoughts*, Locke rejects 'the charging of children's memories [...] with *rules* and precepts, which they [...] as soon forget as given'; he instead imagines a practice of rule-bound action induced by 'mak[ing] them do it over and over again till they are perfect'.[14] The success of a boy's training would be shown by his mechanical repetition of even obviously artificial motions like bowing:

[By] repeating the same action, till it be grown habitual in them, the perform-ance will not depend on memory or reflection, the concomitant of prudence and age and not of childhood, but will be natural in them. Thus bowing to a gentleman when he salutes him and looking in his face when he speaks to him is by constant use as natural to a well-bred man as breathing; it requires no thought, no reflection.[15]

Like Garrick's 'grace', this qualifies as an anti-performative performance because Locke imagines a repetition of prescribed gesture that does not fall into the degraded category of iteration – or, to use Locke's cognate for 'an awkward and forced imitation of what should be genuine and easy', affectation. Instead, to a precisely opposing ontological effect, this boy's bow becomes natural. Unlike poorly mimed or 'constrained motions', gestures first instilled in a boy from the outside 'seem [...] naturally to flow from a sweetness of mind and a well-turned disposition'.[16]

Burney's friend and admirer Edmund Burke adopts Locke's breathing analogy to rate the regulatory power of manners over that of the law:

Manners are of more importance than laws. Upon them, in a great measure the laws depend. The law touches us but here and there, and now and then. Manners are what vex or soothe, corrupt or purify, exalt or debase, barbarize or refine us, by a constant, steady, uniform, insensible operation, like that of the air we breathe in.[17]

A person who insensibly absorbs manners has forgotten something that Locke, in his attention to the parental authority that must, at least initially, 'make them do it over and over', cannot ignore: manners are also 'law'. As Burke's *Philosophical Inquiry into Our Ideas of the Sublime and the Beautiful* (1757) attests, his anti-performative equation of manners and reflex disavows even the attenuated exercise of discipline required to make children bow;[18] in his lack of reference to Lockean childhood, Burke's steadily breathing subject forgets the affinity of manners and the law only to remember it better than ever. Burke is, as much as Thomas Hobbes, a philosopher of political power, but if insuperable fear and awe guarantee the persistence of Hobbesian sovereignty, then Burke envisions an equally insuperable but 'insensible' consensus that operates independently of even parental coercion. For Burke, insensibly mechanized manners claim the unifying force of Hobbesian passion; for Burney, however, naturalized politeness qualifies only one man in an age.

Aside from the rote observation that Lord Orville is 'indeed extremely handsome', Evelina perceives him, as she does Garrick, in the register of gesture.[19] She writes of their first encounter, when Orville dances with her at a '*private* ball' populated by 'half the world!': 'His conversation was sensible and spirited; his air and address were open and noble; his manners gentle, attentive, and infinitely engaging; his person is all elegance, and his countenance, the most animated and expressive I have ever seen'.[20] Even more than in the case of Garrick – the specifics of whose part, though not mentioned by Evelina, are written down – the content of Orville's conversation plays no role in Evelina's assessment of how well his manners are 'animated'. Coming as it does after Evelina's appraisal of Garrick, this evocation of Orville's countenance as 'the most [...] expressive I have ever seen' would seem to grant Orville that superlative precisely because he does *not* express any specifiable script. Orville's elegance makes him noble, along Burkean lines, because it appears to be not even residually prompted by rules and precepts.

Because it is Orville's lack of affectation, rather than the gratuitous content of his conversation, that makes him noble, we can assess the significance of the appeal made to Evelina by her competing suitor Sir Clement

Willoughby. Willoughby, a nobleman the superficiality of whose politeness is most glaringly revealed by his attempt to abduct Evelina, voices his susceptibility to her influence in the following terms: 'your reproofs [...] pierce me to the soul! [...] make me what you please; – you shall govern and direct all my actions, – you shall new-form, new-model me: – I will not even have a wish but of your suggestion'.[21] This more or less meretricious citation of Richardson's *Pamela* anticipates Burney's refusal to lend Evelina the powers with which Pamela ennobles her aristocratic master. Evelina cannot 'govern and direct all [Willoughby's] actions' because she would then become, precisely, a director; whereas the epistolary Pamela supplies a written part distinct from the honour that her future husband initially fails to simulate, Evelina gives neither Orville nor Willoughby such cues. As a throwback to the last age, Orville not only resists 'new-modelling' but defines that process as the hopelessly degraded – or, hopelessly performative – approximation of his embodiment of elegance. As a species of politeness denied to Willoughby – whose iteration of Mr B would subvert the virtue of B's own pleas for direction – Orville's manners do not endorse *Pamela*'s 'progressive' promise.[22] Orville's politeness instead claims an artefactual integrity that renders redundant both *Pamela*'s and Evelina's influence. A product of the last age, Orville's nobility requires the assistance of neither Evelina nor novels.

For Burke, the strictly impossible conditions under which manners 'barbarize' happen only in the apocalyptic event of the French Revolution. Likewise, Burney's protagonist Cecilia Beverly breathes 'tainted air of infectious perdition!' that marks the turn to jeremiad of her second novel.[23] If Evelina tries, albeit ironically, to '*Londonize*' herself, Cecilia is inversely driven by 'air impregnated with luxury and extravagance' to reclaim the domestic space that her dissipated guardian Mr Harrel treats 'merely as an Hôtel': 'she got together her books [...] and secured to herself for the future occupation of her leisure hours, the exhaustless fund of entertainment which reading, that richest, highest, and noblest source of intellectual enjoyment, perpetually affords'.[24] And yet Cecilia's solitary effort to recuperate leisure as enlightened domesticity does not succeed. Upon arriving in London, she accompanies Harrel and his vapid wife to an endless round of assemblies; as a result of the Harrels' duplicity and violence, she gives away the ten thousand pounds of her fortune that were 'peculiarly my own property'; and she falls in love with the single suitor who cannot comply with the requirement attached to her estate, 'that of annexing her name, if she married, to the disposal of her hand and her riches'.[25] All of these events reflect the failure of reading to humanize a public in which 'every one was without restraint, even rank obtained but little distinction; ease was the general plan, and entertainment the general pursuit'.[26] How does *Cecilia*'s ambient impoliteness – evident in the imperviousness of 'every one' to the pleasure of books – throw into relief the qualities that distinguish Orville's successor? How, in other words, does Mortimer Delvile, the noble object of Cecilia's affection, secure his own 'distinction'?

Delvile, the last scion of an ancient and unadulterated aristocratic line, not only deviates from Cecilia's 'crowd of suitors' by sharing her taste for the 'employment, which to a lover of literature [...] is perhaps the mind's first luxury'.[27] For after *Cecilia*'s laboured revelation that 'the change of name is the obstacle' to their marriage, Burney enlists Delvile's 'haughty' mother to substantiate the prospect of her son's 'independant [*sic*] happiness' as a strikingly retrograde bodily lapse: 'How will the blood of your wronged ancestors rise into your guilty cheeks, and how will your heart throb with secret shame and reproach, when wished joy upon your marriage by the name of *Mr. Beverly!*[28] The spectre of the enraged Mrs Delvile, 'extended upon the floor, her face, hands and neck all covered with blood!' (she has, it turns out, 'burst a blood vessel'), seals the antipathy of her son's essence to Cecilia's patronymic.[29]

In *Cecilia*, Burney transforms Orville's anti-performative – but nevertheless still performed – practice of status into Delvile's genetic sensitivity to the threat of plebeian misnomer (Cecilia is the 'only survivor' of 'rich farmers'[30]). Decades earlier, Daniel Defoe's *The Compleat English Gentleman* (1729) spoofed the physiological pretences that would compel Mrs Delvile to swoon in the face of Cecilia's 'blood':

> Nay, I will grant an invisible Influence of the Blood, if they please, as if there were some differing Species in the very Fluids of Nature; that the Spirits of a finer Extraction flow'd in the Vessels, or some *Animalculae* of a differing and more vigorous kind which existed in the Blood, fir'd the Creature with a superiour Heat differing from those which mov'd in the Vessels of a meaner and lower Kind of Creature [...]
>
> [...] [It] is insinuated that there are some Globules in the Blood, some sublime Particles in the Animal Secretion, which will not mix with the hated Stream of a mechanick Race, but preserve themselves pure and entire.[31]

Evelina adheres to the Whiggish redefinition of virtue pronounced by Defoe as 'Manners make the Man',[32] even though Burney's first novel does so, perversely, by demonstrating that the ideally unscripted performance of politeness makes only one man, Orville.[33] In *Cecilia*, however, Delvile materializes as a genetic artefact of the last age. What are the stakes of Burney's regression to this identity of aristocratic value and explicitly mystified 'invisible Influence', an influence aggravated for hundreds of pages by the Delviles' invincible antipathy to Cecilia's last name?

The Materiality of Gentlemen

The strand of conduct-book discourse devoted, in the words of Richard Allestree's *The Gentleman's Calling* (1660), to gentlemen's 'more divine and sublimated part' advances the prospect that Burney rejects with Evelina's refusal to direct the penitent Willoughby: the prospect of manners' transmission between men (or, as in *Pamela*, between women and men).[34] By tracing how masculine politeness is, to borrow Elias's verb, 'reproduced' in three texts[35] – Giovanni della Casa's influential treatise on nobility *Galateo* (1558); Anthony, Earl of Shaftesbury's 'Sensus Communis; An Essay on the Freedom of Wit and Humor' (1709); and Samuel Richardson's *The History of Sir Charles Grandison* (1753–54) – I aim to pursue the significance of Burney's representation of a 'noblest source of intellectual enjoyment' salvaged for *Cecilia* only insofar as it is linked to an anti-communicative metaphysics, in Defoe's words, of 'sublime Particles'. If the dialectical history explained by Elias as a 'double movement: a courtization of bourgeois people and a bourgeoisification of courtly people' was, Elias argues, fuelled in part by the legibility of conduct books that communicated practice to both strata, what can we make of a geneticization of noble enjoyment represented by Burney as both cause and effect of an entire public's immunity to reading?[36]

Reprinted in 1774, its editor states, 'to prevent us from relapsing again into unpoliteness and indelicacy', *Galateo* stages a scene of manners' transmission inconceivable within the sphere of pervasive 'vulgarity' portrayed by *Cecilia*.[37] Here, the courtier Galateo has been charged to deliver his master's message to a visiting count:

> 'The Bishop, my master, esteems your Lordship as a person truly noble [...] Nay, he would have thought your Lordship complete in every respect, without a single exception; but that in one particular action of yours, there appeared some little imperfection: which is, that when you are eating at table, the motion of your lips and mouth causes an uncommon smacking kind of a sound, which is rather offensive to those who have the honour to sit at table with you [...] [The good Prelate] intreats you [...] carefully to correct this ungraceful habit [...]'

> The Count [...] blushed a little at first [...] 'I cannot but esteem myself greatly obliged to the Bishop for this polite instance of his kindness and friendship for me; and you may assure his Lordship, I will most undoubtedly use my utmost endeavours to correct this failing of mine for the future.'[38]

By imaginatively correcting the Bishop's single remaining 'imperfection', Galateo ruptures his lingering continuity with 'those people, whom we sometimes see thrusting, like hogs, their very *snouts* into their soup'.[39] But the Bishop's ennobling difference from a hog is far from a genetic attribute, because it proceeds from an effort of sublimation whose least detail, this passage shows, cannot be taken for granted. In this capacity, Elias repeats the thesis that underscores the Nietzschean, genealogical tendency of his history of manners: 'Nothing in table manners is self-evident or the product, as it were, of a "natural" feeling of delicacy'.[40] And yet della Casa's hypothetical count does possess *some* '"natural" feeling of delicacy'; his willingness to further sublimate himself is signalled by the mechanical readiness of his blush. Although he is deaf to the indelicacy of his lip-smacking, he harbours a susceptibility to correction that makes him, if not as automatically polite as Burke's steadily breathing subject, then just as automatically willing to 'endeavour' to become so.

The willingness of della Casa's count to further refine the sound of the act of eating marks a moment when manners are transmitted between two men. In the following passage, Anthony, Earl of Shaftesbury's 'Sensus Communis' would seem strikingly to illustrate Elias's statement of what, after Michel Foucault, has come to be called the repressive hypothesis: 'The prohibitions supported by social sanctions are reproduced in individuals as self-controls'.[41] For Shaftesbury, manners compel an atomized scene of self-control remote from the exchange navigated by Galateo:

> Should one who had the countenance of a gentleman ask me why I would avoid being nasty when nobody was present, in the first place I should be fully satisfied that he himself was a very nasty gentleman who could ask this question, and that it would be a hard matter for me to make him ever conceive what true cleanliness was. However, I might, notwithstanding this, be contented to give him a slight answer and say, 'It was because I had a nose'.
>
> Should he trouble me further and ask again, 'What if I had a cold or what if naturally I had no such nice smell?', I might answer perhaps that 'I cared as little to see myself nasty as that others should see me in that condition'.
>
> 'But what if it were in the dark?'
>
> 'Why, even then, though I had neither nose nor eyes, my sense of the matter would still be the same: my nature would rise at the thought of what was sordid.'[42]

Here Shaftesbury coordinates the transubstantiation of hygiene into 'nature' with a refinement of gentlemanly acumen that recoils not just from the sight and smell but also from the '*thought* of what was sordid'. Yet Shaftesbury shows some qualms about the pervasiveness of this process, evident in this gentleman's diminished sensibility to external stimuli (whether supplied by other people or his own sense organs) as well as in his diminished capacity to correct others (intimated by his failure to induce politeness in his nasty interlocutor). By basing the imperative that he 'avoid being nasty when nobody was present' upon the increasing ineffability of 'what true cleanliness was', Shaftesbury's reclusive and mutilated gentleman threatens to exacerbate the difficulty with which Allestree introduces *The Gentleman's Calling*: ''twill be no wonder if it be adjudged a ridiculous soloecism [*sic*] to attempt to define his Calling, whose very Essence is thought to consist in having none'.[43] To resolve this dilemma, Allestree cites 'the bright lustre of their exact and exemplary Conversations', thus defining a purpose more bluntly announced by Stephen Penton's *Guardian's Instruction* (1688): 'the Vulgar [...] learn all by gaping and staring on a man in fine Clothes'.[44] According to Jean Gailhard's *Compleat Gentleman* (1678), a gentleman's spectacular exemplarity reciprocally renders those inaccessible to vulgar perception 'useless'.[45]

By so insistently dematerializing the medium of true politeness, Shaftesbury appears to anticipate what Elias evokes as '[the] agency of individual self-control, the super-ego, the conscience or whatever we call it'.[46] Such agency meets the pivotal criterion, somewhat uneasily dramatized by Shaftesbury, of operating 'even when one is alone'.[47] For Elias, the corollary of this change in manners' consistency is the tendency of directives once minutely specified by authors like della Casa to become 'apodictic' or 'categorical':[48] as Shaftesbury's speaker disdainfully suggests, he can never enumerate the criteria of a standard of cleanliness that resides only in 'my sense of the matter'. By embodying politeness that is too refined to be exemplary at all, Shaftesbury's gentleman threatens to diverge from a vindication of his calling that persists through the political economy of Adam Smith, whose *Theory of Moral Sentiments* (1759) bases the 'peace and order of society' on the perceptual priority of 'the plain and palpable difference of birth and fortune' over 'the invisible [...] difference of wisdom and virtue'.[49] And yet the politeness of Shaftesbury's gentleman is not entirely transparent; his justification of solitary cleanliness, if it eludes the registers of smell and sight, remains legible to Shaftesbury's reader as the 'slight answer' that this gentleman does deign to give. Unlike Orville, Shaftesbury's gentleman supplies his audience with a written part, even if he does so in the same gesture that asserts the superfluity of such documentation to the ineffable politeness of 'my nature'.

In *The History of Sir Charles Grandison*, Richardson renovates the medium of gentlemanliness whose limits Shaftesbury's isolated and reticent speaker portends. As resoundingly as does Allestree's *Gentleman's Calling*, Richardson's novel rejects 'private Innocence' in favor of a 'true Publick Spirit',[50] one now transmitted by a man whose 'welfare', an awed onlooker avows, 'is the concern of hundreds, perhaps. He, compared to us, is as the public to the private'.[51] The following scene takes place after a duel precipitated by Grandison's rescue of Harriot Byron from her would-be abductor Sir Hargrave Pollexfen. The audience to the two men's conference, composed of the rakes Bagenhall, Merceda, and Jordan, react to the preternaturally 'great tranquillity' shown by Grandison, who impresses upon the hot-headed Sir Hargrave the 'mischief' of any further violence:

> Sir Hargrave seemed too irresolute either to accept or refuse his [Grandison's] hand.
>
> *Mr. Jor.* I am astonished! – Why, Sir Charles, what a tranquillity must you have within you! The devil take me, Sir Hargrave, if you shall not make up matters with such a noble adversary.
>
> *Mr. Mer.* He has won me to his side. By the great God of Heaven, I had rather have Sir Charles Grandison for my friend than the greatest Prince on earth!
>
> *Mr. Bag.* Did I not *tell* you, gentleman? – D—n me, if I have not hitherto lived to nothing but to my shame! [...]
>
> Sir Hargrave even sobbed [...] like a child. – D—n my heart, said he, in broken sentences – And must I thus put up – And must I thus be overcome? [...]
>
> [The gentlemen] [...] reproached each other, as if they had no notion of what was great and noble in man till now [...]
>
> D—n me, said Sir Hargrave [...] this man, this Sir Charles, is the devil – He has made a mere infant of me.[52]

Richardson's reconstitution of 'what was great and noble in man' is at the same time a reconstitution of Grandison's public, for these rakes are won over by a dispassionate tranquillity whose calming effects are induced by words. By reducing Sir Hargrave to 'a mere infant', Grandison proves the exemplarity of masculine honour in the new medium of literary sentiment. The irrationality of duelling 'Punctilio's' whose influence threatens, Allestree warns, 'that the next Age will be in danger of receiving the Fable of *Don Quixot* for Authentique History' would be undone by the tranquillizing powers of anti-romance, which finally lay to rest 'an observation of

Mr. Locke's' extracted from *Some Thoughts* and cited by Grandison: 'young men, in their warm blood, are forward to think they have in vain learned to fence, if they never show their skill and courage in a duel'.[53] The 'naturally hasty', 'passionate', and much-provoked Grandison, trained in the art of self-government by his mother 'almost from infancy', demonstrates the more impressive virtue of '*true* magnanimity': Grandison sets a standard of masculine honour expressed by the ruefully admiring Hargrave as 'The *devil* could not have made him fight'. Jordan confirms the anti-romantic effect of the feat that proves Grandison 'a wonder of a man': 'I never saw an hero till now'.[54]

Grandison's capacity to convert a hero from a man who fights into a man who cannot be made to fight, as this would be demonstrated by its circle of repentant rakes, supports G. J. Barker-Benfield's suggestion that the eighteenth-century novel 'could be a weapon in the campaign for the reformation of manners'.[55] Richardson's claim for the pleasures of masculine exemplarity – his text's ability to 'enliven as well as instruct'[56] – dissolves the impediment posed, Allestree states, by the 'strangely vitiated palate' that 'will look on Books in no other notion but as Taskmasters'.[57] As Habermas argues, Richardson advances one of literary history's defining appeals to a domestic sphere now represented as 'humanity's genuine site', a sphere in which the cultivation of letters prepares men for an exchange of public opinion governed not by violence but by the 'authority [...] of the better argument'.[58] Novels would, then, enable the pacified practice of representative – or, Grandisonian – human nature. In this capacity, it is worth stressing the irony of Burney's critical classification with, in the words of Nancy Armstrong, the 'conduct-book authors', for characters void of internal sources of entertainment are impervious to the vehicle of Richardsonian virtue.[59]

Like the endeavour of della Casa's count to quiet his eating or the hygiene that still fleshes out Shaftesbury's gentleman, the scene of sentimental communication that enlarges Grandison's public to include the novel's readers represents masculine nobility as an effect of practice. Despite the change in the density of politeness projected by all three authors, each admits the ontological slippage expressed by the anonymous *Institucion of a Gentleman* (1555) with the taxonomy 'gentle gentle', 'gentle ungentle', and 'ungentle gentle'.[60] *Cecilia*'s recourse to a metaphysics of aristocratic birth thus cannot be read as its return to an essentialist past. Rather, *Cecilia* projects the essentialized version *of* a past able to define the quiddity of status only as the '*je ne sçay quoi*' invoked in the Chevalier de la

Chétardie's *Instructions for a Young Nobleman* (1683).[61] As the counterpart of a past where the *je ne sçay quoi* of blood would trump acquired honour, Cecilia occupies a present in which Richardsonian virtue's potential audience, here represented by her relentlessly calculating guardian Mr Briggs, is oblivious to the ennobling influence of print: 'what do you want with books? do no good; all lost time; words get no cash'.[62]

Cecilia's refusal to affirm the humanizing power of books does not reside solely in the crudely progressive self-defence voiced when another one of the novel's businessmen, Mr Hobson, claims to be 'a man of as good property as another man'.[63] It is not only the grossness of a claim to 'wherewithal' which jettisons any pretence to cultivation, but also the insolvency of the one ungentle man in *Cecilia* who feels 'avidity' for the 'polite arts', that signal Burney's restriction of the elevating power of letters.[64] For Cecilia has no career counsel to give her educated but chronically professionless acquaintance Belfield:

> [Cecilia] could suggest nothing, for she was ignorant what was eligible to suggest. The stations and employments of men she only knew by occasionally hearing that such were their professions, and such their situations in life; but with the means and gradations by which they arose to them she was wholly unacquainted.[65]

Given this disclaimer, it is perhaps unsurprising that *Cecilia* reduces 'means and gradations' to the binary clash of attitudes rehearsed by Briggs, according to whom Delvile's father keeps 'all his old grand-dads [...] in a roll; locks 'em in a closet; says his prayers to 'em; can't live without 'em: likes 'em better than cash!'[66] Yet Burney takes some pains to reject the more finely resolved prospect of means and gradations opened by Belfield's literary competence. Rather than winning him 'preferment' or, as his father hopes, making him 'the ornament of the city [...] the best scholar in any shop in London', the skills acquired by Belfield 'at Eaton' prevent him from managing his father's trade; when 'placed in the shop, instead of applying his talents, as his father had expected, to trade, he both despised and abhorred the name of it'.[67] This cautionary tale – Belfield ruins his family and wastes his talents in a series of botched professional endeavours – limits the applicability of a liberal education to men who do not have to practise business, the same proscription Locke makes when he dedicates *Some Thoughts* 'to our English gentry'.[68] The failure of letters to elevate a man who must instead 'understand how to get money' marks *Cecilia*'s most topical and urgent restriction of masculine value.[69]

As the exemplar of a species of nobility that can be communicated only by blood, Delvile accrues his worth against the backdrop of a public that does not profit from Richardson's 'captivating semblance of a *Novel*'.[70] Burney's description of Delvile, composed in the 'flecks of free indirect speech' that, Margaret Doody suggests, punctuate her second novel, sounds much like the one Evelina gives of Orville:[71] 'Mortimer Delvile was tall and finely formed, his features, though not handsome, were full of expression, and a noble openness of manners and address spoke the elegance of his education, and the liberality of his mind'.[72] By citing the 'not handsome' Delvile's liberal education, Burney appeals to a Lockean and Richardsonian standard of gentlemanly practice. This is followed, however, by *Cecilia*'s increasingly regressive specification of the 'obstacle' preventing Delvile's marriage to Cecilia.[73] In what follows, I assess the relation between *Cecilia*'s marriage plot and a public sphere humanized by neither exemplary men nor exemplary texts. Cecilia's love for a suitor deterred by 'the *only* objection that *any* man could form to an alliance with Miss Beverly' stimulates the genetic animosity to her name that lends substance to the Delviles' rank.[74] By thus activating Mortimer's nobility, *Cecilia* conflates its protagonist's exercise of marital choice and her affirmation of the singular value of Delvile's status.

'Misery So Peculiar': *Cecilia*'s Marriage Plot and the Agency of Cecilia's Money

In *Some Reflections upon Marriage, Occasion'd by the Duke & Dutchess of Mazarine's Case* (1700), Mary Astell observes: 'A Woman indeed can't properly be said to Choose, all that is allow'd her, is to Refuse or Accept what is offer'd'.[75] No protagonist would seem more conspicuously to enlarge the extent of feminine amorous choice than the independent heiress Cecilia, whose 'estate of 3000*l*. per annum' guarantees an exponential rate of offers.[76] As one bystander remarks, 'no register-officer keeper has been pestered with more claimants. You know they assault you by dozens'.[77] Even Delvile's particularity would be eroded, this speaker continues, by the volume of 'adulation' Cecilia commands: 'A thousand Mr. Delviles are to Miss Beverly but as one; [...] she regards them not individually as lovers, but collectively as men; [...] she must probably desire, like Portia in the Merchant of Venice [*sic*], that their names may be run over one by one, before she can distinctly tell which is which'.[78] Further hyperbole promises to dissolve the impediment that drives *Cecilia*'s plot: her doctor assures

Cecilia that 'scarcely is there another man you may not chuse or reject at your pleasure', while Mr Briggs attempts to console her by noting that 'if one won't snap, another will'.[79]

The Delviles, headed by a patriarch whose claim to 'over-awing predominance' is repeatedly punctured by Burney's novel ('O 'tis a sad tribe!' one irreverent houseguest remarks), resist inclusion in Briggs's levelling estimate of men's proneness to snap.[80] The 'last of his race', Delvile embodies his singular value – or, the singularity that *is* his value – as his antipathy to Cecilia's fortune, for Burney ennobles Delvile's race as a function of the undesirability of Cecilia's money.[81] In the following paragraphs, then, I underscore *Cecilia*'s departure from the ideological fiction that Habermas and Armstrong assign to the domestic novel. For Armstrong, novels '[represent] sexual relations as something entirely removed from politics'; novels, in a formulation which closely resonates with Habermas's account of domestic literature, '[pass] off ideology as the product of purely human concern'.[82] The fiction of the 'purely human' is, to return to Burney's first novel, deployed by *Evelina* only residually: at the moment that Evelina's birthright seems irrecoverably lost, Lord Orville shows 'the nobleness of his disinterested regard' by declaring himself 'more strongly, more invincibly devoted to you than ever!'[83] And yet the nobleness of Orville's 'disinterested desire' serves, in the end, to ennoble only him.[84] Although occasioned by Evelina's namelessness, his disinterest is made redundant by her recovery of her own exalted patronymic. *Evelina* thus enlists Orville's disinterest to serve what might be called the novel's larger interest – *Evelina*'s suggestion that, unlike the honour of *Pamela*'s Mr B, Orville's nobility requires no repair. *Evelina*'s ideological fiction does not, as Habermas or Armstrong would have it, reside in its representation of a purely human zone of domestic love, but rather in its vision of an antiperformative practice of aristocratic value that trumps the Whiggish articulation of politeness on its own terms.

Delvile is the only suitor in Cecilia's crowd of claimants who elicits her feeling: 'almost every word he spoke shewed the sympathy of their minds, and almost every look which caught her eyes was a reciprocation of intelligence'.[85] Yet the antagonism of his race to Cecilia's name defines 'the man she thought most worthy to be entrusted with the disposal of her fortune' as the man who reduces its value to less than nothing.[86] By granting 'power over her heart' to the suitor who turns an apparently 'trifling' caveat into a betrayal of the essence of his status, Cecilia occupies a 'misery so peculiar' that it escapes the plot permutations contained in Astell's formula:

Cecilia 'was compelled to refuse the man of her choice, though satisfied his affections were her own'.[87] With this synopsis, Burney defines as what can be called an ideological red herring the exclamation Cecilia makes when she hears of the marriage forced upon another eligible daughter: 'how do I rejoice that my independent situation exempts me from being disposed of for life, by thus being set up to sale!'[88] Rather than freeing her to marry the man she loves, Cecilia's independent situation places her within an economy of feminine choice even more miserably restricted than that evoked by Astell. Cecilia finally determines upon a 'sacrifice' that she 'voluntarily' undertakes; assured that this expedient 'has had the approval of Mrs. Delvile', 'the ingenuous Cecilia' relinquishes her estate to marry Delvile and assume his patronymic.[89] Following the disasters caused by her secret marriage to and subsequent separation from Delvile, she is restored to her husband and inherits a compensatory fortune from his aunt.

Like Evelina, Cecilia enters London society to find herself 'merely an object to be gazed at'.[90] Whereas Evelina's anonymity qualifies her as a litmus of the rudeness of almost every man of the present age, Cecilia's fortune serves to distinguish London's last noble man. On the one hand, Cecilia receives proposals from insolvent aristocrats like the 'inoffensive' Lord Derford, whose rejection compels Delvile's snobbish father to exclaim, 'This is a very extraordinary circumstance! […] the son of an earl to be rejected by a young woman of no family, and yet no reason to be assigned for it!'[91] For the prejudiced Mr Delvile, rank should constitute a more than ample reason for her acceptance; for Cecilia's mercenary acquaintance Mrs Belfield, money should oblige Cecilia to elevate an untitled suitor:

> I think when a young lady has such a fine fortune as that, the only thing she has to do, is to be thinking of making a good use of it, by dividing it […] [As] to only marrying somebody that's got as much of his own, why it is not half so much a favour: and if the young lady would take my advice, she'd marry for love, for as to lucre, she's enough in all conscience.[92]

By rejecting the son of an earl, Cecilia would instead confer 'favour' upon Mrs Belfield's literate but obscure son. This especially toxic articulation of the exercise of marrying for love renders Cecilia's choice interested in spite of herself. Faced with options whose 'use' is dictated by her money, Cecilia compares herself to Mrs Belfield's neglected daughter Henrietta, this novel's closest approximation of Evelina: 'happier in that case is the lowly Henrietta […] who can only be sought and caressed from motives of purest regard'.[93] Yet *Evelina* has established that lowly women are sought and caressed 'from motives of purest regard' only by the anachronistically polite Orville.

Cecilia refuses to ratify the ideological promise perfunctorily figured by 'Henny'.[94] By defining the suitor worthy to marry Cecilia as the one man for whom the price of her fortune is too high, Burney does not imaginatively restore their love to a state of purest regard. Rather than shedding the confusion of love and 'good use', Cecilia's fortune serves what *Cecilia's* marriage plot claims as money's noblest possible use: its affirmation of the ineffability of Delvile's value. *Cecilia* thus exploits the apparent antagonism of love and money to an even more conservative end than does *Evelina*, because Cecilia elects to marry the one man who rejects history's most obvious rationale for the transitivity of politeness. As Elias states of the transformation of status into class, 'More exclusively than before, money has become the basis of social differences'.[95]

In this sense, Cecilia *does* give Delvile her fortune. Burney underscores the levelling effect of money – that is, its capacity to determine social differences – by granting Cecilia's wealth the power to divest a nobleman of his name. Money, Burney makes inescapably clear, dissolves status. And yet because Cecilia forfeits her legacy in deference to the radically antithetical value that would be sustained by Delvile's patronymic, her fortune does something else. By not giving Delvile her fortune, Cecilia gives it to him after all. The paradoxical efficacy of this act recalls Jacques Derrida's term *sous rature*, which means, as Gayatri Spivak explains, that a word is both 'inaccurate' and yet remains 'necessary'.[96] The necessity of money to *Cecilia's* vindication of masculine rank is conveyed by the contradiction upon which this plot finally turns: the inconvertibility of Delvile's value can be gauged only in terms of the magnitude of the fortune that he compels Cecilia to surrender.

A plot in which Cecilia gives Delvile her money *sous rature* divests her of the virtuous influence still legible in Evelina's letters. Because Evelina marries the artefactually noble Orville, her epistolary virtue is superfluous; yet the protagonist of Burney's first novel does still incarnate the literary form through which Richardson vindicates a post-aristocratic medium of masculine value. Cecilia, however, assists Delvile's value differently. Rather than revealing in letters the purity of heart that ratifies her suitor's disinterested sentiment – as I discuss below, *Cecilia's* form does something else – Cecilia sanctions the value of the man whom she marries by voluntarily divesting herself of her legacy. In so doing, Cecilia is, as Burney puts it, 'ingenuous'; in the contemporary sense of that word, she affirms the inviolability of Delvile's status without requiring the extrinsic impetus of a command. (Indeed, Burney's synchronization of Cecilia's advance intention 'instantly to agree' to this marital expedient and Delvile's demurrals that 'it would be madness to expect your compliance!' generates the lovers' most substantive and exciting dialogue.[97]) In perhaps the most resonant overlay of *Cecilia*'s marriage plot and this novel's political imaginary, Cecilia exercises her unprecedented amorous freedom to affirm the value of London's last noble man.

By voluntarily making her 'concession' to Mortimer's status, Cecilia does not inhabit the modernity theorized by Elias, who appropriates Sigmund Freud's alignment of 'sociogenesis and psychogenesis' to excavate from conduct books the Western European achievement of sublimation or, as Elias puts it, 'inner pacification'.[98] For the distinction of Delvile from a sea of impolite men places the phylogenetic burden of 'a new self-discipline' upon only one person, Cecilia herself.[99] The fantasy at stake in Burney's second novel resides in Cecilia's single-handed, stoic, and briefly maddened activation of Delvile's value. In this, Cecilia also does not inhabit the modernity theorized by Armstrong or Habermas. By freely divesting herself of her legacy, Cecilia vindicates a form of masculine value that inheres neither in literary sentiment – for then someone like Belfield would claim it – nor in Briggs's wads of cash. Her surrender of her fortune cannot be routed into an ideological fiction of disinterested feeling, because both Cecilia's love and her money are necessary to her ingenuous sanction of Delvile's worth.

Cecilia's surrender of her birthright fixes the opposition of Delvile's status to the pointedly anti-aristocratic powers of her money. This is an unstable, incoherent, and, as many readers have observed, bleak fantasy, one which the character of Delvile does nothing to sweeten. Here I will briefly suggest that Burney offers an alternative vision of the agency – if I may so call Cecilia's vindication of Delvile's value – that Cecilia wields within her impolite public sphere, an alternative distinct from the concession demanded by Delville's rank. In assessing the latter event, Barbara Zonitch suggests that it 'highlights a more personal dilemma: Can the economic and emotional interests of marriage be reconciled?'[100] Yet in *Cecilia*, the 'personal' claims the resolution of the unspecified 'sympathy of their minds' that, as we have seen, defines Mortimer as London's singularly eligible man. By tailoring the personal to the wholesale stipulation of Delvile's worth, *Cecilia* is not so easily legible as a realist novel; beyond a generic statement of their sympathy, Burney does not build characters who sustain an individualized articulation of romantic love.[101] Speaking from a critical vantage which does not presume the accessibility of Cecilia's emotional world, Deidre Lynch argues that Burney invests her heroines with 'psychological' depth to make them 'more three-dimensional than other characters'.[102] The distinguishing dimensionality of these characters 'fuels the fantasy of an inner self that might operate independent of relations of social exchange', thereby serving the ends assigned the domestic novel by Habermas and Armstrong.[103] I conclude this essay with the opposing suggestion that, rather than imagining a self whose depths elude social determination, Burney does just the opposite: she represents novelistic women who lend themselves almost wholly – if always with difficulty – to a conservative or an anti-bourgeois figuration of masculine value. A nameless but virtuous epistolary subject, Evelina proves the consistency of Orville's politeness. Cecilia, however, is composed of free indirect speech. How does *Cecilia*'s departure from the form that vindicates Orville's worth enable this second novel's vision of a public sphere in which politeness cannot be communicated?

At the very level of the narrative technology that would instantiate it, Cecilia's inner self is indelibly social. In the following passage, Cecilia, newly arrived in London, attends the rehearsal of an opera; her interiority contributes to a new species of social value by means of the peculiarly elliptical formal resource of free indirect speech:

> This was the first Opera she had ever heard, yet she was not wholly a stranger to Italian compositions, having assiduously studied music from a natural love of the art, attended all the best concerts her neighbourhood afforded, and regularly received from London the works of the best masters. But the little skill she had thus gained, served rather to increase than to lessen the surprise with which she heard the present performance, – a surprize [*sic*] of which the discovery of her own ignorance made not the least part. Unconscious from the little she had acquired how much was to be learnt, she was astonished to find the inadequate power of written music to convey any idea of vocal abilities: with just knowledge enough, therefore, to understand something of the difficulties, and feel much of the merit, she gave to the whole Opera an avidity of attention almost painful from its own eagerness.[104]

This passage does not herald, to cite once more from Lynch, the novelistic emergence of 'an inner identity that transcends social determination'.[105] Instead, Burney qualifies the gap between 'written music' and 'present performance' to theorize a selectively generalized mode of cultural consumption. And it is precisely 'Cecilia' who measures the profundity of this gap: the 'inadequate power' of a written part to communicate Cecilia's future experience of music parallels the inadequacy of the free indirect speech that can evoke the intensity of this experience only extrinsically. Indeed, Burney's account of Cecilia's first opera can be described as *doubly* extrinsic, because the 'avidity of attention' to which its narrator refers does not compose a transcendent inner identity. Even though Cecilia's avid attention is accompanied by such sentiments as surprise, astonishment, and pain, these feelings operate not to define her particular psychology, but rather to assert the fundamental ineffability of the 'idea' that absorbs her. For what hollows out depth of which Cecilia was previously 'unconscious' is not her inner self but rather her sudden access to a mode of aesthetic receptivity that distinguishes her, among London's throng of auditors, as 'the only person thus astonished'.[106] Writing of Jane Austen, D. A. Miller remarks of free indirect style: 'Narration comes as near to a character's psychic and linguistic reality as it can get without collapsing into it [...] Though free indirect style plainly offers *a third term* between character and narration, it is, or means to be, a nondialectical one: a kind of turnstile'.[107] In Burney's *Cecilia*, however, free indirect style is dialectical, insofar as it recombines character and narration to broach not Cecilia's 'psychic and linguistic reality' but rather the de-personalized incommunicability of her aesthetic experience. Rather than a turnstile, *Cecilia*'s form approximates the always asymptotic approach of words to an experience whose avidity proceeds from the fact that language never comes any closer to this object.

Burney anticipates the divorce, asserted by Immanuel Kant's *Critique of Judgment* (1790), of aesthetic receptivity from 'sensation proper'. Through the novelistic form of her experience, Cecilia diverges, as Kant puts it, from 'people who aim at nothing but enjoyment'.[108] Her pained and incommunicable attentiveness dissociates her from the ambient semi-barbarity of an audience which defines 'the only thing [that] carries one to the Opera' as 'those signores and signoras cutting capers':[109] for, as Kant stipulates, '[any] taste remains barbaric if its liking requires that *charms* and *emotions* be mingled in'.[110] In a striking irony, then, the ennobling vehicle embraced by Burney's own novel is not the book – whose failure *Cecilia* strenuously asserts – but, instead, the very medium of culture that proves the inadequacy of the written. And it is not privatized or psychological sentiment that *Cecilia*'s representation of culture would communicate, but rather the rigorous particularity of a form of value distinguished not because Cecilia finds it enjoyable but because she finds it 'almost painful'.

Cecilia's astonishment affirms her difference from characters, Burney dismissively states at the start of the novel, 'of that common sort which renders delineation superfluous'.[111] Again, it does so not by providing psychological detail but by revising the form of novelistic 'delineation' itself. By briefly materializing as an experience of cultural receptivity whose power to elevate coincides with her narrative's inability to communicate it, Cecilia lends herself to a different kind of value than that to which she does not give her fortune. Burney will elaborate the former species of value only in her final, post-Revolutionary novel.[112] For better or for worse, Burney dedicates Cecilia's almost unencumbered amorous choice to the misery of a marriage plot that would, impossibly, forestall the historical agency of money itself.

Notes

1 Frances Burney, *Cecilia, or Memoirs of an Heiress*, ed. Peter Sabor and Margaret Anne Doody (Oxford: Oxford University Press, 1988), p. 408. My deepest thanks go to Jill Heydt-Stevenson and Charlotte Sussman for their comments on earlier drafts of this essay.

2 Norbert Elias, *The Civilizing Process: Sociogenetic and Psychogenetic Investigations*, trans. Edmund Jephcott (Oxford: Blackwell, rev. edn, 2000), p. 369.

3 See the holograph of *Cecilia, or Memoirs of an Heiress*, held in the Berg Collection, New York Public Library, I, p. 53. Cecilia Beverly is in this edition of the novel still intermittently named 'Albina Wyerly'. For support of this research, I am indebted to a grant from the Department of Women's Studies, Arizona State University, summer 1999. I am also indebted to the Newberry Library for a Mellon-NEH fellowship during the 2002–2003 academic year.

4 Burney, *Cecilia*, p. 43.

5 Jürgen Habermas, *The Structural Transformation of the Public Sphere: An Inquiry into a Category of Bourgeois Society*, trans. Thomas Burger (Cambridge, MA: MIT Press, 1989), p. 56.

6 See my *Ingenuous Subjection: Compliance and Power in the Eighteenth-Century Domestic Novel* (Philadelphia: University of Pennsylvania Press, 2005) for the argument that women's compliance in the domestic sphere signifies in the novel, in political and moral philosophy, and conduct-book literature as an explicitly political practice. Just as post-absolutist men's assent to public power, as theorized by John Locke and others, has the crucially modernizing virtue of being unforced or 'ingenuous', so women in the private sphere who comply freely or ingenuously would determine the modernity of the men who govern them. *Pamela* demonstrates both the logic of this promise and the insoluble contradictions of a domestic modernity where husbands still claim a naturalized, extra-contractual or sex-based right to conjugal rule. (Mr B is not so modern after all: at the close of *Pamela* II, Richardson

shores up B's claim to domestic power not because of B's sex – for although she is a woman, Pamela's virtue exceeds his – but because of his aristocratic excellence.)

Having written this essay before the completion of my book, I regret that I cannot place *Cecilia* in closer proximity to the book's argument. Burney's novels represent perhaps the most forcible literary refusal of the fiction of ingenuous subjection, and, like Mary Astell, Burney reveals the inextricability of certain forms of conservatism and indeed essentialism from her refusal to entertain the promise of the enlightened exercise of power whose arbitrary foundation remains unrevised. See Susan Staves, *Married Women's Separate Property in England, 1660–1833* (Cambridge, MA: Harvard University Press, 1990) for an exhaustive account of the failure of contract ideology to effect the revision of legal impediments that precluded wives' independent ownership of property.

7 Frances Burney, *Evelina, or, A Young Lady's Entrance into the World*, ed. Susan Kubica Howard (Peterborough, Ontario: Broadview Press, 2000), p. 415.

8 Burney, *Evelina*, p. 414.

9 Burney, *Evelina*, pp. 96, 486 (emphasis Burney's).

10 This comedy was originally staged at Covent Garden in 1747. In 1776, Garrick played the character Ranger 'numerous times', according to Susan Kubica Howard (*Evelina*, p. 116, n. 2). Hoadly's play represents the jealous husband and guardian Strictland, who forbids the marriage of his ward Jacintha to her suitor Bellamy. Ranger is the mediator who engineers the play's happy ending.

11 Burney, *Evelina*, pp. 116–17 (emphasis Burney's).

12 See Michael Fried's seminal expression of the eighteenth-century French ideal of absorption, epitomized in '[Denis] Diderot's conception of painting[, which] rested ultimately upon the supreme fiction that the beholder did not exist, that he was not really there, standing before the canvas'. Paradoxically, for Diderot, 'only by establishing the fiction of his [the beholder's] absence or nonexistence could his actual placement before and enthrallment by the painting be secured'. Diderot's writings on painting and drama thus aim, as Fried states, to '*de-theatricalize beholding*' (*Absorption and Theatricality: Painting and Beholder in the Age of Diderot* [Chicago: University of Chicago Press, 1980], pp. 103–104); emphasis Fried's. Fried's terms are transposed into the register of novelistic discourse by William Warner; in *Licensing Entertainment: The Elevation of Novel Reading in Britain, 1684–1750* (Berkeley: University of California Press, 1998). Warner suggests (p. 226) that Richardson's *Pamela* strives to avoid 'a coy and self-conscious theatricality that panders to the gaze of the beholder'.

13 In using the term 'performativity', the theorist of gender and power Judith Butler argues for the apparent essence of a sex fixed only as a result of a person's practice of gender. Butler explicitly draws upon the redefinition of linguistic *meaning* proposed by Ferdinand de Saussure not as the divine or organic truth of a natural language but, because of the arbitrariness of the linguistic signifier, as a differential *value* provisionally secured as the specificity of one word relative to all others. Such value, for Saussure, is achieved only at the cost of its proneness to structural (synchronic) and temporal (diachronic) mutation. Jacques Derrida appropriates Saussure's insight into the structural and temporal contingency of linguistic value to coin the neologism 'différance', whose closest approximation in the realm of a

performance of gender that also only provisionally secures the stability of its agent's sex is, again, performativity. While the actors imagined by Locke, Burke, or Burney do not closely resemble Butler's subject, her term helps articulate the stakes of the opposition between the natural and the affected practice of manners.

14 John Locke, *Some Thoughts Concerning Education*, ed. Ruth Grant and Nathan Tarcov (Indianapolis: Hackett, 1996), p. 39.

15 Locke, *Some Thoughts*, pp. 39–40.

16 Locke, *Some Thoughts*, p. 42.

17 Edmund Burke, *First Letter on a Regicide Peace* (1796), in *The Writings and Speeches of Edmund Burke*, ed. R. B. McDowell (Oxford: Clarendon, 1991), Vol. 9, p. 242.

18 I diverge a bit, however, from assessments of Burke like that made by Frances Ferguson: 'such an extreme empiricism as Burke's purchases its lucidity at the price of the notion of human freedom, as all action is described as a mechanical response to external stimuli' ('Legislating the Sublime', in Ralph Cohen, ed., *Studies in Eighteenth-Century British Art and Aesthetics* [Berkeley: University of California Press, 1985], p. 131). Burke's *Enquiry* lapses from mechanical 'lucidity' at crucial moments: for example, when Burke attempts to reconcile Locke's developmental narrative to words whose sensational origins cannot always be recovered.

19 Burney, *Evelina*, p. 121.

20 Burney, *Evelina*, pp. 120, 122 (emphasis Burney's).

21 Burney, *Evelina*, p. 483.

22 Barbara Zonitch, *Familiar Violence: Gender and Social Upheaval in the Novels of Frances Burney* (Newark: University of Delaware Press, 1997), p. 37. Zonitch invokes 'the progressive Orville' (p. 37) as a model of 'the progressive tenet that honor rests in behavior rather than in one's birth' (p. 36). Yet Orville violates the core promise of a progressive articulation of masculine value: that manners can be acquired. See Michael McKeon's *The Origins of the English Novel* (Baltimore: Johns Hopkins University Press, 1987) for its seminal articulation of progressive ideology and for the argument that masculine honour can be recuperated through feminine virtue (most saliently, chastity).

23 Burney, *Cecilia*, p. 292.

24 Burney, *Evelina*, p. 116 (emphasis Burney's); Burney, *Cecilia*, pp. 33, 53, 31.

25 Burney, *Cecilia*, pp. 181, 6.

26 Burney, *Cecilia*, p. 22.

27 Burney, *Cecilia*, pp. 10, 103.

28 Burney, *Cecilia*, pp. 511, 679, 676, 677.

29 Burney, *Cecilia*, pp. 680, 681.

30 Burney, *Cecilia*, p. 5.

31 Daniel Defoe, *The Compleat English Gentleman*, ed. Karl D. Bülbring (London: David Nutt, 1890), pp. 16–17.

32 Defoe, *Compleat English Gentleman*, p. 18. See J. G. A. Pocock's *Virtue, Commerce, and History* (Cambridge: Cambridge University Press, 1985) for his exemplary discussion of how in an eighteenth-century commercial economy '[v]irtue was redefined [...] with the aid of the concept of "manners"': 'it was preeminently the function of commerce to refine the passions and polish the manners' (pp. 48–49). See also Pocock's discussion of the conflict between an 'agrarian' and 'patriot' ideal of

unspecialized personal autonomy (p. 109) and a commercial ideal 'which stresses exchange and civilisation of the passions' (p. 115).

33 The exhaustiveness with which *Evelina* proves the failed politeness of every man in Evelina's London defeats compression, but a crucial demonstration of Willoughby's inadequacy occurs in the doubled scenes when both he and Orville view Evelina in such compromising situations that she could be taken for an 'actress' (*Evelina*, p. 317). While Orville shows his unshakeable politeness by refusing to concede that Evelina might possibly be a prostitute, Willoughby is swayed by the evidence of his 'senses' to 'make my own interpretation' (*Evelina*, p. 319). Evelina later comments: '[Willoughby's] *changing with the tide*, has sunk him more in my opinion, than any other part of his conduct' (*Evelina*, p. 323). Emphasis Burney's.

34 Richard Allestree, *The Gentleman's Calling* (London: Printed for T. Garthwait, 1660), p. 98.

35 Elias, *Civilizing Process*, p. 109.

36 Elias, *Civilizing Process*, p. 93. Although Pocock does not mention Elias in his *Virtue, Commerce, and History*, Elias's elaboration, here via Mirabeau, of 'the ideal in whose name everywhere in Europe the middle classes were aligning themselves against the courtly-aristocratic upper class, and through which they legitimized themselves – the ideal of virtue' (p. 34) anticipates Pocock's characterization of the Whiggish implication of virtue, commercial intercourse, and manners.

37 Giovanni della Casa, *Galateo: or, A Treatise on Politeness and Delicacy of Manners* (London: Printed for J. Dodsley, 1774), p. xii. The translator notes of this text: 'Mr. Sterne seems to speak of it as a romance, and calls it Galatea; an evident proof that he had not read it at least, if he had ever seen it' (p. vii); Burney, *Cecilia*, p. 100.

38 Della Casa, *Galateo*, pp. 21–23.

39 Della Casa, *Galateo*, p. 24 (emphasis della Casa's).

40 Elias, *Civilizing Process*, p. 92.

41 Elias, *Civilizing Process*, p. 160.

42 Anthony Ashley Cooper, Third Earl of Shaftesbury, *Characteristics of Men, Manners, Opinions, Times*, ed. Lawrence E. Klein (Cambridge: Cambridge University Press, 1999), p. 58.

43 Allestree, *Gentleman's Calling*, p. a3v (italicization Allestree's).

44 Allestree, *Gentleman's Calling*, p. 133. Stephen Penton, *The Guardian's Instruction, or, The Gentleman's Romance* (London: Printed for Simon Miller, 1688), p. 13.

45 Jean Gailhard, *The Compleat Gentleman: Or, Directions for the Education of Youth as to their Breeding at Home and Traveling Abroad* (London: Printed for Thomas Newcomb, 1678), p. A4.

46 Elias, *Civilizing Process*, p. 373.

47 Elias, *Civilizing Process*, p. 127. Elias states: '[S]ocially undesirable impulses or inclinations become more radically suppressed. They become associated with embarrassment, fear, shame or guilt, even when one is alone.'

48 Elias, *The Civilizing Process*, pp. 95, 422.

49 Adam Smith, *The Theory of Moral Sentiments*, ed. D. D. Raphael and A. L. Macfie (Oxford: Clarendon Press, 1976), p. 226. Smith's sanguine assessment of the power of wealthy spectacle to regulate society more effectively than 'even the relief of the

miserable' (p. 226) was proven resoundingly wrong, of course, by the French Revolution.

50 Allestree, *Gentleman's Calling*, p. 155.

51 Samuel Richardson, *The History of Sir Charles Grandison*, ed. Jocelyn Harris (Oxford: Oxford University Press, 1986), Vol. 2, p. 307.

52 Richardson, *Grandison*, Vol. 2, pp. 251, 252–53.

53 Allestree, *Gentleman's Calling*, p. 141; Richardson, *Grandison*, Vol. 2, p. 261; Locke, *Some Thoughts*, p. 152.

54 Richardson, *Grandison*, Vol. 2, pp. 261, 265, 261, 261, 268, 271, 264.

55 G. J. Barker-Benfield, *The Culture of Sensibility: Sex and Society in Eighteenth-Century Britain* (Chicago: University of Chicago Press, 1992), p. 64.

56 Richardson, *Grandison*, Vol. 1, p. 4.

57 Allestree, *Gentleman's Calling*, p. 113.

58 Habermas, *Structural Transformation*, pp. 52, 41.

59 Nancy Armstrong, *Desire and Domestic Fiction: A Political History of the Novel* (Oxford: Oxford University Press, 1987), p. 77. Armstrong states: '[fiction] also had the virtue of dramatizing the same principles sketched out in the conduct books. Burney's *Evelina* is only one of the better-known examples of the fiction by lady novelists, as the women who wrote polite novels were called' (p. 97).

60 Cited in John E. Mason, *Gentlefolk in the Making: Studies in the History of Courtesy Literature and Related Topics from 1531 to 1774* (Philadelphia: University of Pennsylvania Press, 1935), p. 37 (italicized in original). Mason remarks that '[the] argument […] is the familiar one that nobility is dependent upon virtue'.

61 Cited in Mason, *Gentlefolk*, pp. 77–78.

62 Burney, *Cecilia*, p. 181.

63 Burney, *Cecilia*, p. 401.

64 Burney, *Cecilia*, pp. 411, 738, 12.

65 Burney, *Cecilia*, p. 248.

66 Burney, *Cecilia*, p. 753.

67 Burney, *Cecilia*, pp. 12, 214.

68 Locke, *Some Thoughts*, p. 8.

69 Burney, *Cecilia*, p. 215.

70 Samuel Richardson, *A Collection of the Moral and Instructive Sentiments… Contained in the Histories of* Pamela, Clarissa, *and* Sir Charles Grandison (London: Printed for Samuel Richardson, 1755), p. vi (emphasis Richardson's).

71 Doody, Introduction to *Cecilia*, p. xxv. In her *Frances Burney: The Life in the Works* (New Brunswick, NJ: Rutgers University Press, 1988), Doody comments upon 'the usefulness for the author of the third-person narrator' in *Cecilia* and assesses one instance of 'a quick touch of free indirect speech' (p. 124).

72 Burney, *Cecilia*, p. 152.

73 Burney, *Cecilia*, pp. 294, 477, 481, 511.

74 Burney, *Cecilia*, p. 525 (emphasis Burney's).

75 Mary Astell, *Political Writings*, ed. Patricia Springborg (Cambridge: Cambridge University Press, 1996), p. 43.

76 Burney, *Cecilia*, p. 5.

77 Burney, *Cecilia*, p. 597.

78 Burney, *Cecilia*, p. 602.
79 Burney, *Cecilia*, pp. 692, 742.
80 Burney, *Cecilia*, pp. 97, 466.
81 Burney, *Cecilia*, p. 499.
82 Armstrong, *Desire and Domestic Fiction*, pp. 28, 42.
83 Burney, *Evelina*, p. 511.
84 Burney, *Evelina*, p. 512.
85 Burney, *Cecilia*, p. 241.
86 Burney, *Cecilia*, p. 253.
87 Burney, *Cecilia*, pp. 554–55, 294, 643.
88 Burney, *Cecilia*, p. 468.
89 Burney, *Cecilia*, p. 803.
90 Burney, *Cecilia*, p. 37.
91 Burney, *Cecilia*, pp. 525, 319.
92 Burney, *Cecilia*, p. 447.
93 Burney, *Cecilia*, p. 362.
94 Burney, *Cecilia*, p. 442.
95 Elias, *Civilizing Process*, p. 90.
96 Jacques Derrida, *Of Grammatology*, trans. Gayatri Chakravorty Spivak (Baltimore: Johns Hopkins University Press, 1998), Translator's Preface, p. xiv. More could be said about the experience of reading the holograph of this novel, which places large portions of it *sous rature*, and indeed quite explicitly so (they remain legible to the moderately dedicated reader).
97 Burney, *Cecilia*, p. 803.
98 Burney, *Cecilia*, p. 803; Elias, *Civilizing Process*, pp. 109, 389.
99 Elias, *Civilizing Process*, p. 182.
100 Zonitch, *Familiar Violence*, p. 64.
101 See Roland Barthes, *Mythologies*, trans. Annette Lavers (New York: Hill and Wang, 1972), for Barthes's argument that realistic novelistic form participates in 'the process through which the bourgeoisie transforms the reality of the world into an image of the world, History into Nature' (p. 141). For further elaboration of this claim, see Barthes's *Writing Degree Zero* and *S/Z*. By conspicuously refusing to align her novels with the values of 'the bourgeoisie', Burney demands a divergent assessment of the political instrumentality of this genre's form. See my closing pages.
102 Deidre Shauna Lynch, *The Economy of Character: Novels, Market Culture, and the Business of Inner Meaning* (Chicago: University of Chicago Press, 1998), pp. 174, 199.
103 Lynch, *Economy of Character*, p. 201.
104 Burney, *Cecilia*, p. 64.
105 Lynch, *Economy of Character*, p. 200. Here Lynch is discussing Burney's final novel *The Wanderer; or, Female Difficulties* (1814). More broadly, however, Lynch is arguing for the antipathy of 'social determination' and interiority that would provide the coordinates for novel reading in 'a psychological culture' (p. 200).
106 Burney, *Cecilia*, p. 65.
107 D. A. Miller, *Jane Austen, or The Secret of Style* (Princeton: Princeton University Press, 2003), p. 59 (emphasis Miller's).

108 Immanuel Kant, *Critique of Judgment*, trans. Werner S. Pluhar (Indianapolis, IN: Hackett, 1987), pp. 174, 48.

109 Burney, *Cecilia*, p. 61.

110 Kant, *Critique of Judgment*, p. 69 (emphasis Kant's).

111 Burney, *Cecilia*, p. 35.

112 The core criterion of Kant's anti-sensual or anti-'barbaric' refinement of pleasure inheres in his vision of 'pure disinterested liking' (*Critique of Judgment*, p. 46). This criterion occasions Pierre Bourdieu's critique of 'distinction', a mutation of aristocratic value that transposes genetic and artefactual tokens of status into the practical register of aesthetic competence. In 'How the Wanderer Works: Reading Burney and Bourdieu', *ELH* 68 (Winter 2001), pp. 965–89 I argue that Burney theorizes the practice of distinction in her last novel, *The Wanderer; or, Female Difficulties* (1814).

CHAPTER FIVE

'All Agog to Find Her Out': Compulsory Narration in *The Wanderer*

SUZIE ASHA PARK

Mute Eloquence

Brainstorming ideas for *The Wanderer; or, Female Difficulties* (1814), Frances Burney envisions the plot turning on an impenetrable mystery: 'A carried on disguise, from virtuous motives, producing a mystery which the audience themselves cannot pierce. Exciting alternatively blame & pity'.[1] The novel tracks the difficulties of a young woman who appears on the scene disguised as a 'tattered dulcinea' – a French émigrée wearing the plainest clothes, her face swathed in bandages and patches, and her skin coloured black.[2] Yet the disguise is not 'carried on', but falls away so quickly, disappearing within the first few chapters, that it is really immaterial next to the truly unpierceable mystery of the novel: the wanderer's reticence, her stubborn refusal to tell her story. Recent critics have read women's reticence in Romantic novels as the sure sign of psychological depth.[3] In her breathtaking account of the 'economy of character' through the eighteenth and nineteenth centuries, Deidre Lynch identifies the Romantic-period heroine as prototypically reticent and plain, her deep psychology in effect produced by the narrative's free indirect discourse, or what is not directly spoken by the heroine herself: 'One might suppose that the premise that underwrites turn-of-the-century characterization is that declarative sentences do not suit a heroine: they say too much'.[4] Arguing that readers grew accustomed to recognizing such plainness and quietness as the signs of 'retiring, deep femininity', Lynch understands 'depth effects' to be the fruit of new cultural practices, specifically 'reorganiz[ing] Romantic-period reading as an experience in exercising personal preferences'.[5]

The Wanderer complicates this picture of Romantic novels providing expanded venues for exercising choice. In presenting a heroine pressed at every turn to quit or else to justify her 'unrelenting reserve' – 'never to consult, to commune, to speak, nor to hear' – Burney seems rather to bar readers from sharing in the inner life of the heroine than to invite them to exercise any privileged form of knowledge tied to new Romantic reading practices.[6] Rather than facilitate recognition of 'deep femininity', I argue, the wanderer's reserve instead questions and challenges the very pressure to disclose depths that an increasingly Romantic culture both exerts and manages to veil as a gentle invitation to express the self freely. Addressing the larger question of how Romantic novels' representations of psychological depth also carry within them the means for their own critique, this essay examines *The Wanderer* as a limit-case of how to interrogate the Romantic belief in freedom of expression. *The Wanderer* gives us a way to think about where and why the freedom to tell one's story seamlessly becomes the *obligation* to tell one's story. Asking what it means for Burney to stake the very survival of her heroine on her reticence, we can begin to see where the Romantic novel runs a course counter to the cultural fiction that a woman can divulge her story of her own free will – free, that is, from the intrusion of culture and a history of demands for deep narratives.

The novel opens with the wanderer's cry for admission onto a boat carrying a group of English travellers secretly leaving France during the Reign of Terror. Literally shrouded in 'darkness [that] impeded examination', the passengers immediately make demands for disclosure: 'I cannot for my life make out who she is, nor what she wants. Why won't you tell us, demoiselle? I should like to know your history'.[7] Yet such demands for clarification are accompanied by a richly ironic running commentary on the kinds of mysterious stories audiences conventionally expect. Elinor Joddrel, the Wollstonecraftian revolutionary mouthpiece of the novel, teases Albert Harleigh for admitting the wanderer on the basis of sentimental good will towards women in distress:

> 'I wonder what sort of a dulcinea you have brought amongst us! though, I really believe, you are such a complete knight-errant, that you would just as willingly find her a tawny Hottentot as a fair Circassian. She affords us, however, the vivifying food of conjecture, – the only nourishment of which I never sicken! – I am glad, therefore, that 'tis dark, for discovery is almost always disappointment.'[8]

Since Harleigh is a sentimental man of feeling, he would 'find' or determine the wanderer's inner beauties as readily as he would assign her racial identity.[9] In the same way, Elinor suggests, the wanderer's observers expect a story that produces and sustains a mystery fully spelled out by the conventions of mysterious storytelling. Underscoring a key preoccupation of the novel, Elinor points to the Romantic audience's insatiable appetite for inexhaustible character. Crucially, the wanderer's refusal to disclose her story allows observers to feed or 'nourish' their endless speculations on her history, identity, and inner thoughts. When the wanderer remains silent and seems to be praying, Elinor teases, 'She's a nun, then, depend upon it. Make her tell us the history of her convent', and later concludes that the right change in atmosphere would prompt everyone on board the boat to confess their life stories: 'We want nothing, now, but a white foaming billow, or a shrill whistle from Boreas, to bring us all to confession, and surprise out our histories'.[10]

The audience's demands for both disclosure *and* mystery imbricate a larger cultural pressure to seek out the hidden self. Even as other characters doggedly push for the wanderer's story, and withhold assistance because she will not communicate her history, they clearly presume from the outset to know her innermost motives. To Elinor's aunt, Mrs Maple, the wanderer's reticence signals a wholly 'suspicious character'; the wanderer must be a scheming adventuress, a 'black insect' and 'such a body' trying to pass for something more respectable.[11] To Harleigh, on the other hand, the wanderer's reticence means she is the very reservoir of virtue, unspeakable and true: 'The detail, I own, Elinor, is unaccountable and ill-looking: I can defend no single particular, even to myself; but yet the whole, the all-together, carries with it an indescribable, but irresistible vindication'.[12] Yet these two perspectives – one damning, the other eulogizing – end up doing the same thing. As the plainspoken Mr Riley quips, both Mrs Maple and Harleigh expect to 'find' nothing more than what they already suspect in their demands for the wanderer's story:

> 'Every one after his own fashion, Miss Nelly. The best amongst us has as little taste for being thwarted as the worst. He has, faith! We all think our own way the only one that has any common sense. Mine is that of a diver: I seek always for what is hidden. What is obvious soon surfeits me. If this demoiselle had named herself, I should never have thought of her again; but now, I'm all agog to find her out.'[13]

Connecting taste and acquisitiveness with seeking character depth (diving for 'what is hidden'), Riley suggests that the actual *telling* of the wanderer's story hardly matters. Her 'icy, relentless silence' keeps others' interest alive precisely because they can be 'all agog to find her out' at their pleasure.[14]

This opening commentary describes not only the forceful demands for story that the wanderer must continually thwart, but also the habits of the

Romantic-era reader who specifically expects to 'discover' the depths of character. What remains unexamined, however, and what the novel painstakingly questions, is precisely this forceful interest audiences bring to narrative. This essay re-examines how we have come to understand *The Wanderer*, along with contemporaneous novels sharing its concern with feminine reticence, as straightforward purveyors of the so-called Burney school of realism.[15] It questions our most recent critical assumptions about the course charted by novelists writing between 1760 and 1820, years that Joyce Hemlow has called 'the rise of the novel of manners [which] might [also] be called the age of courtesy books for women'.[16] Read as bristling commentary on the tradition of realism that Burney herself helped delineate (typically running a beeline from Burney to Edgeworth to Austen to Eliot), *The Wanderer* does not appear to celebrate the liberating effects of giving consciousness a narrative. In her essay for this volume, Helen Thompson challenges this very assumption when she looks at the striking plotline of Burney's second novel, *Cecilia, or Memoirs of an Heiress* (1782). For all of *Cecilia*'s celebration of the heroine's 'unprecedented freedom of choice' (in husband), Thompson argues, the novel relentlessly aligns this 'freedom' with her utter lack of choice in exercising her desires. Indeed, if Burney made thoughts speak, she did not make them speak of freedom.

Sharing Thompson's wariness in assigning redemptive powers to the Romantic novel's documentation of inner life, I argue that lyrical expressions within the Romantic novel often take the form of obligatory life stories – a cold-pressed lyricism browbeaten or freshly 'surprised out' of characters. I understand Burney's project to be different from that described by new historicist studies. In such accounts, depth becomes one of two things: either a kind of accidental by-product of women's struggles to write covertly against social pressures to be properly indebted to men, or a deliberate effect of formal technique. Nancy Armstrong, for instance, argues that women writers from Burney through the Victorian age produced 'extrasocial depths in the self' – or the effect of dark hidden desires – in their attempts to 'conceal the political power' they wielded in writing novels that dealt in seemingly safe, non-political, exclusively feminine topics of courtship.[17] For Catherine Gallagher, too, female authors like Burney needed to 'clear a linguistic space' by claiming to write about and as 'Nobody', a 'universal subjectivity' transcending the limitations of the marketplace.[18] Depth comes out of secret struggles for these critics, who propose that we understand presentations of elusiveness as being themselves socially produced – as Lynch says, by 'apprehending interiority as an effect of public and social discourses'.[19] Lynch explains that women writers deploy formal techniques such as free indirect discourse in order to produce the effect of psychological 'depth', the illusion of deep subjectivities that are elusive, hidden, and untouched by the social.[20] Women's narratives of this period deliberately produce the effect of depth – 'they had the forms for interiority' – in direct response to social developments in economic and class mobility that created a general crisis in legibility.[21] Reading about the hidden feelings of characters, their unrecognized difference from what the world saw, argues Lynch, allowed consumers a way of understanding and describing their own deep selves.

In contrast, I maintain that this approach to reading presentations of interiority as always already social only underscores the problem at the root of Burney's critique. Instead of naturalizing ready access to interiority, I argue, Burney undermines the very claim that interiority can be fully accounted for. Works like *The Wanderer* are not only much less accommodating to this model – what we might call a recovery-model of interiority – but in fact contest the formal constraints of counting certain subjectivities as transparently deep. The point of elusiveness and reticence in *The Wanderer*, in other words, is not to produce the illusion of depth but to reveal the illusory basis of authoritative forms imposed upon character. Rather than create the effect of depth for better management by readers, then, narrations of the 'inner' thoughts of characters provide the very means for criticizing the authoritative presumptiveness of 'public and social discourses' that claim to account for the interiority of subjects.

Burney poses an alternative to the recovery-model of interiority using what I call *compulsory narration*. Questioning the cultural correspondence between the exercise of free will and an account of free will, compulsory narration shows that the demand for disclosure elicits narratives that merely reinforce prior assumptions. An Admiral on board the boat sailing to England advises the wanderer not to keep secrets, as they will all come out anyhow: 'as everything is sure to come out, sooner or later, it only breeds suspicion and trouble for nothing, to procrastinate telling to-day with your own free will, what you may be certain will be known to-morrow, or next day, with or without it'.[22] Presenting a five-volume drama of 'procrastination' that greatly frustrates other characters as well as the novel's critics, Burney explores this division between direct expression, which presumably exercises a 'free will', and perverse silence, which 'breeds suspicion and trouble for nothing'.

Shuttling deftly between her critique of ideals of feminine modesty and

Romantic self-expression, Burney poses a seemingly radical opposition between the wanderer and Elinor in order to question the models of female expression they represent: quiet modesty and hidden virtue in the former, forthright speech and transparent relations between people in the latter. Specifically, Burney identifies the wanderer's enforced silence – her 'unbroken taciturnity' – with the vexed tradition of mute eloquence.[23] Playing a dual function in the novel, mute eloquence signals both Burney's animated participation in strait-laced convention and her keen rejection of its implicit silencing function. Mute eloquence does the work of making instantly legible the unspeakable emotions 'spoken' by silent eyes; it is shorthand for emotional states, denoting exquisite inexpressibility in the oeuvre of sentimental writing. The tearful parting of the wanderer (later identified as Juliet Granville) and her childhood friend from France, Gabriella, could have been plucked from a sentimental novel written a half-century earlier: 'A tear stole down the cheek of Gabriella as she heard this annunciation; but she offered no remonstrance; she permitted herself no enquiry; her eye alone said, "Why, why this!" Juliet saw, but shrunk [sic] from this mute eloquence'.[24] At the same time, Burney exploits the ambiguities of mute eloquence by making her most forthright proponent of direct expression, Elinor, shun and then embrace the expressive value of women's silence. Initially rejecting everything but the expression of all thoughts 'clearly and roundly', Elinor ends up occupying the reverse position of mute eloquence in her two suicide attempts; believing she could 'prove her sincerity by her own immediate destruction', Elinor shows that the ultimate direct expression she can make is an act of silencing.[25]

Even as the wanderer and Elinor seem to occupy opposing positions, they end up showing that both models of expression are compulsory and conventional. The sheer theatricality Elinor must exercise in order to achieve her ideal of transparent relations indicates that direct speech and silence are both performances of already scripted roles for women, not the exercise of freedom. As we shall see, the novel's energies are spent in showing that both models of female expression – silence and direct expression – actually are compelled versions of each other. Celeste Langan's theorization of negative liberty provides a useful formula for exploring this confusion between negative freedom (freedom from intrusion) and positive freedom (freedom to express oneself). Examining the figure of the vagrant in Romantic poetry, Langan defines negative liberty as a dialectic between 'surplus' and 'distress', produced at once to worry and correct anxieties about liberalism:

> Perfectly expressive of the negative liberty enshrined in liberalism as 'freedom
> from', the alienated condition of vagrancy is the *pathos* of this negative liberty:
> the 'freedom to come and go' becomes the obligation to mobility. Also,
> however, the reverse: freedom, that description of the condition of transcen-
> dental surplus, may be no more than a refracted image of an exigency.[26]

This model of individuality can conceive of freedom only as negative, as
'freedom from' demands and obligations: 'Let us take as the ethical ideal
of liberal democracy Benjamin Constant's imagination of freedom: the
right of individuals "to come and go without permission, and without
having to account for their motives or undertakings"'.[27] The 'transcen-
dental surplus' produced by this presumed freedom to act without account
actually encodes 'obligation to mobility', compelled movement that underwrites the very structure of Romantic freedom. The presumed negative
freedom of Burney's Romantic 'wanderer', that she is free *from* having to
give an account of her thoughts and motives, actually encodes an obligation to express herself, whether expression takes the form of self-narration
or mute eloquence. Observers expect the wanderer to disclose her inner
life to fill up preconceived notions of her interiority.

If Burney's novel does not move along in terms of plot development, it
is precisely because the novel is a long rehearsal of the wanderer's attempts
at thwarting demands for story. The wanderer's numerous ways of delivering the same response – that she cannot tell her story – can even be
captured by a single rhetorical formula: 'there is no medium, in a situation
such as mine, between unlimited confidence, or unbroken taciturnity'.[28]
Exemplary of the novel's compulsory narration, the wanderer's usual
response is to say that she lacks the means for full expression. Whether she
tells all or tells nothing, she cannot reveal anything that her audience does
not already expect to discover through the cultural convention of depth.
What looks like the rehearsal of empty speech, then, actually is a strategy
for conflating the radical distinction between reticence and direct speech
that the novel examines. Critiquing the cultural assumption that both
silence and forthright expression are techniques of depth-production,
Burney shows that both modes of 'free' expression equally involve
compulsion.

'A Very Woman' and her Critics

It seems ironic that *The Wanderer*, a novel about a maximally reticent heroine, should fail to satisfy critics' demands for depth. Surprisingly, Burney's contemporaries show the least patience precisely where today's critics see the greatest potential. According to Lynch, who sees the novel generously 'fuel[ling] the fantasy of an inner self that might operate independent of social exchange', the wanderer's reticence serves the purpose of making interiority legible for readers.[29] William Hazlitt, on the other hand, saw neither method nor matter behind what he considered Burney's 'very woman' failure to produce persuasive representations of a deep self. Indeed, the wanderer's painstaking refusal to tell her story inspired his derisive remarks on the novel's seemingly empty formalism:

> The whole is a question of form, whether that form is adhered to or infringed upon. [...] Because a vulgar country Miss would answer 'yes' to a proposal of marriage in the first page, Madame D'Arblay makes it a proof of an excess of refinement, and an indispensable point of etiquette in her young ladies, to postpone the answer to the end of five volumes, without the smallest reason for their doing so, and with every reason to the contrary. [...] Her ladies 'stand so upon the order of their going', that they do not go at all.[30]

In Hazlitt's portrait of the foolish coquette, Burney gives too much form in exchange for not enough content. The wanderer exercises nothing more than the perverse logic of deferring the expected 'yes' simply in order to prove that she had the power all along to confer the 'yes'. '*The Wanderer*'s central improbability', as Helen Thompson so aptly observes, 'lies in the deferral of the wanderer's "yes"'.[31] For Hazlitt, *The Wanderer* crystallizes the inadequacies of women in general. This revolution in focus – from Hazlitt's critique of Burney's failure to express interiority to today's celebratory, though guarded, observations of her deliberate production of an inner self – provides a framework for thinking about Burney's exploration of the period's conventions of depth. Yet this revolution in focus is just that. Hazlitt's Burney cannot help but stick irrationally to the form of things, never transcending form to express interiority, while the modern-day Burney cannot help but use form to produce depth. While these positions seem to occupy opposite ends of a spectrum of feminine agency, they end up returning us to the project of seeking depth that Burney resists. Rather than read a convincing picture of inner life as the ambition of Burney's novel, I read the pressure to produce such a picture as the object of her critique. Drawing on the terms of Hazlitt's critique and building

upon the more recent work of critics assessing models of feminine subjectivity in *The Wanderer*, I argue that Burney is less concerned with proposing
a successful mode of Romantic expression than she is interested in questioning any claim to objective authority in analyses of inner life.

As the final section of this essay will demonstrate, Burney's novel thoroughly questions claims to discovering the true psychology of subjects,
instead exposing the forceful machinery behind such claims. Kristina
Straub and other critics have identified Burney's agency in being able to
navigate a 'self-division' model of subjectivity, where the 'unresolved
doubleness' between Burney's roles as professional writer and proper
female manifests ways of managing her 'self-divided' state: the woman
writer meets and subverts expectations for feminine propriety using the
'strategy of feminine duplicity', or 'strategies for gaining "unfeminine"
control over self-identification while retaining the traditional power of
femininity'.[32] Yet rather than straddle this fence between feminine passivity
and unfeminine agency, Burney, I argue, strategically occupies the 'very
woman' position Hazlitt envisions for her. The fundamental problem
facing the wanderer stems from the same cultural assumption that Straub
celebrates: women presumably employ the ruse of feminine propriety to
carry out subversive measures to gain '"unfeminine" control'. The
wanderer's entire crisis in credibility has to do with always looking like she
seeks attention when she asks others to put the most 'favourable construction' on her appearances. Burney critiques the need to make this request
of others, when women are presumed to have agency precisely where they
do not. Her narrative stages the harsh probing of the wanderer's reticence,
showing that these 'investigations' of her mind embark from preconceived
ideas about her deepest motivations. Seeming to confirm what Luce
Irigaray has identified as 'a teleology already in operation somewhere',
these investigations paradoxically end up reducing excessive reticence into
predetermined insights.[33] Burney's point, in other words, has less to do
with imagining the wanderer's agency in silence than in showing that the
wanderer has none under the very rubric of Romantic expression that
Hazlitt and others, as we shall see, describe as an option for exercising
freedom.

In exploring the period's conventions of depth, then, Burney exposes
rather than satisfies demands. At the broadest level, Burney exposes these
demands through the wanderer's pattern of responses to pressures for her
story. The wanderer never grows tired of reminding others that her
survival depends on how 'charitably' they interpret her silence rather than

on how much she divulges about herself: 'My past history, Madam, it would be useless to hear – and impossible for me to relate: my present plan must depend upon a charitable construction of my unavoidable, indispensable silence'.[34] Under the strictest orders to keep silent about her past, the wanderer nevertheless sounds 'wilfully obstinate, and causelessly obscure'.[35] Through most of the novel, we only know that the wanderer peruses a letter instructing her never to 'break [her] silence': 'while all is secret, all may be safe; by a single surmise, all may be lost'.[36] Near the end, we finally learn how the wanderer's guardian in France, the Bishop, sends such directives to be silent. The Bishop exhorts her silence because she has fled from a compulsory marriage to an unnamed, ruthless Commissary of Robespierre; knowing that the Commissary threatens to kill the Bishop if the wanderer's hefty dowry cannot be extracted from her relative in England, the wanderer tries to remain unknown and unidentifiable in England until the Bishop can escape and vouch for her identity. Until this information is disclosed, however, the wanderer sounds the single point of her 'unavoidable, indispensable silence' so persistently that it is no wonder critics from Burney's time to our own have complained that the novel goes nowhere.

Specifically, Burney appears to indulge in rhetorical indecision throughout the novel. The charge is unmistakable in Hazlitt's assessment of the wanderer's characterization as 'a perpetual game at cross-purposes': the wanderer's conduct is 'not to be accounted for directly out of the circumstances in which she is placed, but out of some factitious and misplaced refinement on them'.[37] Describing this counterproductive discourse as a rampant cultural phenomenon of Burney's time, Hazlitt argues that women's popular fiction of the 1790s manifests symptoms of political instability, belonging to the tribe of 'frantic novels' that Wordsworth sickens at: 'It is not to be wondered at, if amidst the tumult of events crowded into this period, our literature has partaken of the disorder of the time; if our prose has run mad, and our poetry grown childish'.[38] This thoughtless mirroring of events, in turn, explains the popularity of Ann Radcliffe's 'mouldering castles' and Elizabeth Inchbald's *Nature and Art* (1796), which was popular only because 'it fell in (as to its two main characters) with the prevailing prejudice of the moment, that judges and bishops were not invariably pure abstractions of justice and piety'. Burney is the starting point of this apparently feminine tradition of falling in with prejudices; she is the debased progenitor of a slew of women writers whose narratives, Hazlitt insists, 'come to nothing'. He distinguishes her for being 'quite of the old school, a mere common observer of manners, and also a very woman'; standing for a paradoxically deficient surplus, 'a very woman', as we shall see, is richly endowed with too much of nothing.[39]

Hazlitt's global assumption that both the content and form of women's writings go nowhere invites us to ask what a 'very woman' means in the larger context of sentimentalism and feminism. For Hazlitt, feminine writing figures all that remains external and meaningless: background, situations, manners, form – everything, in short, that looks like a backdrop to plot rather than the psychology of characters.[40] All of this, he argues, fails to become substantial material for Romantic contemplation – 'the internal conception and contemplation of the possible workings of the human mind'.[41] He praises William Godwin's *Caleb Williams* (1794) for its representation of the exemplary Romantic figure, Falkland, a character compellingly 'thrown back into himself and his own thoughts'. Conversely, Hazlitt's main argument about women writers is that they simply cannot represent such character 'depth' – the capacity to be 'thrown back' into the self – because they themselves are all 'surface':

> The surface of [women's] minds, like that of their bodies, seems of a finer texture than ours; more soft, and susceptible of immediate impulses. They have less muscular strength; less power of continued voluntary attention – of reason, passion, and imagination: but they are more easily impressed with whatever appeals to their senses or habitual prejudices. The intuitive perception of their minds is less disturbed by any abstruse reasonings on causes or consequences. They learn the idiom of character and manners, as they acquire that of language, by rote, without troubling themselves about the principles.[42]

Hazlitt's assumptions about women, I argue, perform a crucial Romantic-era revision of, but not solution to, the lingering problem of sentimental transparency. Defining feminine experience as the mechanical expression of 'immediate impulses', Hazlitt conjures a picture stemming from earlier eighteenth-century stereotypes of woman as exquisitely emotional but psychologically vacuous.[43] Alexander Pope famously states, 'Most Women have no Characters at all', while Jonathan Swift describes feminine subjectivity as a self-cancelling process of hoarding and carelessly spending derivative language and actions: 'A set of Phrases learn't by Rote; / [...] While all she prates has nothing in it'.[44] Impulsively collecting and reciting others' words and thoughts, women apparently bypass the reflective process altogether by wasting opportunities to reflect on the 'principles' behind language and action. Wholly deficient in 'continued voluntary attention', a 'very woman' remains exclusively in the realm of acting without thought, mimesis without purpose.

As this tradition attests, a 'very woman' misses the 'principles' behind her prodigal spending of emotion precisely where her observers succeed in recognizing the shortcomings of her mind's 'intuitive perception[s]'. In terms of mimetic faithfulness, Burney seems both estranged and too familiar, entirely off the mark and altogether too absorbed to make a reliable statement about her own psychology. Indeed, when Hazlitt speaks of Burney as though she is cursed by her 'very woman' consciousness, she becomes two things: because she is an insider trapped by her own gendered consciousness of what counts as worth attending to, she is automatically an outsider to what counts as 'realistic' motivation for action. Whereas describing women's inner life as impulsive might suggest a degree of freedom, Hazlitt clearly makes spontaneity a liability for women; 'susceptible of immediate impulses' and 'more easily impressed', women seem to be led passively to a rehearsal of words, behaviour, and desires that are already expected by critics. Predicting the course of feminine 'impulsiveness', Hazlitt makes it a pathological condition of women rather than a possibility for free expression.

Refusing any indication of impulsiveness in her deferral of the heroine's 'yes' for five long volumes, Burney draws our critical attention to the pervasive cultural assumption that woman is not only too much herself, but is also perennially unaware of this condition. Masculine theories of the subject wholly rely on this feminine 'nothing' in order to explain, dialectically, how men, but not women, can be 'thrown back' into the life of the mind. Hazlitt's 'contemplative' Romantic male figure, after all, seems to look more intensely 'inward'-directed only after Hazlitt thoroughly denounces women writers' inevitable concentration on form and the external features of atmospheric setting, character types, and manners. By excluding women from that key Romantic privilege of self-understanding, making them totally unfamiliar with their own state of mind, the concept of the 'very woman' effectively endows women with a rich surplus of invisibility that can be interpreted and critiqued endlessly as a 'nothing you can see'.[45]

If Hazlitt sees evidence of women's biologically determined weaknesses in Burney's regressive habits of making her ladies 'not go at all', Claudia Johnson's much more contemporary perspective strangely hearkens back to Hazlitt's assessment when she detects the counterproductive energies of Burney's practice of 'taking back with one hand what she gives with the other'.[46] Johnson argues that the novel's punitive attitude towards women is symptomatic of Burney's inability to reward her female characters for bringing forth complaints directly. Burney seems unable to imagine a greater payoff for the female complaint than its affirmation of the very systems that hold women in check:

> Wherever race, class, gender, and political stripe are at stake, critique gets strangled in the plethora of the novel's counterexamples, and the novel's very immensity impedes rather than extends insight. [...] I detect neither a protodeconstructive strategy to expose how apparently opposing positions partake of the same logic nor even a simpler determination to complicate our political thinking, but rather a wish to protest the effects of social injustice while making sure that the social structures, customs, and attitudes that produced them remain intact.[47]

The notion that Burney's writing endlessly recuperates the disciplinary energies she seeks to challenge, whether strategically or unintentionally, is felt throughout the criticism on Burney.[48] Here, however, Burney participates unwittingly in a compulsory cancellation policy, where her writing 'impedes rather than extends insight'. While Straub's 'self-division' strategy leads to Burney's empowerment, Claudia Johnson's anti-strategy, in which Burney cannot help but ambush her own attempts at critiquing the 'effects of social injustice', leads to a wholesale negation of feminine agency: 'In The Wanderer, women indeed hold sway, but their rule is never manly, but rather, alas, all too feminine – that is, irrational, out of control, ineffectual'.[49] As Johnson's criticism makes clear, The Wanderer elicits a special kind of frustration from critics. They see in the novel's literalization of feminine powerlessness – a heroine who is unable to say or be who she really is – an overly drawn-out picture of how women cannot act or even think outside the sphere of what is expected of them.

Yet Burney structures the novel as a series of 'trifling pretexts' in an attempt to imagine how a subject might escape being 'pronounced upon only from outward semblance'.[50] In her supposed inability to think outside of prohibitions on what she can express or protest, Burney produces 'cross-purposes' that look at once entirely compliant with the 'social structures, customs, and attitudes' Johnson describes and thoroughly unaccountable to them. Yet what Johnson and Hazlitt vigorously discredit is precisely what they cannot forgive: Burney's 'inability' to credibly narrate the wanderer's, and, apparently, her own, motives looks too much like an evenhanded refusal to produce anything but 'cross-purposes'. The novel appears ungenerous in all of its excess, belying a certain pleasure and blindness in presenting what Johnson calls 'excess [that] carries no meaning'.[51] Burney seems blind to, yet perversely satisfied by, this 'perpetual game' at offering no legible or persuasive motivation for the wanderer's actions. Reading naïve hopelessness in Burney's attempt to defend the 'DIFFI-CULTIES OF WOMAN', this vein of criticism misses the main conflict of the novel. Indeed, in saying that the novel fails as social commentary because it does not imagine women acting outside the 'stranglehold of propriety', the criticism ends up exerting the very pressure to disclose legible motives that the novel works against.

Commissioning Inner Life

Turning now to a closer examination of the novel, I propose that its counter-intuitive movements serve a crucial critical purpose. Rather than simply index a 'very woman's' weaknesses, as some critics above suggest, the wanderer's 'relentless reserve' stages hidden depth itself in order to show that it is an enforced convention, not the end goal of writing about a heroine compelled to tell her story. Specifically, Burney resists commis-sioned interiors by representing the hidden self as the product of a rote performance. Neither able to tell her story nor persuasively exonerate her silence, the wanderer tests and blurs the line between spontaneous glances at genuine depth and premeditated displays of expected 'depth'. The novel militates the wanderer's 'commissioned' interiority against the long-standing discourse of feminine modesty and the emerging discourse of Romantic mystery. In an early instance of such commissioned perform-ances, the wanderer is forced to perform in a private production of John Vanbrugh's comedy, *The Provok'd Husband* (1728). Staying at Mrs Maple's house, and having nowhere else to go, the wanderer cannot refuse Elinor, Mrs Maple's niece, when she orders her to perform the lead role of Lady Townly:

> The stranger [wanderer] now saw no alternative between obsequiously submitting, or immediately relinquishing her asylum.
>
> How might she find another? she knew not where even to seek her friend, and no letter was arrived from abroad.
>
> There was no resource! She decided upon studying the part.
>
> This was not difficult: she had read it at three rehearsals, and had carefully copied it; but she acquired it mechanically because unwillingly, and while she got the words by rote, scarcely took their meaning into consideration.[52]

This rush of free indirect discourse and the scene of theatrical performance that follows broadly outline the wanderer's performative resistance
to 'public and abrupt inquiry'.[53] Here the wanderer looks like a faithful
picture of Hazlitt's 'very woman', acting strictly 'by rote' and missing the
meaning behind her mechanically acquired words when she 'scarcely
[takes] their meaning into consideration'. Yet she fully occupies the
conventional role imposed on her: 'When called down, at night, to the
grand final rehearsal, she gave equal surprise to Harleigh, from finding her
already perfect in so long a part, and from hearing her repeat it with a tame-
ness almost lifeless'.[54] In giving 'surprise' to Harleigh, the wanderer cannot
be anything other than always 'already perfect' in playing her role. While
her observers believe they witness her sparkling progress from studied role
to spontaneous displays of genuine depth, the wanderer merely plays her
scripted role.

The narrative drives this paradox home in the wanderer's mechanical
'expression' of feeling in her actual stage performance. At the same time
she expresses anxiety over her audience not knowing 'how little [her]
choice has been consulted', her audience reads radical progress in her
movement from being 'hardly audible' to delivering a wholly persuasive
performance of Lady Townly: 'her performance acquired a wholly new
character: it seemed the essence of gay intelligence, of well bred animation,
and of lively variety. [...] Every feature of her face spoke her discrimination of every word; while the spirit which gave a charm to the whole, was
chastened by a taste the most correct; and while though modest she was
never aukward; though frightened, never ungraceful'.[55] The utter comprehensiveness of her delivery is formally perfect, as 'every feature' speaks and
clarifies 'every word'; it delivers the perfectly legible 'essence' of deep qualities. Strikingly, though, it is the wanderer's performance, rather than the
wanderer herself, that 'acquire[s] a wholly new character'. Blurring this
distinction between her performance and identity, her audience can speculate simultaneously on the source of her learned 'excellence' in
performance and the source of her deep self:

> Whether this excellence were the result of practice and instruction, or a sudden
> emanation of general genius, accidentally directed to a particular point, was
> disputed by the critics amongst the audience; and disputed, as usual with a
> greater vehemence, from the impossibility of obtaining documents to decide,
> or direct opinion. But that which was regarded as the highest refinement of her
> acting, was a certain air of inquietude, which was discernible through the
> utmost gaiety of her exertions, and which, with the occasional absence and

sadness, that had their source in her own disturbance, was attributed to deep research into the latent subjects of uneasiness belonging to the situation of Lady Townly.[56]

The term 'deep research' puns on a conventional set of techniques for studying how to communicate the inner self in a wholly spontaneous way. It signifies both the extensive study of the physical signs others would recognize as masking an 'air of inquietude', as if the wanderer were a method actor studying what it would be like to experience Lady Townly's 'latent subjects of uneasiness', and the irrepressibility of authentic Romantic genius. Determining the cultural value of depth requires precisely this ongoing activity of disputation amongst the audience, which thrives upon the absence of 'documents to decide, or direct opinion'. Fully occupying what Helen Thompson calls the 'interiorizing premise that would make the wanderer's performance [reveal depth]', Burney carefully characterizes this language as an instance of her culture's growing doctrine of enforced interiors.[57] Like conceptions of Romantic genius, the inner self is a rhetorical convention supposed to be both ineffable and incontrovertible, buoyed up by nothing more than the rich lack of concrete evidence.

If the audience's fruitless debates on whether the wanderer's expressions on stage are wholly studied or wholly spontaneous ultimately expose the artificiality of such distinctions, it is Harleigh who tries to suture such differences. Harleigh represents the Romantic audience *par excellence*. Throughout the novel, he evinces an overwhelming desire to know or, rather, confirm what he already knows to be 'the whole, the all-together [about the wanderer that] carries with it an indescribable, but irresistible vindication'.[58] Harleigh's attempts to verbalize the wanderer's ineffable depths, however, always frame any response she could make in the language of romantic accident, spontaneity, and surprise discovery. For example, Harleigh's career in seeking the wanderer's hidden self really begins when he accidentally discovers the wanderer sketching landscapes in the closet.

> Harleigh, who had not seen the stranger turned into the closet, now entered it, in search of a pencil. Not a little was then his surprize to find her sketching, upon the back of a letter, a view of the hills, downs, cottages, and cattle, which formed the prospect from the window.
>
> It was beautifully executed, and undoubtedly from nature. Harleigh, with mingled astonishment and admiration, clasped his hands, and energetically exclaimed, 'Accomplished creature! who....and what are you?'[59]

Metaphorically wandering into the wanderer's mind, Harleigh seems to uncover the transparency of her hidden feelings merely by stumbling upon a set piece of framed detection. The window serves to frame not only the conventions of picturesque landscape that the wanderer sees, but also Harleigh's view of her looking at the landscape.[60] Alighting upon this Romantic 'closet' drama, he becomes the primary actor in the scene, theatrically exclaiming his disbelief and pleasure at the wanderer's silent demonstration of natural talent. Her sketch, resourcefully executed on the exterior of a letter, transparently demonstrates her nature within; for Harleigh, 'it', that is, her inner mind inscribed on the outer letter, can only be 'undoubtedly from nature' because she seems to sketch only for herself. Burney deploys this set of conventions on a miniature, concentrated scale, moving from Harleigh's recognition of all the right attractions – the wanderer's drawing is skilful, faithful to nature in a picturesque manner, and performed in private – to his punctuating question about her identity: 'who....and what are you?'.

Striking a perfect blend of sentimental masochism and jouissance, Harleigh's questioning underscores the forceful nature of Romantic lines of inquiry.[61] Yet his search for spontaneity is certainly a throwback to the heyday of masculine questing after sentimental pleasures, from Laurence Sterne's Yorick in *A Sentimental Journey* (1768) to Henry Mackenzie's Harley in *The Man of Feeling* (1771). Harleigh's determination to know the wanderer's undoubtedly mired past resembles Yorick's fascination with mad Maria, the 'disorder'd maid' Yorick seeks out after reading about her plight: ''Tis going, I own, like the Knight of the Woeful Countenance, in quest of melancholy adventures – but I know not how it is, but I am never so perfectly conscious of the existence of a soul within me, as when I am entangled in them'.[62] Yet the main difference between *this* Harleigh, refitted for a Romantic culture, and his sentimental predecessors is that he can endlessly spin out the wanderer's Romantic mystery only by actively denying any role in producing it. When Elinor wants to question the wanderer in order to 'fathom her', Harleigh instructs Elinor to view the wanderer just as she requests to be viewed: 'Pardon me, Elinor, that I have stopt any further enquiries. It is not from a romantic admiration of mystery, but merely from an opinion that, as her wish of concealment is open and confessed, we ought not, through the medium of serving her, to entangle her into the snares of curiosity'.[63] Thus a standing irony of the novel is that Harleigh chastens others into renouncing 'romantic' habits, only to become the most earnest inquisitor as he presses harder than anyone else to find out the wanderer's romantic history.

Unlike the wanderer's female patrons who overtly withhold financial assistance from the wanderer simply because she will not divulge her story, Harleigh gives his money and advice freely, but more and more expects in return that the wanderer confide in him. As she herself accuses, showing confidence in Harleigh would mean her implicit reciprocation of his desire for her: 'You probe me, Sir, too painfully! – I appear, to you, I see, wilfully obstinate, and causelessly obscure: yet to be justified to you, I must incur a harsher censure from myself!'[64] While she insists that she has been 'utterly misunderstood', Harleigh need only infer her positive rejoinder from her mass of negative exclamations. At the height of exerting such pressures on the wanderer, Harleigh demands just 'One word, – one little word' from her to confirm or dispel his suspicion that she has given her heart to another:

> 'Confide to me your name – your situation – the motives to your concealment – the causes that can induce such mystery of appearance, in one whose mind is so evidently the seat of the clearest purity: – the reasons of such disguise – '.
>
> 'Disguise, I acknowledge, Sir, you may charge me with; but not deceit! I give no false colouring. I am only not open.'
>
> 'That, that is what first struck me as a mark of a distinguished character! That noble superiority to all petty artifices, even for your immediate safety; that undoubting innocence, that framed no precautions against evil constructions; that innate dignity, which supported without a murmur such difficulties, such trials.'[65]

Harleigh attributes a wealth of positive content – 'that noble superiority', 'that undoubting innocence', 'that innate dignity' – to the wanderer's wholly negative construction of her expressions.[66] Saying that she is 'only not open', the wanderer triggers Harleigh's deluge of happy 'discovery'. The distinction she tries to communicate to Harleigh – that she practises compelled 'disguise', not intentional 'deceit' – is engulfed instantly by his preconceived method of accounting for her behaviour. And when the wanderer (here called 'Ellis') complains that he is missing the point of her real inability to explain her need to be silent, he exhorts exactly this:

> 'Mr. Harleigh,' interrupted Ellis, with strong emotion, 'there is no medium, in a situation such as mine, between unlimited confidence, or unbroken taciturnity: my confidence I cannot give you; it is out of my power – ask me, then, nothing!'[...]
>
> 'Speak, I implore you, speak! – Is that heart, which I paint to myself the seat

of every virtue..... is it already gone? – given, dedicated to another?'

He now trembled himself, and durst not resist her effort to open the door, as she replied, 'I have no heart! – I must have none!'[67]

From the first, then, whatever action she could take is a foretold demonstration of Harleigh's taste in contemplating the beauty of the wanderer's unknowability. 'Who, who art thou?' is really a question that needs no answer: the wanderer, without divulging the smallest hint of information about herself, abundantly meets his request for disclosure. Harleigh reiterates the object of his demands: 'one word, one word', 'who, who', 'that, that is what first struck me'. His use of repetition, in fact, infuses the narrative with a sense of redoubled meaning, where his demands echo their own force and require nothing more than a confirmation of his expected picture of 'distinguished character' and 'undoubting innocence'. It seems fitting, then, that his request to hear just 'one word' should actually require nothing less than the wanderer's complete self-disclosure: 'your name – your situation – the motives to your concealment – the causes that can induce such mystery of appearance'. The totalizing nature of his little request effectively crowds out any place for her reply to be seriously heeded – 'I am only not open' – and reinforces the 'mystery' of the wanderer that is not one. Harleigh repeatedly practises this act of simultaneously covering over the wanderer's clear message that she cannot disclose anything about herself and 'discovering' her hidden depths in each of her refusals to speak.

Standing in seeming opposition to Harleigh's passive-aggressive renunciation of a 'romantic admiration of mystery' is Elinor's imperious demand for absolutely transparent relations between people. Elinor rejects her fiancé, Dennis (Harleigh's brother), because she loves Albert Harleigh instead. She constantly trumpets her desire to fly in the face of custom, especially codes of feminine propriety, since her awakening to women's oppression in revolutionary France. When arguing with Harleigh on the merits of revolutionary thinking, for example, Elinor rejoices that her two-year-long residence in France 'opened [her] eyes on that side of the channel' and made her free to 'dar[e] think for [herself]'.[68] In rooting out mystery, Elinor specifically focuses on exposing Harleigh's engineering of the wanderer's mystery. For while Harleigh refuses to acknowledge his own activity of romantic seeking, Elinor continually points to the false distinctions he tries to maintain between artfulness and genuine depth. She accuses him of viewing the wanderer through the very lens of romantic mystery that he claims to denounce: 'Oh, Harleigh! how is it you thus can love all you were wont to scorn? double dealing, false appearances, and lurking disguise! without a family she dare claim, without a story she dare tell, without a name she dare avow!'[69]

Trying to make her thoughts transparent to others, Elinor seems to espouse transparent relations between herself and Harleigh, to whom she declares her love: 'I come to explain to you the principles by which I am actuated, clearly and roundly; without false modesty, insipid affectation, or artful ambiguity'.[70] Even as Elinor clamours for transparent relations between people, however, she paradoxically demands mediation by producing layers of theatrical intervention between her message and Harleigh.[71] She 'commissions' the wanderer to tell Harleigh of Elinor's passionate attachment to him: 'My design, as you will find, in making you speak instead of myself, is a stroke of Machievalian [sic] policy; for it will finish both suspences [sic] at once; since if, when you talk to him of me, he thinks only of my agent [the wanderer], how will he refrain, in answering your embassy, to betray himself?'[72] Using the wanderer in this way as a go-between, Elinor compels the wanderer to speak *for* her. Like a stage director, Elinor directs a 'play' of disclosures to make supposedly transparent relations legible: 'My operations are to commence thus: Act I. Scene I. Enter Ellis, seeking Albert. Don't stare so; I know perfectly well what I am about. Scene II. Albert and Ellis meet. Ellis informs him that she must hold a confabulation with him the next day; and desires that he will remain at Lewes to be at hand'.[73]

By showing that Elinor's Jacobin, rationalist ideals of forthright speech and transparency are themselves theatrical performances, Burney makes visible the rhetorical machinery behind any demand for disclosures of an 'ineffable' inner life. When Elinor charges the wanderer with performing false reserve, the wanderer resorts to a strictly pro forma defence of feminine modesty: 'when a young female, not forced by peculiar circumstances, or impelled by resistless genius, exhibits herself a willing candidate for public applause; – she must have, I own, other notions, or other nerves, than mine!'[74] Because feminine modesty is diametrically opposed to theatricality, the wanderer suggests, the theatrical impulse must stem from 'other notions, or other nerves'. Elinor's quest for a 'new doctrine' of feminism as a practice of display – to 'avow to the whole world, that I dare speak and act, as well as think and feel for myself!' – provides this 'other' theatrical impulse. In this seemingly radical opposition between the wanderer and Elinor, Elinor is firmly aligned with masculine self-display and the wanderer with feminine modesty and hidden virtue.[75] The novel clearly subordinates Elinor's revolutionary 'system'-seeking to the virtues of the wanderer's doctrine of never deliberately putting herself in the public eye.[76] At the same time it presents this caricatured difference, however, the novel thoroughly questions the apparent division between feminine modesty and theatricality, ultimately making modesty a compelled version of theatricality. This radical distinction borders on collapse as Elinor's claims to being roundly misunderstood and dismissed in her 'system'-seeking sound more and more like the wanderer's claims to looking 'causelessly obscure' in her silence.

Elinor's fanaticism in seeking inner motives – 'I shall now know the truth! [...] Is he glad of a pretence to stay on my account? Or impelled irre-sistibly upon yours? I shall now know all, all, all!' – is taken to a comic pitch when she pushes the reluctant wanderer to read Harleigh's countenance for signs of loving either the wanderer or Elinor: 'Take this [letter of decla-ration] to him immediately; and, while he reads it, mark every change of his countenance, so as to be able to deduce, and clearly to understand, the sensations which pass in his mind'.[77] What ensues between the wanderer and Harleigh is a highly sentimental exchange of inferences and omissions. Burney uses the conventional language of romantic depth-seeking to stage this parodic 'courtship', where the wanderer is commissioned to 'court' Harleigh for his transparent thoughts ('the sensations which pass in his mind'). Because the wanderer is too modest to spell out the content of Elinor's commission, Harleigh must fill in the blanks: 'Her embarrassment now announced something extraordinary; but it was avowedly not personal, and Harleigh eagerly besought her to be expeditious. "You must make me so, then," cried she, "by divining what I have to reveal!"'[78] By playing the form of conventional expectations for feminine modesty, the wanderer excuses herself from directly having to clarify her feelings about Harleigh.

This tortuous series of exchanges between Harleigh and the wanderer culminates in her absolute refusal of his Romantic seeking and speculation: 'I beg you, Sir, to consider all that was drawn from you this morning, or all that might be inferred, as perfectly null – unpronounced and unthought'.[79] And later: 'you must not any where seek me; – I must avoid you every where!' Harleigh urges the wanderer to explain her rejection of his atten-tions: '"Was it extorted?" cried he, detaining her, "or had it your heart's approbation?"' She responds that, given his pressure to find her out, in spite of her requests for privacy, there is no difference between her compulsion and consent: '"From whatever motives it was uttered", answered she, looking away from him, "it has been pronounced, and must be adhered to religiously!"[80] The most salient features of the wanderer's pattern of response to demands are present here. The only self-assertion she can make is an act of negation: 'unpronounced', 'unthought', 'null', a 'void'. Yet by nullifying and even 'unthinking' Harleigh's thoughts for him – 'avoiding' and voiding his presumptions – the wanderer produces a striking reversal of her earlier request that he fill in and 'divine' everything she could not say. Using these terms of transparent sentimental exchange, she empties out the meaning of his inferences, showing that he presumes to know any 'vindication' or statement she could possibly make about herself before she speaks, or even if she never speaks.

If self-assertion for the wanderer takes the form of rhetorical negation, self-expression amounts to literal self-negation in the case of Elinor. After concluding that Harleigh's desire is directed towards the wanderer, Elinor stages the final act of her 'play' by attempting to render herself null and void by committing suicide before both of them. Following her rule of making all motives legible and transparent, Elinor tries to 'prove her sincerity by her own immediate destruction'.[81] Thus she imagines her self-destruction as the strongest, sincerest expression of self. Attributing such an extreme expressive value to her silence, Elinor moves from being a caricature of direct expression to a caricature of mute eloquence. She begins by demanding transparency and direct expression from others, slides into theatrical indirection in order to achieve transparency, and finally tries to express her innermost feelings by silencing herself. Early on, Elinor sums up what will be her attitude towards the wanderer throughout the novel: 'Now that she is so ready to tell her story […] I am confident that there is none to tell. While she was enveloped in the mystical […] I was dying with curiosity to make some discovery'.[82] The most striking feature of Elinor's doggedness in self-display is, in fact, this ability to frame her positive desires only in relation to the absence of the wanderer's. Elinor's theatrical moves between these models of female expression – between direct expression and mute eloquence – show that the two are versions of one another: direct speech and silence are compulsory, scripted performances.

Elinor's rhetorical strategy of pointing to the wanderer's empty silence as a resource for 'discovering' full Romantic depths has an interesting analogue in a physical object. Elinor totes around and lavishes attention on a 'shagreen case' holding the knife that she will use to attempt suicide. Sounding like a materialization of Elinor's 'chagrined' case against the wanderer, this 'shagreen case' reappears several times throughout the rounds of questioning and evasion that take place due to Elinor's commissioning of the wanderer to tell Harleigh Elinor's desires for him. Each time, the wanderer grows closer to correcting her assessment of its contents: '[Elinor] took from her bureau the shagreen case which she had so fondly caressed, and which Ellis [the wanderer's temporary name] concluded to contain some portrait, or cherished keep-sake of Harleigh'.[83] The wanderer's initial mistake here is important, for it shows that the case could hold interchangeable objects: a 'cherished' picture of Harleigh that preserves sentimental attachment, or, a 'poniard' meant to cut Elinor's attachments to life. Equally important is the 'painfully [...] encreasing embarrassment' that haunts their interactions centring on the discovered contents of the case.[84] Whether the case contains signs of continuity with or a break away from sentimental tradition, it represents a larger embarrassment over the cultural pressures in seeking for depth that so often pass for invitations to self-expression.[85]

In the end, Elinor is left with 'one regret alone': 'this was, having suffered her dagger to be seen and seized. She feared being suspected of a mere puerile effort, to frighten from Harleigh an offer of his hand, in menacing what she had not courage, nor, perhaps, even intention to perform'.[86] Separating her views from those of what she calls 'the tribe of sentimental pedants, who think it a disgrace to grow wiser; or who suppose that they must abide by their first opinions', Elinor points to the manufactured quality of any 'ineffable something', any preconceived idea of inner life, coming into view.[87] In staging her suicide attempts (there are two of them), Elinor mocks the very conventions of romantic disclosure that she puts to use: 'The rest of my plot is not yet quite ripe for disclosure. But all is arranged'.[88] In presenting this triumvirate of characters who demand and resist disclosure precisely where they utilize its most culturally legible forms, Burney ponders the problem of how to show and critique pressures to display depth in a recognizable form, how to show that 'women's difficulties' are *both* entirely persuasive and real, and entirely conventional and shop-worn.

Notes

In researching and writing this article, I am indebted to the Huntington Library and to the Mellon Foundation for a fellowship to participate in its Interpretive Seminar in the Humanities, 'The 1790s: British Culture in a Revolutionary Decade'. I thank the directors Kevin Gilmartin and Saree Makdisi, all of the participants of that Seminar, and Julie Carlson, Jon Mee, and Jonathan Grossman for their conversation and suggestions. I especially thank Charlotte Sussman, Jill Heydt-Stevenson, Steve Goldsmith, Anne-Lise François and C.C. Wharram for their unflagging support. A brief version of this essay appears as 'Resisting Demands for Depth in *The Wanderer*', *European Romantic Review* 15.2 (2004 June), pp. 307–15.

1   Margaret Anne Doody, *Frances Burney: The Life in the Works* (New Brunswick, NJ: Rutgers University Press, 1988), p. 25. Doody identifies this fragment from Burney's notes on her third novel, *Camilla*, as Burney's initial thoughts on what would eventually become *The Wanderer*.

2   Frances Burney, *The Wanderer; or, Female Difficulties* (1814), ed. Margaret Anne Doody, Robert Mack, and Peter Sabor (Oxford: Oxford University Press, 1991), p. 13. For an incisive reading of the wanderer's performance of aristocratic essence through the redundant revelation of her whiteness, see Helen Thompson, 'How the Wanderer Works: Reading Burney and Bourdieu', *ELH* 68 (2001), pp. 965–89.

3   In thinking about psychological depth as just one choice among many in Romantic-era representations of subjectivity, I am indebted to Andrea Henderson, *Romantic Identities: Varieties of Subjectivity, 1774–1830* (Cambridge: Cambridge University Press, 1996).

4   Deidre Lynch, *The Economy of Character: Novels, Market Culture, and the Business of Inner Meaning* (Chicago: University of Chicago Press, 1998), p. 154.

5   Lynch, *The Economy of Character*, pp. 155, 151. For historical overviews of women as consumers of popular sentimental novels, see also: Nancy Armstrong, *Desire and Domestic Fiction: A Political History of the Novel* (New York: Oxford University Press, 1987); G. J. Barker-Benfield, *The Culture of Sensibility: Sex and Society in Eighteenth-Century Britain* (Chicago: University of Chicago Press, 1992); and Catherine Gallagher, *Nobody's Story: The Vanishing Acts of Women Writers in the Marketplace, 1670–1920* (Berkeley: University of California Press, 1994).

6   Burney, *The Wanderer*, pp. 341, 861.

7   Burney, *The Wanderer*, p. 16.

8   Burney, *The Wanderer*, pp. 12–13.

9   Noting Harleigh's sentimental lineage in her excellent introduction to *The Wanderer*, Margaret Anne Doody writes, 'This hero of *The Man of Feeling* (1771) is nothing but sentiment and delicacy, a censor of the coarse world who applies to it standards of delicacy and sensibility that the world usually lacks'. Margaret Anne Doody, 'Introduction', in Burney, *The Wanderer*, p. xxvi.

10 Burney, *The Wanderer*, pp. 13, 15.

11 Burney, *The Wanderer*, p. 16.

12 Burney, *The Wanderer*, p. 30.

13 Burney, *The Wanderer*, p. 29.

14 Burney, *The Wanderer*, p. 861.

15 Burney is generally understood to be at the forefront of a group of women writers who could constitute a 'school of realism' by their attention to similar post-*Clarissa* concerns: finding husbands and navigating worlds of consumer spending and threats to chastity. These writers denounce theatrical publicity and write almost claustrophobically of 'self-enclosure', as Nancy Armstrong puts it: 'For Austen

obviously wrote to an audience who willingly granted fiction the status of a special-
ized kind of truth. The key to such authority was self-enclosure. Like Burney and
the other lady novelists, Austen appeared more than willing to leave the rest of the
world alone and deal only with matters of courtship and marriage. While
Richardson introduced conduct-book materials into the novel as a strategy of
conversion, then, novels of manners settled on various strategies of containment'.
Armstrong, *Desire and Domestic Fiction*, p. 135.

16 Joyce Hemlow, 'Fanny Burney and the Courtesy Books', *PMLA* 65.5 (September
1950), pp. 732–61 [p. 732].

17 Reversing previous understandings of novels by women – thought to represent
women and their domestic roles as merely privative – Nancy Armstrong concludes
that social convention did less to suppress sexuality than the representations of
such suppression in novels of manners from Burney through the Victorian age.
Armstrong, *Desire and Domestic Fiction*, p. 165.

18 Gallagher, *Nobody's Story*, pp. 204, 233.

19 Lynch, *The Economy of Character*, p. 168. See in particular 'Inside Stories', Part II of
Lynch's book, where Burney is a forerunner of Romantic depth-seeking:
'[Burney's] novels, with those of the "Burney school" generally, prepared the
ground for the novel reader's persisting preoccupation with recovering inside,
untold stories. They anchor a tradition that has valued psychological fiction for its
enshrinement of a real self misrepresented by its appearances in the social realm
and objectified by society's commercial arrangements. In a psychological culture,
this privatized notion of the self is the telos of novel writing and reading' (p. 205).

20 In her essay in this volume, Helen Thompson identifies a thoroughly socialized
interiority – 'Cecilia's inner self is indelibly social' – directly challenging the assumption that delineating rich psychology is the goal of Burney's writing. More generally,
Thompson interrogates the 'humanizing agency of books' that, since Richardson's
Pamela (1740), is assumed to teach readers domestic literature's ability to 'transmute
power into uncoerced sentiment'.

21 Lynch, *The Economy of Character*, pp. 151–52.

22 Burney, *The Wanderer*, p. 36.

23 Burney, *The Wanderer*, p. 341.

24 Burney, *The Wanderer*, p. 654.

25 Burney, *The Wanderer*, pp. 173, 186.

26 Celeste Langan, *Romantic Vagrancy: Wordsworth and the Simulation of Freedom*
(Cambridge: Cambridge University Press, 1995), p. 19.

27 Langan, *Romantic Vagrancy*, p. 15.

28 Burney, *The Wanderer*, p. 341.

29 Lynch, *The Economy of Character*, p. 201.

30 William Hazlitt, *Lectures on the English Comic Writers* (1819), in *The Collected Works of
William Hazlitt*, ed. A. R. Waller and Arnold Glover (London: J. M. Dent, 1903),
pp. 124–25.

31 Thompson, 'How the Wanderer Works', p. 966.

32 Kristina Straub, *Divided Fictions: Fanny Burney and Feminine Strategy* (Lexington:
University Press of Kentucky, 1987), pp. 6–7.

33 Luce Irigaray, 'Any Theory of the "Subject" Has Always Been Appropriated by the

"Masculine'", in *Speculum of the Other Woman*, trans. Gillian Gill (Ithaca: Cornell University Press, 1985), p. 139. For Irigaray, theories of the 'subject' – including but not limited to psychoanalytic theories – invariably set up interpretive stumbling blocks for delving into women's subconsciousness merely in order to confirm 'the discourse of the same, through comprehension and extension'. These theories continually pare down excesses in order to prove that a woman cannot recognize the inner workings of her mind; thus the validity of such insight rests entirely on the guarantee of women's self-ignorance.

34 Burney, *The Wanderer*, p. 216.

35 Burney, *The Wanderer*, p. 348.

36 Burney, *The Wanderer*, p. 220.

37 Hazlitt, *Lectures*, p. 125.

38 Hazlitt, *Lectures*, p. 123. 'Lecture VI', as Hazlitt explicitly states, is an attempt to 'sett[le] the standard of excellence, both as to degree and kind' in English novel-writing of the eighteenth and early nineteenth centuries (p. 108). In standardizing excellence, Hazlitt tries to do for novels what Wordsworth purports to do for poetry in Preface to *Lyrical Ballads* (1802): 'For the human mind is capable of being excited without the application of gross and violent stimulants [...]. For a multitude of causes, unknown to former times, are now acting with a combined force to blunt the discriminating powers of the mind, and unfitting it for all voluntary exertion to reduce it to a state of almost savage torpor'; in *William Wordsworth*, ed. Stephen Gill (Oxford: Oxford University Press, 1990), p. 599.

39 Hazlitt, *Lectures*, p. 123. For a recent overview of the crisis in political controls induced by this burgeoning of Romantic novels, see Amanda Gilroy and Wil Verhoeven, eds., 'The Romantic-Era Novel', a special issue of *Novel: A Forum on Fiction* 34.2 (2001), pp. 147–62.

40 Hazlitt, *Lectures*, pp. 126–27. Although Radcliffe's story 'comes to nothing', Hazlitt muses, her 'dramatic power' depends wholly in working up chilling 'situations' and 'back-ground' that make the reader believe there is something ('mysterious agency') behind the *form* of what turns out to be nothing.

41 Hazlitt, *Lectures*, p. 130.

42 Hazlitt, *Lectures*, pp. 123–24. Hazlitt inserts this gloss on 'women, in general', his metaphorical link between women's anatomy and psychology, in the middle of his critical analysis of Burney's penchant for creating stock characters and phrases 'by rote': 'Her heroes and heroines, almost all of them, depend on the stock of a single phrase or sentiment, and have certain mottoes or devices by which they may always be known'.

43 In her famous remonstrance against these stereotypes, Mary Wollstonecraft critiques the 'system of dissimulation' imposed on women, who are encouraged to cultivate 'the shew instead of the substance' and so become like sentimental 'reed[s] over which every passing breeze has power'. Mary Wollstonecraft, *A Vindication of the Rights of Men; A Vindication of the Rights of Woman*, ed. D. L. Macdonald and Kathleen Scherf (Peterborough, Ontario: Broadview Press, 1997), pp. 223, 270, 138.

44 Alexander Pope, 'Epistle to a Lady: Of the Characters of Women' (1735), in Roger Lonsdale (ed.), *The New Oxford Book of Eighteenth-Century Verse* (Oxford: Oxford University Press, 1992), pp. 248–54. Jonathan Swift, 'The Furniture of a Woman's

Mind' (1727), in *The Writings of Jonathan Swift*, ed. Robert Greenberg and William Piper (New York: Norton, 1973), pp. 529–31.

45 Luce Irigaray, 'The Blind Spot of an Old Dream of Symmetry', in *Speculum of the Other Woman*, pp. 46–47. Following the logic of Freud's theory of castration anxiety, Irigaray describes what women (or 'woman') could logically possess: 'She exposes, exhibits the possibility of *a nothing to see*. [...] Woman's castration is defined as her having nothing you can see, as her *having* nothing. In her having nothing penile, in seeing that she has No Thing. Nothing *like* man. That is to say, *no sex/organ* that can be seen in a *form* capable of founding its reality, reproducing its truth'.

46 Claudia Johnson, *Equivocal Beings: Politics, Gender, and Sentimentality in the 1790s: Wollstonecraft, Radcliffe, Burney, Austen* (Chicago: University of Chicago Press, 1995), p. 169. Johnson argues that Burney is unwittingly complicit with the impossible demands of sentimentality placed on women: 'Rather than stretching our notions of what a woman can do without sacrifice to propriety, she tightens the stranglehold of propriety itself'.

47 Johnson, *Equivocal Beings*, p. 170.

48 For various considerations of Burney's ambivalent negotiation of feminine propriety and strategies of resistance, see Julia Epstein, *The Iron Pen: Frances Burney and the Politics of Women's Writing* (Madison: University of Wisconsin Press, 1989); Juliet McMaster, 'The Silent Angel: Impediments to Female Expression in Frances Burney's Novels', *Studies in the Novel* 21.3 (1989), pp. 235–52; and Katherine Rogers, *Frances Burney: The World of 'Female Difficulties'* (New York: Harvester Wheatsheaf, 1990).

49 Johnson, *Equivocal Beings*, p. 175.

50 Burney, *The Wanderer*, p. 344.

51 Johnson, *Equivocal Beings*, p. 173.

52 Burney, *The Wanderer*, p. 87.

53 Burney, *The Wanderer*, p. 87.

54 Burney, *The Wanderer*, p. 90.

55 Burney, *The Wanderer*, p. 94.

56 Burney, *The Wanderer*, p. 95.

57 Thompson, 'How the Wanderer Works', pp. 969, 971. Reading the novel through the lens of Bourdieu's concept of *habitus* as the 'ceaselessly transitive activity of embody*ing*', Thompson asserts that the wanderer 'consistently evinces aristocratic quality at the same time that it must be iterated as revelation'. Departing from Thompson's point that Burney 'rejects the interiorizing premise' in an attempt to affirm aristocratic difference after the French Revolution, I argue that Burney fully occupies this premise in order to critique the cultural fiction that subjects could choose to be understood as standing outside this premise.

58 Burney, *The Wanderer*, p. 30.

59 Burney, *The Wanderer*, p. 88.

60 See Jill Heydt-Stevenson, 'Liberty, Connection, and Tyranny: The Novels of Jane Austen and the Aesthetic Movement of the Picturesque', in Thomas Pfau and Robert Gleckner, eds., *Lessons of Romanticism: A Critical Companion* (Durham, NC: Duke University Press, 1998), pp. 261–79.

61 For a discussion of the Romantic trope of forceful male questing, see Marlon Ross,

'Romantic Quest and Conquest: Troping Masculine Power in the Crisis of Poetic Identity', in Anne Mellor, ed., *Romanticism and Feminism* (Bloomington: Indiana University Press, 1988), pp. 26–51.

62 Laurence Sterne, *A Sentimental Journey Through France and Italy*, ed. Ian Jack (Oxford: Oxford University Press, 1984), p. 113. See Claudia Johnson's argument in *Equivocal Beings* that these days never really ended for sentimental men, who appropriated the authority of traditionally feminine roles of distress.

63 Burney, *The Wanderer*, p. 34.

64 Burney, *The Wanderer*, p. 348.

65 Burney, *The Wanderer*, p. 340.

66 See Andrea Henderson, 'Burney's *The Wanderer* and Early-Nineteenth-Century Commodity Fetishism', *Nineteenth-Century Literature* 57.1 (2002), pp. 20–21. Arguing for the wanderer's primary role as an 'anonymous and aloof' commodity, Henderson puts a premium on the wanderer's ability to conjure endless speculative desires in her observers: 'The plasticity and obscurity of Juliet's identity [...] enable her to function as a screen for the projection of the desires of others'.

67 Burney, *The Wanderer*, p. 341.

68 Burney, *The Wanderer*, pp. 18, 173.

69 Burney, *The Wanderer*, p. 181.

70 Burney, *The Wanderer*, p. 173.

71 Julie Carlson locates debates on women's agency on stage within a rich history of anti-theatrical criticism that strategically shifts affective authority from women to men, from theatre back to poetry: 'Romantic antitheatricalism seeks to efface what romantic discourse on, and practice of, theatre renders visible: the contradictions that structure the place of 'women' in early nineteenth-century aesthetics, formulations of nationhood, and conditions of theatre'. Julie Carlson, *In the Theatre of Romanticism: Coleridge, Nationalism, Women* (Cambridge: Cambridge University Press, 1994), p. 136. See also Judith Pascoe, *Romantic Theatricality: Gender, Poetry, and Spectatorship* (Ithaca: Cornell University Press, 1997).

72 Burney, *The Wanderer*, p. 161.

73 Burney, *The Wanderer*, p. 157.

74 Burney, *The Wanderer*, pp. 398–99.

75 Andrea Austin identifies homosocial rivalry, following Eve Sedgwick, between the wanderer and Elinor. Andrea Austin, 'Between Women: Frances Burney's *The Wanderer*', *English Studies in Canada* 22.3 (1996), pp. 253–66.

76 William Galperin locates the novel's 'authentically Romantic' as well as 'authentically feminist moments' in Elinor's faulty radicalism: 'Elinor's conventionally progressive claims for liberty are transformed midway into a critique of a conventionally progressive narrative'. William Galperin, 'What Happens When Austen and Burney Enter the Romantic Canon?', in Pfau and Gleckner, eds., *Lessons of Romanticism*, pp. 383, 385.

77 Burney, *The Wanderer*, pp. 160, 187.

78 Burney, *The Wanderer*, p. 164.

79 Burney, *The Wanderer*, p. 192.

80 Burney, *The Wanderer*, p. 205.

81 Burney, *The Wanderer*, p. 186.

82 Burney, *The Wanderer*, p. 28.

83 Burney, *The Wanderer*, p. 172.

84 Burney, *The Wanderer*, p. 171.

85 For another study that addresses the role of objects in *The Wanderer*, see Jillian Heydt-Stevenson's '"Changing her Gown and Setting her Head to Rights": New Shops, New Hats and New Identities', in Jennie Batchelor and Cora Kaplan, eds., *Women and Material Culture, 1660–1830* (Basingstoke: Palgrave Macmillan, 2007), pp. 52–68.

86 Burney, *The Wanderer*, p. 186.

87 Burney, *The Wanderer*, p. 151.

88 Burney, *The Wanderer*, p. 157.

CHAPTER SIX

A Select Collection: Barbauld, Scott, and the Rise of the (Reprinted) Novel

MICHAEL GAMER

> The art of fictitious narrative appears to have its origin in the same principles of selection by which the fine arts in general are created and perfected. [...] Thus, in the process of time, a mass of curious narrative is collected, which is communicated from one individual to another.
>
> – John Dunlop, *The History of Fiction* (1814)[1]

To the extent that literary periods define themselves by the works they canonize as well as by the books they print, the year 1774 should stand as a doubly conspicuous marker to Romanticists and to historians of genre. The year of *Donaldson v. Beckett*, the House of Lords' decision that ended perpetual copyright in Britain, 1774 saw fundamental changes in book production as publishers rushed to reprint titles suddenly thrust into the public domain. Representing the decision as nothing less than a wholesale assault on property rights, *The Morning Chronicle* of 23 February identified the magnitude of the loss: 'By the above decision of the important question respecting copy-right in books, near 200,000 £. worth of what was honestly purchased at public sale, and which was yesterday thought property is now reduced to nothing'.[2] With the term of copyright now set at twenty-one years and with a host of British writers from John Milton to James Thomson thrust into the public domain, *Donaldson* did more than affect the profits of British publishers; it directed their attention to British authors and away from foreign ones who, repackaged in the form of new translations, had previously been the staple of new editions, anthologies, and collections. In this sense, the year that ended perpetual copyright in Britain brought with it permanent changes in the economic practices and cultural politics of British publishing – and, as such, stands as one of many strong candidates for dividing the literary period we call 'the Eighteenth

Century' from that we call 'Romantic'. At the very least, the decades that followed *Donaldson v. Beckett* constitute, if not an Age of Canonization, a span of years in which venture publicists, aided by two revolutions and over two decades of world conflict, became canon-builders by reprinting British authors on an unprecedented scale.

Yet, as various commentators from Barbara Benedict to Barbara Herrnstein Smith have reminded us, reprinting and canon-building are hardly the same activity: none of the acts of valuation involved in reprinting a text necessarily overlap with those attending processes of canonization. An essentially economic decision involving risk and return, reprinting presupposes only a publisher's willingness to print based on the expectation of some kind of profit, that expectation almost always taking the form of a belief that customers will buy. Where a title is not protected by copyright, reprinting becomes, whether in the eighteenth century or today, an even more speculative act because a bookseller must engage in it without customary protections from competition.[3] In contrast, the project of canonization, as Trevor Ross and others have contended, was for much of the eighteenth century the domain of early literary critics and historians if not the basis for their activities:

> It is during this period [the eighteenth century] that the modern terms of value first entered critical discourse. [...] The emergence of these conceptual categories went hand in hand with significant changes in critical practice, including what René Wellek identified as 'the awakening of the historical sense and modern self-consciousness that led to the development of literary history as a discipline', culminating during the period with the publication of Thomas Warton's *History of English Poetry* (1774–81).[4]

Extending Wellek's argument, Lawrence Lipking has suggested that Warton's work ought to be seen alongside Samuel Johnson's *Lives of the Poets* (1779–81) as answering a larger cultural need for an 'ordered' canon.[5]

Where Ross seeks to connect such canon-building activities to those earlier ideas 'of an English canon [that] predate the eighteenth-century',[6] my own essay begins by connecting these same changes in critical practice to the innovations in British publishing brought about by *Donaldson*, with the particular goal of exploring the effects of this partnership of critics and booksellers on the canonization of the British novel during the Romantic period.

My contention is that the late-eighteenth-century 'need' for an ordered canon – epitomized for Ross and others in the critical writings of Hugh Blair, Warton, and Johnson – found, if anything, even more potent expression through an already existing and heavily commodified publisher's vehicle: the multi-volumed, many-authored form I here call the 'select collection'. Transformed in the aftermath of *Donaldson v. Beckett*, the select collection merged the discriminating practices of the anthology with the representative claims of the collection. Bolstered by the new eighteenth-century criticism, whether the retrospective 'history' of Warton or the author's 'life' epitomized in Johnson, it became a literalized, material embodiment of the literary canon, its critical apparatus a register of the collection's particular claims to prestige and importance. Within the domain of prose fiction, this combination of critical preface and publisher's reprint took on a wide variety of forms through the several *'Novelist's'* collections published between 1780 and 1830: from James Harrison's *Novelist's Magazine* (1779–88), to Anna Laetitia Barbauld's (1810) and William Mudford's (1810–16) respective *British Novelists*, to Walter Scott's *Ballantyne's Novelist's Library* (1821–24). In each, one finds succinct claims for a particular novelistic canon and pointed replies to earlier collections. Perhaps more important, the collections as a whole constitute at once a sustained critical discourse and a specific kind of literary text – one governed, moreover, by its own set of material constraints, literary politics, and generic conventions.

Before *Donaldson*

> So that, in every Respect we have mention'd, it may be said, without the least Appearance of Presumption, that so Choice a Collection as this has not hitherto appear'd in this Kingdom.
>
> — Samuel Croxall, Preface to *A Select Collection of Novels* (1720)[7]

'Select collections' of novels existed long before *Donaldson* and even before the 1710 Copyright Act of Queen Anne. While I take the name from an early eighteenth-century collection of fiction edited by Samuel Croxall, earlier models exist in compilations such as Richard 'novel' Bentley's twelve-volume *Modern Novels*, published in 1692. In this latter case, Bentley had published novels and plays throughout the 1680s, and *Modern Novels* appears to be a kind of second edition of selected works previously published by him and perhaps bound to order, all still with their original title pages and imprint dates.[8] Croxall's 1720 *Select Collection*, on the other hand, presents us with a body of fiction specifically prepared as a collection rather than cobbled together from earlier printed copies. His full title

– A Select Collection of Novels in Four Volumes; written by the most Celebrated Authors in several Languages; many of which never appear'd in English before; and all New Translated from the ORIGINALS, by several Eminent Hands – captures not only the dual urges of selection and collection at work in the genre, but also its pre-1774 reliance on newly translated foreign texts unprotected by British copyright.

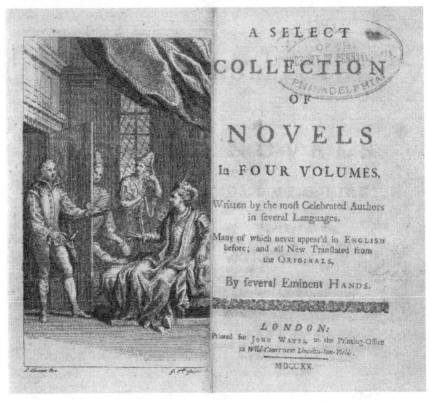

Figure 1 Frontispiece and title page to Vol. 1 of *A Select Collection of Novels* (1720). Permission granted by the University of Pennsylvania Library.

As its preface confirms, the collection culls existing non-English fiction, drawing only on the 'Originals' of 'the most Celebrated Authors', and relying on the skills of 'several Eminent Hands' to translate them into English. Its several frontispieces and dedications – each volume containing one of each – elaborate upon these tropes of selectivity and representativeness while at the same time feminizing its contents and imagined audience. The frontispiece to Volume 1 (Fig. 1) presents an exotic female space, its occupants engaged in conversation until interrupted by a male cavalier. Each volume's dedication, in turn, selects an eminent lady as protector to the volume, proceeding hierarchically. In addition, Volume 1 adds an editor's preface and a treatise on romances to further frame the edition and testify to its quality and seriousness. When two subsequent volumes were added in 1721 to the initial four, Croxall's opening dedication to Mrs Mary Chambers in Volume 5 made explicit the connection between his select collection of female dedicatees, the site of female conversation, and the contents of his work:

> Tho' every one, who has the Happiness of being acquainted with your Manner of thinking and conversing with the World, must be sensible how far Entertainments of this Kind fall below your Taste; yet, when I profess that I am making an impartial disinterested Choice of such among your Sex, as are able to give Reputation to the Author that mentions them, I should have been inexcusable if I had left You out of the Number.[9]

Here, one finds language and argumentation very similar to Croxall's preface (quoted above). Both wield vocabularies of distinction, assuming the principles of selection governing the assembly of 'so Choice a Collection' of novels and female dedicatees to be largely the same. Yet what such assemblies themselves collectively represent, aside from one another, is less clear. This ambiguity stems in part from the rhetorical demands of any dedication, which require abundant superlatives and matchless dedicatees. But it also arises from a problem in representation apparent in the term 'select collection', which describes a grouping of objects at once peerless and yet representative of some larger body. Croxall's solution to this quandary, of course, is to stress the shared principles of 'Choice' that have guided his selection of both groupings, half asserting and half suggesting a mutually constitutive relationship between them. Typical novels, he asserts, necessarily must fall below the taste of a Mrs Mary Chambers, whose 'Manner of thinking and conversing' outshines 'such among [her] Sex' who read fiction. But in the presence of such a select collection of novels, this compliment produces an implied analogy that operates as follows: just as Mrs Mary Chambers (and, by extension, the rest of the dedicatees) must surpass other women, so also must the *Select Collection of Novels* surpass other 'Entertainments of this Kind'. The comparison made, the dedication can conclude with the hope that so exemplary a woman will not be displeased to be associated with so exemplary a collection of fiction.

Half-made and half-hidden by the language of elaborate compliment, such an argument about the exemplary nature of select collections attempts to have it both ways. Whether in his choice of novels or of dedicatees, Croxall projects a fantasy of perfect representation, where well-chosen members purportedly embody what is essential and what is best about their species. As part of a coterie of representative women, Mrs Mary Chambers stands forth as 'exemplary' in both senses of that word – as illustrative of women and as a model of perfection for them to follow. The same goes for the contents of Croxall's *Select Collection*, its simultaneous claims of typicality and excellence contained in its very title. One even finds this dual tendency in Croxall's decision to reprint a translation of Pierre Daniel Huet's *Treatise on the Origin of Romances* (1672) to open the first volume. For Croxall, Huet's essay at once perfectly represents the origins of prose fiction and stands as a model of literary history, treating its subject 'so amply, so pertinently, [and] so perspicuously [...] that it might well supersede the Necessity of any other Preface':

> Had not the original Design of these Imitations of History been to instill the Noblest Sentiments after the most Agreeable Manner [...]. A Person of no less unspotted a Reputation, than universal Learning, as Monsieur *Huet* the Bishop of Avranches in *France*, wou'd never have been at the Pains to write the History of such Works.[10]

As such, both Huet and his essay occupy a position within the collection similar to that of its patrons and contents, the capacious excellence of each part of the collection perfectly representing its essential character as a whole.

Considered in a more general sense, select collections like Croxall's display this divided sense of their own representative functions because their stated principles of selectivity and collectivity cannot coexist entirely without friction. In this sense, the form shares some of the aims of early anthologies and miscellanies, particularly in the expansive sense in which Barbara Benedict has described these latter forms. Each parades its selectivity, and each clusters its chosen texts under categories in an attempt to mediate between individual readers and broader cultural values.

Yet the inevitable differences are equally striking. By typically printing unabridged texts rather than extracts, for example, select collections do not share the same 'logic of the exception' that Leah Price has found characteristic of anthologies.[11] Where select collections print texts in their entirety across several volumes, anthologies usually abridge, extract, and expunge works into single volumes to render them suitable for imagined audiences of superior taste. Resembling in their editorial practices the readerly activities of skimming and skipping through a volume, anthologies distinguish quotable passages from unquotable ones, and through these acts of distinction create similar divisions between worthy and unworthy authors, critics, and readers. As Price notes, the anthology's 'culture of the excerpt' is especially foreign to the novel, whose scale and prescribed reading rituals render it unsuitable for anthologies unless utterly transformed by anthologizing editors into those volumes of excerpted 'Beauties' and 'Elegant Extracts' that replace the pleasures of narrative with those of aphorism and lyric.[12] Thus, while anthologies' habits of selectivity render them constant accessories to canon-formation, their habits of extraction bring with them decidedly *un*representative practices not found in select collections, not to mention the implication that in gathering their flowers they have left nothing but weeds behind.

We begin to address some of these complexities inherent in select collections, I believe, by joining to these ideas of selectivity the idea of the 'collection' as developed by Jean Baudrillard, Susan Pearce, and (quoted below) Susan Stewart, for whom collections of objects pose a particularly rich set of questions about representation through the acts of substitution they perform:

> [The] collection offers example rather than sample, metaphor rather than metonymy. [...] Like other forms of art, its function is not the restoration of a context of origin but rather the creation of a new context, a context standing in a metaphorical, rather than a contiguous, relation to the world of everyday life. [...] [E]ach element within the collection is representative and works in combination toward the creation of a new whole that is the context of the collection itself. The spatial whole of the collection supersedes the individual narratives that 'lie behind it'.[13]

Taking up such terms with regard to *A Select Collection of Novels*, we find Croxall's preface and dedications claiming two separate tropological functions for that collection. On one hand, Croxall's chosen texts stand in metaphoric (exemplarily typical) relation to the bulk of published novels; on the other, they stand in metonymic (exemplarily peerless) relation to this same body of fiction.

Select collections thus bring with them the claims of both Price's anthology and Stewart's collection, usually operating somewhere between these two poles of exemplarity. The latter, metaphorical nature of select collections, moreover, arises out of the *substitutable* nature of their component parts – not in the sense that those parts can be interchanged with other objects in the collection, but rather in the sense that they can be replaced by other objects not currently part of the collection. For Stewart, a perfectly representative collection would be as efficiently representative as Noah's Ark, having 'both the minimum and the complete number of elements necessary for an autonomous world [...] both full and singular, which has banished repetition and achieved authority'.[14] Beyond their metonymic claims to selectivity, then, select collections always commit two fundamental, metaphorical acts of signification inherent to their status as collections. While their component parts stand in for objects not in the collection, these same parts also work in combination with one another to produce an autonomous entity (the collection itself) through acts of compilation, arrangement, and classification. The collection thus functions as a complex system, its arrangement of objects playing a constitutive role in constructing a 'new whole' that has the power to exceed its parts and supersede the original contexts of those parts.

Looking beyond Croxall, one finds such considerations presiding over Robert Dodsley's formative *Select Collection of Old Plays* (1744), the publication that arguably popularized 'select collection' as the name for an already existing form. Consisting of medieval and Renaissance English plays either never before printed or not printed for a century,[15] Dodsley's twelve-volume collection went through multiple editions during the century, galvanized interest in theatre history, and functioned as the period's standard edition of non-Shakespearean early drama. It also led Dodsley to print other *Select Collections* regularly, his own activities comprising part of the explosion of publications in the mid-1740s bearing the name of 'select collection'. Where London publishers had produced little more than half a dozen such works in the previous quarter of a century, they published nearly the same number in 1744–45 alone. Besides Dodsley's *Select Collection of Old Plays* published in early February,[16] we find Gilmour's *Select Collection of Poems* (1744), Anderson's *Select Collection of Remarkable Trials* (1744), Cooper's *Leisure Hours' Amusements: Being a Select Collection of One Hundred and Fifty of the Most Diverting Stories Dispersed in the Writings of the Best English Authors* (1744), and Thompson's *The Atalantis Reviv'd: Being a Select Collection of Novels, of Illustrious Persons of Both Sexes; Taken from the Best Authors* (1745). All make the dual representative claims of Croxall. All deal in uncopyrighted material – Gilmour's *Select Collection* printing Milton's *Comus*, for example, alongside occasional poems by Addison, Dryden, Congreve, Gay, Hughes, Parnell, and Pope.

Taken as a whole, however, their titles are even more suggestive for the awareness they show of one another. Here one finds select collections of 'plays', 'poems', 'trials', 'stories', and 'novels' without overlapping – a division of generic territory that continued over the next decade, with London booksellers commissioning select collections of 'secret histories', 'lampoons', 'tales of the fairies', 'questions and answers', 'rational arguments', and 'letters' (see Works Cited). With its avoidance of redundancies and its carving up of conceptual space, such a pattern of publication resembles a series of proprietary claims to monopolize individual genres, in which the publication of a given select collection makes unnecessary the publication of others in the same genre.[17] It also itself resembles the process of assembling a collection, only here issues of economic substitutability combine with aesthetic and taxonomic ones. In this case, the independent behaviour of several publishers over several years has the effect of producing a select collection of *Select Collections*. And with these effects comes a further, secondary effect of collectively bestowing authority, since in projecting print culture onto an ordered, literary space, publishers of select collections lay claim to specific genres while honouring rival claims to other genres. The result between 1744 and 1755 is a perfect partitioning of an explicitly genred, exemplary literary space – a kind of Noah's Ark of genres.

Certainly this is the practice of Dodsley's *Select Collection of Old Plays*, whose paratextual materials present that work as authoritative and exhaustive – from the 'Dedication', which links the collection's value to the infinite 'Generosity' and intellectual 'Stores' of its aristocratic patron, to the 'Postscript', which informs readers that two extra volumes will be added to round out the collection based on the suggestions of 'the Publick'.[18] Standing between these two modest essays, moreover, is Dodsley's substantial prefatory essay. It presents a narrative of developing consciousness, in which a publisher originally bent on producing a workmanlike edition comes to realize the potential of his adopted form, the select collection:

When I first conceiv'd the Design of collecting together the best and scarcest of our old Plays, I had no intention to do more than search out the several Authors, select what was good from each, and give as correct an Edition of them as I could. [...] But as the Publick has been so kind to favour me with much greater Encouragement than I expected, I thought it my Duty to omit nothing that might conduce either to the greater Perfection of the Work, or their better Entertainment. It was this Consideration which led me to think of prefixing to each Play, where any Materials were to be had, a brief Account of

the Life and Writings of its Author; and also, by way of Preface, a short historical Essay on the Rise and Progress of the *English* Stage, from its earliest
Beginnings, to the Death of King *Charles* the First, when Playhouses were
suppress'd. [...] Another End which I thought such a Collection might answer,
was, that it would serve very well to Shew the Progress and Improvement of
our Taste and Language. For this better Purpose, in the six Pieces which
compose the first Volume, and also in the remarkable Tragedy of *Gorboduc*, I
was even so scrupulous as to preserve their very original Orthography.[19]

Several kinds of 'Duty' present themselves here, from Horatian imperatives
to please and instruct to the codes that govern business–client relations. Yet
what vies with these largely social and economic obligations is something
closer to an aesthetic commitment to the project itself, what Dodsley calls
his duty 'to the greater Perfection of the Work'. It is this sense of the collection as complex system that leads him not only to construct elaborate
paratextual materials for the collection, but also to reconceive of each play
as worthy of its own textual apparatus, comprising preserved orthography,
critical essay, and editorial notes. As the essay summarizes at its opening,
the goal of 'this better Purpose' is to provide as perfect a representation as
possible of early English drama and dramatic history: 'This I thought
would at once serve as a Specimen of the different Merits of the Writers,
and shew the Humours and Manners of the Times in which they lived'.[20]

Composed of national materials either never printed or for which
permission to print had been purchased, Dodsley's *Select Collection* provides
an early model of canon-building by a publisher before *Donaldson v. Beckett*
– one in which we see that publisher addressing issues and discovering
principles in 1744 that would become increasingly important after 1774.
Prominent among these is Dodsley's stated belief in collectedness as a
form of value in and of itself: that the most valuable collections are those
that most truthfully represent their signifieds; and that hastily, cheaply, or
ignorantly constructed collections are little better than frauds perpetrated
on the public. In this way, the collection's faithfulness as a representation
becomes an index of Dodsley's knowledge, character, and connections.
For Baudrillard, such issues explain why collections always function as
representations that inevitably include either the authoring or collecting
self: 'a given collection is made up of a succession of terms, but the final
term must always be the person of the collector'.[21] Stewart puts the matter
even more succinctly: 'When one wishes to disparage the souvenir, one
says that it is not authentic; when one wants to disparage the collected
object, one says "it is not *you*"'.[22]

When we move from personal collections to the large publishing ventures that are select collections, however, the status of collector and collection, and their relation to one another, shift perceptibly. Where private collection becomes public commodity, one finds similar transformations in the cultural identity of the collection. No longer a private eccentric or individual connoisseur, the collector-proprietor acquires an institutional presence, becoming a guarantor of the collection's cultural value. The quality and character of the collection, in turn, reflect the quality and character of the firm standing behind it. Publishers' names begin to function like brands, particularly where no individual editor or compiler appears on the title page to share ownership of the work. Thus we find *Poets of Great Britain from Chaucer to Churchill*, published by John Bell, customarily referred to as '*Bell's British Poets*', and publishers such as John Nichols marketing his *Select Collection of Poems* (1780) in *The Gazetteer and New Daily Advertiser* as a publication compatible with other brand-name collections of stature:

> This day is published, in Four Volumes small Octavo,
>   price Half a Guinea neatly sewed in Boards,
>   A SELECT COLLECTION OF POEMS:
> With notes, Biographical and Historical, by J. NICHOLS; adorned with Four Portraits, by J. Lely, &c. elegantly engraved by Basire, Collyer, and Cook.
>   Printed by and for the Editor, in Red Lion Passage, Fleet-street; and sold by all the Proprietors of the late elegant Edition of the English Poets, with which Work these Volumes are uniformly printed. They are also a proper Companion to the Collections of Dodsley and Pearch.[23]

'Dodsley' and 'Pearch' here nearly form a small select collection in themselves, functioning as exemplars of the bookselling establishment and as benchmarks of taste and standardization. Nichols presents himself in a similarly solid light as a 'proprietor' of 'proper' collections – in short, as a bulwark of propriety. Shepherding the best English poetry into public life, he becomes chaperone and protector of poems attired 'uniformly' and 'elegantly' under his care. Appropriately 'adorned' with portraits painted and engraved by the best artists, the *Select Collection of Poems* will cut a respectable figure even among the best society, and will prove 'a proper Companion' even to such 'elegant' progeny as the collections of Dodsley and Pearch.

Such metaphors of parenting and protectorship appear especially where select collections identify themselves as national in character, as if the claim of representing a country's culture necessitated a more serious and patriotic air. Certainly such figures became even more prevalent in the wake of *Donaldson v. Beckett*, when publisher reprints took the decidedly national turn anticipated thirty years earlier by Dodsley and other publishers of uncopyrighted materials such as Robert Baldwin and James Magee. Baldwin's *The Goldfinch; Being a select collection of the most celebrated English songs* (1748) and Magee's *Select Collection of English Songs* (1751) set off a spate of songbooks bearing the name 'select collection', so that by the year of *Donaldson v. Beckett* they accounted for nearly half of the books bearing that name (Table 1).

Year	1694–1703	1704–13	1714–23	1724–33	1734–43	1744–53	1754–63	1764–73	1774–83
Total 'select collections' published	1	1	2	4	2	14	20	32	38
'Select collection' songbooks published	0	0	0	0	1	4	4	13	21

Table 1 Total number of 'select collections' and number of 'select collection' songbooks published, 1694–1783. I begin each decade with a '4' year (1714–23, for example) to make clearer the effects of Dodsley's *Select Collection* (1744) and of *Donaldson v. Beckett* (1774).

The success of these publications understandably produced changes in the practices of editors and booksellers, who, eager to exploit a fashionable form, began to deploy 'select collection' on the title pages of a variety of publications as a secondary and tertiary generic term. Single-volume 'select collections' like *The Goldfinch* gave rise not only to dozens of songbooks in the second half of the eighteenth century; they also produced other miscellaneous 'select collections' like *The Repository, or General Review: consisting chiefly of a select collection of literary compositions, extracted from all the celebrated periodical productions now publishing* (1756) and *Adultery Anatomized: in a select collection of tryals, for criminal conversation* (1761).

As with most publishing fashions, these titling practices eventually produced their own backlash. It came primarily in the form of antiquarian collections whose simpler titles – wielding 'select collection' as a primary titular term – recall those of Croxall and Dodsley. The most famous of these is Joseph Ritson's three-volume *A Select Collection of English Songs* (1783), whose traditional title was followed by an even more conservative preface calling for fewer and more authoritative collections:

Publications of this nature are already so numerous that, if a preface had not, on any other account, been necessary, something of the kind would, doubtless, have been required, by way of apology, for adding one more to the number, particularly under so plain and unalluring a title as that with which the present volumes are ushered into the world. [...] Perhaps, indeed; if the above circumstance be viewed in a proper light, we shall find that the multiplicity of similar compilations afford rather an argument for, than an objection to an additional undertaking, upon an improved plan. There is not, it may be fairly asserted, any one language in the world possessed of a greater variety of beautiful and elegant pieces of lyric poetry than our own. But, so long as these beauties, this elegance, continue to be scattered abroad, suppressed, and (if one may be allowed the expression) buried alive, in a multitude of collections, consisting chiefly of compositions of the lowest, and most despicable nature; one or more being annually hashed up (*crambe repetia*) by needy retainers to the press, and the most modern being, always, infinitely the worst [...] the greater part of this inestimable possession must, of course, remain altogether unknown to the generality of readers. For who, let his desires and his convenience be what they may, will think it worth his while to peruse, much less to purchase, two or three hundred volumes, merely because each of them may happen to contain a couple of excellent songs?[24]

Ritson's 'improved plan' is essentially one of 'plain and unalluring' antiquarian restoration, one that will call forth books from a bygone golden age. Where modern publications decay in quality as they multiply in number, his *Select Collection of English Songs* proposes to reverse this process by replacing the waste and duplication of some three hundred modern volumes with three authoritative ones. In the process, Ritson invokes the proprietary language of Nichols and others so that the project becomes its own act of chivalry: his collection will rescue the incomparably 'beautiful and elegant' figure of English Song (so lately degraded by company 'of the lowest, and most despicable nature') and re-present it in its 'proper light'.

Ritson's other, more buried metaphor is decidedly national. Rather than providing the 'hash' of modern editions, he plans to reconstitute for his readers the textual equivalent of the entire (and original) English roast beef – unmodernized and in all its imperfections – so that what emerges is an entirely restored literary corpus and national treasure:

Impelled by no lucrative or unworthy motives, the publisher of the present volumes has been solely careful to do justice to the work; a purpose, to effect which neither labour nor expence has been spared. And he is vain enough to flatter himself that the public will have now in their possession, what has been so long wanted, so much desired, so frequently attempted, and hitherto, he thinks, so imperfectly executed, A NATIONAL REPOSITORY OF

MELODY AND SONG. The intrinsic value of the work, in both respects, will be left to pronounce its own eulogium.[25]

Opposing profiteering to patriotism, he expresses the same sense of national duty to 'the work' as Dodsley had four decades earlier. With no language in his account possessing songs of greater variety and beauty than English, only a collection of 'intrinsic value', free from the 'unworthy motives' that propel jobbing and profiteering, will 'do justice to the work' of building a national canon.

National Collections

I cite Ritson's *Select Collection of English Songs* because it provides a dual case study both in the history of literary nationalism and in the history of that largely forgotten generic term. Privileging originary models 'as they have come down to us', Ritson attempts to reclaim the title of '*Select Collection*' from modern (mis)appropriation just as surely as he seeks to retrieve English songs from modern (mis)spelling.[26] Yet most contemporary editors and publishers producing similar multi-volume collections after 1774 did not follow his example. Whether because 'select collection' had become, as Ritson saw it, corrupted by modernization or because it simply seemed old-fashioned, the booksellers who most aggressively capitalized on the *Donaldson* decision chose to abandon the term at the very moment they were inaugurating select collections of unparalleled size and exhaustiveness. Put another way, the term 'select collection' dropped from the titles of multi-volume collections at the very moment when venture publicists were printing collections of poetry, drama, and non-fiction prose more ambitious than anything before seen from London booksellers.

Arguably the most conspicuous of these pioneers in print collections was circulating librarian and newspaper owner John Bell. With *Donaldson* yet undecided in the House of Lords, Bell began work on a series of reprinted collections of fairly monumental scale. His signature format – the small pocket-sized volume, affordable and elegantly printed with a single frontispiece – produced impressive collections of many volumes that were popular both with lending libraries and with individual book-buyers. Bell had become the successor to Bathoe's circulating library in the 1760s; he had eventually changed that library's name to 'The British Library'. Subsequent publications were imprinted with 'John Bell, British Library, Strand', the words 'British Library' increasingly appearing in the

PRINTED BY

John Bell, British Library, Strand,

Figure 2 Title page to *Bell's British Theatre* (1776–78). Permission granted by the University of Pennsylvania Library.

same special gothic type that Bell later used for the masthead of his newspaper, *The World* (1787–93) (Fig. 2).

Beginning in 1774 with an eleven-volume edition of Shakespeare, the representative national dramatist, Bell over the next few years launched or helped to launch several collections, including *A Select Collection of Oriental Tales* (1776), the 21-volume *Bell's British Theatre* (1776–78), and *Poets of Great Britain Complete from Chaucer to Churchill* (1777–82), which extended to 109 volumes. Published in the wake of *Donaldson*, it was these latter two works that had finally broken the economic monopoly of London booksellers on reprints. In 1776, 27 publishers, headed by John Rivington, had brought out *The New English Theatre* (12 vols., 1776–77) to rival *Bell's British Theatre*, complete with frontispieces, portraits, fonts, borders, and editorial apparatuses to match Bell's successful edition (Fig. 3).[27]

Figure 3 Frontispiece to *Bell's British Theatre* (1776); frontispiece to *The New English Theatre* (1776). Permission granted by University of Pennsylvania Library

In 1779, an even larger group of 36 publishers had gone farther, boycotting Bell and recruiting Samuel Johnson to write prefaces for the even more elaborate sixty-volume *Works of the English Poets* (1779). Within such collections, paratexts – from frontispieces and critical essays to editorial apparatuses and prefaces – become acts of marketed patriotism, the bookseller's only just homage to great national authors. Just as Hugh Blair's *Lectures on Rhetoric and Belles Lettres* (1783) had come from his editorial and critical work on Shakespeare (1753) and Ossian (1763) – the former reprinted by Donaldson himself – so Johnson's critical monument to canon-building (*Lives of the Poets*) began as a series of prefaces for a highly leveraged select collection of national authors printed in response to the case that bore Donaldson's name.

Groundbreaking in their typography and style,[28] Bell's advertisements also self-consciously exploited the 'Britishness' of his imprint. The usual Bell ad wields the word 'British' at least twice and usually either in italics or capital letters. But the advertisements for his select collections go even further, presenting the collections and his library as a 'national conveniency [...] worthy of general encouragement' and as a museum in which 'the BRITISH [...] merits of each respective Author be handed down to posterity with the utmost degree of reputation'.[29] His announcement for the *Supplement to Bell's British Theatre* stands as a fairly typical specimen of his marketing of select collections after 1774:

> AS a *Supplement* to BELL's BRITISH THEATRE, comprising *fifty-seven* of the best and most modern FARCES and ENTERTAINMENTS now performing on the *British Stage*, which would cost *Two Guineas and an Half*, if purchased in any other way, although they are now sold at Three Shillings per volume, sewed, at the British Library in the Strand; where may be had also, the most valuable Collection of English Plays that has ever been printed, viz. BELL's BRITISH THEATRE.[30]

While Bell may have shown more flair than others in his attempts to transform 'British' into a brand-name and marketing tool, he was hardly alone in such endeavours. His competitors engaged in similar practices, titling their works and pitching their wares along largely the same lines. Within a single day's issue of the 1780 *Morning Chronicle*, for example, we find a Bell advertisement; nearby we also find Nichols' advertisement for *A Select Collection of Poems* simply carrying the headline '*ENGLISH POETRY*' in the largest possible italics, while the conglomerate of firms publishing *Works of the English Poets* advertises that work by quoting the following passage from the *Critical Review*: 'As the general character of every polished nation depends in a great measure on its poetical productions, too much care cannot be taken, in works of this nature, to impress on foreigners a proper idea of their merit'.[31] 'Works of this nature' might no longer bear the name *Select Collection* on their title-pages, but the age of the British select collection – and of the publisher as canon-builder – had begun.

A Magazine of Novels

> I must be very stupid but I cannot think what I have to say about the Novelist's Magazine.
>
> – Walter Scott to John Ballantyne (April 1822)[32]

While in the immediate aftermath of *Donaldson*, Bell brought out select collections of British poetry, legitimate drama, farces, and tales, neither he nor his competitors attempted anything like a similarly representative collection of British fiction. The absence is telling, all the more so when considered alongside publishers' aggressive building of 'national reposito- ries' in other genres. The few collections of fiction published during the latter half of the 1770s, in fact, avoid these newer formats, preferring the earlier models instituted by Bentley and Croxall. George Kearsly's *A Collec- tion of Novels, Selected and Revised by Mrs. Griffith* (1777), for example, adapts the format and even the costume of earlier select collections (Fig. 4). Forward-looking only in its steady bowdlerization of its late-seventeenth- and early-eighteenth-century contents,[33] Kearsly's collection bears little resemblance to the ambitious poetic and dramatic collections that domi- nated the London trade after 1774. Like the earlier *Novelist; or Tea-Table Miscellany, containing select tales of Dr. Croxall* (1766), it borrows the majority of its contents from Croxall's *Select Collection*, supplementing these transla- tions of foreign works with short works by Aphra Behn and Eliza Haywood. Its two frontispieces, each facing a title page featuring Athena addressing a chastened Eros while pointing to Parnassus, also recall earlier formats and eras, though now with a cautionary air. Even its working defi- nition of the 'novel' – denoting a shorter work of fiction (rather than a longer 'romance') – smacks more of the 1690s and 1720s than of the decade of *Humphry Clinker* (1771) and *Evelina* (1778).

The need to present such a collection of fiction as chaperoned by a married woman of known respectability points to other, more obvious reasons for the absence of select collections of the British novel in the wake of *Donaldson*. As the 1770s closed, the novel's place in British literary

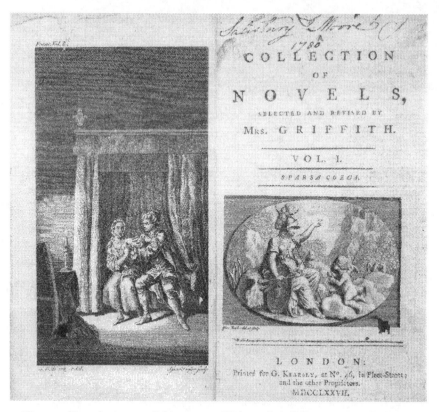

Figure 4 Frontispiece and title page to Vol. 1 of *A Collection of Novels* (1777).
Permission granted by University of Pennsylvania Library.

culture was hardly secure, as literary historians from J. M. S. Tompkins and
Ioan Williams to Terry Lovell and Ina Ferris have demonstrated. With the
novel occupying a less prestigious position than other literary forms, it is
hardly surprising that the publishing firm of Harrison took a more cautious
approach than publishers in other genres to collecting and republishing
British fiction in unabridged form. Printed in October of 1779, its
prospectus for *The Novelist's Magazine* (1779–88) followed the example of
Bell's British Theatre in proposing periodical publication; beyond this similarity, however, it studiously avoided the national bent of other
contemporary collections. Harrison instead only promised a 'very capital
and agreeable Publication' rather than a national repository or patriotic
act.[34] The address 'To the Public', printed on the reverse side of the
prospectus, begins in a more modest vein as well. Rather than making

claims for the novel's value as work of art or as contribution to Britain's literary glory, Harrison opens by defending its moral and didactic tendencies and pointing to its power to place 'every feeling Heart, every susceptible Mind [...] at the Shrine of suffering Virtue!'[35] The only national service Harrison claims for his publication, in fact, is economic. With each weekly number printed in double-columned large octavo format and priced at sixpence, his readers will be able to purchase works of fiction for one-third of their usual price, unabridged and without the shortcomings of other inexpensive reprints: 'Lest the Cheapness of this elegant Work should induce some Persons to imagine the several Pieces of which it is to consist, will be mangled and abridged; the Proprietors beg Leave most respectfully to assure the Public, that every Tale, Novel, &c. will contain the exact Words written by each Author; nor will a single sentence by any means be omitted'.[36]

Like most eighteenth-century publishers, little is known about James Harrison beyond his advertisements and title pages.[37] His fondness for fiction extended at least to that of occasional authorship: his stories 'The Criminal' and 'The History of Captain Winterfield' open each of the two volumes of *The New Novelist's Magazine* (1786–87), the collection of short fiction designed to be a companion to the longer works of *The Novelist's Magazine*. Plot-driven and moving easily between tale of exotic adventure and moment of romantic discovery, these stories partake of narrative traditions similar to those governing the contents of the first volumes of *The Novelist's Magazine*. In one of the few modern commentaries on the collection, Richard C. Taylor has concluded Harrison's choice of texts to be essentially canonical; noting Harrison's fondness for oriental romance and foreign translations, he argues for their loss from later collections of fiction as an effect of canonization.[38] Such an assessment represents *The Novelist's Magazine*'s 23 volumes with a fair degree of accuracy, filled as they are with familiar works by Richardson, Sterne, Goldsmith, and Fielding.

What Taylor's account overlooks, however, is the strange drama of the collection's unfolding. Unlike the poetic and dramatic collections of contemporaries like Bell and Warton, Harrison's venture attempts neither the chronological ordering nor the generic categorization that usually characterize select collections. Confronted with the myriad risks attending any publishing innovation, *The Novelist's Magazine*'s first three full years of publication (1779–82) show Harrison (understandably) choosing the most popular authors of his day no longer protected by copyright. Recent work on reprints by Peter Garside and James Raven, in fact, shows Harrison in

these first years to be almost a barometer of popular taste.[39] Volume 1 of
The Novelist's Magazine opens with John Hawkesworth's *Almoran and Hamet*
followed by Henry Fielding's *Adventures of Joseph Andrews* and *Amelia*.
Volumes 2 and 3 repeat this pattern of varying between exotic tale and
homegrown history: the former with John Langhorne's *Solyman and Almená,
an Oriental Tale* followed by Oliver Goldsmith's *The Vicar of Wakefield, a Tale*,
Tobias Smollett's *The Adventures of Roderick Random*, Francis Ashmore's
Zadig; or, The Book of Fate; An Oriental History, and Alain René Le Sage's *Devil
upon Two Sticks*; the latter with Sir Charles Morell's *Tales of the Genii* and
Fielding's *History of Tom Jones* (Fig. 5). The choices of Harrison's first nine
volumes are most striking for how quickly they establish and adhere to a
publishing formula that combines what we now call the traditional novel
with a rich assortment of tales, travels, and adventures. Of writers traditionally considered canonical, Smollett appears in these volumes five
times, Fielding four, and Le Sage and Sterne twice; Defoe, Goldsmith, and
Swift also make appearances, while epistolary fiction and works by women
writers are virtually absent (see Appendix 1).

It was not until 1783, when *The Novelist's Magazine* had reached weekly
circulations nearing 10,000, that Harrison varied this pattern. When he did,
it was to announce in a special prospectus the publication of Samuel
Richardson's *Sir Charles Grandison*:

> The Publishers of the Novelist's Magazine flatter themselves they need make
> no apology for inserting, in a work which has received such marks of universal
> approbation, a production which has very deservedly been esteemed, by men
> of the first literary and moral characters, the most perfect of its kind that ever
> appeared in this or any other language.[40]

The advertisement is interestingly defensive in tone. In spite of declaring
itself 'no apology', the text that follows consists entirely of quotations
praising Richardson by Warton, Johnson, Lord Lyttleton, Jean-Jacques
Rousseau, and Diderot, its final paragraph concluding it 'unnecessary to
dwell on merit which has been universally admitted […]. [T]hose who read
Sir Charles Grandison will need no guide to direct them to its beauties'.
Noticeably absent are references to the novel's lasting popularity or its
ability to move readers; the scene of reading constructed in Harrison's original prospectus of 1779 is here replaced by the praise of learned male critics
and by readers who need no guidance to discover the 'beauties' of a writer
of such 'merit'.

Requiring eight months and the whole of Volumes 10 and 11 to print,
Harrison's edition of *Sir Charles Grandison* inaugurated a more permanent

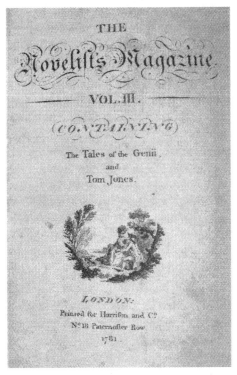

Figure 5 Title page of Volume 3 of *The Novelist's Magazine* (1781). From the author's own collection

change in *The Novelist's Magazine*'s self-representation and claimed social function. It was a transformation, moreover, that went beyond merely printing epistolary works and authors like Sarah Fielding, Charlotte Lennox, and Frances Sheridan. As the language of the *Grandison* prospectus and later advertisements demonstrate, Harrison in these years moved to conceiving of *The Novelist's Magazine* less as a consumable serial and more as a permanent repository of long fiction in the tradition of Ritson –as a 'work' of lasting value on which 'men of the first literary and moral characters' bestowed 'marks of universal approbation'. Popular success, apparently, not only brought increased national prominence and dignity; it also produced an accompanying change in the principles of selection governing the collection. By the time he reached Volume 10 and a weekly circulation pushing into five figures, Harrison could gamble on a work less certain to generate sales. The result is a prospectus that posits an inverse relationship between the economically viable and the culturally prestigious. Similar issues inform subsequent select collections published by Harrison. The three words comprising the title of *Harrison's British Classics* (1785–97) – featuring essays by Joseph Addison, George Colman, Thomas Fitzosborne, Samuel Johnson, Hugh Kelly, William Shenstone, Richard Steele, and Launcelot Temple, among others – at once appropriate Bell's habits of collection-naming and patriotic marketing while making the project of canon-creating explicit. These same assumptions even find their way into the prospectus for *The New Novelist's Magazine* where, alongside the familiar claims of high quality and low cost, Harrison deploys the language of Bell, promising to provide 'an elegant collection of the many beautiful little TALES and STORIES scattered throughout innumerable voluminous Miscellanies [...] [in] entirely NEW TRANSLATIONS [...] from learned and ingenious Friends, willing to assist him in exposing the deformities of Vice, and displaying the loveliness of Virtue'.[41]

Harrison ended *The Novelist's Magazine* in 1788 after 23 volumes and 60 novels. In nine years of publication, he achieved sales exceeding not only other contemporary select collections but also periodicals like the *Gentleman's Magazine* (1731–1833) and *Monthly Review* (1749–1845). His effect on the history of the novel can be felt in literary reviews' increasingly historical and comparatist notices of fiction after 1780, in the correspondence of Walter Scott and other novelists, and in the sheer number of volumes of *The Novelist's Magazine* held in library collections and still available for sale by antiquarian booksellers. Put another way, the subsequent collections and critical work of Walter Scott and Anna Barbauld (to whom I turn to in the final section of this essay) – not to mention the self-conscious intertextuality and generic experimentation of Romantic-period fiction in general – would not have happened had publishers such as Harrison not been painstakingly collecting the novel's history into select collections. In a genre notorious for flooding the market with new productions, Harrison almost single-handedly filled his country's bookshops and circulating libraries with reprinted fiction. Yet the success of his venture registers most clearly in the repeated attempts of booksellers to duplicate his publishing success in the years that followed by privileging the same 'standard' authors in their own collections. J. H. Emmert's *The Novelist: or, A Choice Selection of the Best Novels* (1792–93), for example, ceased publication after only two volumes devoted to Richardson and Fielding. *Hogg's New Novelist's Magazine* (1794) also largely failed to attract readers, while William Mudford's *The British Novelist* (1810–11, 1816) sputtered to a halt five volumes into what had become a *de rigueur* reprinting of Fielding, Goldsmith, Smollett, and Sterne (see Appendix 2). Even Leigh Hunt's *Classic Tales, Serious and Lively* (1806) enjoyed at best moderate success by reprinting shorter works by Goldsmith, Hawkesworth, Johnson, Mackenzie, Marmontel, and Sterne, nearly all of which had appeared in *The Novelist's Magazine* and *The New Novelist's Magazine*.

From Cabinet to Collection

It is within this context that Walter Scott, flushed with the success of his poem *Marmion* and deep in planning the *Quarterly Review* and the *Edinburgh Annual Register*, first proposed a select collection of fiction to bookseller John Murray late in October of 1808:

> I have been also turning over in my mind the plan of the Novels & Romances. In my opinion they should be set about without loss of time beginning with the Novels of Richardson. Fielding & Smollett will lead the van with a very short memoir of each of their lives & a prefatory Essay on the peculiarities of their stile. These will be follow[e]d by a good selection of novels of less name.[42]

The rapid correspondence that followed shows Scott at his most entre-preneurially sanguine. Over the next two weeks he, James Ballantyne, and Murray tentatively agreed to produce a series entitled 'The Cabinet of Novels, being a collection &c',[43] the title inspired probably by the recent *Cabinet of Poetry* (1808) published in six volumes. Scott's first six volumes would be published together 'with a full detail of [the] plan, and an assur-ance to the public that it was in speedy progress'.[44] Combining collected works of major novelists with a 'good selection of novels of less name' and consisting of approximately twenty double-columned royal octavo volumes, the full collection would deliberately resemble Harrison's serial, though in updated and improved form:

> To give the selection some appearance of arrangement, it will be necessary to separate the Translations from the original Novels, to place those of each author together – which I observe is neglected in Harrison's series – and to keep the Novels, properly so-called, separate from Romances and Tales. I have little doubt that 20 volumes of 700 pages will hold all the Novels, &c. that are worth reprinting.[45]

In the ensuing months, Scott's strategies of organization quickly multiplied the number of texts to be included, and thus the projected number of volumes, from twenty to 200. The number arose, moreover, from the same urges as those shaping his proposed critical apparatus and plan of publication. Through them, he seeks to impose a sense of collectedness – the 'appearance of arrangement' – on what would otherwise be a serial form. Yet, in his enthusiasm, Scott cannot help but invoke the language of *The Novelist's Magazine*'s own advertisements when he imagines making his domain 'all the Novels, &c. that are worth reprinting'. Throughout its nine-year run, Harrison's advertisements for *The Novelist's Magazine* had sold the series as comprised of 'all English and foreign novels, tales, and romances, worth reading'.[46] While the shift from 'worth reading' to 'worth printing' is suggestive in itself, the presence of Harrison's publishing model is nevertheless clear, and extends even to Scott's ambivalence over Richardson. 'Beginning with the Novels of Richardson' yet somehow 'lead[ing]' with Fielding and Smollett, he reproduces Harrison's own division between economic profitability and cultural authoritativeness. Writing to Archibald Constable fourteen years later, Scott put the matter even more bluntly: 'Having printed Smollett and Fielding, Richardson undoubtedly comes next in order. But then his works are so insufferably long, that they will take a great deal of room in the proposed edition – while, on the other hand, a collection of novels without Richardson would be very incomplete. What are you to say of Defoe?'[47]

What is most striking about the *Ballantyne's Novelist's Library* (1821–24), the ten-volume series finally begun over a decade after Scott first wrote to Murray, is the tenacity with which Scott clung to his original scheme and Harrison's model. Though updated and organized by author, its finished contents still essentially follow the trajectory of Harrison's series, devoting a volume to Fielding and two to Smollett before moving on to works by Alain Le Sage and Charles Johnstone, followed by Oliver Goldsmith, Samuel Johnson, Henry Mackenzie, Horace Walpole, and Clara Reeve (see Appendix 3). As with *The Novelist's Magazine*, Richardson appears in *Ballantyne's Novelist's Library* only at its midpoint – *after*, rather than before, 'a good selection of novels of less name'. Even Scott's omission of pre-1740 works published by Harrison, among them *Gulliver's Travels* and *Robinson Crusoe*, appears to have arisen not from dissatisfaction with Harrison's choice of works but rather from his partner John Ballantyne's having already published them in *Popular Romances: Consisting of Imaginary Voyages and Travels* (1812), a collection edited by Scott's assistant Henry Weber that also included Murray.[48] With Harrison's choice of texts apparently unimpeachable, onlookers such as Constable looked to the collection's formatting to explain its poor sales: 'I suppose the scheme of the *British*

Novelists will now be given up – it was I believe by no means a successful one in point of sale, arising altogether, as a Bookseller would say, from the mode in which it was got up. A collection of Novels must not be printed in small type like a Newspaper, a *Corpus Juris*, or as a book of reference, and in the present times of good and rather expensive taste, there will be no very great number of readers for works requiring a magnifying glass or at all events spectacles'.[49]

However just his criticisms, Constable's slip of the pen points to more likely reasons for the failure of the *Ballantyne's Novelist's Library*, which he mistakenly calls 'the *British Novelists*' rather than by its rightful name. In doing so, he points to a rival publication that had recently gone through its second edition in 1820, and whose first edition in 1810 arguably laid the intellectual groundwork for the novel's ascent to cultural dominance during the Regency. This publication was *The British Novelists* in fifty volumes, edited and introduced by Anna Laetitia Barbauld, and published by a conglomerate led by Lowndes and the Rivingtons. Announced at the same time as Mudford's *The British Novelist* and as Scott was preparing his own materials for Murray, Barbauld's collection trumped its rivals because of its richly authoritative editorial apparatus and its innovations in formatting and publication. Breaking with the traditional double columns and royal octavo format – which, in Scott's words, made 'the book [...] heavy [though] the subject is light' – it adopted the larger print and smaller size of earlier poetic and dramatic collections.[50] For the first time in decades, here was a collection of longer British fiction published in a form unassociated with newsprint and professional records, and that more closely resembled Bell's elegant pocket volumes than Harrison's economic tomes. Yet equally important to Barbauld's success was the timing and mode of *The British Novelists*' publication – in particular the simple fact that its fifty volumes appeared as single collection rather than serial. As such, they presented a body of work fully organized and assembled, clear in its conceptual boundaries and chronologies, and noticeably different from previous collections of fiction assembled piecemeal and given coherence only in retrospect when publication terminated. In this way, *The British Novelists* exhibited to its audience for the first time a single body of fiction under a national banner whose claims to exemplarity and representativeness could not be mistaken.

Such claims were confirmed by the comprehensiveness and rhetoric of Barbauld's introductory essay. In both its historical scope and its claims for the novel, 'On the Origin and Progress of Novel-Writing' resembles the 'Introductory Discourse' of Joanna Baillie's *Plays on the Passions* (1798). Both essays counter longstanding moral prejudices by arguing for the historical, aesthetic, and pedagogical importance of their respective genres. With this purpose in mind, Barbauld's opening presents the novel as universal in its appeal and deserving a distinguished place in literary hierarchies:

> A Collection of Novels has a better chance of giving pleasure than of commanding respect. Books of this description are condemned by the grave, and despised by the fastidious; but their leaves are seldom found unopened, and they occupy the parlour and the dressing-room while productions of higher name often gather dust upon the shelf. It might not perhaps be difficult to show that this species of composition is entitled to a higher rank than has been generally assigned it.[51]

Such terms do more than anticipate Jane Austen's own defence of the novel in *Northanger Abbey*;[52] they present the genre as possessing traits similar to those possessed by select collections. Just as select collections purport to represent both what is typical and what is best in a species, the novel in Barbauld's account embodies what is typical and best in people – as is reflected by novels being found in both the best and the most intimate rooms in the house. Part of Barbauld's argument about the exemplarity of fiction, then, depends on her dextrous handling of generic tags, where 'fictitious narrative', 'romance', and 'novel' function as interchangeable yet historically specific terms. Thus, the universal appeal of 'fictitious narrative' transcends divisions of class, gender, nationality, and historical period even as its various forms are expressive of specific peoples and cultural moments:[53]

> To measure the dignity by the pleasure he [the novelist] affords his readers is not perhaps using an accurate criterion; but the invention of a story, the choice of proper incidents, the ordonnance of the plan, occasional beauties of description, and above all, the power exercised over the reader's heart by filling it with the successive emotions of love, pity, joy, anguish, transport, or indignation, together with the grave impressive moral resulting from the whole, imply talents of the highest order, and ought to be appretiated [*sic*] accordingly. A good novel is an epic in prose, with more of character and less (indeed in modern novels nothing) of the supernatural machinery.[54]

Within this logic, the novel's universality of appeal becomes the basis for its deserving the highest cultural standing, with the 'modern novel' in contemporary literary hierarchies rightfully possessing the position once held by the ancient epic.

Barbauld employs a similarly two-pronged argument about the transcendent and progressive nature of the British novel, which forms the *telos* of her broad sweep of the history of fiction. Within this narrative, British writers at once contribute to a longstanding tradition originating in ancient Greece even as they break from that tradition to invent the 'modern novel' early in the eighteenth century. Foreign works from these same years – particularly *Zayde* and *The Princess of Cleves* (both published in Croxall's *Select Collection of Novels*) – understandably occupy interestingly liminal spaces. Resembling 'pre-Romantics', these texts are somehow pre-novels, 'approaching the modern novel of the serious kind' yet, like Cervantes, not managing to bring that formal ideal fully into existence. That accomplishment is instead reserved for Defoe:

> The first author amongst us who distinguished himself by natural painting, was that truly original genius De Foe. His *Robinson Crusoe* is to this day an *unique* in its kind, and he has made it very interesting without applying to the common resource of love. At length, in the reign of George the Second, Richardson, Fielding, and Smollett, appeared in quick succession; and their success raised such a demand for this kind of entertainment, that it has ever since been furnished from the press, rather as a regular and necessary supply, than as an occasional gratification.[55]

Drawing on a rhetorical tradition established through essays such as Edward Young's *Conjectures on Original Composition* (1759), Barbauld presents Defoe as a genius of native growth, 'original' both in his uniqueness and in that he provides the origin of the modern novel. Nourished on Hanoverian soil, the modern novel becomes in Barbauld's representation at once organic and locally grown – its genealogy sharing of the same number of generations as the reigning royal family, its flourishing state suggesting a similar state of health for the British nation.

In focusing on this narrative of origins, I seek at once to rebut and to applaud Claudia Johnson's recent essay on Barbauld's collection, which asserts that Barbauld eschews 'politically freighted mythoses of origin' in order to argue for *The British Novelists* as a 'contending canon' of prose fiction.[56] As I hope I have shown, these two considerations need not be mutually exclusive. The narrative of origins is plainly there, as is the attempt to represent the 'modern novel' as a new and distinctly British variety of narrative art. My own point, in a sense, is that Barbauld inscribes these very same contending canons into *The British Novelists'* apparatus, and that she carries off these acts of inscription seamlessly by exploiting the select collection's formal properties. For Barbauld's primary concerns are indeed canonical; the arrangement she bestows and the critical apparatus she erects in many ways constitute *The British Novelists'* overarching argument.

After all, given the pains with which Barbauld's introduction constructs a family tree of the British novel – in which Defoe is succeeded by Richardson, Fielding, and Smollett, who in turn are succeeded by successively larger generations – it is all the more striking to see her abandon this narrative in *The British Novelists'* arrangement and contents. There, rather than finding strict chronology, we find chronological, hierarchical, and generic organizing principles at work simultaneously. While its fifty volumes proceed in roughly chronological order, chronology is upset at key places as a way of asserting one author's or one work's primacy over another. A small instance of this occurs at Volume 22, where Clara Reeve's *Old English Baron* (1778) appears before Horace Walpole's *Castle of Otranto* (1764); the most stunning reversal, however, involves Barbauld's decision to open with Richardson's *Clarissa* (Vols. 1–8) and *Sir Charles Grandison* (Vols. 9–15) rather than with her own proclaimed point of origin, *Robinson Crusoe* (Vols. 16–17). Yet chronology comprises only one of the contending canons present in the collection. Tallying the number of volumes a given author receives, for example, strongly confirms the primacy of Richardson, who at fifteen volumes outstrips all rivals by a threefold margin. Coming second, however, is not Fielding but Frances Burney (Vols. 38–42) and Ann Radcliffe (Vols. 43–47), on whom Barbauld bestows five volumes each. And tracking the number of prefatory pages devoted to each author presents us with still a third hierarchy of authors – one more in line with the history outlined in Barbauld's introduction. There, Richardson again exceeds all others, receiving 66 pages, followed by Fielding with 32, Smollett with 18, Goldsmith with 12, and Burney with 11.[57]

Such analyses yield at least two distinct views of the history of the novel present in *The British Novelists* – views that exist silently though uneasily alongside one another. In this sense, while Barbauld's introduction provides a kind of official historiography, its contents and arrangement present readers with very different view. Using these latter registers, we find a novel that opens with Richardson and closes with Edgeworth – a novel, moreover, epistolary in nature and dissenting in flavour, dominated by women writers after 1770. While Barbauld's introduction also notes the 'great proportion [...] of ladies' who have distinguished themselves as writers of fiction,[58] my point here is the stunning degree to which her specific acts of selection and commentary overturn a canon of British fiction established by Harrison and perpetuated by subsequent editors.

With *The British Novelists'* fifty volumes published as a single entity and in a single blow, Barbauld found herself at least partially freed from the economic constraints of serial publications. As a result, she could – to paraphrase Scott's words – begin with Defoe but lead with Richardson, and in the process shift the novel's centre of gravity back to the epistolary and the domestic.

I opened this essay with an epigraph from John Dunlop's *History of Fiction*, printed by Ballantyne on the eve of *Waverley* (1814),[59] the novel to which Scott returned in 1810 after *The British Novelists* forced him to abandon (for the time being, at least) his plans to publish his own select collection of fiction.[60] I close with Barbauld's collection rather than Scott's because, in spite of Scott's own triumphs as a novelist, *The British Novelists* constitutes the first fully intact select collection of British fiction – the first unhampered by the demands of serial publications and capturing the generic experimentation of writers such as Radcliffe and Edgeworth – published after *Donaldson v. Beckett*. Put another way, I end with Barbauld because she is the first collector of novels to exploit fully the select collection's powers as a signifying form, and it was through this same form that publishers most powerfully shaped the idea of a British canon in other genres after 1774. Under Barbauld's handling, the result was an authoritative collection of fiction that acted as a powerful corrective to earlier attempts at canonization.[61]

Still, as the final paragraph of Barbauld's introductory essay states, the freedom of the collector only extends so far:

> Variety in manner has been attended to [...] [and s]ome regard it has been thought proper to pay to the taste and preference of the public, as was but reasonable in an undertaking in which their preference was to indemnify those who are at the expense and risk of the publication. Copyright also was not to be intruded on, and the number of volumes was determined by the booksellers. Some perhaps may think that too much importance has been already given to a subject so frivolous, but a discriminating taste is no where more called for than with regard to a species of books which every body reads. It was said by Fletcher of Saltoun, 'Let me make the ballads of a nation, and I care not who makes the laws'. Might it not be said with as much propriety, Let me make the novels of a country, and let who will make the systems?[62]

Given how frequently commentators have cited Barbauld's two closing sentences, it is surprising how infrequently one finds them quoted in their full context. Preceded by a formidable list of constraints, the tone of Barbauld's closing shifts from something like defensiveness to something more triumphantly pointed. It is as if, proud as Barbauld is of her achievement, she asks her readers to imagine what she might have accomplished if unimpeded by copyright and popular taste, both of which have dictated that in places she substitute one text for another. Hints elsewhere in *The British Novelists* point to Barbauld's original intention to have included more volumes and a greater number of living authors;[63] but far more important is the fundamental act of imagination to which she exhorts her readers who, with minds unmediated by publishers and unconstrained by intellectual property laws, ultimately hold the final responsibility of 'mak[ing] the novels of a country'.

Appendix 1: Contents of *The Novelist's Magazine* (1779–88)

Volume(s)	Year published	Author	Title
1	1780	John Hawkesworth	*Almoran and Hamet. An Oriental Tale*
		Henry Fielding	*The History of the Adventures of Joseph Andrews*
		Henry Fielding	*Amelia*
2	1780	John Langhorne	*Solyman and Almená. An Oriental Tale*
		Oliver Goldsmith	*The Vicar of Wakefield. A Tale*
		Tobias Smollett	*The Adventures of Roderick Random*
		Voltaire (tr. Ashmore)	*Zadig; or, The Book of Fate. An Oriental History*
		Alain Le Sage (tr. Smollett)	*The Devil upon Two Sticks*
3	1781	Sir Charles Morell	*The Tales of the Genii*
		Henry Fielding	*The History of Tom Jones, a Foundling*
4	1781	Alain Le Sage	*The Adventures of Gil Blas of Santillane*
		Daniel Defoe	*The Life and Adventures of Robinson Crusoe*
5	1781	Laurence Sterne	*The Life and Opinions of Tristram Shandy, Gentleman*
		Rev. Mr. Stackhouse	*Chinese Tales*
		Rev. Dr. Dodd	*The Sisters; or, The History of Lucy and Caroline Sanson*
6	1782	Tobias Smollett	*The Adventures of Peregrine Pickle*
		Marmontel	*Moral Tales*
7	1782	de Mouhy	*The Fortunate Country Maid*
		Hugh Kelly	*Memoirs of a Magdelen; or, The History of Louisa Mildmay*
		John Langhorne	*Letters between Theodosius and Constantia*
		Tobias Smollett	*The Adventures of Ferdinand Count Fathom*
8	1782	Cervantes (tr. Smollett)	*The History and Adventures of the Renowned Don Quixote*
9	1782	Laurence Sterne	*A Sentimental Journey*

		Jonathan Swift	*Gulliver's Travels*
		Sarah Fielding	*The Adventures of David Simple*
		Tobias Smollett	*The Adventures of Sir Launcelot Greaves*
		Francis Ashworth	*Letters of a Peruvian Princess*
		Henry Fielding	*The History of Jonathan Wilde the Great*
10–11	1783	Samuel Richardson	*Sir Charles Grandison*
12	1783	Charlotte Lennox	*The Female Quixote; or, The Adventures of Arabella*
		Henry Fielding	*A Journey from this World to the Next*
		Kimber	*The Life and Adventures of Joe Thompson*
		Robert Paltock	*The Life and Adventures of Peter Wilkins, a Cornish Man*
13	1784	Eliza Haywood	*The History of Miss Betsy Thoughtless*
		tr. Ambrose Philips	*The Thousand and One Days: Persian Tales*
14–15	1784	Samuel Richardson	*Clarissa, or The History of a Young Lady*
16	1784	de Avellaneda (tr. Yardley)	*A Continuation of Don Quixote*
		Marivaux	*The Virtuous Orphan; or The Life of Marianne, Countess of **
17	1785	Salignac (tr. Hawkesworth)	*The Adventures of Telemachus, the Son of Ulysses*
		de Vergy	*Henrietta, Countess Osenvor. A Sentimental Novel*
		Eliza Haywood	*The History of Jemmy and Jenny Jessamy*
18	1785	Galland	*Arabian Nights Entertainments*
19	1785	Tobias Smollett	*The Expedition of Humphry Clinker (1785).*
		Francis Coventry	*The History of Pompey the Little*
		Sarah Fielding	*The History of Ophelia*
		Thomas Flloyd	*Tartarian Tales; or, A Thousand and One Quarters of Hours*
20	1786	Samuel Richardson	*Pamela*
21	1786	Samuel Humphreys	*Peruvian Tales, Related in One Thousand and One Hours*
		'tr. from the Italian'	*The Adventures of Signor Gaudentio di Lucca*
		Tobias Smollett	*The History and Adventures of an Atom*
		Voltaire (tr. Ashmore)	*The Sincere Huron. A True History*
		Peter Longueville	*The English Hermit*
22	1787	John Shebbeare	*Lydia; or, Filial Piety. A Novel*
		Frances Sheridan	*Memoirs of Miss Sidney Bidulph*
23	1788	Samuel Johnson	*The History of Rasselas, Prince of Abissinia. A Tale*
		Charlotte Lennox	*Henrietta*
		Frances Sheridan	*The History of Nourjahad*
		Mr. Collyer	*Letters from Felicia to Charlotte*
		Sir John Hill	*The Adventures of Mr. George Edwards, A Creole*
		Eliza Haywood	*The Invisible Spy*

Appendix 2: Contents of *The British Novelist*, ed. William Mudford (1810–16)

Volume	Year published	Author	Title
1	1810	Tobias Smollett	*Peregrine Pickle*
		Tobias Smollett	*Humphry Clinker*
2	1810	Tobias Smollett	*Roderick Random*
		Tobias Smollett	*Ferdinand Count Fathom*
		Tobias Smollett	*Sir Launcelot Greaves*
3	1811	Laurence Sterne	*Tristram Shandy*
		Laurence Sterne	*A Sentimental Journey*
		Jonathan Swift	*Gulliver's Travels*
		Oliver Goldsmith	*The Vicar of Wakefield*
4	1811	Henry Fielding	*Tom Jones*
		Henry Fielding	*Jonathan Wild the Great*
5	1816	Henry Fielding	*Joseph Andrews*
		Henry Fielding	*Amelia*

Appendix 3: Contents of Ballantyne's Novelist's Library (1821–24)

Volume(s)	Year published	Author	Title
1	1821	Henry Fielding	*Joseph Andrews*
		Henry Fielding	*Tom Jones*
		Henry Fielding	*Amelia*
		Henry Fielding	*Jonathan Wild*
2	1821	Tobias Smollett	*Roderick Random*
		Tobias Smollett	*Peregrine Pickle*
		Tobias Smollett	*Humphry Clinker*
3	1821	Tobias Smollett	*Count Fatham*
		Tobias Smollett	*Sir Launcelot Greaves*
		Tobias Smollett	Cervantes' *Don Quixote*
4	1822	Le Tobias Smollett	*Gil Blas*
		Alain Le Sage	*The Devil on Two Sticks*
		Alain Le Sage	*Vanillo Gonzales*
		Charles Johnstone	*The Adventures of a Guinea*
5	1823	Laurence Sterne	*Tristram Shandy*
		Laurence Sterne	*Sentimental Journey*
		Oliver Goldsmith	*The Vicar of Wakefield*

		Samuel Johnson	*Rasselas*
		Henry Mackenzie	*The Man of Feeling*
		Henry Mackenzie	*The Man of the World*
		Henry Mackenzie	*Julia de Roubigne*
		Horace Walpole	*The Castle of Otranto*
		Clara Reeve	*The Old English Baron*
6–8	1824	Samuel Richardson	*Pamela*
		Samuel Richardson	*Clarissa*
		Samuel Richardson	*Sir Charles Grandison*
9	1824	Jonathan Swift	*Gulliver's Travels*
		Robert Bage	*Mount Henneth*
		Robert Bage	*Barham Downs*
		Robert Bage	*James Wallace*
		Richard Cumberland	*Henry*
10	1824	Ann Radcliffe	*Sicilian Romance*
		Ann Radcliffe	*Romance of the Forest*
		Ann Radcliffe	*Mysteries of Udolpho*
		Ann Radcliffe	*The Italian*
		Ann Radcliffe	*Castles of Athlin & Dunbayne*

Appendix 4: Contents of *The British Novelists*, ed. Anna Laetitia Barbauld (1810)

Volume(s)	*Author*	*Title*	*Original date of publication*	*Length of Barbauld's preface (pages)*
1–8	Samuel Richardson	*Clarissa*	1748	66
9–15	Samuel Richardson	*Sir Charles Grandison*	1753	
16–17	Daniel Defoe	*Robinson Crusoe*	1719	8
18	Henry Fielding	*Joseph Andrews*	1742	32
18–21	Henry Fielding	*Tom Jones*	1749	
22	Clara Reeve	*The Old English Baron*	1777	3
22	Horace Walpole	*The Castle of Otranto*	1764	3
23	Samuel Coventry	*Pompey the Little*	1751	no preface
23	Oliver Goldsmith	*The Vicar of Wakefield*	1766	12
24–25	Charlotte Lennox	*The Female Quixote*	1752	4
26	Samuel Johnson	*Rasselas*	1759	8
26	John Hawkesworth	*Almoran and Hamet*	1761	2
27	Frances Brooke	*Lady Julia Mandeville*	1763	2
27	Elizabeth Inchbald	*Nature and Art*	1796	4

28	Elizabeth Inchbald	*A Simple Story*	1791	
29	Henry Mackenzie	*The Man of Feeling*	1771	3
29	Henry Mackenzie	*Julia de Roubigné; A Tale*	1777	
30–31	Tobias Smollett	*Humphry Clinker*	1771	18
32–33	Richard Graves	*The Spiritual Quixote*	1773	no preface
34–35	John Moore	*Zeluco*	1789	7
36–37	Charlotte Smith	*The Old Manor House*	1793	8
38–39	Frances Burney	*Evelina*	1778	11
40–42	Frances Burney	*Cecilia*	1782	
43–44	Ann Radcliffe	*The Romance of the Forest*	1791	8
45–47	Ann Radcliffe	*The Mysteries of Udolpho*	1794	
48	Robert Bage	*Hermsprong*	1796	3
49–50	Maria Edgeworth	*Belinda*	1801	1
50	Maria Edgeworth	*The Modern Griselda*	1805	

Notes

1 John Dunlop, *The History of Fiction* (London: Longman, Hurst, Rees, Orme, and Brown, 1814), Vol. 1, pp. v–vi.

2 Quoted in Mark Rose, *Authors and Owners: The Invention of Copyright* (Cambridge, MA: Harvard University Press, 1993), p. 93.

3 A 10 February 2003 *New York Times* article asserted that reprinting English classics was arguably the most aggressive corner of the twenty-first-century book trade: 'The stiffest competition in the book business may be among the publishers staking claim to Dickens and Austen'. Bill Goldstein, 'Publishers Give Classics a Makeover', *The New York Times* (10 February 2003), sec. A, p. 9, col. 1.

4 Trevor Ross, *The Making of the English Literary Canon: From the Middle Ages to the Late Eighteenth Century* (Montreal: McGill-Queen's University Press, 1998), p. 247. See also Terry Eagleton, *The Function of Criticism: From the Spectator to Post-Structuralism* (London: Verso, 1996), pp. 34–35; John Guillory, *Cultural Capital* (Chicago: University of Chicago Press, 1993), p. 33.

5 See Lawrence Lipking, *The Ordering of the Arts in Eighteenth-Century England* (Princeton: Princeton University Press, 1970), quoted in Ross, *Making*, p. 247.

6 Ross, *Making*, p. 5. Ross represents his own project as one of demonstrating that an earlier 'version of canon-formation, one largely non-institutional and hence unfamiliar to us now, informed the production and reception of English literature well before the eighteenth century. My aim is to provide a sense of this earlier version of canon-formation and to trace its history and eventual displacement in early modernity'.

7 Samuel Croxall, Preface to *A Select Collection of Novels* (1720), Vol. 1, pp. iv–v.

8 The Clark Library in Los Angeles owns the only full set of *Modern Novels*. Several other archives, from Carlisle Cathedral to the British and Huntington libraries,

contain individual copies, some of which correspond in their contents to the Clark copy. Others, such as the Huntington copy of Volume 11, present corresponding though expanded contents, the extra novels contained intermixed with those comprising the Clark volumes rather than simply appended.

9 Croxall, *Select Collection*, Vol. 5, pp. i–ii.

10 Croxall, *Select Collection*, Vol. 1, pp. i–ii.

11 Leah Price, *The Anthology and the Rise of the Novel: From Richardson to George Eliot* (Cambridge: Cambridge University Press, 2000), p. 7.

12 Price, *Anthology and the Rise of the Novel*, p. 5.

13 Susan Stewart, *On Longing: Narratives of the Miniature, the Gigantic, the Souvenir, the Collection* (Durham, NC: Duke University Press, 1993), pp. 151–53.

14 Stewart, *On Longing*, p. 152.

15 Regarding the question of whether there existed a public domain for books before 1774, see William St Clair, *The Reading Nation in the Romantic Period* (New York and Cambridge: Cambridge University Press, 2004), pp. 52, 132n. St Clair argues convincingly that in England there effectively was no public domain before 1774 – i.e., that the practices of London booksellers insured that even dormant titles were owned if they had ever been printed. While my own essay was originally written before the publication of *The Reading Nation in the Romantic Period* (2004), it has benefited considerably from St Clair's comments and suggestions.

16 Dodley's Advertisement of 14 January 1744 announced publication at '[the] beginning of next month'. See *The Eighteenth Century*, reel 9720, no. 12.

17 The only exception is the explosion of songbooks published, beginning with *The Goldfinch; Being a Select Collection of the Most Celebrated English Songs* (London: R. Baldwin), 1748. See Works Cited.

18 *A Select Collection of Old Plays*, 12 vols. (London: R. Dodsley, 1744), Vol. 1, n.p.; Vol. 1, p. xl.

19 Dodsley, *Select Collection of Old Plays*, Vol. 1, pp. i–ii; Vol. 1, pp. xxxvi–xxxvii. What intervenes between the first and second parts of the quotation is an introductory essay on the origins of European theatre.

20 Dodsley, *Select Collection of Old Plays*, Vol. 1, p. i.

21 Jean Baudrillard, 'The System of Collecting', in John Elner and Roger Cardinal, eds., *The Cultures of Collecting* (London: Reaktion Books, 1994), p. 12.

22 Stewart, *On Longing*, p. 159.

23 *The Gazetteer and New Daily Advertiser* (2 March 1780), no. 15,929, p. 1.

24 Joseph Ritson, *A Select Collection of English Songs*, 3 vols. (London: J. Johnson, 1783), Vol. 1, pp. i–ii.

25 Ritson, *Select Collection*, Vol. 1, pp. xiii–xiv.

26 Ritson, *Select Collection*, Vol. 1, pp. ix–x.

27 See Stanley Morison, *John Bell, 1745–1831* (Cambridge: Cambridge University Press, 1930). Bell's own Prospectus took pains to assure customers that British authors would receive their pictoral, editorial, and critical due: 'AT the end of the year will be printed one Volume, consisting of an INDEX of the CHARACTERS, SENTIMENTS, SIMILIES, SPEECHES, and DESCRIPTIONS contained in the preceding Volumes of the BRITISH THEATRE. – And, in the course of the Work will be published another Volume, containing the LIVES of the DIFFERENT

AUTHORS whose works compose this publication, with a PORTRAIT of each, finely engraved, from pictures of the best authority; including also, an HISTOR-ICAL ACCOUNT of the RISE and PROGRESS of the ENGLISH STAGE, from its earliest beginning to the present time'; John Bell, 'To the Public', Prospectus for *Bell's British Theatre* (London: John Bell, 1774), Vol. 1, pp. 2–3.

28 While competing newspapers usually employed two or three kinds of type for their advertisements – usually one font in two sizes and italics – Bell frequently employed two and three times that number (Morison, *John Bell*, p. 10).

29 Advertisement, *The World*, 5 January 1787; John Bell, 'To the Public', p. 3.

30 Advertisement, *The World*, 5 January 1787.

31 Advertisement, *Morning Chronicle*, 22 January 1780.

32 Walter Scott, *The Letters of Sir Walter Scott*, ed. H. J. C. Grierson, 12 vols. (London: Constable, 1932), Vol. 7, pp. 124–25.

33 Mrs Griffith's *Collection of Novels* contains Segrais' *Zayde* and its *Sequel*, Behn's *Oroonoko*, *The Princess of Cleves*, Haywood's *The Fruitless Enquiry*, Behn's *Agnes de Castro*, and Aubin's *The Noble Slaves*.

34 'A Pleasing Publication', Advertisement for *The Novelist's Magazine* (London: Harrison, 1779), British Library call number 823c.1, p. 1.

35 'A Pleasing Publication', p. 2.

36 'A Pleasing Publication', p. 2.

37 This situation, however, may soon change thanks to Eleanor Shevlin, who has begun to present but not to publish her primary work on Harrison.

38 Richard C. Taylor, 'James Harrison, *The Novelist's Magazine*, and the Early Canon-izing of the English Novel', *Studies in English Literature 1500–1900* 33 (1993), p. 637.

39 James Raven, *The British Novel 1750–1770: A Chronological Checklist of Prose Fiction Printed in Britain and Ireland* (Newark: University of Delaware Press, 1987), p. 14; P.D. Garside, 'Walter Scott and the "Common" Novel, 1808–1819', *Cardiff Corvey: Reading the Romantic Text* 3 (1999), available at http://www.cf.ac.uk/encap/corvey/articles/cc03–n02.html (last accessed 25 June 2008).

40 Advertisement for *Sir Charles Grandison* for *The Novelist's Magazine* (London: Harrison, 1783), p. 1.

41 *The New Novelist's Magazine*, 2 vols. (London: Harrison, 1786–87), Vol. 1, p. 1.

42 Scott, *Letters*, Vol. 2, p. 114.

43 Scott, *Letters*, Vol. 2, p. 120.

44 Samuel Smiles, *A Publisher and his Friends: Memoir and Correspondence of the Late John Murray, with an account of the origin and progress of the house, 1768–1843*, 2 vols. (London and New York: John Murray and Charles Scribner's Sons, 1891), Vol. 2, p. 88.

45 Scott, *Letters*, Vol. 2, p. 119.

46 *London Chronicle*, 2–4 November 1780; quoted in Taylor, 'Early Canonizing of the English Novel', p. 635.

47 Thomas Constable, *Archibald Constable and his Literary Correspondents*, 3 vols. (Edin-burgh: Edmonston & Douglas, 1873), Vol. 1, pp. 198–99. Scott's assertion about 'order' comes not from a mistake in chronology, but rather from the fact that he and Ballantyne had already printed Fielding and Smollett for *Ballantyne's Novelist's Library*. The passage quoted comes from a letter Scott wrote to Archibald Constable; with the *Ballantyne's* series faltering after James Ballantyne's death in

1821, Scott and Constable attempted to negotiate a reconceived collection whose formatting more closely resembled Barbauld's *The British Novelists* (1810; 2nd edn 1820).

48 From its contents – none of which appear in Barbauld's *The British Novelists* – it appears that *Popular Romances* took on its final form only after the publication of Barbauld's collection caused Scott to abandon his own project. For a contrasting interpretation comparing Scott's and Harrison's choice of texts, see Taylor, 'Early Canonizing of the English Novel', p. 637.

49 Scott, *Letters*, Vol. 7, p. 15n.

50 Scott, *Letters*, Vol. 2, p. 119.

51 *The British Novelists*, ed. Anna Laetitia Barbauld, 50 vols. (London: F. C. and J. Rivington and others, 1810), Vol. 1, p. 1.

52 Claudia Johnson, "'Let Me Make the Novels of a Country'": Barbauld's *The British Novelists* (1810/1820)', *Novel: A Forum on Fiction* 34 (2001), p. 163.

53 Barbauld, ed., *The British Novelists*, Vol. 1, pp. 1–2.

54 Barbauld, ed., *The British Novelists*, Vol. 1, pp. 2–3.

55 Barbauld, ed., *The British Novelists*, Vol. 1, pp. 37–38.

56 Johnson, "'Novels of a Country'", p. 169.

57 I provide data on Barbauld's *The British Novelists* and other select collections in the appendices to this essay.

58 Barbauld, ed., *The British Novelists*, Vol. 1, p. 59.

59 Its publication is announced in the April 1814 *Critical Review*, Vol. 5, p. 557. *Waverley* was published that August.

60 Garside, 'Walter Scott and the "Common" Novel'.

61 For readings of *The Ballantyne Novelist's Library* as itself a corrective to earlier collections of novels, see Johnson, "'Novels of a Country'", pp. 173–75; Taylor, 'Early Canonizing of the English Novel', pp. 637–38; and Homer Obed Brown, *Institutions of the English Novel from Defoe to Scott* (Philadelphia: University of Pennsylvania Press, 1997).

62 Barbauld, ed., *The British Novelists*, Vol. 1, pp. 60–61.

63 Among other things, Barbauld expresses reservations about the early gothic fiction of Reeve and Walpole (preferring Reeve), criticizes Hawkesworth's *Almoran and Hamet*, praises William Beckford, William Godwin, and Amelia Opie, and voices a decided preference for Bage's *Man As He Is* over *Hermsprong*.

CHAPTER SEVEN

Austen, Empire and Moral Virtue

SAREE MAKDISI

Much of the recent scholarship on Jane Austen has been gripped by a controversy concerning the relationship between Austen and imperialism, especially in *Mansfield Park*. As the essay by Miranda Burgess in this volume also attests, some critics have worked to retrieve and elaborate the subtle cues that link the quiet, settled order of Austen's domestic setting with the drama of imperial conquest, while others have read the novel as a critique of British imperialism, and Austen herself as a sister and friend to the wretched of the earth. What I want to propose in this essay is that *Mansfield Park*'s engagement with the cultural politics of imperialism is at once less straightforward and more profound than has been suggested so far, but that that engagement can only be elaborated in relation to the novel's treatment of questions seemingly far removed from the blood and sweat of imperial conquest, to which they are, however, inexorably tied. For in *Mansfield Park*, we can see Austen articulating – precisely in connection with Britain's changing national and imperial project – some of the key cultural and political concerns underlying the emergent culture of modernization; above all, the vital new role of moral virtue as the key to the self-regulating subject who would form the core of modern culture, and the new role for women as the ideological guarantors of that moral virtue. In many ways, this makes *Mansfield Park* one of the key texts for understanding the profound cultural, political and psycho-affective transformations that took place all through the Romantic period, and that have continued to play a role in an age of conflict extending into our own time.

What made Austen's novel interesting from the geoaesthetic perspective elaborated by Edward Said in his book *Culture and Imperialism* (whose chapter on *Mansfield Park* ignited the recent controversy) is the way it links together the space of the Bertram slave plantation in Antigua with the domestic estate at Mansfield.[1] Said argues that although the two spaces (domestic and imperial) are structurally essential to each other, representationally they are utterly separate. Some of Said's critics have, however, drawn attention to the novel's expression of moral outrage against the slave trade, and, arguing against Said's reading of *Mansfield Park* as an essentially imperialist novel, they see this moral outrage as an indicator of what they take to be the novel's critique of imperialism.[2] Now, it could be argued that one shortcoming of Said's reading of the novel, to which I will return shortly, is that its privileging of geoaesthetic questions ends up understating the complexity of Austen's interest in empire (which was, I would argue, not simply geoaesthetic in nature). Some of his critics, however, have overcompensated for this shortcoming, and they have done so not simply by overstating the novel's expression of moral outrage but rather by taking it at face value and hence misreading it altogether, conflating slavery and imperialism, and hence treating a critique of the one necessarily as a critique of the other.

Slavery and imperialism have not shared an entirely continuous history, of course, and the late eighteenth and early nineteenth centuries marked a significant divergence between them. Indeed, Austen was working precisely at a moment when it was not just well-meaning novelists and poets who were writing against the slave trade or slavery itself. We have to remember that throughout the period of her novel's publication, the British empire itself was working to jettison slavery and turn towards other, more productive and efficient modes of imperial rule.[3] By the time of *Mansfield Park*'s publication, then, a critique of either the slave trade or slavery as such would not merely have been irrelevant to a critique of imperialism, it would have fitted seamlessly into ongoing efforts to strengthen and revitalize the British empire; that is, efforts to shore up the empire's moral resources and to prepare it for what was at the time an entirely new preoccupation of imperial politics, namely, a civilizing mission against decadence and idleness, against inefficiency, against barbarism, against moral failing and unregulated desire.

Thus, the first point I want to register here is that readings of the novel that take its moral and ethical stance at face value will be unable to engage with its historical and political complexity. The second point, however, essentially the flip-side of the first, is that any investigation of the novel's political and historical complexity, especially its relationship to empire, must take into account its moral and ethical dimension. For in *Mansfield Park*, moral critique serves as the expression of an underlying political stance, precisely because of the politicization of morality and ethics in Jane Austen's lifetime.

It is essential to bear in mind that imperialism really only became a moral issue during the lifetime of Jane Austen. The transition towards a form of imperial domination and the imposition of new and specifically modern institutions, manners, morals, virtues, and ways of life on other cultures – in other words the attempt to bring civilization to supposed barbarism, a process whose bankruptcy would receive perhaps its most scathing damnation in Conrad's *Heart of Darkness* at the other end of the nineteenth century – took place throughout the decades around 1800. (One of the key signs of this transition was the trial of Warren Hastings, who was accused of having been corrupted by the lusts and passions of Oriental despotism, rather than upholding true British values in confrontation with the moral degradations of the East.)

Once it had successfully jettisoned slavery (thanks in no small part to the ferocious resistance put up by slaves themselves, of course), the new British empire would use the moral virtues as the spearhead of new imperial adventures, which lends credence to Blake's furious assertion that 'The Moral Virtues are continual Accusers of Sin & promote Eternal Wars & Domineering over others'.[4] For it was precisely in the name of the moral virtues that Austen's novel celebrates in Fanny Price that the British empire would ransack the world, at home as well as overseas, looking for the sources of 'barbarism' in order to extirpate them, crush them, stamp and burn them out and replace them with sober, productive, efficient – and above all respectably proper – prosperity. We see precisely this moral crusading at work when Sir Thomas goes through his estate after his return from Antigua, organizing, computing, calculating, and moralizing, burning every copy of the play *Lovers' Vows* that he could find and erasing every trace of the aborted performance staged by his children and their friends.

Ironically, then, morality and moralism were hardly weapons to be used against empire but instead themselves defined the sharpest cutting edge of the new imperialism that was emerging in Austen's time. At the same time, morality – or, more precisely, a certain conception of moral virtue – was also, however, essential to an emergent understanding of subjectivity that was simultaneously taking on new significance as the cornerstone of a new and properly modern cultural, political and psycho-affective order. As I have argued in other contexts, this new conception of subjectivity was inseparable from the new understanding of Britain's national and imperial destiny. Moral virtue, then, offers the key to understanding both Romantic subjectivity and Romantic imperialism, and, indeed, the seamless discursive, conceptual and material continuities between them. What all this raises in turn, then, is the all-important question of how morality and the cultural politics of subjectivity itself would come to serve the needs of a growing empire.

Austen's novel anticipates the new role of the British empire as a machine for the production of a new form of subjectivity, one appropriate to its needs both at home and abroad, needs that cannot be understood simply in terms of national interest and national identity, let alone geopolitical organization. In this sense, what is perhaps most remarkable about the novel's treatment of imperialism is that it demonstrates the extent to which a certain disciplinary logic, namely, the logic animating the self-regulating modern subject, must operate seamlessly *across* the empire's domain, unifying rather than separating domestic and imperial space. In the project to replace the outmoded logic of slavery (in other words, discipline enforced by external brutality) with a disciplinary regime based on self-regulation – a far more efficient mode of governmentality – the subject would become one of the key sites for the intensification of imperial activity. For if the logic of slavery would be abandoned because it could be replaced by a much more effective form of control and exploitation – one in which the exercise of self-regulating moral virtue would be a central constituent feature – that new form of control and exploitation was one that would necessarily be centred on the individual self-regulating subject. In other words, what was at stake in the new imperialism was not merely the subjectivity of the slave but the subjectivity of the master, and perhaps above all the subjectivity of the mistress herself.

My claim here, then, is essentially the opposite of the one proposed by Katie Trumpener in her reading of Austen in *Bardic Nationalism*. For rather than tracing what Trumpener calls the 'long reach of the plantation system into the heart of England',[5] I argue that *Mansfield Park* traces the development of an entirely new form of imperialism, reaching out from the empire's heart to tie masters and slaves, colonizers and colonized, all the more thoroughly – however unequally and brutally – together, not just geopolitically but in terms of a narrowly and instrumentally understood conception of self-regulating subjectivity. In this sense, however, what I am suggesting is also quite different from the argument put forward by Said; for if *Mansfield Park* is an imperialist novel – which I believe it to be – its imperialism is one that is comprehensive and indeed potentially universal, rather than being geopolitically restricted to distant settlements

beyond the scope of narrative and representation. In fact I would say that
what we are dealing with in *Mansfield Park* is the articulation *avant la lettre*
of a kind of imperialism whose intensities exceed the actually existing geot-
emporal scale of empire itself.

In order to assess the ways in which Austen's novel integrates, rather
than separates, the imperial and the domestic, consider, for example, the
way in which Sir Thomas's return to Mansfield Park following his stay in
Antigua is staged, in grossly and hence rather satirically exaggerated terms,
as something of an imperial counter-insurgency – or search-and-destroy –
operation. For during Sir Thomas's absence from Mansfield, things had
clearly got out of hand. When he returns, he restores order to the estate's
material well-being ('He had to reinstate himself in all the wonted concerns
of his Mansfield life, to see his steward and his bailiff – to examine and
compute – and, in the intervals of business, to walk into his stables and his
gardens, and nearest plantations'[6]). But above all he restores the estate's
moral well-being, especially in the wake of the abortive attempt to perform
the scandalous play *Lovers' Vows*. The narrator of *Mansfield Park* tells us that
the preparations for the play, by allowing a certain degree of moral loose-
ness, had threatened the material well-being of the estate, which Sir
Thomas also has to put to order upon his return ('The scene painter was
gone, having spoilt only the floor of one room, ruined all the coachman's
sponges, and made five of the under-servants idle and dissatisfied; and Sir
Thomas was in hopes that another day or two would suffise to wipe away
every outward memento of what had been, even to the destruction of every
unbound copy of "Lovers' Vows" in the house, for he was burning all that
met his eye'[7]). Sir Thomas's return then precipitates a series of crises, the
end result of which is that all those bad, undisciplined, unproductive,
wasteful, frivolous, inappropriate, indulgent, pleasure-seeking, degenerate
characters, associated with the *Lovers' Vows* performance – the unfortunate
Maria and Julia as well as the Crawfords and the aiding and abetting Aunt
Norris – are essentially purged, leaving us with a much happier Sir Thomas,
his wife, and their still recovering (and hence somewhat negligible) eldest
son, and, of course, an ultimately happily married Fanny and Edmund.

Thus the key feature of the novel's ending is that the moderate, sober,
disciplined, and relentlessly proper Fanny and Edmund now dominate the
representational space of Mansfield Park, though – crucially – they don't
actually own the estate itself, and indeed on the contrary find themselves
happily squeezed into the confines of Thornton Lacey. For the master of
the property in England as well as in Antigua – that is, Sir Thomas – the

story's denouement offers a lesson in something far more profound than mere property management. By the end of the novel, he learns, and we presumably learn with him, that moral and material well-being are inseparable. In other words, the real lesson that Sir Thomas learns is that self-discipline counts far more than a mere show of obedience to an overlord, such as Sir Thomas had demanded, and received, both from his slaves and from his children. For, at the end of the novel, 'Sir Thomas, poor Sir Thomas, a parent, and conscious of errors in his own conduct as a parent', recognizes his earlier

> grievous mismanagement; but, bad as it was, he gradually grew to feel that it had not been the most direful mistake in his plan of education. Some thing must have been wanting *within*, or time would have worn away much of its ill effect. He feared that principle, active principle, had been wanting, that they had never been properly taught to govern their inclinations and tempers, by that sense of duty which can alone suffice. They had been instructed theoretically in their religion, but never required to bring it into daily practice [...]. He had meant them to be good, but his cares had been directed to the understanding and manners, not the disposition; and of the necessity of self-denial and humility, he feared they had never heard from any lips that could profit them.
>
> Bitterly did he deplore a deficiency which now he could scarcely comprehend to have been possible.[8]

What was 'wanting within' the four Bertram children, then, is the very sense of principle and moral virtue that Edmund only learns by the end of the novel (from Fanny) – but that Fanny, 'my Fanny', as the narrator calls her, of course, had known all along. For it is precisely on the basis of her principles, which she – unlike Maria, Julia, and Tom – had learned from an early age because she received such strict disciplinary treatment at Mansfield, that Fanny learns to govern her inclination and temper, 'by that sense of duty which can alone suffice'. It is, in other words, precisely thanks to her strict governance that Fanny learns 'the necessity of self-denial and humility', and all of the other principles which are so lacking in Crawford, because of which she rejects him. For Fanny sees right away that all these good, moral virtues are lacking in him. Sir Thomas is angered at Fanny's rejection of Crawford only because he (Sir Thomas) had been deceived and was not as aware of Crawford's moral failings as Fanny had been all along: otherwise, he would surely have agreed with her judgement of him (as in fact he does in the end, almost, but not quite, too late). Clearly, if Fanny is such an admirable character in the novel's terms (even though, as Marilyn

Butler argues, as a flatly one-dimensional character she also represents the weakest moment of Austen's novel from a technical and aesthetic point of view[9]), it is because she, unlike the others, learns to internalize self-regulatory discipline; for which, presumably, she can be thankful for her harsh treatment at the hands of Aunt Norris. Far from a critique of authority, far from a celebration of human freedom and women's liberation, what the final pages of Austen's novel yield to is a celebration of the virtues of discipline and moral virtue generally: hard work, self-denial, and above all the internalization (that is, the rendering far more efficient) of the policing mechanisms which for the other children had been merely external signs and hence not really taken seriously. For it turns out that the real enemies here are indulgence, pleasure, luxury, excess, idleness, and the host of quasi-Oriental corruptions that they give rise to; whereas the principles vindicated by the end of *Mansfield Park* are sobriety, self-discipline, self-denial, frugality, composure, etc., which Sir Thomas so happily acknowledges in Fanny, and which enable her living happily ever after with an appropriately reformed Edmund. Of course, part of the point here is that Sir Thomas learns this lesson a little too late for the benefit of his children; thus what the novel narrates is the passing of the torch of moral virtue to the next generation, to Fanny and Edmund.

Indeed, the union of Fanny and Edmund expresses the affirmation of a new form of marriage, a new form of family, or, as Clara Tuite puts it, 'the tight and reluctant squeeze of the aristocratic family [...] into the smaller, narrower space [...] of the bourgeois-identified nuclear family'.[10] Hence, according to Tuite, *Mansfield Park* narrates not so much the qualified rise of the bourgeoisie as its compression into the 'confines of the bourgeois ideology of domesticity'.[11] And this emergent ideology of domesticity centred on the affirmation of a new role for women in a domestic sphere which, as Linda Colley demonstrates, was paradoxically understood to be separate from the sphere of politics, nation, and empire and yet at the same time absolutely essential to its survival and prosperity.[12] It falls, of course, to Fanny – rather than to any of the dissipated and indulgent Bertram women – to play this new role called for by the emergent ideology of what Colley calls 'womanpower'. For Fanny sees, long before the narrator explicitly admits it to us, that Crawford was 'ruined by early independence and bad domestic example', that he 'indulged in the freaks of a cold-blooded vanity a little too long'.[13]

The emphasis of the novel's end, then, is not so much on Sir Thomas's contrition as it is on the positive role that Fanny plays in securing the happy ending. As Clara Tuite argues, the 'domestic improvements' that Mansfield undergoes are specifically middle-class and feminine-gendered and are effected 'by the specifically feminine-gendered agency of Fanny Price'.[14] Maaja Stewart points out that by the end of the novel the drooping and sentimental Fanny has replaced the dazzling, witty, and independent-minded Mary Crawford, in a process that Stewart says itself 'involves a redefinition of "feminine" character and a radical increase of male authority',[15] whose institutions (e.g., the church, the Royal Navy) Mary Crawford refuses to idolize and even makes fun of, whereas Fanny reveres them through her love for Edmund and her brother William, that shining young servant of Britain's imperial power who is perhaps the novel's most consistently charming character. But by the end, as Stewart says, Fanny has also replaced the daughters of the house 'as the one who will sustain the Mansfield values into the next generation'. Again I think Marilyn Butler is right to argue that it is when the novel is bluntest in the expression of ideological commitments – as in the ending – that it is least interesting in aesthetic terms; for by the end Fanny ceases to be a genuinely believable character and becomes more a flattened-out marker of an ideological position.[16]

Although I agree with Stewart that 'class formation in *Mansfield Park* occurs at the expense of kinship relations',[17] it is important to bear in mind here that the class whose formation we witness in these pages, in which merit is privileged over inheritance, in which discipline and self-denial are privileged over idleness and luxury, and in which hard work is privileged over privilege itself, is properly bourgeois in nature, replacing at once the values of the slave-plantation and of the landed gentry with the values of a new class and a new way of life – that is, a new form of exploitation – in whose reproduction and regulation women would play a central ideological role, and in which, as Gary Kelley has argued, 'a certain figure of "woman" was constructed to represent a professional middle-class discourse of subjectivity'.[18] Thus by the time of the novel's ending the values of bourgeois – rather than aristocratic – marriage have been affirmed, as critics including Tuite, Butler and others have demonstrated, even if as a result of the compression of the former aristocracy into a new role, rather than as a result of the autochthonous emergence of a fully fledged bourgeoisie.

This is surely the first of the links between Mansfield itself and the estate in Antigua, and indeed the whole question of empire. Said argues that 'what assures the domestic tranquility and attractive harmony of one is the productivity and regulated discipline of the other'.[19] But the problem with this reading is that in *both* cases, at home and abroad, tranquillity and discipline are shown to be essential, and in this sense the imperial pressure in the novel is far more extreme than it is revealed to be in such an account. Yes, this is a novel saturated with the discourse of empire, not only in the ways that Said discusses, and in the presence of goods and property derived from unequal exchange, and in the perpetual celebration of Fanny's brother William, his promotion and successful career in the armed services of the British Empire, but also in a few other things – Fanny's own obsession with the colonial estate in Antigua and the fact that at one point we discover her reading Lord Macartney's account of his 1793 colonial expedition to China. Of all the characters, Fanny and William are not only the ones rendered in the most positive light: they are also the ones who are most closely aligned with the interests of the new empire and its clean and shiny imperial quest for moral virtue.

One point that I would like to emphasize, then, is that the operations of empire here involve not only the subjugation and exploitation of distant colonial possessions, but *also* the ever more efficient and productive exploitation of property and possessions – people and capital – in the domestic sphere, and more than that the ever more efficient regulation of subjectivity itself. We might even say that the real enemy that is hunted down and destroyed in *Mansfield Park* is pleasure for its own sake, that is, unproductive pleasure. By the time of the novel's ending, we are presented with the triumph of the ideology of duty, self-denial, humility, internalized self-regulating discipline, frugality, and above all the relentless productivity and nourishment of property consummated in the marriage of Fanny and Edmund, whose greatest enemy is pleasure for its own sake, that is, the kind of momentary gratification henceforth taken to be typical of degraded Orientals suffering from all the worst excesses of femininity, effeminacy, licentiousness, ungoverned sexuality and moral corruption, and who are hence all the more in need of the civilizing mission, the weaning and tutelage, that it would fall to a morally virtuous empire to so reluctantly provide.

This in turn leads to the second point I want to emphasize, which is that this new imperial discourse is also intimately concerned with the production and regulation of subjectivity. In fact one of the most remarkable things about this conclusion is that Austen's elaboration of subjectivity is most readily aligned not with a putative conservatism (with which she is often misleadingly identified) but rather with the so-called English

Jacobins of the 1790s. I don't mean to understate the very real differences between Austen and 1790s' radicalism, but on the other hand it is hardly a coincidence that the regulation of subjectivity was an essential component of a dominant strand of radicalism in the 1790s. Most of the English radicals of the 1790s would have been as keen as Jane Austen to distance themselves from the excess and indulgence of the Crawfords or the Bertram children. For most of the radicals of the 1790s – with the notable exception of Blake – individual self-control was the key to Liberty.[20] We can be free, they argued, only when we are free to exercise control over ourselves, rather than having that control imposed on us by a tyrannical government. 'Let us exert over our own hearts a virtuous despotism,' the radical Coleridge writes, 'and lead our own Passions in triumph, and then we shall want neither Monarch nor General'.[21]

In fact, it is in a radical position like Coleridge's that we can best see the link between the discourse of subjectivity and the discourse of governmentality in a broader sense in the years around 1800. For Coleridge, the self-regulation offered by what he calls Liberty is not an antidote to despotism; it is, on the contrary, an extension and intensification of the logic of despotism, through its internalization. Liberty, or at least this kind of liberty – the liberty of the self-regulating subject – represents, in other words, not the opposite of despotism, but rather its purification, rendering it morally virtuous (hence 'virtuous despotism'). Despotism becomes virtuous, then, when it becomes self-regulating, rather than externally imposed; just as the empire becomes virtuous when it moves from the logic of whips and chains to the logic of self-regulated good behaviour. The key to such good behaviour is of course a proper education, and Austen's interest in education, and particularly the education of women, provides another link to 1790s' radicalism, for which this was a major concern. Various critics have, for example, pointed out the centrality of the abortive *Lovers' Vows* performance in *Mansfield Park*, which ties Austen's novel to Elizabeth Inchbald's adaptation of one of those sickly and stupid German tragedies derided by Wordsworth. Even more interesting, however, is *Mansfield Park*'s relationship to Inchbald's 1791 novel *A Simple Story*. Paula Byrne argues that what Austen offers in effect is a kind of rewriting of both *Lovers' Vows* and *A Simple Story*, in both of which we see a charming, but dangerously mis-educated, coquette fall in love with an erstwhile clergyman. Byrne suggests that that theme is replayed in *Mansfield Park* with the transition from the abortive Mary Crawford/Edmund relationship – interestingly played out through their roles in the *Lovers'*

Vows performance – to the Fanny/Edmund relationship.[22] With the failure of the former and the successful consummation of the latter, it is no longer the witty and dangerous coquette who wins the clergyman's heart but rather the morally virtuous (though admittedly somewhat boring) woman, who has her stern education to thank for her moral propriety, and, ultimately, her material prosperity. A similar move happens in Inchbald's *Simple Story*, where the operative contrast is between the flighty and ill-educated, but nevertheless attractive, Miss Milner, whose life ends in failure (following her husband's voyage to tend to *his* West Indian estate), and her daughter Matilda, who, thanks to her harsh upbringing at her tutor's hands, learns to regulate her subjectivity appropriately, and who, after a difficult period of alienation from her moody and tyrannical father, ends up succeeding in life and romance (with her self-regulated and submissive male equivalent, Rushbrook), thanks, in the novel's famous last line, to a 'proper education'.[23]

What goes for 'education' here, as in much of the 1790s, has little to do with pedagogical content and much to do with form; for here education means learning – as we are reminded by the subtitle of Mary Wollstonecraft's *Original Stories from Real Life*, a children's training manual – how to 'regulate the affections and form the mind to truth and goodness'.[24] Matilda and Rushbrook – a figure of the kind of submissive masculinity that would later drive Nietzsche over the edge – are so successful at learning how to regulate themselves that the tyrannical Lord Elmwood revokes many of the rules he has devised to keep them in check; as Eleanor Ty points out, 'Matilda and Rushbrook have so thoroughly internalized the Law of the Father that they will police themselves'.[25] For with such self-regulating virtuous despotism in place, there is no longer any need for an external despotism; though Ty also points out that in her novel Inchbald kills off the vital threat to patriarchal power represented by the vivacious Miss Milner just in case. It is interesting, in fact, to note that Mary Wollstonecraft, who reviewed *A Simple Story*, wrote approvingly of the novel's lessons for 'thoughtless and unprincipled minds', but lamented that Mrs Inchbald did not reinforce it by even more sharply contrasting the 'vain, giddy miss Milner' and Matilda, who, 'educated in adversity', should 'have learned (to prove that a cultivated mind is a real advantage) how to bear, nay, rise above her misfortunes'.[26] After all, for Wollstonecraft as much as for Coleridge, the key to success in life is the kind of self-regulation that we see perfected in the characters of Matilda and Rushbrook – which would resurface in Fanny Price and Edmund Bertram.

For most of the radicals of the 1790s (and again Blake is a notable exception), such self-restraint is the main feature differentiating modern culture from the barbarous excesses of European aristocrats and Oriental despots.[27] Saturated to its very core with Orientalist discourse, in fact, 1790s' radicalism consistently deployed the image of the Orient as the ultimate locus of the culture of excess (despotic, enthusiastic, exotic, erotic) that it also identified with the aristocratic European regimes whose legitimacy it had set out to challenge. This Orientalism cut both ways, however; for if, on the one hand, the Orient could serve as an imaginary representation of all the bad features of the *ancien régime* (despotism, patronage, ritual, corruption) that the radicals sought to overturn, it could also serve – and indeed it did – as a very real sphere for European intervention and modernization. It is, in other words, hardly a coincidence that Volney's *Ruins; OR Meditation on the revolutions of empire* served as one of the key texts for both Romantic radicalism and European imperialism, beginning with Napoleon, who carried Volney's works with him to Egypt as handbooks for imperial conquest.[28] Decades later, in Egypt, in India, in Palestine, in Arabia, Cromer, Balfour, and Lawrence would justify their own imperialism in terms of bringing order and systematization to the East – an argument that has its origins in Romantic-period radicalism and its zeal for self-regulation. For, after all, the proclaimed mission of European imperialism was precisely to teach non-Europeans how to regulate themselves. 'You may look through the whole history of the Orientals in what is called, broadly speaking, the East,' wrote Lord Balfour (author of the notorious 1917 declaration that carries his name), 'and you never find traces of self-government. [...] [C]conqueror has succeeded conqueror; one domination has followed another; but never in all the revolutions of fate and fortune have you seen one of those nations of its own motion establish what we, from a Western point of view, call self-government'.[29] Balfour's point, however, is that Orientals are incapable of self-government at the collective or the national level exactly because they are incapable of self-government at an individual level, at the level of the subject.

If it was a zeal for self-regulation that would align the interests of 1790s' radicalism with the new imperial project that began to emerge in the Romantic period, it can hardly be a coincidence that it was precisely in its relationship to self-regulation that the logic of virtuous despotism here articulated by the 1790s' radicals would be seized on by the advocates of British imperialism early in the nineteenth century. I have already suggested that *Mansfield Park* anticipates the new role of the British empire as a machine for the production of a new form of subjectivity. Lest we forget how essential the question of subjectivity would become to British imperialism in the nineteenth century, it is worth recalling Macaulay's dictum that, in view of the practical difficulty of ruling hundreds of millions of Indians with a relatively small number of colonial administrators, 'We must at present do our best to form a class who may be interpreters between us and the millions whom we govern; a class of persons, Indian in blood and colour, but English in taste, in opinions, in morals, and in intellect'.[30] It is no coincidence that Macaulay's articulation of a new imperial mission in the *Minute on Indian Education* took place exactly when slavery itself (and not merely the slave trade) was finally being abolished throughout the British empire, that is, in the mid-1830s. Clearly, in the new empire only just coming into being as slavery was finally being done away with, imperial power would operate not merely on the battlefield and on the high seas; its most important zone of operations would be the newly discovered terrain of morals, manners, and intellect, that is, in the manufacture and regulation of individual subjectivities (whose traumas and neuroses Frantz Fanon would so clearly document in *Black Skin, White Masks*[31]). And in thus announcing the centrality of the question of subjectivity to the new imperial mission, Macaulay was drawing on the logic of Paine, Wollstonecraft, Coleridge and Volney, and the other radicals of the 1790s for whom self-regulation was of such profound importance. It is in Macaulay then that we see the extent to which not only morally virtuous abolitionism but moral virtue itself in the years around 1800 laid the foundations for a new kind of empire which would now begin its extraordinary expansion, by the end of which it would control a quarter of the globe. (I am not saying that the abolition of slavery necessarily led to the intensification of empire; I am merely saying that the form that abolitionism took in alliance with moral virtue contributed to this outcome. There were of course far more radical articulations of the cause of freedom, but they were pushed to the margins.)

Mansfield Park, published in 1814, is situated exactly half-way between the radical discourse of subjectivity in the 1790s and the new imperial discourse of the 1830s. It came to light at a moment in which the prerogative of imperialism – the torch of the imperial mission – was passing in fact from what had been a radical position in favour of progress, efficiency and the moral virtue of the self-regulating subject to an entirely new brand of colonial administrators. We can trace this transmission in the work of various radicals, in the networks linking together old 1790s' activists such as Francis Place with the new voices of Thomas Malthus, James Mill and Thomas Macaulay. We can also trace it in terms of the evolution of a new-found role for women as the guarantors of social order. Linda Colley's point is that the consolidation of a 'separate spheres' ideology actually (though to us it may seem contradictory) implied a major role for women in the nation, as the centralizing source of domestic virtue. On the uses to which women put their influence, according to Hannah More, 'will depend, in no low degree, the well-being' of the state, 'nay perhaps the very existence of [...] Society' itself.[32] According to Colley, 'this (to us) contra-dictory set of arguments, an insistence that women must stay within the private sphere, while at the same time exerting moral influence outside it, dominated though it did not exhaust discussion of female rights in Great Britain in the first half of the nineteenth century'.[33] Moreover, as Moira Ferguson points out, while 'the historical intersection of a feminist impulse with anti-slavery agitation helped secure white British women's political self-empowerment', it did so at the expense of race relations, so that, as Ferguson argues, 'anti-slavery colonial discourse [...] played a significant role in generating and consolidating nineteenth-century British imperialist and "domestic-racist" ideology'.[34] In fact, the development of early English feminism, as Deirdre Coleman has cautioned, at times anticipated and at times replicated some of the central axioms of a new imperialist ideology.[35]

Given all the new cultural, ideological and political work being expressed in the pages of Austen's novel, it would therefore be misleading to identify *Mansfield Park*, or Austen herself, with something called 'conser-vatism', especially with regard to its position on empire. For on the question of empire we see an older form of conservatism (namely, Burke's) dropping away, to be replaced by a remarkable political and intellectual convergence in which it is virtually impossible to distinguish putatively conservative from would-be radical voices. In the early nineteenth century, then, the mission of empire would become almost universal as the discourse of self-regulating moral virtue took hold in Britain. Even later on in the century, the voices of dissent – for example, the organized women's movement, the trades union movement – explicitly shared in the imperialist vision in their bid for respectability and centrality, a role in the consensus constitutive of the culture of modernization as we have come to understand it.

There were of course dissenting voices amidst all this happy consensus, voices calling for the creation of an alternative modernity based on sharing, cooperation and being in common, an alternative modernity that has never really (or has not yet) had a chance. But to hear these voices we have to turn away from those cultural forms and political struggles which have by now attained a certain degree of respectability; we have to turn to a long tradition that resisted all forms of exploitation and inequality.[36] Here I am thinking of the long line of anti-colonialist and anti-capitalist writing and agitation, going back through the eighteenth century to at least the seventeenth century, and in which women such as Anne Hutchinson, Catherine Despard, and Elizabeth Campbell played a crucial role in articulating the voices of those disenfranchised and marginalized by the very same global system of production and exchange that is celebrated in *Mansfield Park*.

Notes

1   Edward Said, *Culture and Imperialism* (New York: Knopf, 1993), pp. 80–97.
2   See, in particular, Susan Fraiman, 'Jane Austen and Edward Said: Gender, Culture and Imperialism', in Deidre Lynch, ed., *Janeites: Austen's Disciples and Devotees* (Princeton: Princeton University Press, 2000), pp. 206–24; and Katie Trumpener, *Bardic Nationalism: The Romantic Novel and the British Empire* (Princeton: Princeton University Press, 1997), esp. pp. 161–92.
3   One of the classic works on this subject remains C. L. R. James, *The Black Jacobins* (New York: Vintage, 1989). Also see Robin Blackburn, *The Overthrow of Colonial Slavery, 1776–1848* (London: Verso, 1989); and Eric Williams, *Capitalism and Slavery* (Chapel Hill: University of North Carolina Press, 1994).
4   Blake, annotations to Berkeley, in *The Complete Poetry and Prose of William Blake*, ed. David Erdman (New York: Anchor Books, 1988), p. 664.
5   Trumpener, *Bardic Nationalism*, p. 175.
6   Jane Austen, *Mansfield Park*, ed. James Kinsley (Oxford: Oxford University Press, 1980), pp. 171–72.
7   Austen, *Mansfield Park*, p. 172.
8   Austen, *Mansfield Park*, pp. 420–21, 422–23.
9   Marilyn Butler, *Jane Austen and the War of Ideas* (Oxford: Clarendon Press, 1975), pp. 247–49.
10 Clara Tuite, 'Domestic Retrenchment and Imperial Expansion: The Property Plots of *Mansfield Park*', in You-me Park and Rajeswari Sunder Rajan, eds., *The Postcolonial Jane Austen* (London: Routledge, 2000), p. 99.
11 Tuite, 'Domestic Retrenchment', p. 99.
12 See Linda Colley, *Britons: Forging the Nation, 1707–1837* (New Haven: Yale University Press, 1994).
13 Austen, *Mansfield Park*, p. 426.
14 Tuite, 'Domestic Retrenchment', p. 95.
15 Maaja Stewart, *Domestic Realities and Imperial Fictions: Jane Austen's Novels in Eighteenth Century Contexts* (Athens: University of Georgia Press, 1993).

16 See Butler, *Jane Austen and the War of Ideas*.

17 Stewart, *Domestic Realities*, pp. 110, 131.

18 Gary Kelley, *Women, Writing and Revolution* (Oxford: Clarendon Press, 1993), p. 5.

19 Said, *Culture and Imperialism*, p. 85.

20 This is a question I discuss at length in *William Blake and the Impossible History of the 1790s* (Chicago: University of Chicago Press, 2003).

21 Samuel Taylor Coleridge, 'Lectures on Revealed Religion: Lecture 6', in *Collected Works*, ed. Kathleen Coburn and Bart Winer (Princeton: Princeton University Press, 1969), Vol. 2, p. 229.

22 Paula Byrne, 'A Simple Story: From Inchbald to Austen', *Romanticism* 5.2 (Fall 1999), pp. 161–71.

23 See Elizabeth Inchbald, *A Simple Story*, ed. Anna Lott (Peterborough, Ontario: Broadview Press, 2007).

24 See Mary Wollstonecraft, *Original Stories from Real Life* (London: Joseph Johnson, 1791).

25 Eleanor Ty, *Unsex'd Revolutionaries: Five Women Novelists of the 1790s* (Toronto: University of Toronto Press, 1993), p. 100.

26 See Mary Wollstonecraft, review of *A Simple Story* for the *Analytical Review*, in Inchbald, *A Simple Story*, ed. Anna Lott, p. 381.

27 This is, again, an issue I discuss at much greater length in *William Blake and the Impossible History of the 1790s*.

28 See Said, *Orientalism*, p. 81.

29 Balfour, quoted in Said, *Orientalism*, pp. 32–33.

30 See Thomas Macaulay, *Minute on Indian Education*, in Barbara Harlow and Mia Carter, eds., *Archives of Empire, Vol. 1: From the East India Company to the Suez Canal* (Durham, NC: Duke University Press, 2003), pp. 227–39.

31 See Frantz Fanon, *Black Skin, White Masks*, trans. Constance Farrington (New York: Grove Press, 1994).

32 Hannah More, quoted in Colley, *Britons*, p. 275.

33 Colley, *Britons*, p. 275.

34 Moira Ferguson, *Subject to Others: British Women Writers and Colonial Slavery, 1670–1834* (London: Routledge, 1992), p. 6.

35 See Deirdre Coleman, 'Conspicuous Consumption: White Abolitionism and English Women's Protest Writing in the 1790s', *ELH* 61 (Summer 1994), pp. 341–62.

36 A sense of this tradition is compellingly conveyed in Peter Linebaugh and Marcus Rediker, *The Many-Headed Hydra: The Hidden History of the Revolutionary Atlantic* (New York: Beacon Press, 2001).

CHAPTER EIGHT

Fanny Price's British Museum:
Empire, Genre, and Memory in *Mansfield Park*

MIRANDA BURGESS

This essay seeks to answer two questions: how does Fanny Price, the heroine of Jane Austen's 1814 novel *Mansfield Park*, experience imperialism, and what might Fanny's experience, and the novel's ways of representing it, tell readers about the novel's, Austen's, or Britain's relation to empire itself? In making the question of experience and its representation the focus of this essay and the novel it discusses, I depart from the recent critical orthodoxy that has made it difficult to read *Mansfield Park* other than as a synecdoche for contemporary imperial history.[1] In so doing, however, I aim not so much to reclaim the novel from postcolonial approaches as to propose methods for investigating imperial questions that take into renewed account this novel's specifically Romantic character.

Edward Said's most significant contribution to the study of *Mansfield Park* was the respatialization of a novel that had, as Said put it, been read as 'constituted mainly by temporality', and his insistence on the dynamic interconnectedness of transatlantic space.[2] Yet in establishing Sir Thomas Bertram's Mansfield Park estate in the geographic context of colonialism and plantation slavery, Said represented his approach as supplementary, even prosthetic, in character, a matter of giving voice to what Austen's novel, like nineteenth-century Britain in general, had forgotten or failed to say about its imperial dependency. As a result of this essentially corrective stance, a number of influential readers have responded by defending Austen against Said's charges of inattention or complacency, most often by treating her domestic narrative as an extended metaphor for imperial injustice or suggesting that her characters' forgetfulness of empire is an ironic rebuke to the Britain whose landed interests they represent.[3]

Like Saree Makdisi, whose essay in this volume proposes a similar turn to the 'psycho-affective' dimension of Austen's novel, I want to redirect these debates away from Austen's own geopolitical consciousness – the question of what she knew about empire, and when she knew it – towards the emotion and cognition of the heroine, Fanny Price. Indeed, before the 1990s *Mansfield Park* was most often read in a way that emphasized the protagonist's subjectivity, and the atypically Romantic breadth of detail with which her psyche is represented in Austen's novel.[4] Unlike Makdisi, however, I will not suggest that a focus on the heroine's affective experience is intrinsically at odds with a reading focused on what he calls 'geoaesthetic questions'. Rather, the visible workings of the heroine's understanding are what demarcate the place of empire in *Mansfield Park*, and they are represented, precisely, in terms that are simultaneously spatial and textual: geographical and literary-aesthetic. The novel's detailed mapping of the movements of a consciousness as it mediates representations of empire and feels its own place in relation to them points to an arena within Romantic fiction more broadly where the representation of empire can be fruitfully observed and investigated.

Said's questions of memory remain central to this discussion. The novel's, or Austen's, marginalization of imperial questions is, as Said suggests, a consequence of forgetting or deliberate erasure, but the forgetfulness in question is Fanny Price's and not Austen's. Moreover, and this is my primary focus here, it is not completely successful. The relation of *Mansfield Park* to empire can be charted by revisiting Fanny's processes of remembering and by tracing the novel's detailed anatomy of her memory's failures and successes. That Fanny is weak of memory, and that retentive recollection is the chief index of intelligence and learning at Mansfield Park, are claims made very early in the novel by members of the Bertram family. Before long, however, Fanny trades forgetfulness and a head apparently empty of rote information for a mind that seems, however hard it tries, to be unable to forget.[5] Once unable to recall the accumulated details of the schoolroom, Fanny now finds herself haunted by the recollection of the *process* by which she comes to learn them: by her passage from an impecunious Portsmouth childhood to Mansfield Park and the education that prepares the landed class for participation – imaginative as much as economic – in Britain's imperial enterprise.

If, as I am suggesting, Fanny's aristocratic achievements are troubled by her memories of class subordination that persist despite all efforts to suppress them, then it is worth investigating the ways in which Fanny's history enables her collection of, and sympathy with, the historical remainders, the costs and consequences of imperial triumph. At the same time, it is the proposition of this essay that Austen's rendering of Fanny's cognitive and affective processes, her experience, memory, and sympathy, not only testifies to the reliance of empire abroad on class distinctions at home but actually serves as a record of the processes of reading, thinking, feeling and forgetting that make imperialism possible.

In their essay in this volume, Jill Heydt-Stevenson and Charlotte Sussman characterize the Romantic novel as a form of writing whose 'heterogeneity […] of approaches to the real', and the genre mixing that serves as its textual register, provoke its readers 'to understand different kinds of communal imagining'. In keeping with this observation, this essay examines the intersections between textual form and human cognition in Austen's portrait of Fanny and her education. It argues that print culture, and the mixing of genres that would later give way to separate disciplines of geography, imperial history and travel writing, provide Fanny's memory with the content that Austen's novel will anatomize.

First, I propose that an apt memory for the political organization of space, the proper object of schoolroom geographic learning, is a key index of imperial competence in the novel, a competence that is both a register and a product of socioeconomic privilege. Second, I trace Austen's mapping of memory through metaphors of space that lay bare the historical content of spatial description and spatial experience. When Fanny looks at the Mansfield Park estate, she sees a museum where memories of her past are stored and an arena within which memory can be transcended by means of a picturesque imagination. The perspectival tension the novel establishes between these two ways of seeing defines Fanny's memory as at once a crucial part and a characteristic, class-marked failure of imperial imagining. Third, I demonstrate that memory and imagination, like imperial space itself, are shown in *Mansfield Park* to be thoroughly mediated. Shaped and imprinted by print culture, Fanny's cognition is marked, in particular, by the picturesque pamphlets that serve as the canonical texts of genteel geographical learning and by peripheral nationalist antiquarian texts that unsettle the orthodoxies of the British imperial landscape. The narrative of Fanny's growth, and the representation of her memory, is haunted by the competing genres of imperial and anti-imperial nationalist geography, and by the even more troubling, conflicted historiography produced by the encounter between them.

It is in the representation of Fanny's mind as a locus of empire and a product of print culture that a distinctively Romantic and distinctly critical account of British imperialism emerges in *Mansfield Park*: a process unfolding in national and personal experience, in imagination and affect as well as in history, and in the memories that alternately feed and haunt the heroine's imaginings.

Education

Mansfield Park begins with an act of importation caught in a web of imperial connections and perceptions. Born to a family with more children than money, the ten-year-old Fanny Price is taken or sent – some readers say torn – from her Portsmouth home to make the 'long journey' to Mansfield Park.[6] Moira Ferguson and Said have compared Fanny's transportation to the contemporary traffic in slaves, Ferguson because of the lack of agency Fanny experiences at Mansfield and Said because she is 'brought in [...] and set to work'.[7] In the eyes of her well-married aunt Lady Bertram and her plantation-owning husband, however, Fanny's family, like the Bertrams' Antigua plantations, is a provider of raw materials. The goal of her labours is what Lionel Trilling termed a 'hygiene of the self', for Fanny herself, as Makdisi also emphasizes, is the stuff on which the young Fanny works.[8] She as closely resembles the imported produce as she does the labourer who processes and transforms it. And she is as much a local product as a source of imported labour, for it is both her kinship to the Bertram family and her distance and difference from them that motivates her importation.[9] Her trajectory within England reproduces the completed circuit of Mansfield Park's, and Britain's, colonial trade: she is brought in to work and be worked on and readied to be sent out again. When Fanny is read metaphorically as an indentured colonial subject, she must also be read within a complex context that requires her to be simultaneously domestic and unfamiliar, at once alien and at home.

Fanny's education at Mansfield Park confirms her ambiguous imperial status. Brought in by a scheme of her mother's family, she becomes subject, alongside the Bertram daughters, to the discipline of the governess Miss Lee. The lessons are structured around the history of empires, Roman as well as British, and the systematic comprehension of space and the systems that order it, from the table of the elements to the geography of Europe.[10] The self-discipline Fanny and her cousins are encouraged to cultivate belongs to an imperial self. At the same time, however, Fanny receives lessons that sustain her difference from her cousins and equate it with inferiority. In planning for her arrival, Sir Thomas Bertram balances his desire to integrate her fully into the household with his need 'to make her remember that she is not a *Miss Bertram*'.[11] The object of both educations is Fanny's memory; their shared tool is her memory's instruction. As an essential part of her adoption into her uncle's family and into the imperial economy in which the Bertrams participate, Fanny's memory training produces a consciousness in line with Homi Bhabha's account of colonized subjectivity: 'a difference that is almost the same, but not quite'.[12]

The novel frames Fanny's growth to maturity between two contrasting scenes, which introduce and recapitulate the imperial investments of *Mansfield Park*. The assessment of her inadequate geographical knowledge by Sir Thomas's daughters begins the first volume and her informed discussion of the West Indian slave trade with her uncle introduces the second. The treatment of geography in these scenes, and in the representation of Fanny's memory and its training throughout the rest of the novel, reveals suggestive parallels with contemporary discussions within and about the emerging discipline of geography, which were taking place in the periodical and pamphlet press, as well as in public lectures and scientific institutions, throughout the early nineteenth century.

As Felix Driver has shown in his history of the discipline, geography was in the process of diverging from the polite literature of tourism and travel. Practitioners in these fields of inquiry were negotiating the relations and bounds between them through two intersecting debates: on the necessity and propriety of expertise in each, the appropriate genres for geographical and tourist writing, and whether or not these genres should appeal to leisured but unlearned reading audiences, especially upper-class women; and on the relation of geography, its genres, and their newly defined groups of readers to the formation and development of empire.[13] Austen's investigation of the effects of geographical reading and instruction on Fanny's memory offers a broader comment on the role of a geographical education conducted through polite letters in maintaining the conventions of upper-class femininity and the relation of these conventions to the maintenance of British national and imperial competence. The inconsistencies evident within Fanny's experience of geography, as within the contemporary field of geography itself, enact the complexity of Fanny's imperial relations.

Space and its mastery, its techniques, and their genres are at issue from the moment of Fanny's arrival at Mansfield Park. Her cousins waste no time in taking her measure as uncharted terrain, beginning with 'a full survey of her face and her frock' and 'reflections on her size' before assessing her potential as the designated colonizer of her own still-uncivilized self.[14] Their investigations document, and convey to Austen's readers, a child remarkable only for an 'awkward' demeanour and a total ignorance of geography:

> Fanny could read, work, and write, but she had been taught nothing more; and as her cousins found her ignorant of many things with which they had been long familiar, they thought her prodigiously stupid, and for the first two or three weeks were continually bringing some fresh report of it into the drawing-room. 'Dear Mamma, only think, my cousin cannot put the map of Europe together – or my cousin cannot tell the principal Rivers in Russia – or she never heard of Asia Minor – or she does not know the difference between water-colours and crayons! – How strange! [...] Do you know, we asked her last night, which way she would go to get to Ireland; and she said, she should cross to the Isle of Wight. She thinks of nothing but the Isle of Wight, and she calls it the Island, as if there were no other island in the world.'[15]

The apparent randomness of the areas of competency in which Fanny is examined and found wanting belies the systematic character of the education Maria and Julia Bertram expect, and which they themselves receive. Contemporary conduct writers such as James Fordyce include geographical learning – 'VOYAGES and TRAVELS' as well as 'GEOGRAPHY', for these categories have not yet become fully detached from each other – among the 'pleasing' arts such as drawing that, as part of feminine education, 'prevent many a folly, and many a sin which proceed from idleness' and are 'useful in conversation'.[16] Such views of education come under ironic scrutiny in Austen's *Pride and Prejudice*, in which Mr Collins, wielding Fordyce's *Sermons*, is no more able than anyone else to prevent Lydia Bennet's elopement.[17]

Although Julia and Maria Bertram both repeat the 'folly' of elopement in *Mansfield Park*, however, something more than Fordyce's assumption that the ornamental guarantees the ethical is called into question by Austen's ironic exit survey of the Bertram 'plan of education'.[18] While the testing of Fanny displays an overriding concern with accomplishments as indices of upper-class feminine learning, the list of tests makes clear that a sense of place and of global position are paramount among them. To be unable to tell Ireland from the Isle of Wight, or to discern the relations that unite Northampton to both within the map of Europe, is a climactic defect of knowledge far worse then a confusion among painting implements. Fanny's cousin Edmund, in particular, works to remedy the deficit, recommending the latest narratives by official and imperial travellers and explorers, such as John Barrow's edition of George, Earl of Macartney's voyages in Russia, Ireland and China.[19] Geography is an acquirement of the landed class, to be learned and practised by young ladies in the school-room, making the propertied British woman a creature of imperial scope.

That this educational theory participates in a larger context of British thought about the relations between geography and imperial process is emphasized by Austen's narration. The novel draws the reader's attention to the Bertram sisters' equation of Fanny's educational differences from themselves with an inborn incapacity to learn. Moreover, the narrative emphasizes that in equating ignorance with stupidity, and in taking themselves as the standard against which ignorance and knowledge must be measured, Maria and Julia share the perspective of the adults who oversee their education as well as of the moralists who recommend its plan. To the sisters' complaints about Fanny, their Aunt Norris responds that they 'are blessed with wonderful memories', while their 'poor cousin has probably none at all. There is a vast deal of difference in memories, as well as in every thing else, and therefore you must make allowance for your cousin, and pity her deficiency'.[20] Like Enlightenment stadial historians, or like Enlightenment travellers looking at the New World or Ireland or the High-lands of Scotland, a class of writers and writings with whom genteel education must have familiarized them, the Bertrams assume that all human intelligence and knowledge exists on a single, developmental scale.[21] Learning is not measured according to any contingent body of knowledge but held up to an ideal of comprehensiveness, which issues in a judgement of perfection or imperfection, primitiveness or maturity that alone accounts for individual variation. A unified grasp of the world and its systems is the endpoint of this uniform intellectual history. In the hands of the Bertrams, educational assessments founded on these principles are both an expression of imperial participation and a scale for its measure-ment. Where empire as well as education is concerned, Fanny's empty memory places her at the beginning of the developmental scale.

The novel's initial emphasis on Fanny's limited knowledge of the world beyond her Portsmouth home contrasts markedly with the later scene, the capstone of her education, in which she asks her uncle an informed ques-tion about his Antigua estates and 'the slave trade' that demonstrates the 'curiosity and pleasure' with which she receives colonial 'information'.[22] Taken together, the two moments establish a parallel, noted by Katie Trumpener and Clara Tuite in particular, between the heroine's growth into maturity and the growth of her imperial awareness.[23] World-making in this novel – 'putting the map together' – is an instrument of self-making that must take place in order for the obverse, self-making in the service of empire-building, to occur. The class dimension of these intersecting processes, in which geopolitical space and the selves that inhabit it are manufactured, has gone relatively undiscussed.[24] Yet the 'hygiene of the self' through which Fanny transforms herself demands much in terms of 'carrying', 'fetching', 'pains', and other class-marked forms of labour not demanded of her cousins.[25] The transformations of subjectivity that result are integrally linked to Fanny's visible rise in class position. As a result, any continuing failures of geographical learning can be seen as evidence of imperfect social mobility – in the heroine and her memory – even as the failures themselves carry an imperial significance.

By documenting Fanny's origins in the milieu of her father, a 'Lieutenant of Marines, without education, fortune, or connections' who elopes with her mother, a small-town lawyer's niece, *Mansfield Park* demonstrates that its heroine's imperial grasp develops only as a result of her movement to her uncle's landed estate.[26] From the house Lieutenant Price rents at Portsmouth, the Isle of Wight looms large across the harbour, screening in Fanny's view of the world and establishing an outer limit for any aspiration his daughter might have to travel: wherever she might choose to go, 'she should cross to the Isle of Wight' first.[27] At Mansfield, however, Fanny's education eventually gives her the credentials to take her place as 'the only young woman in the drawing-room, the only occupier of that interesting division of a family in which she had hitherto held so humble a third'.[28] With her passage into the heart of the estate, coinciding with her maturation and with the integration of imperial knowledge that defines it, 'not only at home did her value increase', but in society as well.[29] An eye that takes in Britain's place in its empire and the world, in this novel, is contingent not only on a memory for geographic knowledge, but also on the privileged class position of which such an imperial eye is an expression.

Yet despite the apparent competence Fanny achieves and the novel's affirmation of her value, her rise in position is never fully realized. Although education closes the gap that exists in childhood between her geographical ignorance and the expansive knowledge of her Bertram cousins, a new and jarring fracture opens in adulthood between her eager expressions of concern for colonial matters and her cousins' jaded disinclination for geographical discussion. While Julia and Maria preserve what Fanny calls a 'dead silence' about the history of Caribbean slavery, 'sitting by without speaking a word, or seeming at all interested in the subject',

Fanny asks her uncle a question that declares a lively interest in human conditions in the Caribbean and in the economic dependencies that yoke Mansfield Park to Sir Thomas's plantations.[30]

The difference between Fanny and her cousins can be understood in two ways. First, unlike Bertram's daughters, Fanny cannot wear her learning lightly. To be perceived as a gentlewoman, especially by her uncle, who has engineered and cannot fail of remembering the whole history of her adoption from the indigent household of his wife's sister, she must remind her relations of her geographic understanding. She does so even as she recognizes that she may give the impression of wishing 'to set myself off at their expense' by speaking when they are silent.[31] Second, because she carries with her the lingering memory of her childhood inability to 'put the map of Europe together' and the class distinction exposed by her failure, the adult Fanny emerges not only with the requisite understanding of the physical and political geography of the British empire, but also with an active interest in the human history that has produced it.

Perhaps, like Austen herself, Fanny has been reading Thomas Clarkson's *History of the Rise, Progress and Accomplishment of the Abolition of the African Slave Trade by the British Parliament* (1808).[32] What conditions Fanny's interest, however, is what she remembers: the special position, with regard to empire, of the low end of the urban lower-middle class, to which she by birth belongs. Fanny's father belongs to 'a subordinate and inferior branch of the Navy' that acts as an oceangoing bodyguard to protect ships' officers from mutiny and from onshore attack, not least on imperial adventures.[33] His 'profession' is unlike the church and the law, and equally unlike the army or navy, in being, as the narrator puts it, 'such as no interest could reach'.[34] Fanny's mother, meanwhile, has a continually increasing, imperfectly documented, and uncountable number of offspring, a 'superfluity of children' particularly ill-suited to her 'want of almost everything else', financial or educational. Her sister Mrs Norris, who attempts to keep up with the Prices' birthrate, 'now and then' tells the Bertrams 'in an angry voice, that Fanny had got another child'.[35] Though the Prices are above the reach of charitable institutions, they are equally far beyond the pale of the Mansfield social circles. They produce children who seem to the Bertrams likely to suffer, at the very least, from 'gross ignorance' and 'vulgarity', if not a 'really bad' disposition, and who require to be 'introduced into the society of this country', as Mrs Norris puts it, through what the Prices view, in their turn, as a 'foreign education'.[36] Although three of the Price children eventually learn the polite geographies that initiate them into this society, the family continues to share much with the Bertrams' perception of the colonized peoples that are among geographers' chief subjects.

Yet although they are analogous in the Bertrams' minds to the natives of colonized places, the Price family, like other members of the contemporary lower-middle class, do the daily work of empire, participating in the colonizing of lands they will not own and from which they earn no more than wages.[37] As a naval midshipman, Fanny's older brother William takes tours of duty to the West Indies; a younger brother, 'midshipman on board an Indiaman', has joined the merchant marine.[38] Having placed William and Fanny decisively among the transactors and beneficiaries of imperialism, Mrs Price's ambitions for her remaining children include the hope of one son's becoming 'useful to Sir Thomas in the concerns of his West Indian property' – 'No situation would be beneath him' – and another's being 'sent out to the East', and it is likely that their father has also laboured at imperial work.[39] Like Fanny herself, they are simultaneously positioned as quasi-colonial raw materials and as eager participants in empire. Their involvement in imperial exploration and commerce is of a sort equally different from the landed stake held by Sir Thomas Bertram and from the consumption of polite tourist literature by his daughters and by Fanny.

To the imperious gaze of Mansfield Park, the Price household is at once domestic and beyond the pale, as peripheral and mysterious as a tract of uncharted ground yet as familiar as those who are sent out to cultivate it. In their relationship to empire, the closest resemblance of the Prices, as the Bertrams' condemnation of their feckless fecundity suggests and as their own desperate willingness to take part in colonial projects equally implies, is to the migrant Irish poor who preoccupied the moralists, political arithmeticians, and political economists of the eighteenth and early nineteenth centuries.[40] As the longstanding subject of British geographical investigation and colonial intervention, Ireland had come, in the wake of the Union in 1801, to confront the United Kingdom with a domestic and increasingly urban set of problems.[41] That Austen's heroine feels some such connection is underlined by the ten-year-old Fanny's striking sense of Ireland's closeness and accessibility: to the Price children, only the Isle of Wight seems to stand between Ireland and their Portsmouth home. Fanny is mistaken, of course, so far as the map is concerned, but in the context of the novel's representation of her own imperial experience, she may not be far wrong in her imaginings, however hard she tries later on to forget.

The novel's paradoxical representation of the Price family as at once the soldiers and objects of empire emphasizes that theirs is work carried out by those who must first, in a practical sense, be colonized. *Mansfield Park* ends with Sir Thomas's affirmation of the sameness and the difference of the Prices and Bertrams and his own contribution to each. Conducting a final survey of Fanny, William, and Susan, he believes he has 'reason to rejoice in what he had done for them all, and acknowledge the advantages of early hardship and discipline, and the consciousness of being born to struggle and endure'.[42] To be useful to Mansfield and Britain, the Prices' stationary daughters and seafaring sons must be taught a sense of themselves and their world that is 'almost the same, but not quite' as the imperial eye of the landed classes that employ them. Yet in producing difference, Sir Thomas also emphasizes existing differences, in this case the history of class difference and class subordination that divides the Bertram family from the Prices.

There remains something awkward about Fanny in particular, something poorly adapted to her situation at Mansfield Park, which troubles the landed estate and its imperial investments. The fate of the differences between Fanny and the Bertrams charts the history of class within the novel. Not least, it highlights the effects of domestic class relations on Austen's representation of Britain's imperial interests. This is not to suggest that empire is a vehicle for the exploration of class in this novel, which, as I have been arguing, presents the process of making Britain's empire as both analogous to and reliant on class subordination. Rather, the relation between empire and class as it is represented in *Mansfield Park* provides a context for the narrative of the heroine's incomplete class rise as it is played out in her recollections. Faulty at first and then inescapably stubborn, it is, above all, Fanny's memory that registers the presence in Austen's novel of empire's troubling history, in Britain and abroad.

Perspective

In outlining a context in imperial history for the way in which Fanny Price's memory is portrayed in *Mansfield Park*, I have come some way from the account of her geographical learning and thinking with which I began. But the journey has been shorter than it first appears, for I want now to propose that Fanny's memory is itself a colonial terrain. To make this argument, let me turn to Austen's representation of her heroine's processes of remembering through metaphors of space, or, to put it another way, to

Austen's depiction of geographies as historic sites and devices for the storage of memory. In the two key scenes in the novel in which Fanny reflects on her own history, her change of homes, her education, and her consequent rise in class position, she finds her memory of past events figured in the landscape. Under Fanny's gaze, Mansfield Park and its environs register the contrast between the territory of the past, recalled in its uncultivated natural state, and the tamed and polished landscape of the present, even as Fanny tries and fails to efface the distinction from remembrance. Like Fanny herself, the terrain this novel charts is haunted by historical process.

To turn to these scenes is also to return, in a double sense, to the question of *Mansfield Park*'s Romanticism: its mixing and quotation of contemporary genres, especially poetry, and its relevance to later debates about the significance of these genres. In depicting Fanny's perception of the spaces around her and her attempts at comprehending them, the novel takes up the problem of relations between history and imagination that is the subtext, as New Historicist scholarship especially emphasized, of much Romantic poetry. It is not my intention to rehearse the debates about history and transcendence that dominated the field of British Romantic studies in the 1980s and early 1990s, but rather to consider the question of Austen's intervention in the contemporary conversations that were their object. In *Mansfield Park*, Fanny Price tries and fails to imitate the Romantic approaches to thinking about space that were provided by contemporary locodescriptive poetry and by manuals of picturesque description – genres that outlined many of the assumptions and techniques with which, as William Galperin has shown, Romantic writers approached the depiction of history.[43] When Fanny engages in explicit quotation, and imitation, of William Wordsworth's 'Lines composed a few miles above Tintern Abbey' and William Gilpin's *Observations Relative Chiefly to Picturesque Beauty*, it is precisely in order to grapple with the problem of historical experience. Repeatedly demonstrating Fanny's inability to surmount her past in an imaginative relation to landscape, the novel advances and rejects the idea that nineteenth-century Britons can fully achieve, through imagination, any transcendence of a context that necessarily includes imperial history.

This rejection of the possibility of forgetfulness in *Mansfield Park* raises questions for Said's account of the novel's blind-spots about history – an imperviousness or forgetfulness, he suggests, that it shares with Romantic novels more broadly. At the same time, however, Fanny's failed imitation of the cognitive processes she borrows from canonical Romantic genres establishes Austen's novel in a relation of critical distance to these contemporary forms. It is in these scenes that Austen most concretely and insistently raises the question of mediation: the shaping of memory and imagination by print culture and, in particular, by the competing genres of geographical writing – poetic, tourist, scientific – that mark the early-nineteenth-century scene of the discipline's emergence.

The first of Austen's paired scenes takes place between Fanny and Mary Crawford on the grounds of the Parsonage at Mansfield. As the two young women sit in the garden of Mary's sister Mrs Grant, Fanny expresses her admiration of its arrangement:

> 'Every time I come into this shrubbery I am more struck with its growth and beauty. Three years ago, this was nothing but a rough hedgerow along the upper side of the field, never thought of as any thing, or capable of becoming any thing; and now it is converted into a walk, and it would be difficult to say whether most valuable as a convenience or an ornament; and perhaps in another three years we may be forgetting – almost forgetting what it was before. How wonderful, how very wonderful the operations of time, and the changes of the human mind! [...] If any one faculty of our nature may be called more wonderful than the rest, I do think it is memory. There seems something more speakingly incomprehensible in the powers, the failures, the inequalities of memory, than in any other of our intelligences. The memory is sometimes so retentive, so serviceable, so obedient – at others, so bewildered and so weak – and at others again, so tyrannic, so beyond controul! – We are to be sure a miracle every way – but our powers of recollecting and of forgetting, do seem peculiarly past finding out.'[44]

Fanny's denization at Mansfield is evident in her reflections on this scene, for although she has travelled no farther than across the park, she borrows the language of the picturesque tour to describe her surroundings. Fanny's rhetorical borrowing from a genre that remains the linchpin of her and her cousins' imperial education points toward what I will argue is the heart of this garden scene: the metaphoric relation between the development of the garden and Fanny's memory training.

Fanny assesses the shrubbery in the terms of Gilpin's *Observations*, drawing her evaluative vocabulary from his strictures on the design of gardens belonging to houses. Because 'a house is an *artificial* object', Gilpin writes,

> the scenery around it, *must*, in some degree, partake of *art*. Propriety requires it: convenience demands it. But if it partake of *art*, it should also partake of *nature*, as belonging to the country. It has therefore two characters to support;

and may be considered as the connecting thread between the regularity of the house, and the freedom of the natural scene [...]. [The] business of the embellished scene, is to [...] remove offensive objects, and to add a pleasing foreground to the distance.[45]

For Gilpin, two processes are crucial in producing such picturesque scenes: the creation of 'distance' and the removal of 'offensive objects' that have become, over time, a part of the garden site. Through these two methods, the gardener enables the viewer to rise, as it were, above the two existing, conflicting characters of the garden, perceiving a new and harmonious beauty in the scene. In advocating such a distanciated perspective on landscape, Gilpin prefigures New Historicist readings of poems such as 'Tintern Abbey', which emphasizes the speaker's self-positioning above the prospect he describes and his pleasure in the way the elements of his scene, including evidence of pollution and poverty, 'lose themselves' among the harmonious picture of the landscape.[46] Elsewhere in *Observations*, Gilpin writes that although the 'regular intermixture' of domestic, industrial, and natural elements in landscape

produces often deformity on the nearer grounds; [...] when all these regular forms are softened by distance – when hedge-row trees begin to unite, and lengthen into streaks along the horizon – when farm-houses, and ordinary buildings lose all their vulgarity of shape, and are scattered about, in formless spots, through the several parts of a distance, it is inconceivable what richness, and beauty, this mass of deformity, when melted together, adds to landscape.[47]

In *Observations*, Gilpin provides a manual, a groundbreaking set of aesthetic instructions, for viewers who wish, through the achievement of what for him remains a physical and spatial kind of transcendence, to distance themselves from the pain and disorder of history and to understand the distance as improvement. In making use of Gilpin's aesthetic practice in her account of Mrs Grant's shrubbery, Fanny makes the implied connection between transcendent landscape and history more explicit. It is only with the passage of time, she suggests, that the 'beauty' and 'convenience' of the garden have become impossible to distinguish from each other. It is a consequence of passing time that the viewer is distanced from the rough history of the scene, which is lost in a pleasing landscape.

In conjoining time and space, memory and landscape, Austen's scene unfolds a metaphoric as well as a physical geography. Its cohesion, when considered from close up, yields irreconcilable elements that form a counterpart to the contradictions within the narrative of Fanny's geographical education that I discussed earlier in this essay. Yet the rhetoric and outcomes of Fanny's reverie about the shrubbery also replicate the narrator's account of Fanny's own development from roughness into 'value' and from domestic 'convenience' to an ornamental role as 'the only young woman in the drawing-room'.[48] The novel's metonymic linkage of the geography of the tour to polite education intersects with its metaphoric treatment of memory as a terrain to be emptied of disregarded content, refilled, and then charted.

Even so, despite its formal sophistication, the correspondence between Fanny and the landscape that emerges in this scene is attributed to the heroine rather than to the narrator. It is Fanny's own recognition of the parallel that prompts her thoughts in the direction of the nature of memory, whence they move in a now-familiar pattern from a mind that is empty of recollection to one that is uncomfortably retentive. Although Fanny begins her reflections by declaring her awe at the human capacity to forget the past, she stumbles – as Gilpin and Wordsworth never stumble – over the chasm between 'forgetting' and 'almost forgetting' and comes to wonder, equally, at memory's insistence. As it is metaphorized in landscape, memory to Fanny is both marvellous and painful, at times forgetting what needs to be remembered (as in her childhood struggles to make a coherent whole of the map of Europe) and at other, more 'tyrannic' times, stubbornly remembering what she wishes to forget (hence the adult Fanny's uncomfortable recollection of her struggles with education, imitation, and difference).

As in the scene of Fanny's earlier display of geographical memory in conversation with Sir Thomas, it is apparently only the heroine, with her lower-middle-class history, whose glance at the successful transformation of the garden fails to forget the difference between present beauty and past roughness. Instead Mary Crawford sees the reflection of her polished, perfected, aristocratic self.[49] While her way of looking replicates Fanny's self-absorption, Mary is, in two senses, a better viewer of the garden than Fanny, for she does not recognize, and cannot remember, the history of its transformation. Mary has, that is, fully internalized both the explicit and the implicit lessons of the picturesque: that viewers should notice only the finished landscape if they wish to take pleasure from it, and that their pleasure derives from their own perspective on the landscapes they perceive. Like Maria and Julia Bertram, moreover, Mary makes light of her polite but tutored knowledge, so that its origins in the contemporary picturesque tour are no longer visible. Fanny, with her remembrance and quotation of Gilpin's teachings, is unable, once again, fully to inhabit her own learning and so to forget the history of class mobility that complicates it.

As with the earlier scenes of geographical memory to which I have been comparing Fanny's landscape experience, I want to underline the national and imperial as well as the class dimensions of Austen's narrative. An incipient nationalism is evident in Gilpin's text in a form that sets the perspective of the native viewer in natural harmony with the national landscape his or her perspective organizes. Even as Gilpin protests that he does not 'wish to speak merely as an Englishman', he insists that the act of appreciating landscape is peculiarly and locally English, because, he writes, 'this country exceeds most countries in the variety of it's [sic] picturesque beauties'.[50] The supremacy exists because the process of harmonizing the disparate marks history leaves on the land – such as the Wordsworthian 'intermixture of wood and cultivation' – is a strength 'found oftener in English landscape than in the landscape of other countries'.[51] In creating smoothness and sameness from the coming together of discordant elements, Britain, it seems, has colonized its own landscape. The sentiment that takes particular pleasure in this achievement matters more than class divisions among the tourists Gilpin addresses.

Tim Fulford has emphasized Gilpin's detachment of his tourist-readers' pleasure in landscape from the necessity of owning or inheriting the land they view.[52] Reading 'Tintern Abbey' in conversation with Gilpin's relatively egalitarian literature of the tour has allowed readers, such as Fulford, who wish to rethink the New Historicist examinations of the poem to argue that Wordsworth seeks not to transcend historical conflicts and sufferings but rather to enact them metaphorically in the new form of landscape aesthetics.[53] Such readings stress that the poem's scene includes the 'houseless' charcoal burners and the evidence of Enclosure Acts in 'hedgerows', however 'sportive', and in farms that are 'green to the very door'.[54] More recently, Debbie Lee has re-examined this revisionist reading of Wordsworthian 'aesthetic distance' in the context of contemporary abolitionism, suggesting that an imagination that transcends the merely local and individual becomes, for such writers, an imagination capable of trans-imperial empathy.[55] It is distance, that is, that allows the imaginative viewer to see common ground in particularity, though, as Lee points out, such a perception does not necessarily oppose itself to imperialism.[56]

To achieve such empathy requires a viewer who has access to a judicious spatial and historical distance. In Austen's depiction, however, the process of viewing landscape by Gilpin's rules – learning to take the long view, and to look with explicitly English eyes – remains unperfected by those who do not participate, or who like Fanny must grow into participation, in landed Britain. The gaze of such participants notes the residue of their own class history in the landed English scene they witness. The scene of Fanny's reveries reveals the mistake the Bertram sisters make when they assume that every education, every intellect, and, by extension, every place and people follows an identical trajectory of development with greater or lesser success. In learning to put the map of England together as Fanny literally does in the Parsonage garden, she follows a path that, as Austen demonstrates, is wholly distinct from theirs. I have argued that Fanny's distinctness is framed by Austen's account of her imperial education and that the framing allows Fanny's experience of her memory training to dramatize her own and her family's ambiguous relation to empire. If Austen's garden set-piece demonstrates that Fanny's relations to Britain remain equally distinct, so, I would like to suggest, the picture of Britain's relation to its imperial entanglements that emerges in the novel not only calls Gilpin's achievement of transcendence into doubt but also questions the perspective that makes Wordsworth's discordant elements 'lose themselves' in harmony.

The second of the paired scenes in which Austen maps the colonial terrain of Fanny's memory brings together an act of landscape appreciation that is founded on Gilpin's, and that refers to Wordsworth's, while enumerating the imperial stakes of such figurings of Britain. Left alone in the former schoolroom at Mansfield, Fanny contemplates the collection of objects that have accumulated there.[57] Deliberately acquired or consigned by chance, all are artefacts of the history that has brought her among a landed class that benefits from empire:

> Her plants, her books – of which she had been a collector, from the first hour of her commanding a shilling – her writing desk, and her works of charity and ingenuity, were all within her reach; – or if indisposed for employment, if nothing but musing would do, she could scarcely see an object in that room which had not an interesting remembrance connected with it. – Everything was a friend, or bore her thoughts to a friend; and though there had been sometimes much of suffering to her – though her motives had been often misunderstood, her feelings disregarded, and her comprehension undervalued; though she had known the pains of tyranny, of ridicule, and neglect, yet almost every recurrence of either had led to something consolatory [...] – and the whole was now so blended together, so harmonized by distance, that every former affliction had its charm. The room was most dear to her [though] [...] its greatest elegancies and ornaments were a faded footstool of Julia's

work, too ill done for the drawing-room, three transparencies, made in a rage for transparencies, for the three lower panes of one window, where Tintern Abbey held its station between a cave in Italy, and a moonlight lake in Cumberland; a collection of family profiles thought unworthy of being anywhere else, over the mantle-piece, and by their side and pinned against the wall, a small sketch of a ship sent four years ago from the Mediterranean by William, with H.M.S. Antwerp at the bottom, in letters as tall as the main-mast.[58]

'Harmonized by distance': here again, Fanny, and thus Austen's novel, is talking about time in conventional, spatial terms. Surveying the borrowed demesne of the schoolroom, Fanny echoes Gilpin's account of diversity 'softened by distance', or, as the first of the transparencies stationed between her eye and her view of the Park seems to suggest, she imitates the Wordsworth of 'Tintern Abbey'.

For Fanny, however, the tyrannic waywardness of memory means that the disparate elements that make up the landscape of the schoolroom are imperfectly 'blended together'. Every object in the room serves as a repository for memories of emotional experience and the history that has produced them. The long perspective lent by the privileged present cannot entirely harmonize, let alone erase or 'lose', these isolated, painful traces of the past Fanny shares with objects 'thought unworthy of being anywhere else'. And so her 'works of charity', signs of the social role of a woman of the landed classes, lie side by side with objects marked with her experience of 'tyranny'; with the remnants of an education designed at once to highlight and to remedy an 'under-valued' intellect by alternating 'ridicule and neglect'; and with the artefact most visibly linked to the imperial role of her family and her native class and place: a sketch of the *Antwerp*, the ship on which her older brother serves not just in the Mediterranean but also in the West Indies of the Bertrams' colonial plantations, all the while failing to rise beyond his position at the bottom of the ranks.[59] The schoolroom is Fanny's British museum, where the artefacts of a complex personal and imperial history are stored. But the broken relics of this history never resolve themselves, as the collections of an imperial nation must, into a narrative of upward and outward progress.[60] Instead they persist, each in its irreducible quiddity, bearing the fractured traces of competing histories.

In *Mansfield Park*, Austen rewrites the scene of 'Tintern Abbey' with an eye to the details of British landscape, the physical leavings of a domestic history that is also a history of colonial involvement, which refuse to harmonize or vanish. Fanny's schoolroom musings are more in line than Wordsworth's poem with what Fulford and others argue about the persistence of history in the Romantic poetics of landscape. The citation of 'Tintern Abbey' coupled with the reduction of its scene to a transparency – an object to be seen through, remnant of a brief 'rage for transparencies' and only one among the discordant objects that have found their way into Fanny's museum – emphasizes the perspectival differences that distinguish the novel from the poem and its picturesque apparatus. For Austen, the gulf between these perceptions of Britain arises from the distinction between 'forgetting' and 'almost forgetting'. Born of domestic differences in birth and landed power, the distinction has implications for the experience of empire at home and for the character of Britons' imperial participation abroad.

Mediation

The history of readers' responses to 'Tintern Abbey' opens a window on the larger topic of history and transcendence in British Romantic writing. Austen's representation of the tension between 'forgetting' and 'almost forgetting' in *Mansfield Park* allows us to open another that is specific to the Romantic novel. From readings of 'Tintern Abbey' for its aesthetic of 'oversight' to assertions that historicist criticism reinscribes Romantic transcendence, scholars have spent much of the past two decades exploring the relation between the Romantic imagination and history.[61] More recently, revisionist readers have revived the topic of imagination as something more than ideology, emphasizing its continuing historical engagement, or argued that the local and the particular persist in Romantic writing as hallmarks of British nationalism.[62] Still others have suggested that not only what post-Romantic readers notice in Romantic texts, but also which texts they continue to notice, is a consequence of the naturalization of British nationhood, and of a developing national literature, in nineteenth-century criticism, and the novel in particular.[63] In order to fulfil the last of the promises with which this essay began, an account of the mediated character of psycho-affective processes such as 'almost forgetting' in *Mansfield Park*, I want to bring these approaches together. The scenes of Fanny Price's geographical education and her response to the landscapes of Britain provide the contours of an aesthetic imagination whose historical engagement is founded on inescapable memory. I will conclude by proposing that Austen's depiction of Fanny's memory as an accumulation of historical details is indeed associated with nationalism, but that the lineaments are drawn from the anti-imperial nationalism of the United Kingdom's peripheries, and that the significance inheres in what the heroine remembers: a mix of British picturesque writing and peripheral nationalist print production.

It will be useful to restate what I have been arguing throughout this essay: that the protagonist's memory, as it is represented in *Mansfield Park*, is a thoroughly textual one. Both as a consequence of its training at Mansfield and as a result of Austen's techniques for portraying it, Fanny's mind is an aggregate of imperfectly harmonized passages from books. Picturesque tours and Lake School poetry figure especially prominently in her recollected reading. But Fanny also reads beyond the official Bertram syllabus. All kinds of current books accumulate in the schoolroom, in part because Fanny has early become a 'collector' of them but also, perhaps, because those Bertram acquisitions that do not hold the interest of Maria and Julia – from the picturesque manuals and abolition history whose influence is implicit in Fanny's conversations to Macartney's travels and the narrative poems by Walter Scott and William Cowper Fanny quotes in the novel – are likely to wash up there. Moreover, during Fanny's brief return to Portsmouth, she subscribes *'in propria persona'* to a circulating library, becoming, in her state of textual deprivation, 'a renter, a chuser of books'.[64] As Fanny's reading diverges from Maria's and Julia's, so Austen's mapping of her memory comes to hinge on a genre whose conventions Fanny, alone among the occupants of Mansfield and its neighbourhood, appears to recognize and recall.

Along with the English picturesque tourism of Gilpin and his followers, Fanny's perspective on landscape and history bears the markers of a closely related competitor: the antiquarian tour of Britain's peripheries. Now little read, the antiquarian tour is among the genres whose literary-historical 'forgetting' took place through what Clifford Siskin has theorized as a retrospective attribution of ephemerality.[65] Yet notwithstanding the Bertrams' indifference, the peripheral tour was a popular and diverse Romantic literary form with a readership in Britain.[66] Irish examples encompass poetry as well as prose, ranging from esoterica such as those Charles Vallancey published in his *Collectanea de Rebus Hibernicis* (1781–82) to expensive quartos such as Charlotte Brooke's *Reliques of Irish Poetry* (1789), an urbane collection whose subscribers included Charlotte Smith and Anna Seward.[67] In the work of Irish and Scottish writers alike, the genre often takes the form of included set-pieces within novels and narrative poems, among them Sydney Owenson's *Wild Irish Girl* (1806), Maria

Edgeworth's *The Absentee* (1812) and Scott's *Lay of the Last Minstrel* (1805) and *Lady of the Lake* (1810), all of which Austen or her characters cite in writing and conversation.[68]

The peripheral antiquarian tour, as Trumpener has shown, responds dialectically to metropolitan tourist writing, including picturesque tours that considered Ireland as a colonized and thus as an increasingly system-atized and coherent terrain.[69] Its techniques centre on imitation of British picturesque writing, in the oblique form of parody and pastiche.[70] What differentiates the genre from the metropolitan picturesque tour, despite an identical range of generic markers, then, is its concentration on landscape, in particular that of colonized Ireland, as 'a site simultaneously of historical plenitude and historical loss'.[71] In this genre, as in Fanny Price's memory and Austen's *Mansfield Park*, histories are played out across geographic space and landscape observation becomes a source of histor-ical testimony.

Peripheral nationalist tourists read historical details back into a land-scape that has been rendered harmonious by what they see as a distanciated and thus as a superficial perspective. So, for example, the picturesque pleasure Owenson's English tourist Horatio M. takes in his travels from London to the far west of Ireland, where castle ruins 'grand even in deso-lation, and magnificent in decay' crown a 'wildly romantic' peninsula, is tempered by learning that his ancestors have pushed the castle's owners off more arable land.[72] Similarly, when Edgeworth's Lord Colambre jour-neys to Ireland to view the effects of his father's absenteeism on his Irish estates, a tenant informs him that 'the desolation of the prospect' is a consequence of mismanagement and distance rather than the intrinsically wild or barren character of the land.[73] The historical breakdown of the picturesque in these novels provides a model for Fanny's querying of harmonious distance and forgetting in the schoolroom and in Mrs Grant's garden. In the antiquarian scenes that Owenson and Edgeworth include in their own Romantic novels, territories once viewed as well-composed romantic landscapes are repopulated and re-historicized in being seen up close.

In recovering the history of each landscape that gives aesthetic pleasure to its viewer, these writers defend the significance of material artefacts, not just as objects to be preserved in picturesque scenes but also as essential sources in the writing of history and historical accounts of landscapes. For Owenson, the assertion that 'manuscripts, annals, and records, are not the treasures of a colonized or a conquered country' because 'it is always the policy of the conqueror, (or the invader) to destroy those mementi' amply justifies an obsessive focus on caches of rusting weaponry, the history of musical instruments, and the details of 'ancient Irish' dress that prefigures Fanny's enumeration of the disparate objects in the East Room at Mansfield Park.[74] In substituting antiquities for narrative, Owenson suggests not only that the evidence of the linguistic past is a kind of frozen history but also that artefacts can speak and be heard.[75] Unlike Fanny, who attempts to divorce her privileged state at Mansfield from her remembered past experience, Owenson demonstrates through the recovery and description of antiquarian fragments that the Irish present is a product of Ireland's past, and of its colonial experience in particular. Yet Fanny's enumeration of the relics in her schoolroom museum, and the almost forgotten memories she unwillingly acknowledges amid attempts to find harmony in distance, recapitulate this accounting of the past, its pains, and the costs of progress. In Fanny's memory, despite her best efforts, the fragments of the past persist and speak.

Conventions drawn from the antiquarian tour give shape to Austen's presentation of what Fanny remembers. The inclusion of these genres in *Mansfield Park* marks the return of the heroine's early sense of strangeness. Dividing Fanny from the Bertrams by complicating her relation to the English picturesque of Mansfield Park, these generic recollections simultaneously re-establish Fanny's childhood affinity for Ireland. Bhabha has posited a variety of uncanny experience, a 'paradigmatic colonial [...] condition', that reveals itself as a subject moves between a culture and its colonial others. What should feel familiar is estranged by intra-imperial travel, and painful histories that should have been forgotten return to haunt the present.[76] Fanny's memory, I suggest, is the site of such a haunting: a print cultural uncanny.

In his analysis of Irish Romantic texts such as Owenson's novels, Leerssen identifies 'auto-exoticism' as the means by which their writers distinguished Ireland from Britain and, after Union, from the United Kingdom that had absorbed it. He concludes that 'Romantic exoticism' is 'chronological as well as [...] geographical': Irish writers looking at the Irish past appropriate this strange history in much the same way as Britain weaves strange countries and their produce into its seamless imperial fabric.[77] In this way Irish antiquarian tourists transform the history of Ireland into 'an undifferentiated pool of diverse mementos and memories', paradoxically homogeneous in its calculated difference from the modern British present – a kind of historiographic bog that is, of course, the forerunner of Fanny's schoolroom, equally crowded with mementos.[78] To Leerssen, antiquarian thinking is an essentially reactionary phenomenon, a nationalism that defends itself against the British impulse towards modernizing the colonies by clinging to the traces of a past the colonial present supersedes.

The characteristic fragmentation of antiquarian objects, however, along with the loss of their lived context, provides material for a history that is alternative to nationalist nostalgia as well as to imperialism, as Yoon Sun Lee has pointed out.[79] There are numerous moments in Owenson's writing that exemplify such a history. Praising a Sligo landscape in *Patriotic Sketches of Ireland* (1807), Owenson begins by echoing Gilpin and Wordsworth as well as her own *Wild Irish Girl*: what she sees is a 'scene of romantic variety', which frequently combines the most cultivated and harmonious traits, with the wildest and most abrupt images of scenic beauty'; an 'expansive prospect' that 'dissolve[s] every object into one mild and indistinct hue'.[80] But Owenson's landscape, like the garden at Mansfield Parsonage and like Fanny's similarly 'blended' and 'harmonized' schoolroom memories, turns out to be imperfectly harmonious. Viewed more closely, the rural Irish picturesque discloses the contrast between past and present, juxtaposing 'opulent' towns with 'ruinous and wretched villages' marked alike by the 'violence of the tide' and 'the vicissitudes of civil dissension'. Owenson concludes that the landscape's details are 'an epitome of the fate of all earthly states' and of 'the rise, climacteric, decline, and fall of every empire', including Britain's.[81]

In describing the process in which Fanny Price reflects on landscape, Austen mirrors the kind of analytic progression that Owenson establishes in *Patriotic Sketches* and *The Wild Irish Girl*. In her reveries on the Parsonage garden and the schoolroom, Fanny wishes to emphasize the evidence of progress she finds in the present scene: her wonder at the shrubbery's 'valuable' present and her pleasure in the 'charm' of objects 'blended together' in a schoolroom prospect 'harmonized by distance'.[82] Yet, like Owenson, she cannot help falling back into the scene from whose history she has raised and distanced herself, recovering and enumerating the traces of 'rough hedgerow' that lurk in the one and of 'the pains of tyranny, of ridicule, and neglect' preserved in the artefacts of the other.

Perhaps most significantly, Fanny, unlike Owenson, never attempts to exoticize the past or seek out history's traces. Rather they haunt her, emerging unwilled in her memory and appearing randomly in her schoolroom at the whim of the Bertrams: even as she strives to develop a grateful pleasure in the harmony of past and present with which her hardscrabble origins blend into her imperial education, the traces of her history trouble her precisely as 'almost forgetting' troubles the prospect of forgetfulness.

Conclusion

In her experience of haunting by her half-forgotten past, Fanny Price is haunted by genre, and by a generic competition for the authority to define the relation between the national present and its imperial history. Pulled between the inescapable remnants of the past and the desperate quest to forget them, the unstable narrative form of Fanny's historical reveries emerges from the clash between imperial picturesque and colonial anti-quarianism. Austen's account of Fanny's cognition itself forms a kind of textual museum, preserving the fragmentary traces of the competing genres that surface in their shared, repeated keywords: harmony, blend, and distance; suffering, tyranny, neglect, object. The mind that emerges is an assemblage of shards from contemporary print culture. This textual form – a new, unstable, and internally conflicted genre – of the heroine's memory is also the genre of empire in this novel as it explores the media of what Heydt-Stevenson and Sussman call 'communal imagining'.

The mapping of memory and imagination in Austen's *Mansfield Park* offers an exemplary opportunity for investigating the mediation of empire in the novel of British Romanticism. In representing a consciousness thematically as a product of literary form and in enacting this representa-tion generically, Austen's novel allows its readers to propose anew the ties between mind, letters, and history – not as an evasion of Britain's troubled political past but precisely as an encounter with it. At the same time, in demonstrating the mediated character of its heroine's Romantic mind, *Mansfield Park* makes a case for literary writing and reading as a historically active process, capable of serving the British nation's geographical ends but equally capable of preserving the memorials that allow a questioning of Britain's imperial history.

Notes

1 One could instance the literalness with which Patricia Rozema's 1999 film addressed Fanny's curiosity about Antigua. But there is also an extended history in the criticism. Although neither Alistair M. Duckworth nor Marilyn Butler

addresses the issue of empire in their ground-breaking political readings of Austen's novels, *The Improvement of the Estate: A Study of Jane Austen's Novels* (Baltimore: Johns Hopkins University Press, 1971) and *Jane Austen and the War of Ideas* (Oxford: Clarendon Press, 1975) respectively, later in the decade Julia Prewitt Brown suggests, in *Jane Austen's Novels: Social Change and Literary Form* (Cambridge, MA: Harvard University Press, 1979), pp. 87–88, that Sir Thomas Bertram's journey to Antigua, and Fanny's interest in it, point to an enclosed national and domestic world that is no longer 'self-sufficient' but marked by 'fear of [political] contamination.' See also Margaret Kirkham's argument, in *Jane Austen: Feminism and Fiction* (Sussex: Harvester, 1983), pp. 116–20, that Fanny's views on gender might comment more largely on the history of slavery indicated by the title's reference to the Mansfield Decision that abolished slavery in Britain, and the related arguments of Claudia Johnson in *Women, Politics, and the Novel* (Chicago: University of Chicago Press, 1988), pp. 107–108, and Moira Ferguson, '*Mansfield Park*: Slavery, Colonialism, and Gender', *Oxford Literary Review* 13 (1991), pp. 118–39.

2   Edward Said, *Culture and Imperialism* (New York: Vintage, 1993), p. 84.

3   Susan Fraiman, 'Jane Austen and Edward Said: Gender, Culture, and Imperialism', in Deidre Lynch, ed., *Janeites: Austen's Disciples and Devotees* (Princeton: Princeton University Press, 2000), pp. 206–23; Katie Trumpener, *Bardic Nationalism: The Romantic Novel and the British Empire* (Princeton: Princeton University Press, 1997), pp. 161–92. See also You-me Park and Rajeswari Sunder Rajan, eds., *The Post-Colonial Jane Austen* (London: Routledge, 2000), especially Clara Tuite, 'Domestic Retrenchment and Imperial Expansion: The Property Plots of *Mansfield Park*', pp. 93–115.

4   See, variously, Marvin Mudrick, *Jane Austen: Irony as Defence and Discovery* (Berkeley: University of California Press, 1968), p. 166; Butler, *War of Ideas*, pp. 221, 230, 249; Laura G. Mooneyham, *Romance, Language and Education in Jane Austen's Novels* (New York: St Martin's Press, 1988), p. 69. The readings of the novel as a feminist document that predominated in the 1980s also emphasized the role of represented thought and affect. See especially Johnson, *Women, Politics, and the Novel*, p. 96.

5   Mary Lascelles, in her pioneering *Jane Austen and her Art* (Oxford: Oxford University Press, 1939), pp. 189, 194, highlighted the significance of Fanny's consciousness of time both in the development of the character and in what Lascelles saw as Austen's developing 'technique for using the consciousness of her characters as a means of communication with the reader'.

6   Jane Austen, *Mansfield Park*, ed. James Kinsley (Oxford: Oxford University Press, 1980), p. 9.

7   Said, *Culture and Imperialism*, p. 92; Moira Ferguson, *Colonialism and Gender Relations from Mary Wollstonecraft to Jamaica Kincaid: East Caribbean Connections* (New York: Columbia University Press, 1993), pp. 67, 71–74.

8   Lionel Trilling, *The Opposing Self* (New York: Viking, 1955), p. 218.

9   Clara Tuite, *Romantic Austen: Sexual Politics and the Literary Canon* (Cambridge: Cambridge University Press, 2002), p.104.

10 Austen, *Mansfield Park*, p. 15. As a discipline, contemporary chemistry was newly systematized. David Knight (in 'Chemistry on an Offshore Island: Britain, 1789–1840', in Knight and Helge Kragh, eds., *The Making of the Chemist: The Social History of Chemistry in Europe, 1789–1914* (Cambridge: Cambridge University Press, 1998), pp.

101–102) suggests that by the turn of the nineteenth century systematic thinking and synthetic analyses within the discipline of chemistry had ceased to be associated only with 'overweening science' and revolutionary French theory. It influenced even popular textbooks for young ladies, such as Jane Marcet's *Conversations on Chemistry* (London: Longman, 9th edn, 1824), which refers to the 'great change chemistry has undergone since it has become a regular science' (p. 7). The Bertram sisters' tabular conception of the 'Metals' and 'Semi-Metals' reflects this new influence. The reading together of Norse, Greek and Roman legend implied in Austen's reference to 'Heathen Mythology' is part of the prehistory of 'Western civilization' as an Anglocentric concept, inculcated in popular children's literature throughout the nineteenth and early twentieth centuries; see Siân Echard, *Printing the Middle Ages* (Philadelphia: University of Pennsylvania Press, forthcoming 2008).

11 Austen, *Mansfield Park*, p. 8.

12 Homi Bhabha, 'Of Mimicry and Man: The Ambivalence of Colonial Discourse', in *The Location of Culture* (London: Routledge, 1994), p. 86.

13 Felix Driver, *Geography Militant: Cultures of Exploration and Empire* (Oxford: Blackwell, 2001), pp. 8–20, 50–52.

14 Austen, *Mansfield Park*, pp. 10–11.

15 Austen, *Mansfield Park*, p. 15.

16 James Fordyce, *Sermons to Young Women*, 2 vols. (London: Millar, 1794), Vol. 1, pp. 200–201; Vol. 1, p. 215. See also the insistence of Laetitia Matilda Hawkins (*Letters on the Female Mind, its Powers and Pursuits, Addressed to Miss H. M. Williams, with particular reference to her Letters from France*, 2 vols. (London: Hookham, 1793), Vol. 1, pp. 11, 13) that every 'ornamental science or study' is appropriate to women; Hawkins includes 'geography, natural philosophy, natural history, civil history' and music and drawing among these. Thomas Gisborne, in *An Enquiry into the Duties of the Female Sex* (London: Cadell, 1797), pp. 20–21, is more explicit, dividing polite reading from geographical practices, including 'the acquirements subordinate to navigation; the knowledge indispensable in the wide field of commercial enterprise; the arts of defence, and of attack by land and sea'.

17 Jane Austen, *Pride and Prejudice*, ed. James Kinsley (Oxford: Oxford University Press, 1970), p. 60.

18 Austen, *Mansfield Park*, pp. 412, 422.

19 Austen, *Mansfield Park*, p. 140. John Barrow, *Some Account of the Public Life, and a Selection from the unpublished Writings, of the Earl of Macartney, the latter consisting of extracts from an account of the Russian Empire; a sketch of the political history of Ireland; and a journal of an embassy from the King of Great Britain to the Emperor of China* (London: Cadell, 1807).

20 Austen, *Mansfield Park*, p. 16.

21 When Austen's Miss Tilney wishes to cite the important historians she has read, she names the Scottish Enlightenment stalwarts David Hume and William Robertson (*Northanger Abbey*, ed. John Davie (Oxford: Oxford University Press, 1971), p. 85). See also Margaret Anne Doody, 'Jane Austen's Reading', in *The Jane Austen Companion*, ed. J. David Grey (New York: Macmillan, 1986), pp. 350–54; Christopher Kent, 'Learning History with, and from, Jane Austen', in *Jane Austen's Beginnings: The Juvenilia and Lady Susan* (Ann Arbor: UMI, 1989), pp. 59–72. On Enlightenment universal/stadial history, see Ronald L. Meek, *Social Science and the*

Ignoble Savage (Cambridge: Cambridge University Press, 1976).

22 Austen, *Mansfield Park*, p. 178.

23 Trumpener, *Bardic Nationalism*, p. 180; Tuite, 'Domestic Retrenchment', p. 111.

24 Examinations of social and economic status in *Mansfield Park* tend to view the novel as an affirmation of or a brief for the bourgeois improvement of the imperially dependent landed aristocracy, or to view the heroine's anomalous class position in isolation from the matter of the nation and its empire. For the former perspective, see for example Ferguson, *Colonialism*, pp. 66–67; for the latter, see Johnson, *Women, Politics, and the Novel*, pp. 107–108.

25 Austen, *Mansfield Park*, p. 17.

26 Austen, *Mansfield Park*, pp. 1–2.

27 Austen, *Mansfield Park*, p. 15.

28 Austen, *Mansfield Park*, p. 184.

29 Austen, *Mansfield Park*, p. 184.

30 Austen, *Mansfield Park*, p. 178.

31 Austen, *Mansfield Park*, p. 178.

32 Jane Austen, Letter to Cassandra Austen, 24 January 1813, in *Letters*, ed. Deirdre Le Faye (Oxford: Oxford University Press, new edn, 1997), p. 198. That Fanny quotes from a contemporary work from the same publisher, Walter Scott's *Lay of the Last Minstrel* (London: Longman, 1805) suggests that she would have had access to Clarkson's text through her uncle's account with the bookseller.

33 Brian Southam, *Jane Austen and the Navy* (London: Hambledon, 2000), p. 202.

34 Austen, *Mansfield Park*, p. 2.

35 Austen, *Mansfield Park*, p. 2. In the first chapter of *Mansfield Park* (p. 3), Mrs Price is 'preparing for her ninth lying-in' a year before Fanny departs to be adopted by the Bertrams, and she is later described (p. 355) as the 'mother of nine children'. But the list of her named children includes William, Fanny, and Susan, as well as Mary (p. 351), who dies young, 'Betsey […] and John, Richard, Sam, Tom, and Charles' (p. 355). That Mary is five years old when Fanny leaves for Mansfield, and that Charles and Betsey have both 'been born since Fanny's going away', suggests that the total number of Price children has reached at least eleven, with at least one name going unrecorded.

36 Austen, *Mansfield Park*, pp. 4, 8, 356.

37 See Linda Colley, *Britons: Forging the Nation* (London: Vintage, 1996), pp. 69–71; Benedict Anderson, *Imagined Communities: Reflections on the Origins and Spread of Nationalism* (London: Verso, rev. edn, 1991), pp. 93–94.

38 Austen, *Mansfield Park*, pp. 213, 347.

39 Austen, *Mansfield Park*, p. 3.

40 See Ina Ferris, *The Romantic National Tale and the Question of Ireland* (Cambridge: Cambridge University Press, 2002), pp. 26–37; Mary Poovey, *A History of the Modern Fact: Problems of Knowledge in the Sciences of Wealth and Society* (Chicago: University of Chicago Press, 1998), pp. 120–38; Trumpener, *Bardic Nationalism*, pp. 37–66.

41 See especially Ferris, *The Romantic National Tale*, pp. 3–4, 31–32. Ferris's account is a suggestive supplement to debates on Ireland's status as a colony or a subject of domestic imperialism; see Michael Hechter, *Internal Colonialism: The Celtic Fringe as a Subject of British Colonial Development, 1536–1966* (London: Routledge, 1975); S. J. Connolly, 'Eighteenth-Century Ireland: Colony or Ancien Régime?', in D. George

Boyce and Alan O'Day, *The Making of Modern Irish History: Revisionism and the Revisionist Controversy* (London: Routledge, 1996), pp. 15–33. The ubiquity of the term 'plantation', an Anglicization of *colonia*, in contemporary Anglo-Irish historiography implies that Ireland's domestic and colonial status continued, however uneasily, to coexist.

42 Austen, *Mansfield Park*, pp. 431–32.

43 William Galperin, *The Historical Austen* (Philadelphia: University of Pennsylvania Press, 2003), pp. 44–81.

44 Austen, *Mansfield Park*, pp. 187–88.

45 William Gilpin, *Observations Relative Chiefly to Picturesque Beauty, Made in the Year 1772, on Several Parts of England; Particularly the Mountains, and Lakes of Cumberland, and Westmoreland*, 2 vols. (London: Blamire, 1788), Vol. 1, p. xiv.

46 William Wordsworth, 'Lines composed a few miles above Tintern Abbey, on revisiting the Banks of the Wye during a Tour. July 13, 1798', in *Poems*, ed. Thomas Hutchinson (London: Oxford University Press, 1911), Vol. 1, l. 13. See also Marjorie Levinson, *Wordsworth's Great Period Poems* (Cambridge: Cambridge University Press, 1986), pp. 31–32.

47 Gilpin, *Observations*, Vol. 1, pp. 7–8.

48 Austen, *Mansfield Park*, p. 184.

49 Austen, *Mansfield Park*, p. 189. Fanny's obsessive rememberings, and the way they contrast with Mary's lack of interest while mirroring her reading of the scene as a reflection of herself, complicate Tuite's recent argument, in 'Domestic Retrenchment', that *Mansfield Park* argues for a bourgeois reform, through Fanny, of a landed aristocracy represented by Mary.

50 Gilpin, *Observations*, Vol. 1, p. 5.

51 Gilpin, *Observations*, Vol. 1, p. 7.

52 Tim Fulford, *Landscape, Liberty and Authority: Poetry, Criticism and Politics from Thomson to Wordsworth* (Cambridge: Cambridge University Press, 1996), p. 142.

53 Fulford, *Landscape, Liberty and Authority*, p. 164; see also Elizabeth K. Helsinger, *Rural Scenes and National Representation: Britain, 1815–1850* (Princeton: Princeton University Press, 1997), pp. 177–79.

54 Wordsworth, 'Tintern Abbey', ll. 15–20.

55 Debbie Lee, *Slavery and the Romantic Imagination* (Philadelphia: University of Pennsylvania Press, 2002), pp. 29–43, 202.

56 Lee, *Slavery and the Romantic Imagination*, p. 22.

57 Sonia Hofkosh, in *Sexual Politics and the Romantic Author* (Cambridge: Cambridge University Press, 1998), p. 123, points out that Fanny's schoolroom is known as 'the East room', associating it with the geographic East as well as with the class marginality of the governesses who once occupied it.

58 Austen, *Mansfield Park*, p. 137.

59 Austen, *Mansfield Park*, pp. 213, 270; William does not join the *Thrush* until he gains a lieutenancy, which happens only when Henry Crawford uses his connections in the admiralty.

60 See Thomas Richards, *Knowledge and the Fantasy of Empire* (London: Verso, 1993), p. 11; see also Anderson, *Imagined Communities*, p. 181.

61 Levinson, *Wordsworth's Great Period Poems*, pp. 14–57; Alan Liu, 'Local Transcendence: Cultural Criticism, Postmodernism, and the Romanticism of Detail',

Representations 32 (1990), p. 76.

62 See, respectively, Lee, *Slavery and the Romantic Imagination*; David Simpson, *Romanticism, Nationalism, and the Revolt Against Theory* (Chicago: University of Chicago Press, 1993).

63 See Clifford Siskin, *The Work of Writing: Literature and Social Change in Britain, 1700–1830* (Baltimore: Johns Hopkins University Press, 1998).

64 Austen, *Mansfield Park*, p. 363.

65 Siskin, *The Work of Writing*, p. 218.

66 On British readers, see Ferris, *The Romantic National Tale*, p. 18. Trumpener (*Bardic Nationalism*, pp. 37–66) and Joep Leerssen (*Remembrance and Imagination: Patterns in the Historical and Literary Representation of Ireland in the Nineteenth Century* (Cork: Cork University Press, 1997) and *Mere Irish and Fíor-Ghael: Studies in the Idea of Irish Nationality, its Development and Literary Expression prior to the Nineteenth Century* (Cork: Cork University Press, 2nd edn, 1997), pp. 329–76) document the large and diverse range of these texts that appeared during the Romantic period.

67 Charlotte Brooke, *Reliques of Irish Poetry: Consisting of Heroic Poems, Odes, Elegies, and Songs, Translated into English Verse* (Dublin, 1789), pp. x–xxiii; Charles Vallancey, *Collectanea de Rebus Hibernicis*, 6 vols. (Dublin: Marchbank).

68 Jane Austen, Letter to C. Austen, 17–18 January 1809, in *Letters*, p. 166; Letter to Anna Austen, 28 September 1814, in *Letters*, p. 278; *Mansfield Park*, p. 77; Letter to C. Austen, 18 June 1811, in *Letters*, p. 194.

69 Trumpener, *Bardic Nationalism*, pp. 37–66.

70 See my 'The National Tale and Allied Genres, 1770s–1840s', in John Wilson Foster, ed., *The Cambridge Companion to the Irish Novel* (Cambridge: Cambridge University Press, 2006), pp. 49–54.

71 Trumpener, *Bardic Nationalism*, pp. 45–46.

72 Sydney Owenson, *The Wild Irish Girl*, ed. Kathryn Kirkpatrick (Oxford: Oxford University Press, 1999), pp. 42–44.

73 Maria Edgeworth, *The Absentee*, ed. Heidi Thomson and Kim Walker (London: Penguin, 1999), p. 137.

74 Owenson, *The Wild Irish Girl*, p. 174.

75 See also Yoon Sun Lee, 'A Divided Inheritance: Scott's Antiquarian Novel and the British Nation', *ELH* 64 (1997), pp. 537–67 [p. 563].

76 Homi Bhabha, 'Introduction: Locations of Culture', in *The Location of Culture*, p. 11.

77 Leerssen, *Remembrance and Imagination*, pp. 37, 49.

78 Leerssen, *Remembrance and Imagination*, p. 50.

79 Yoon Sun Lee, 'A Divided Inheritance'.

80 Sydney Owenson, *Patriotic Sketches, written in Connaught* (London: Phillips, 1807), pp. 2–3, 5, 6.

81 Owenson, *Patriotic Sketches*, pp. 7–8. Richard C. Sha, in *The Visual and Verbal Sketch in British Romanticism* (Philadelphia: University of Pennsylvania Press, 1998), pp. 132–33, sees Owenson's comments as a revolutionary threat to Britain; I read them as a reminder, heralding Austen's in *Mansfield Park*, that the disparate pieces that make up empires have their own complex, continuing histories.

82 Austen, *Mansfield Park*, pp. 137, 187.

CHAPTER NINE

Between the Lines: Poetry, *Persuasion*, and the Feelings of the Past

MARY JACOBUS

Walking, in town or country, is one of the devices used in Jane Austen's novels to depict intimacy, private reflection, or the possibility of transgressing – by however little – the boundaries of consciousness and polite social intercourse. The Romantic-era novel as Austen practises it admits transgression, in this sense, between the little sportive lines of a country hedgerow. In *Persuasion* (1815–16), overhearing is the other device used to render porous the estranged yet linked consciousness of the novel's two former lovers, Anne Elliot and Captain Frederick Wentworth. The effect of such devices is to create an interstitial space in which the minds and feelings of the characters can meet; it is this space that renders *Persuasion* the most Romantic and private of Austen's novels. Each of the former lovers is the survivor of an earlier, failed romance that has been marginalized and apparently forgotten. Their recovery of this earlier romance involves the recovery of shared memory. Just as the 'revisit' poem returns the Romantic poet, often in the company of a second self, to a recollected landscape, so *Persuasion* revisits a landscape of former feeling and finds it changed.[1]

The most memorable scene of overhearing in *Persuasion* occurs at the end of the novel, in the famous revised chapter, when Captain Wentworth overhears Anne discussing the relative constancy of men and women. But an equally important instance occurs early on in the novel, during an autumnal walk when Anne, resting on a bank, overhears a conversation between Captain Wentworth and the high-spirited younger of the two Musgrove sisters, Louisa, as they make their way along 'the rough, wild sort of channel, down the centre' of a double West Country hedgerow.[2] The conversation is about persuasion – tellingly, given Austen's concern with the legitimacy (or otherwise) of one person's influence over another. In this novel, the words 'persuasion' or 'persuaded' rarely occur innocently.

When what takes place between the lines is as important as anything that gets said directly, overhearing becomes a privileged form of inter-subjective communication. Like an aside, or a digression, or a story within a story, overhearing occupies a kind of interstice in the narrative. Neither inside nor outside, Austen's interstice resembles what the psychoanalyst D. W. Winnicott calls 'potential space'.

An inter-subjective space, neither merged nor separate, Winnicott's potential space is at once the space of cultural experience and of its childhood precursor, play. As Winnicott writes, play is *'neither a matter of inner psychic reality nor a matter of external reality'*.[3] It occupies a liminal position where subjectivities blur and new meanings emerge. Is it a 'found' space, or an imaginary one? We should never ask this question, according to Winnicott. On this occasion, Louisa Musgrove energetically declares that she would not be 'easily persuaded' by anyone: 'When I have made up my mind, I have made it'.[4] Captain Wentworth takes her literally, rather than hearing this as the expression of adolescent fantasy. Praising her 'character of decision and firmness', he reflects: 'It is the worst evil of too yielding and indecisive a character, that no influence over it can be depended on. – You are never sure of a good impression being durable'.[5] Picking a glossy hazel-nut from the autumn hedgerow, he playfully imagines it to be 'in possession of all the happiness that a hazel-nut can be supposed capable of', and wishes that Louisa may be equally firm in order to assure her own continued beauty and happiness 'in her November of life'. It is not her life he has in mind, however, but that of the hidden overhearer, Anne – no longer 'a beautiful glossy nut' but faded and disregarded in her 27-year-old November of life. Pained and agitated by what she rightly understands as an allusion to her earlier lack of firmness, Anne is glad of the shelter of a holly bush; then, as so often, she takes refuge in 'the solitude and silence which only numbers could give'.[6]

In this scene of overhearing, we learn that Captain Wentworth judges Anne harshly, although pained to see her beauty and happiness diminished since their youthful parting eight years before. Anne (like the reader) overhears enough to understand that Captain Wentworth 'could not forgive her, – but he could not be unfeeling'.[7] We also see him interested despite himself to learn that Anne, since breaking off their engagement, had refused Charles Musgrove (who has married her querulous and self-centred younger sister Mary instead). And once again, we learn that Lady Russell – the original persuader – is held responsible: 'Charles might not be learned and bookish enough to please Lady Russell, and [...] therefore, she persuaded Anne to refuse him'.[8] Persuasion, in the sense of exercising influence over another, remains the issue that divides hero and heroine still. But there is another kind of influence at stake here, one that pertains not so much to one person's influence over another as to literary influence. Along with asking what constitutes a legitimate form of influence, *Persuasion* seems to be asking what makes it transient or durable, and how it makes itself felt. What kind of influence, for instance, causes Captain Wentworth to wax sentential over a hazel-nut while enjoying the company of a lively and attractive girl? Between the lines – just as he and Louisa are making their way along the overgrown path at the heart of the hedgerow – Austen probes and tests the extent of the influence exercised by books and poetry over persons and feelings.

The question of literary influence, along with its relation to mood, the formation of character, and the longevity of affection, crops up on a number of different occasions in *Persuasion*. On this walk, for instance, whose ostensible aim is to renew relations between the older, less lively Musgrove sister and her clergyman cousin, Anne has been supplementing her pleasure in 'the view of the last smiles of the year upon the tawny leaves and withered hedges',

> repeating to herself some few of the thousand poetical descriptions extant of autumn, that season of peculiar and inexhaustible influence on the mind of taste and tenderness, that season which has drawn from every poet, worthy of being read, some attempt at description, or some lines of feeling. She occupied her mind as much as possible in such like musings and quotations [...].[9]

'Lines of feeling' are inseparable from seasonal description in the eighteenth-century loco-descriptive tradition to which Anne's mind inevitably turns during her walk, as she repeats 'some few of the thousand poetical descriptions extant of autumn'. The peculiar Englishness of this construction of mood in terms of seasonal landscape marks Austen as an attentive and self-conscious practitioner of the same loco-descriptive genre. But this being rural England, 'the sweets of poetical despondence' are 'counteracted' by the sight of 'the ploughs at work, and the fresh-made path' which 'spoke the farmer [...] meaning to have spring again'.[10] And not just the farmer. The farmer's calendar hints at the author's romantic plot: the recovery of Anne's hopes and happiness with the return of spring. But Austen is also letting us know that Anne's poetic sensibility – her blend of literary quotation and seasonal affective disorder (SAD) – is an aspect of her secluded inner life, to which we only gain access via quotation, another form of interstitial overhearing on the part of the reader.

Austen is being just the slightest bit ironic about Anne's self-protective need for distraction in the presence of the large and not always harmonious family group that now includes her former lover ('She occupied her mind as much as possible in such like musings and quotations'), just as there is a touch of hyperbole about referring to 'the sweets of poetical despondence'. Such language implies that musings and quotations, like poetical melancholy, are a kind of secretion of Anne's mind – a defence against distress, appropriately counteracted by the sight of freshly ploughed fields. Later, Austen's implied critique is developed by Anne herself, when the bookish and retiring Captain Benwick (defined by his mourning for a dead fiancée, Fanny Harville) proves 'intimately acquainted with all [Scott's] tenderest songs' and Byron's 'impassioned descriptions of hopeless agony'.[11] Anne urges him to read less poetry and more prose, prescribing an impromptu alternative reading-list to counteract his melancholy tendency – 'such works of our best moralists, such collections of the finest letters, such memoirs of characters of worth and suffering, as occurred to her at the moment as calculated to rouse and fortify the mind'.[12] Yet for many readers, the mood of *Persuasion*'s autumnal reprise of an abortive courtship plot is coloured by Anne's own 'poetical despondence'. Like the interpolated lyrics in a gothic romance by Ann Radcliffe, evoking unde-fined states of feeling or linking hero and heroine in a song-haunted landscape, poetic quotation represents an affective register that is never entirely counteracted by the farmer's plough. Poetry similarly provides fertile ground for feelings that burgeon between the lines of Austen's well-cultivated agricultural landscape. One might call it the novel's literary unconscious. But it is also one of the ways in which the novel's larger polit-ical and historical contexts make themselves indirectly felt.

Poetry marks *Persuasion* as among the most Romantic of all Austen's novels – a novel that privileges constancy to the past even when all hope is gone. Poetic quotation gives access to a range of reference that is not automatically available to the West Country land-owning classes of England, especially those whose favourite (perhaps only) reading is Debrett's Baronetage, sporting almanacs, or the Navy List to which Anne herself turns for news of her former lover's navel career. The novel's literary allusions expand its horizons beyond the vicinity of Somerset, Dorset, and Bath, while accurately depicting the reading habits of the educated classes of the time, including those, like Anne (or Austen herself) possessing 'minds of taste and tenderness'. As well as introducing elements of exoticism and tragic violence excluded from *Persuasion*'s setting (whether domestic, rural, or urban) poetry constitutes an indirect commentary on the national background against which the novel requires to be read, given its near-contemporary time-frame of 1814, after two decades of Napoleonic wars. But, while preserving and transforming the past, quotation also signals a kind of addiction to melancholy on Anne's part. It implies repetition and stasis, clinging to the past rather than living in the present. This is the diagnostic gist of *Persuasion*'s critique of the poetical tendency. At the end of the novel, Anne's recovery of happiness occasions one of Austen's rare flights of metaphor. The overtaking of literary allusion by the poetry of everyday life signals a shift from the feelings of the past to hope for the future. The quotation that had helped to preserve Anne's vulnerable interiority, while perpetuating her mood of grief, is integrated into Austen's own prose. The romance of the everyday displaces the rhetoric of older forms of persuasion, sportively forecasting renewal. This 'lyricization of the novel' has been identified with *Persuasion*'s use of free indirect discourse.[13] I will be arguing that it also signals a subtle, tactical, and discriminating relation to the poetical tendency.

Lines of Feeling

'Forced into prudence in her youth', Anne 'learned romance as she grew older'.[14] *Persuasion* invites us to reflect on the ambiguity of romance, especially when it comes to poetical influence. For Anne, poetry enshrines feelings that have been banished from the world of Kellynch Hall, although privately kept alive in her by reading, musing, and quotation. It preserves the beleaguered capacity for feeling and reflection which characterizes Anne (alone of her family). But what form of mental activity is constituted by her 'musings and quotations'? What is the status of silent reflection in a novel full of conversation, dancing, walks, excursions, concerts, and parties? – a novel whose dramatic turning-point takes the form of an excited teenager being jumped down from a not-very-great height during an impulsive expedition to a picturesque sea-side resort. Stasis and movement are counter-poised. Literary taste in *Persuasion* resembles the Musgrove family – 'in a state of alteration, perhaps of improvement', with one generation 'in the old English style, and the young people in the new'.[15] Austen's poetical allusions reveal the perennial appeal of the old eighteenth-century canon that coexisted with the new Romantic canon of best-sellers by Scott and Byron. Longstanding eighteenth-century favourites such as Thomson's *Seasons* (1730) jostle with another, more topical and fashionable index of literary taste. Scott and Byron are both mentioned prominently in *Persuasion* during Anne's conversations about contemporary poetry. We know that Austen's own favourites included Samuel Johnson's prose and William Cowper's verse, neither of which is explicitly mentioned in the novel.[16] Her love of Cowper especially places Austen on the cusp of late-eighteenth-century moralized sensibility, mingling evangelical religion, patriotism, and anti-slavery politics with a taste for retirement and reflective country pursuits. But the poetic inter-texts of *Persuasion* are equally revealing from a cultural point of view. While they locate a significant form of activity in solitude, they also enlarge the sphere of the social affections beyond the family, opening a window onto wider geopolitical landscapes.[17] They reveal a society in a state of alteration, looking both back and forward: a society in transition.

Among the poetical descriptions Anne might plausibly have repeated to herself during her autumnal walk would have been lines from 'Autumn', excerpted from Thomson's much-reprinted *Seasons*. Austen also alludes to more modern sonnets, perhaps by William Bowles or Charlotte Smith, 'fraught with the apt analogy of the declining year, with declining happi-ness'.[18] 'Autumn', on the face of it, is a representative tone-poem of eighteenth-century seasonal melancholy. 'Solitary, and in pensive Guise', the poet wanders 'through the sadden'd Grove', haunt of 'the lonesome Muse'.[19] But Thomson is a moralist as well as a loco-descriptive poet; Autumn is the season

> For those whom Wisdom and whom Nature charm.
> To steal themselves from the degenerate Croud,
> And soar above this little Scene of Things;
> To tread low-thoughted Vice beneath their Feet;
> To soothe the throbbing Passions into Peace;
> And wooe lone Quiet in her silent Walks.[20]

Bracing advice for Anne Elliot – who, as it happens, will steal away from the degenerate crowd to visit an old school friend in Bath and soar above the low-thoughted vice of her calculating cousin, the future Sir William Elliot. Notice, however, that Anne, rather than 'woo[ing] lone Quiet in her silent Walks', is always in the company of others: paradoxically, she often seeks 'the solitude and silence which only numbers can bring'. Anne, in fact, is most solitary when in the company of other people. Sociability offers her an opportunity to be pensive, even as her fingers automatically play the tunes to which others dance. This slight but significant deviation from Thomson's autumnal poet-wanderer becomes more striking as the passage from *The Seasons* unfolds. Silenced birds, falling leaves, whistling winds, fallen fruit – 'The desolated prospect thrills the soul' – serve to introduce the 'POWER OF PHILOSOPHIC MELANCHOLY'. This is stronger stuff than either Anne or Austen would endorse, and certainly exceeds the sentimentality of Captain Wentworth's nut-gathering reflections.

Characterized by 'the sudden-starting Tear, / The soften'd Feature, and the beating Heart', Philosophic Melancholy is a power that 'Inflames Imagination', 'Infuses every Tenderness', and 'exalts the swelling Thought'. It induces a deliriously creative state of mind, raises and elevates the Passions, and transforms 'Devotion' into 'rapture and divine Astonishment'. Thomson's philosophic melancholy leads to 'love of Nature'; but above all, it leads to the wish to do good to the human race. Thomson's substantial social agenda includes the following: sighing for 'suffering Worth', 'Scorn, / Of Tyrant Pride', 'the fearless great Resolve', wondering at the dying Patriot, throbbing for Virtue and Fame, and finally 'The Sympathies of Love and Friendship dear; / With all the *social Offspring of the Heart*'.[21] This social agenda reads like the ideological subtext of all that Captain Wentworth represents in *Persuasion* – the patriotic and courageous world of male friendship that Austen associates with the Navy during the period of the Napoleonic wars. Anne Elliot on her walk is no more overwhelmed by the access of Thomson's 'Ten thousand fleet Ideas' than Austen herself. Yet something of this passion and quickness, ambition and scorn, resolve and social sympathy, arguably converge in the irrepressible brightness of Captain Wentworth's eye and the curl of his lip – all the youthful idealism, brilliance, and impetuosity that Lady Russell had so mistrusted, but that bring him success in the Napoleonic wars. At the end of *Persuasion*, we see him – soul-pierced, in an agony of uncertainty and hope – apostrophizing Anne in the highly wrought language of an eighteenth-century lover: 'I have loved none but you […]. Too good, too excellent creature!', as he places in her hands the letter he has been writing 'with eyes of glowing entreaty'.[22] Patriotic endeavour abroad and social sympathy at home undergird the reawakening of romantic love.

Austen is drawing on an eighteenth-century tradition that had associated pleasure in landscape not just with predictable analogies between the declining year and declining happiness, but with the interweaving of deep emotion, high moral aspiration, and national sentiment. The politics of solitary autumnal musings and quotation in *Persuasion* turn out to be anything but abstracted from the situation of England in 1814, when peace broke out after the enforced abdication and first exile of Napoleon.[23] As Sir Walter Elliot's agent shrewdly observes to his cash-strapped employer: 'This peace will be turning all our rich Navy Officers ashore. They will all be wanting a home' – and wives too.[24] The Navy is the profession from which young, unlanded, unconnected Captain Wentworth has grown independently wealthy. During the same period, Sir Walter, living snobbishly and beyond his means on an inherited baronetcy, has grown poor.[25] The peace of 1814 allows Austen to differentiate sharply between those who had risked their lives at war – profiting from the courage and enterprise for which the Navy provided chancy but substantial rewards – and those who had grown wealthy by staying at home and marrying for money, like William Elliot, the calculating heir to Sir Walter's baronetcy. The Navy is also the professional group that supplies Anne with a surrogate family, lacking as she does an appreciative family of her own. 'The Sympathies of Love and Friendship dear' are depicted in the unassuming hospitality of the Harville family circle, making do on shore in their cramped cottage at Lyme. Anne reflects regretfully on what might have been hers: 'These would have been all my friends'.[26] A temporary inmate of their household by virtue of his engagement to Captain Harville's recently dead sister, the melancholy Captain Benwick allows Austen (and her readers) to make a cross-gender comparison between the capable Anne and a grieving lover more thoroughly addicted to poetry than she is.

Anne's conversations with Captain Benwick provide the opportunity for the other prominent moment of literary allusion in *Persuasion*. The family man, Captain Harville, is 'no reader', preferring do-it-yourself projects, fishing, and toy-making for his children to books and reading. But he has 'fashioned very pretty shelves, for a tolerable collection of well-bound volumes, the property of Captain Benwick'.[27] Described as '[a] young man of considerable taste in reading, though principally in poetry', Captain Benwick is easily coaxed into talking poetry with Anne – in fact, 'it had rather the appearance of feelings glad to burst their usual restraints'.[28] Their discussion concerns the poets who constituted the new Romantic canon – not Wordsworth and Coleridge, but the best-selling Scott and Byron, who represent 'the richness of the present age':

> having talked of poetry, the richness of the present age, and gone through a brief comparisons of opinion as to the first-rate poets, trying to ascertain whether *Marmion* or *The Lady of the Lake* were to be preferred, and how ranked the *Giaour* and *The Bride of Abydos*, and moreover, how the *Giaour* was to be

pronounced, he shewed himself so intimately acquainted with all the tenderest songs of the one poet, and all the impassioned descriptions of hopeless agony of the other; he repeated, with such tremulous feeling, the various lines which imaged a broken heart, or a mind destroyed by wretchedness, and looked so entirely as if he meant to be understood, that she ventured to hope he did not always read only poetry, and to say, that she thought it was the misfortune of poetry, to be seldom safely enjoyed by those who enjoyed it completely; and that the strong feelings which alone could estimate it truly, were the very feelings which ought to taste it but sparingly.[29]

Poetry (Anne implies) may demand strong feelings for its proper appreciation, but strength of feeling has its own dangers. Complete enjoyment (or, as we might say, identification) is not safe enjoyment. Poetry should be sparingly tasted and counteracted by a healthy diet of prose moralists.

In response to Anne's therapeutic prescription, Captain Benwick – 'with a shake of his head, and sighs which declared his little faith in the efficacy of any books on grief like his, [...] noted down the names of those she recommended, and promised to procure and read them'.[30] But Anne's proposed course of bibliotherapy suggests that books do have an influence on grief, whether to heighten or moderate it. Captain Benwick believes that books can have little efficacy when it comes to his own grief, since he believes that his feelings exist independently of literature; poetry simply gives expression to grief rather than shaping it (or even leading him to imitate its contemporary poetic forms). By contrast, Anne seems to believe that reading can in fact exercise an influence over one's feelings, for good and ill. Austen's implied argument – that reading both constructs and colours feeling – puts literary persuasion in the dock alongside the influence exercised by one person over another. Anne herself is privately amused at the idea of 'preach[ing] patience and resignation to a young man whom she had never seen before' and suspects that 'like many other great moralists and preachers, she had been eloquent on a point on which her own conduct would ill bear examination'.[31] She preaches, of course, from experience. We could apply these ironic self-reflections to Anne's taste in reading. She was presumably as familiar as Captain Benwick (and Austen herself) with the subtle distinctions to be made between the respective recent poems of Scott (a favourite of Austen's) and Byron. We don't know whether Scott's best-selling *Marmion* (1808) was preferred to *The Lady of the Lake* (1810), or Byron's *The Giaour* to *The Bride of Abydos* (1813). But we do know that these Romantic narrative poems were pointedly topical in ways that turn out to be strategic, given the date and setting of *Persuasion*.

Marmion's combination of seasonal melancholy and political reflection explicitly announces itself as having been written in the wake of the deaths of Nelson and Pitt. Scott's patriotic and nationalist commemoration of the Battle of Flodden Field, three centuries before, centres on a fictional hero whose proto-Byronic remorse for an earlier erotic betrayal earns him an anonymous grave; a medieval tale of romantic intrigue is spliced onto Scott's commemoration of one of the most tragic defeats of Scottish history. Canto I of *Marmion* opens by evoking an autumnal Scottish land-scape – 'November's sky is chill and drear, / November's leaf is red and sear [...] No longer Autumn's glowing red / Upon our Forest hills is shed'.[32] The mountain children ask if spring will return, to which the poet answers: 'the daisy's flower / Again shall paint your summer bower; [...] To mute and to material things / New life revolving summer brings'.[33] But a deeper mourning provides the underlying inspiration for its seasonal melancholy. *Persuasion*, too, has claims to be thought of as a novel of mourning. Most obviously, Anne is in mourning for lost love and lost youth, although not, as it happens, the death in action of Captain Went-worth – an outcome that Lady Russell may well have feared, but does not mention as a cogent reason for her opposition to a long engagement. But we glimpse this alternative narrative in its mirror-image, Captain Benwick's pathetic history of bereavement (the 'little history of his private life, which rendered him perfectly interesting in the eyes of all the ladies'):

> He had been engaged to Captain Harville's sister, and was now mourning her loss. They had been a year or two waiting for fortune and promotion. Fortune came, his prize-money as Lieutenant being great, – promotion, too, came at *last*; but Fanny Harville did not live to know it. She had died the preceding summer, while he was at sea. Captain Wentworth believed it impossible for man to be more attached to woman than poor Benwick had been to Fanny Harville, or to be more deeply afflicted under the dreadful change. He consid-ered his disposition as of the sort which must suffer heavily, uniting very strong feelings with quiet, serious, and retiring manners, and a decided taste for reading, and sedentary pursuits.[34]

Change the gender of the pronouns, and we see Anne Elliot's union of strong feelings with quiet, serious, and retiring manners and a taste for reading. Just so might she have suffered under 'the dreadful change' of young Captain Wentworth's death at sea had they been engaged.

Anne shudders privately at Captain Wentworth's account of his voyage on the decrepit ship, the *Asp*, whose command he took with such alacrity after his disappointment at the breaking-off of their engagement.

Although he turns out to have been lucky at sea, he was even luckier (he relates) to have put into port before a terrific storm that would have sunk his leaky sloop: 'Four-and-twenty hours later, and I should only have been a gallant Captain Wentworth, in a small paragraph at one corner of the newspapers'.[35] But this is not the only occasion on which we learn about the risks of death at sea. Mrs Musgrove's mourning for her ne'er-do-well midshipman son in *Persuasion* is treated with comic realism and notoriously scant sympathy. The spectacle of her 'large fat sighings over the destiny of a son, whom alive nobody had cared for' picks up on Austen's earlier, unsentimental mention of young Dick Musgrove, sent to sea 'because he was stupid and unmanageable on shore' and 'seldom heard of, and scarcely at all regretted' until the news of his death reaches his family.[36] Captain Wentworth, who has briefly had Dick Musgrove under his command, shows his consideration 'for all that was real and unabsurd in the parent's feelings'.[37] But this is more than can be said of Austen herself: 'the Musgroves had had the ill fortune of a very troublesome, hopeless son; and the good fortune to lose him before he reached his twentieth year'.[38] The Musgroves are depicted as a large and loving family, sincerely and unpretentiously devoted to the well-being of all their children. There is something altogether too brusque in *Persuasion*'s dismissal of 'thick-head, unfeeling, unprofitable Dick Musgrove'. Death at sea from the fevers to which sailors in the tropics were all too prone, let alone death at sea in storm or battle, renders this son troublesome in ways that Austen does her best to repress. Arguably, Anne's silent eight-year grief stands in for a more pervasive form of national mourning for sons and lovers lost at sea.

The multiple losses produced by decades of war would certainly have been enough to justify national mourning, not just the mourning of one fat mother over a troublesome son. In particular, England was in mourning for its national heroes, as *Marmion* announces in the introduction to its opening canto. Scott explicitly frames his historical tragedy with the present-day losses which would have been uppermost in his readers' minds:

> But oh! my country's wintry state
> What second spring shall renovate?
> What powerful call shall bid arise
> The buried warlike, and the wise?
> The mind that thought for Britain's weal,
> The hand that grasped the victor's steel?
> The vernal sun new life bestows

Even on the meanest flower that blows;
But vainly, vainly, may he shine,
Where glory weeps o'er NELSON's shrine;
And vainly pierce the solemn gloom,
That shrouds, O PITT, thy hallowed tomb!

    Deep graved in every British heart
O never let those names depart![39]

The names of Nelson and Pitt are never so much as mentioned in *Persuasion*. Yet even a self-proclaimed Border Minstrel is constrained to lament these national heroes before he turns to the Scottish past. England newly at peace in 1814 was in a different mood from that of 1808, but Austen surely had sufficient historical perspective to know that the haven which Kellynch Hall or Lyme provided for naval officers on shore was a comparatively recent development (and was in fact to prove short-lived).[40] Significantly, 1808 (the date of *Marmion*) takes the reader back to the time when Captain Wentworth, returning to England a few thousand pounds richer by virtue of his prize-money, might have written to Anne asking her to renew their engagement. The period of their original engagement and its breaking off was two years before that, in 1806. This was the time when the nation was in mourning for the death of Admiral Nelson in 1805, during the Battle of Trafalgar, while Pitt – the architect of Britain's opposition to Napoleon – had died in 1806.

    There is, then, a double historical time-scheme – a double chronology – at work in *Persuasion*. The date of Anne Elliot's and Captain Wentworth's youthful engagement coincides with an earlier period of emergency, instability, and danger, precisely the period to which Scott's *Marmion* explicitly alludes. The precariousness of the young Captain Wentworth's future corresponded to a time of national uncertainty and risk. Even supposing *The Lady of the Lake* (1810) had been the poem preferred by Anne or Captain Benwick, one reason might have been its enshrining of a time of exile and pining for home, as expressed in its minstrel songs. The hopes of the absent soldier are high, his sword true, his friend sincere, his lady constant, but (so the minstrel sings) he may still encounter exile and misfortune at war:

    'Or if on life's uncertain main
      Mishap shall mar thy sail;
    If faithful, wise, and brave in vain,
    Woe, want, and exile thou sustain
      Beneath the fickle gale;

Waste not a sigh on fortune changed,
On thankless courts, or friends estranged [...].[41]

'Waste not a sigh on [...] friends estranged' is an injunction heeded too well by angry Captain Wentworth. *The Lady of the Lake* echoes with tumultuous alarms and calls to battle as young warriors and clansmen gather at the summons, while a Marmion-like chieftain submerges his unrequited love and dark misdeeds in war. Peace breaks out after long strife (as it was eventually to do in 1814). The constant heroine whom we first encounter in rural seclusion moves to centre-stage and takes resolute action. Attributes celebrated in *The Lady of the Lake* include faithfulness, disinterested love, and respect for worthy foes, interspersed with the enchantments of interpolated lyrics. 'And now the mountain breezes scarcely bring / A wandering witch-note of the distant spell – / And now, 'tis silent all! Enchantress, fare thee well!' So ends the poem, returning us to the present. War is made safe by being consigned to a melancholy past, but melancholy leaks into the present, as it does in *Persuasion*.

Scott writes self-consciously as a loyal patriot about long-ago conflicts between worthy foes. Although fierce and bloody, war remains an internal struggle between the heroes of English and Scottish history. His poetry represents a form of national myth-making – a consolidation of national unity under the sign of romance. Byron's oriental tales invoke a different geopolitical landscape. They provide a window onto more disturbing emotions, and more ambiguous politics, as well as the exotic terrain of the eastern Mediterranean (along with the Azores, the scene of war for Captain Wentworth). The popularity of *The Giaour* and *The Bride of Abydos* was virtually unparalleled at the time of *Persuasion*. Captain Benwick suggests that while Scott's poems pathetically 'imaged a broken heart', Byron's poems (more risky and pathological in emphasis) depict 'a mind destroyed by wretchedness'. Byron's taboo-breaking disregard of British manners, morals, and erotic conventions, along with the tangled politics of his near-eastern settings, expresses a dissident and revolutionary impulse that is absent from Scott's chivalric conservative patriotism (implicitly identified with the pre-history of Anne Elliot's romance). In 1814, these oriental tales were swiftly followed by two others, *The Corsair* and *Lara* – too recent, perhaps, for Captain Benwick and Anne to compare – although Austen may be alluding to the opening lines of *The Corsair* when the vista at Lyme brings to both their minds 'Lord Byron's "dark blue seas"':[42] 'O'er the glad waters of the dark blue sea, / Our thoughts as boundless, and our souls as free [...] Survey our empire, and behold our home!'.[43] For both of them, at the very least, thoughts of a British imperial war in which the Navy had played a key part would have been hard to separate from the sight of the sea.

But to Anne (although not presumably to Captains Benwick and Wentworth), the Eastern Mediterranean – 'These Edens of the eastern wave'[44] – would have been a closed book. In Byron's oriental tales, the time-travel of Scott's chivalric northern romances relocates to a theatre of war associated with exoticism and unbridled passion. This was a region currently in decline – 'There passion riots in her pride, / And lust and rapine wildly reign'.[45] Needless to say, the wildness of lust and rapine is tactfully erased from Austen's *Persuasion*, or takes only urban social forms like William Elliot's seductive behaviour. Byron's 'farewell beam of Feeling past away' speaks of lost glory and freedom, mingled decay and decline, and an exhausted Hellenic culture overrun by the Turks.[46] Comparison with Sir Walter Elliot's need for retrenchment and his slavish dependence on social recognition can only be inadvertent, ironic, and sidelong: ''Twere long to tell, and sad to trace, / Each step from splendour to disgrace'.[47] With Greece in mind, Byron diagnoses 'Self-abasement' as the cause of the Greek fall under Turkish rule. Both *The Giaour* and *The Bride of Abydos* address the complexities of imperialism as they were currently being played out in the Levant. British sympathies were strongly identified with the Greek past, yet British foreign policy was supporting the decaying Ottoman Empire as a counterweight to Russian designs on the Mediterranean. Leila, the dead Circassian slave of *The Giaour*, is tacitly equated with the corpse of Greece over whom East and West struggle – beautiful, betrayed, and forever lost to the outlaw hero. In contrast to Scott's patriotic nationalism and his depiction of a tragic past, Byron (it has been argued) depicts 'the moral hopelessness of the war-torn Levant and, by extension, war-torn Europe'.[48] Although the enemy is Turkish, commentators rightly observe that Byron never equates cultural difference and European moral superiority.[49] Islamic and Christian religions are equally characterized by despotism, injustice, and superstition.

The Giaour (a generically Christian Venetian entrepreneur) personifies the complexities of British relations to a region that it preyed on with its naval strength, just as imperial Venice had once exploited it for gain by means of its own naval supremacy in the Mediterranean. The morally ambiguous Giaour is as much caught up in the confused mix of violence and vengeance as his Turkish opponent, Hassan, who has Leila sewn up in a sack and drowned to punish her infidelity with a Christian. The Giaour is marked by the quintessential attribute of the Byronic hero ('a mind destroyed by wretchedness', in Austen's paraphrase) – remorse. But no actual misdeeds ever quite account for his guilt, whether it is the death of the erotically compromised Leila or his murder of Hassan. By contrast, *The Bride of Abydos* – a tale of quasi-incestuous love – pays tribute to wild hearts and wild farewells, and to love that defies patriarchal despotism. The love-story of Zuleika and Selim is played out against the mythical past of the Hellespont that had once separated Hero and Leander. Selim's crew of pirates – 'So let them ease their hearts with prate / Of equal rights [...] I have a love of freedom too' – define him as a philhellenic freedom-booter who owes fealty to none, so long as he has his beloved Zuleika on board: 'Ay – let the loud winds whistle o'er the deck, / So that those arms cling closer round my neck'. [50] Byron's theme of unsuccessful revolt is accompanied by the traditional oriental motif of nightingale and rose, forever entwined in love and grief.

Orientalism (whether cruel or pathetic, immoral or poetic) could hardly be further from the ethos of *Persuasion*. Austen satirizes Captain Benwick's poetical tastes by making him fall in love with the formerly exuberant, now convalescent and quiescent Louisa Musgrove: 'she would learn to be an enthusiast for Scott and Lord Byron; of course they had fallen in love over poetry'.[51] Falling in love over poetry is the fate of superficial lovers. But Byron's oriental tales implicate the politics of British imperialism. They place the Napoleonic wars in an international frame, gesturing towards what *Persuasion*'s enthusiasm for the Navy excludes – any discussion of British war-objectives, other than the increased wealth and upward mobility that compensated naval officers for the hazards of their chosen career. Just as loco-descriptive seasonal poetry allows both melancholy and national sentiment to invade the subtext of *Persuasion*, Scott's patriotic nationalism and Byronic disaffected philhellenism allow both tragedy and a critique of imperialism to filter into the novel's political unconscious. *Persuasion*'s poetic inter-texts render its novelistic boundaries porous, like the consciousnesses of its two main characters. In this transitional poetic space, *Persuasion* gestures towards what Winnicott calls 'the search for the self' while hinting at the potential addictiveness – the repetitiveness – of both poetry and the feelings of the past.

'Our Feelings Prey Upon Us'

When Captain Benwick 'repeated, with such tremulous feeling, the various lines which imaged a broken heart, or a mind destroyed by wretchedness', he makes the same consolatory use of poetry as Anne Elliot, 'repeating to herself some few of the thousand poetical descriptions extant of autumn'.[52] The repetition of poetry helps them both to endure their losses, but it prevents them returning fully to life. 'We live at home, quiet, confined, and our feelings prey upon us', Anne famously confides to Captain Harville at the end of the novel.[53] She means women like herself, but Captain Benwick is also a literary melancholic confined to the domestic sphere by naval unemployment. Austen implies that a feeling for poetry can feed a defensive – even pathological – attachment to the past that is synonymous with domestic confinement. Two essays included in Winnicott's *Playing and Reality* (1971), 'Playing: Creative Activity and the Search for the Self' and its companion-piece, 'Dreaming, Fantasying, and Living: A Case-History describing a Primary Dissociation', address this double relation to poetry in psychoanalytic terms. The patients in both essays – perhaps the same person – are both middle-aged women living in a state of dissociation from their lives. Occupied by fantasying and daydreaming, the patient in each consumes her days in repetitive, time-killing card-games like playing patience. While apparently sitting in her room, she may in fantasy have painted a picture, done an interesting piece of work, or gone for a walk – 'but from the observer's point of view nothing whatever has happened'.[54] Winnicott tells us that this is a woman who 'knows enough about life and living and about her potential to realize that in life terms she is missing the boat, and that she has always been missing the boat'.[55] When we first meet the 27-year-old Anne Elliot, she too has missed the boat, and realizes it.

The unexplained enigma in *Persuasion* is why intelligent, brilliant, head-strong young Captain Wentworth should ever have fallen in love with quiet nineteen-year-old Anne Elliot in the first place. Austen explains that while he 'had nothing to do, she had hardly any body to love'; despite his own temperament, he is drawn to her 'gentleness, modesty, taste, and feeling'.[56] But when it comes to the point, Anne proves unable to stand up for herself or her feelings: 'She was persuaded to believe the engagement a wrong thing – indiscreet, improper, hardly capable of success, and not deserving it'.[57] Comforted 'under the misery of parting' by the thought that she is being 'self-denying principally for *his* advantage', she perversely sacrifices her happiness for his, only to encounter the resentment of a lover 'feeling himself ill-used by so forced a relinquishment'.[58] Yet the last chapter of *Persuasion* strikes an appropriately upbeat note: 'Who can be in doubt of what followed? When any two young people take it into their heads to marry, they are pretty sure by perseverance to carry their point'.[59] But this was not the case for Anne Elliot and Frederick Wentworth previously, when lack of a secure income was all that divided them. Captain Wentworth's anger, as much as Anne's silent wretchedness, informs their meeting eight years later – 'She had used him ill; deserted and disappointed him; and worse, she had shown a feebleness of character in doing so [...]. It had been the effect of over-persuasion. It had been weakness and timidity'.[60] We hear his point of view, expressed with characteristic energy. Captain Wentworth is forced to recant, but the question remains: why was Anne so persuadable in the first place?

Austen makes it clear from the outset that Anne, the overlooked middle sister – her birth followed two years later by that of a still-born son and heir, and later a younger sister – is of little account in the Elliot family since the death of her mother, 'an excellent woman, sensible and amiable', when she was only fourteen.[61] Her vain father and handsome older sister ignore her, locked in mutual self-regard, fixated on appearances, each other, and the baronetcy, while Anne is consigned to the role of soother, supporter, and home-help for her fretful younger sister, Mary. In *Playing and Reality*, Winnicott describes his patient as the youngest of several siblings who 'found herself in a world that was already organized before she came into the nursery. She was very intelligent and she managed somehow or other to fit in'.[62] But despite this, 'she was never really very rewarding as a member of the group from her own or from the other children's point of view, because she could fit in only on a compliance basis'.[63] Compliance, as always, is a central problem for Winnicott, suppressing as it does what he calls the 'spontaneous gesture' of the hidden or true self. We learn that the communal games his patient played as a child were unsatisfactory – 'she was simply struggling to play whatever role was assigned to her, and the others felt that something was lacking in the sense that she was not actively contributing-in'.[64] But from the patient's point of view, while she appeared to be playing, she was actually fantasying: 'over long periods her defence was to live here in this fantasying activity, and to watch herself playing the other children's games as if watching someone else in the nursery group'.[65] She is in the group but not part of it.

In a different sense, we see Anne simultaneously watching herself playing and watching others play. When she plays the piano so that the others can dance at Uppercross, 'she was extremely glad to be employed, and desired nothing in return but to be unobserved'.[66] But as she plays, she herself observes Captain Wentworth's high spirits, surrounded by a bevy of admiring young women ('If he were a little spoilt by such universal, such eager admiration, who could wonder?'); she even observes Captain Wentworth's covert observation of her. And as she will again do on her walk, she overhears a conversation that concerns herself:

> These were some of the thoughts which occupied Anne, while her fingers were mechanically at work, proceeding for half an hour together, equally without error, and without consciousness. *Once* she felt that he was looking at herself – observing her altered features, perhaps, trying to trace in them the ruins of the face which had once charmed him; and *once* she knew that he must have spoken of her, – she was hardly aware of it, till she heard the answer, but then she was sure of his having asked his partner whether Miss Elliot never danced? The answer was, 'Oh! no, never; she has quite given up dancing. She had rather play. She is never tired of playing.'[67]

'Playing […] as if watching someone else' comes close to describing Anne at the piano ('her fingers were mechanically at work […] equally without error, and without consciousness'). Her mechanical playing expresses a habitual relation not only to her family-group but to her own life. She has given up dancing along with what it signifies in courtship and comedy, becoming the accompanist only: 'She had rather play. She is never tired of playing.'

As she grew older, Winnicott's patient, we are told, 'managed to construct a life in which nothing that was really happening was fully significant to her. Gradually she became one of the many who do not feel that they exist in their own right as whole human beings'.[68] This tragic dilemma underlies her inactivity and her addiction to daydreaming. On one occasion, she fantasizes hectically cutting out and planning the pattern for a dress. Winnicott interprets this fantasy in the light of a childhood that 'seemed unable to allow her to be formless but must, as she felt it, pattern her and cut her out into shapes conceived by other people'.[69] This could be a description – even a deconstruction – of the 'persuasion' exercised by Anne's god-mother, the well-meaning but insensitive Lady Russell, who successfully bullies Anne into submitting to her views about an engagement to Captain Wentworth:

> Anne Elliot, with all her claims of birth, beauty, and mind, to throw herself away at nineteen; involve herself at nineteen in an engagement with a young man, who had nothing but himself to recommend him […]. [This] would be, indeed, a throwing away, which she grieved to think of! Anne Elliot, so young, known to so few, to be snatched off by a stranger without alliance or fortune;

or rather sunk by him into a state of most wearing, anxious, youth-killing dependence! It must not be, if by any fair interference of friendship, any representations from one who had almost a mother's love, and mother's rights, it would be prevented.[70]

Here Austen's free indirect speech ventriloquizes Lady Russell's strenuous 'representations' to Anne of the consequences of her rash engagement ('a throwing away, which she grieved to think of!') in such a way as to suggest how she is bullied into conformity with Lady Russell's forceful views: 'She deprecated the connexion in every light'.[71] Lacking an alive and understanding mother, coerced into confusing 'prudence' with obedience to 'almost a mother's love, and mother's rights', Anne respects the views of her surrogate mother and gives up Captain Wentworth. Not for nothing did Mary Wollstonecraft denounce the ideology of parental rights for its potential tyranny over daughters. But *Persuasion* can be read (between the lines) as making more than a feminist point. Caught between overbearing Lady Russell on one hand, and headstrong Captain Wentworth on the other, Anne takes refuge in the ambiguous (perhaps habitual) consolations of self-sacrifice. And so far as anyone else is aware, Austen tells us, that is the close of 'this little history of sorrowful interest'.[72]

Winnicott suggests that his patient has lacked the true '*formlessness*' necessary for creative dreaming and living. If his patient had dreamed about the cutting out of a dress as opposed to fantasying it, 'this would be a comment on her own personality and self-establishment'.[73] He equates conformity to the shapes of others with 'compliance and a false self organization'.[74] Compliance brings into being a defensive self whose main purpose is at once to defend and to maintain communication with a hidden or secret self.[75] Winnicott's patient is so afraid of the loss of her own identity that she can hardly allow herself to make any progress in the analysis. She fantasizes that her flat is being taken over by other people. In a dream, Winnicott says, the same scenario 'would have to do with her finding new possibilities in her own personality [...]. This is the opposite of feeling patterned and gives her a way of identifying without loss of identity'.[76] By the end of *Persuasion*, Anne is able to identify both with the immature self who had once been guided by her surrogate mother, Lady Russell, and with the mature self who would never give the same advice: neither merging her identity with Lady Russell's nor losing it in Captain Wentworth's equally strong personality, she can now assert her own feelings. Winnicott goes on to underline the need for a poetic form of communication with his patient. Fantasying has no poetic value, but dreaming has poetry in it:

> To support my interpretation I found a language which was suitable through knowing my patient's great interest in poetry. I said that fantasying was [...] a dead end. *It had no poetic value.* The corresponding dream, however, *had poetry in it,* that is to say, layer upon layer of meaning related to past, present, and future, and to inner and outer, and always fundamentally about herself. It is this poetry of the dream that is missing in her fantasying [...]. She then made some excursions into imaginative planning of the future which seemed to give a prospect of future happiness that was different from the here-and-now fixity of any satisfaction that there can be in fantasying.[77]

The theme of Winnicott's essay is his patient's need for formlessness and her gradual ability to take charge of her own life and potential happiness. Recognizing that her endless games of patience are played in a room that is empty of herself, she comes to realize that uncertainty is the necessary complement of the freedom to choose for herself in a potential future.

Winnicott's companion essay, 'Playing: Creative Activity and the Search for the Self', recapitulates some of the same themes, specifically in the context of his patient's interest in poetry. As with the difference between fantasying and dreaming, so with poetry. Winnicott contrasts repetitive, addictive quotation, used as a defensive organization, with a form of quotation that symbolically expresses layers of unconscious meaning as a dream might do. Here as elsewhere, creative play is located along with cultural activity in what Winnicott calls the third area, or 'potential space', between mother and baby. Only in creative play does the individual discover the self and truly communicate with it. But for this free-associative activity, formlessness and non-purposiveness are necessary prerequisites. Winnicott's essay records a three-hour session during which his deeply regressed woman patient moves from a profound and disorganized depression to a newly found self. The different stages are punctuated by copious reference to books and poems, and by what Winnicott calls 'coming into the room' (the room that had been empty of herself). At the outset of the session, his patient complains: 'It's as though there isn't really a ME. Awful book of early teens called *Returned Empty.* That's what I feel like.'[78] She follows up this hopeless allusion with a reference to Christina Rossetti's lugubrious 'Passing Away', with its refrain of religious exhaustion and unfulfilled potential for living: '"My life finishes with a canker in the bud"' These desultory, formless utterances hint at an early, unremembered trauma, and the fundamental conviction that she is 'of no consequence' to anyone. An 'apt quotation from the poet Gerard Manley Hopkins' continuous in the same vein – 'there's no God and I don't matter' – accompanied by hopelessness and sobbing.[79] After nearly two hours (as Winnicott emphasizes), '*the patient seemed to be in the room with me*',[80] her presence signalled by contact with the analyst. Filled with hatred, she makes a memorial card with a black pen for her birthday, which she calls her 'Deathday' – negating Christina Rossetti's joyous pre-Raphaelite religious epithalamium, 'A Birthday' ('My heart is like a singing bird').

Along with thoughts of positive and negative birthday experiences, Winnicott's patient finally arrives at the question of her self-denied, negative, and abortive existence: 'But what is so awful is existence that's negatived! There was never a time when I thought: a good thing to have been born!'[81] What André Green has called 'the intuition of the negative' in Winnicott's work provides a crucial means of understanding this patient.[82] A negatived existence is not just non-existence – it is an existential disaster. Each quotation leads to another, equally apt in its negativity: 'It was in my mind: "Don't make me wish to BE!" That's a line of a poem by Gerard Manley Hopkins.'[83] Even her choice of Hopkins's darkest sonnet is couched in the negative, as a reversed suicide wish. Winnicott footnotes: 'Actual quotation, from the poem "Carrion Comfort", would be: "Not, I'll not [...] / [...] Most weary, cry *I can no more.* I can; / Can something, hope, wish day come, not choose not to be"'.[84] At this point, and in this connection, Winnicott offers his central insight about the uses of poetic quotation by his chain-quoting woman patient:

> We now talked about poetry, how she makes a great deal of use of poetry that she knows by heart, and how she has lived from poem to poem (like cigarette to cigarette in chain-smoking), but without the poem's meaning being understood or felt as she now understands and feels this poem. (Her quotations are always apt, and usually she is unaware of the meaning). I referred her to God as I AM, a useful concept when the individual cannot bear to BE.[85]

Could one also say of Anne Elliot on her autumnal walk that she has 'lived from poem to poem', addictively, perhaps mechanically, like a chain-smoker? Or is the point of *Persuasion* that Anne – unlike Winnicott's patient, but like the melancholic of Thomson's 'Autumn' – can wander unpurposively and philosophically? Here is Winnicott's patient again: 'If I let my hands wander I might find a me – get in touch with a me [...] but I couldn't. I would need to wander for hours. I couldn't let myself go on.'[86] By contrast, poetry is Austen's way of conveying the 'ME' that Anne gets in touch with by keeping open the lines of feeling to her hidden self, however circumscribed her outward life has become.

Winnicott's patient tells him that her long sequence of quotations and allusions has been a way to represent '*me being alone* [...] that's the way I go on when alone, though without words at all, as I don't let myself start talking to myself'.[87] Her addiction to snatches of poetry paradoxically approximates to wordlessness – to silence. For Winnicott, 'talking *to oneself* does not reflect back, unless [...] reflected back by *someone not oneself*'.[88] His patient's search for a self involves searching for someone or something (at once self and not-self, a person or a mirror) to reflect back; only then can she experience herself as alive. Winnicott ventures '*It was yourself that was searching*' – deliberately misquoting Hopkins's poem, 'Spring and Fall' ('It is Margaret you mourn for'). In the next session, the patient comes up with an answer to this implied question about her own existence: 'She said, slowly and with deep feeling: "Yes, I see, one could postulate the existence of a ME from the question, as from the searching"'.[89] This un-purposive searching, which for Winnicott 'can come only from desultory formless functioning, or perhaps from rudimentary playing', allows for the re-finding of a creative self.[90] In Winnicott's view, compliance is incompatible with being fully alive. His patient's repetitive activities – playing solitary games of patience, fantasying, or living from one poem to another – are equated with a defence organization. By contrast, expressive quotation, poetry that has 'layer upon layer of meaning related to past, present, and future, and to inner and outer', is equated with the active quest for a self.[91]

Winnicott invokes Coleridge's definition of the creative Imagination as a repetition of the 'infinite I AM' to suggest an alternative form of poetic repetition. Like playing and culture, which belong to 'an area that is inter-mediate between the inner reality of the individual and the shared reality of the world that is external to individuals', poetry can function as a form of potential space or dreaming.[92] Recognizing his patient's poetic allusions, and distinguishing between different uses (and abuses) of quotation, allows Winnicott to explore the difference between negatived existence and psychic living. He contrasts automatic quotation with making meaningful (and unconscious) use of poetry. While his interpretive stance involves letting the patient arrive at her own interpretations, his analytic presence in itself constitutes a form of mirroring. We might recall that narcissistic Sir Walter Elliot needs an excessive number of mirrors (as Admiral Croft shrewdly notices) in order to reassure himself of his own continued good looks in middle age. Winnicott's patient makes similar use of mirrors in her search for a self. But Winnicott suggests that only the Other can truly perform this mirroring function: 'talking *to oneself* does not reflect back, unless this is a carry-over of such talking having been reflected back by *someone not oneself*.[93] Poetic quotation has the potential to be a form of 'talking *to oneself*' that involves 'having been reflected back by *someone not oneself*'. That is, addictive quotation may function as a negative mode of being, but it also provides the form of words in which Winnicott's patient asks real and urgent questions of her inner reality, and ultimately enters 'the shared reality of the world that is external to individuals'.[94] One form of this world is poetry.

In *Persuasion*, Austen takes a more conventional route to suggesting that Anne Elliot has 'come into the room': masculine admiration for her suddenly regained looks at Lyme and the part she plays in coping with Louisa's accident. Rivalry with her unknown admirer and cousin, William Elliot, recaptures Captain Wentworth's attention – along with her self-possession and management of the crisis caused by Louisa's concussion: 'The passing admiration of Mr. Elliot had at least roused him, and the scenes on the Cobb [...] had fixed her superiority'.[95] Not so much indifferent as piqued by her long-ago rejection, he begins to understand his feelings in the wake of the accident. But when do the feelings of the past cease to prey upon Anne? And what makes it possible for her to reclaim her life? Lyme provides an important sequel to her first literary conversation with Captain Benwick: 'they walked together some time, talking as before of Mr. Scott and Lord Byron, and still as unable, as before, and as unable as any other two readers, to think exactly alike of the merits of either'.[96] In her conversation with Captain Harville, Anne characterizes Captain Benwick as 'a young mourner' in view of his recent bereavement. She also learns from his friend, Captain Harville, that Captain Wentworth had broken the news of his fiancée's death to him, 'and never left the poor fellow for a week; that's what he did, and nobody else could have saved poor James. You may think, Miss Elliot, whether he is dear to us!' Austen continues: 'Anne did think on the question with perfect decision, and said as much in reply as her own feelings could accomplish, or as his seemed able to bear'.[97] Recognizing Captain Benwick as a fellow-reader and fellow-mourner, Anne is shown not only as discussing which poet to like best, but deciding which man is dear to her. We see her expressing her own tastes, which are not exactly like any other reader's, and then (in pointed juxtaposition) thinking on a different question 'with perfect decision'. Literary discrimination and thinking for oneself – 'Anne did think' – are brought into deliberate proximity. But what has a discriminating literary taste to do with love?

Captain Benwick is described as 'a reading man'.[98] But when the opportunity arises, his attachment to his dead fiancée is overtaken by 'perfectly spontaneous, untaught feeling' for all his pierced, wounded, and broken heart.[99] He needs no instruction from books once Louisa, convalescing in the same household, is thrown in his way. Falling in love with the newly sobered Louisa (convalescing 'in an interesting state') suggests that his melancholy taste for Scott and Byron had only ever been skin-deep. As Anne perceives, 'Captain Benwick was not inconsolable [...]. He had an affectionate heart. He must love somebody' – so why not Louisa?[100] But the story is not yet over. Quotation surfaces once more during Anne's argument with Captain Harville about the relative constancy and durability of men's and women's feelings that occupies the rewritten chapter at the end of *Persuasion*:

> '[...] let me observe that all histories are against you, all stories, prose and verse. If I had such a memory as Benwick, I could bring you fifty quotations in a moment on my side the argument, and I do not think I ever opened a book in my life which had not something to say on woman's inconstancy. Songs and proverbs, all talk of woman's fickleness. But perhaps you will say, these were all written by men.'
>
> 'Perhaps I shall. – Yes, yes, if you please, no reference to examples in books. Men have had every advantage of us in telling their own story. Education has been theirs in so much higher a degree; the pen has been in their hands. I will not allow books to prove anything.'
>
> 'But how shall we prove any thing?'
>
> 'We never shall. We never can expect to prove anything upon such a point. It is a difference of opinion which does not admit of proof.'[101]

Famous as this debate is, the sequel is worth emphasizing. Anne points out that men have always had the pen in their hands (although Captain Wentworth has symptomatically let his pen slip as he listens), and the chapter opens with a reference to the greatest of all women story-tellers, Scheherazade. In Austen's version of an Arabian Nights' tale, delay is productive not only of a deeper, more tried and fixed love, but also of emancipation from 'examples in books'. Nothing can be proved on this point, insists Anne, because 'It is a difference of opinion which does not admit of proof'. She knows what she thinks. Her opinions can differ from someone else's.

This unexpected trust in the individual's own opinions is one of the ways in which *Persuasion* declares itself to be a Romantic novel – at least when it comes to the politics of romance. Anne's playful refusal to allow books to prove anything places the burden of proof elsewhere. Dismissing previous literary authority challenges the concept of normative histories – indeed, of history itself. Inherited wisdom, whether derived from mother-surrogates or from books, turns out to be an unwanted Burkean legacy, like Lady Russell's adherence to the status quo and her insistence that she knows better than nineteen-year-old Anne. When Captain Wentworth recounts his anguish at seeing Anne with Lady Russell –'the recollection of what had been, the knowledge of her influence, the indelible, immoveable impression of what persuasion had once done'[102] – Anne replies: 'You should have distinguished'. In the same way, after Louisa's accident at Lyme, he 'had learned to distinguish between the steadiness of principle and the obstinacy of self-will, between the darings of heedlessness and the resolution of a collected mind'.[103] Unlike Captain Wentworth, smarting under his feelings, Anne (and Austen with her) does distinguish. Love is an informed difference of opinion, and – as with literary taste – two people may think differently about it. While it does not admit of proof, it admits distinctions. Lady Russell has nothing less to do 'than to admit that she had been pretty completely wrong, and to take up a new set of opinions'.[104] Austen reflects on a form of cognition amounting to 'quickness of perception in some, a nicety in the discernment of character, a natural penetration [...] which no experience in others can equal'.[105] Lady Russell (we know already) is 'less gifted in this part of understanding' than Anne, who has learned from experience to trust her own discernment.

Captain Wentworth acknowledges at the end of *Persuasion* that 'he had been constant unconsciously, nay unintentionally; that he had meant to forget [Anne] and believed it to be done'.[106] Austen's reference to unconscious constancy gives another turn to the gender-debate. He has been constant in his own way. But, thinking of Anne 'only as one who had yielded', he had been unable to benefit from his more recent knowledge of her character – 'I could not bring it into play'.[107] Both the constancy and the obduracy of the unconscious are evident here. Captain Wentworth's intention is thwarted by unconscious love, just as what he knows cannot be brought into play. These intuitive and affective forms of cognition, even when they take the form of resistance, return us to the vicissitudes of romance and to the function of poetry in *Persuasion*. As the end of the novel nears, when almost nobody can be in doubt of what followed, poetry ceases to be something to be consoled by or fall in love over (as it has been for Anne Elliot, for Captain Benwick, and for Louisa Musgrove). Instead, it flourishes playfully between the lines of Austen's ironic prose. As Anne makes her way through the streets of Bath, her hopes rekindled, Austen editorializes: 'Prettier musings of high-wrought love and eternal constancy, could never have passed along the streets of Bath, than Anne was sporting with from Camden-place to Westgate-buildings. It was almost enough to spread purification and perfume all the way.'[108] The small luxuriating flourishes of Austen's prose allow her readers to drift into pleasurable identification with Anne's musings of high-wrought love and eternal constancy, and still more pleasurable anticipation of what is now surely to come. We even enjoy a touch of perfumed exoticism, sharing Anne's confidence that 'her affection would be [Captain Wentworth's] for ever'. Later, when the lovers are reunited with one another on their outwardly decorous walk back to Camden-place, the present hour will become 'a blessing indeed; and prepare it for all the immortality which the happiest recollections of their own future lives can bestow'.[109] Poetry, we see, can have as much to do with guaranteeing the blessings of the future as with addiction to the past; it immortalizes happy recollections.

History in *Persuasion* – which starts by recapitulating Anne's 'little history of sorrowful interest'[110] – involves repetition with a romantic difference. The perfectly balanced cadences of Austen's prose perform a private epithalamium: 'There they returned again into the past, more exquisitely happy, perhaps, in their re-union, than when it had been first projected; more tender, more tried, more fixed in knowledge of each other's character, truth, and attachment; more equal to act, more justified in acting'.[111] Austen's mobile catalogue of all that the pair are oblivious to on their walk – 'seeing neither sauntering politicians, bustling house-keepers, flirting girls, nor nursery-maids and children' – provides a generic backdrop for lovers so often conscious of being separated by the presence of others and by their previous estrangement. But although they return into the past at this moment, present action is what they now feel more equal to, and (importantly) more justified in. Persuasion, in the form of influence exercised over one person by another, gives way to the assumption of risk involved in any action whose outcome is uncertain. Of Anne's happiness, we are told: 'the dread of a future war [was] all that could dim her sunshine'.[112] The future is unknown – although not entirely so to Austen, in the time-present of *Persuasion*'s writing (after the Battle of Waterloo and Napoleon's second exile). At the start of the novel, Anne's autumnal musings had been the product of confinement and inaction. By the end of the novel, Austen's unobtrusive metaphor ('dim her sunshine') is equated with the uncertainty that inevitably attends all choice, even the author's choice of words. *Persuasion* can be read as a vindication of the rights of women to have their own opinions about both love and poetry – the right to distinguish one man, or poem, from another. The close of the novel allows us to see the author herself at play, sporting between the lines. Like Wordsworth's 'little sportive lines of wood run wild' above Tintern Abbey, Austen's lines of feeling sketch the imprint of romance on a revisited landscape, a changed self. Poetry in *Persuasion* is doubly transitional, recapitulating an inland plot of estrangement and return, of time's elapse and renewed memory, while voyaging into an open-ended future.

Notes

1 For an admirably penetrating and intelligent account of Austen's relation to the literary in *Persuasion* and its relation to both feeling and persuasion, see Adela Pinch, 'Lost in a Book: Jane Austen's *Persuasion*', in *Strange Fits of Passion: Epistemologies of Emotion* (Stanford, CA: Stanford University Press, 1996), pp. 137–63. For a psycho-analytically inflected reading of *Persuasion*, see also Anita Sokolsky, 'The Melancholy Persuasion', in Maud Ellmann, ed., *Psychoanalytic Literary Criticism* (London: Longman, 1994), pp. 128–42, and Jill Heydt-Stevenson, '"Unbecoming Conjunctions": Mourning the Loss of Landscape and Love', *Eighteenth-Century Fiction* 8.1 (October 1995), pp. 51–71, who draws on Freud and Kristeva to analyse Anne's melancholy.

2 Jane Austen, *Persuasion*, ed. Gillian Beer (Harmondsworth: Penguin, 1998), p. 78.

3 See D. W. Winnicott, 'The Location of Cultural Experience', in *Playing and Reality* (London and New York: Routledge, 1971), p. 96: '*if play is neither inside nor outside, where is it?*' Winnicott calls it 'this *third area*, that of cultural experience which is a derivative of play' (p. 102), and relates it to the concept of 'potential space' between mother and baby.

4 Austen, *Persuasion*, p. 78.

5 Austen, *Persuasion*, p. 79.

6 Austen, *Persuasion*, pp. 79, 80.

7 Austen, *Persuasion*, p. 82.

8 Austen, *Persuasion*, p.80.

9 Austen, *Persuasion*, p. 76.

10 Austen, *Persuasion*, p. 77.

11 Austen, *Persuasion*, p. 90.

12 Austen, *Persuasion*, p. 91. We know that from her childhood on, Austen herself 'was well acquainted with the old periodicals from the *Spectator* downwards', along with Richardson (especially *Sir Charles Grandison*), Johnson's moral writings (*Rasselas*), and Goldsmith's *History of England*; see William Austen-Leigh and Richard Arthur Austen-Leigh, *Jane Austen: A Family Record* (Boston: G. K.Hall, 1989), pp. 54–55.

13 For 'the lyricization' of the novel, see Clifford Siskin, *The Historicity of Romantic Discourse* (Oxford: Oxford University Press, 1988), pp. 132, 138–42. For the argument that free indirect discourse displaces poetry itself in *Persuasion*, see also Clara

Tuite, *Romantic Austen: Sexual Politics and the Literary Canon* (Cambridge: Cambridge University Press, 2002), pp. 71–75.

14 Austen, *Persuasion*, p. 27.

15 Austen, *Persuasion*, p. 36.

16 Austen's own poetic favourites included Scott as well as Crabbe and Cowper; see Austen-Leigh and Austen-Leigh, *A Family Record*, p. 54.

17 See the edition of *Persuasion* edited by Linda Bree (Peterborough, Ontario: Broadview Press, 1998) for extracts from the most obvious poetic inter-texts, poems by Thomson, Scott, and Byron discussed here.

18 Austen, *Persuasion*, p.76.

19 James Thomson, 'Autumn', in *The Seasons*, ed. James Sambrook (Oxford: Clarendon Press, 1981), 1744 edn, ll. 960ff.

20 Thomson, 'Autumn', 1744 edn, ll. 974-79.

21 Thomson, 'Autumn', 1744 edn, ll. 1015-40 passim, italics original.

22 Austen, *Persuasion*, pp. 208–209.

23 *Persuasion* was begun next year, after Napoleon's escape and final defeat at the Battle of Waterloo in June 1815; Austen knew that the peace was temporary.

24 Austen, *Persuasion*, p.17.

25 See, however, Brian Southam, *Jane Austen and the Navy* (London and New York: Hambledon and London, 2000), pp. 109–32 for the uncertainties of prize money and promotion – which could leave Captain Harville in straitened circumstances as well as making Captain Wentworth a man of independent means. Austen knew of the vicissitudes of naval fortunes at first hand from her two sailor brothers.

26 Austen, *Persuasion*, p.88.

27 Austen, *Persuasion*, p. 89.

28 Austen, *Persuasion*, p. 90.

29 Austen, *Persuasion*, p. 90.

30 Austen, *Persuasion*, p. 91.

31 Austen, *Persuasion*, p. 91.

32 Walter Scott, *Marmion*, in *Scott: Poetical Works*, ed. J. Logie Robertson (London: Oxford University Press, 1904, reprinted 1967), Canto I, ll. 1-2, 15-16.

33 Scott, *Marmion*, Canto I, ll. 45-46, 53-54.

34 Austen, *Persuasion*, p. 87.

35 Austen, *Persuasion*, p. 59.

36 Austen, *Persuasion*, pp. 61, 45.

37 Austen, *Persuasion*, p. 60.

38 Austen, *Persuasion*, p. 45.

39 Scott, *Marmion*, Canto I, ll. 57-70.

40 As Brian Southam argues, the Army was in the ascendant over the war-weary Navy by the time Austen began *Persuasion*, which deals with the fate of naval officers on shore, variously living on prize money, pensions, or half-pay. Southam suggests that Austen was mounting a rear-guard action – 'Righting and Re-Writing History' (the title of his chapter on *Persuasion*) – in order to rehabilitate the Navy, and possibly to recompense her own much-loved but slow-to-advance naval brother, Francis, in the wake of the recent scaling-down of the Navy; see *Jane Austen and the Navy*, pp. 257–98.

41 Walter Scott, *The Lady of the Lake*, in *Scott: Poetical Works*, ed. Robertson, Canto II, ll. 37-43.

42 Austen, *Persuasion*, p. 98.

43 Byron, *The Corsair*, in *Byron, Poetical Works*, ed. Frederick Page (new edn, ed. John Jump; Oxford: Oxford University Press, 1975), ll. 1-4. Alternatively, Austen has in mind Canto II of *Childe Harold's Pilgrimage* (1812) with its 'dark blue sea', 'fresh breeze', and 'white sail set, the gallant frigate tight'; in *Byron*, ed. Jerome J. McGann (Oxford: Oxford University Press, 1986), Canto II, ll. 145, 147, 148.

44 Byron, *The Giaour* (1813), in *Byron*, ed. McGann, l. 15.

45 Byron, *The Giaour*, ll. 59-60.

46 Byron, *The Giaour*, l. 100.

47 Byron, *The Giaour*, ll. 136-37.

48 See Nigel Leask, *British Romantic Writers and the East: Anxieties of Empire* (Cambridge: Cambridge University Press, 1992), p. 33, as well as for an extended consideration of Byron's oriental tales.

49 See Leask, *British Romantic Writers and the East*, p. 29.

50 Byron, *The Bride of Abydos*, in *Byron, Poetical Works*, ed. Jump, ll. 385-87; ll. 453-54.

51 Austen, *Persuasion*, p. 149.

52 Austen, *Persuasion*, pp. 90, 76.

53 Austen, *Persuasion*, p. 205.

54 Winnicott, *Playing and Reality*, p. 27.

55 Winnicott, *Playing and Reality*, pp. 27–28.

56 Austen, *Persuasion*, p. 24.

57 Austen, *Persuasion*, p. 25.

58 Austen, *Persuasion*, p. 25.

59 Austen, *Persuasion*, p. 218.

60 Austen, Persuasion, p. 55.

61 Austen, *Persuasion*, p. 6.

62 Winnicott, *Playing and Reality*, p. 28.

63 Winnicott, *Playing and Reality*, p. 28.

64 Winnicott, *Playing and Reality*, p. 28.

65 Winnicott, *Playing and Reality*, p. 29.

66 Austen, *Persuasion*, p. 64.

67 Austen, *Persuasion*, p. 64.

68 Winnicott, *Playing and Reality*, p. 29.

69 Winnicott, *Playing and Reality*, p. 34.

70 Austen, *Persuasion*, pp. 24–25.

71 Austen, *Persuasion*, p. 25.

72 Jane Austen, *Persuasion*, p. 26.

73 Winnicott, *Playing and Reality*, p. 33.

74 Winnicott, *Playing and Reality*, p. 34n.

75 See Winnicott's essay 'Ego Distortion in Terms of True and False Self' (1960), in D. W. Winnicott, *The Maturational Processes and the Facilitating Environment* (London: Hogarth Press, 1965), pp. 140–52.

76 Winnicott, *Playing and Reality*, p. 35.

77 Winnicott, *Playing and Reality*, p. 35.

78 Winnicott, *Playing and Reality*, p. 58. See Florence L. Barclay, *Returned Empty* (London: G. P. Putnum's Sons, 1920).

79 Winnicott, *Playing and Reality*, p. 59.

80 Winnicott, *Playing and Reality*, p. 60.

81 Winnicott, *Playing and Reality*, pp. 61–62.

82 For a reading of Winnicott's essay, 'Transitional Objects and Transitional Phenomena', see André Green, 'The Intuition of the Negative in *Playing and Reality*', in Gregorio Kohon, ed., *The Dead Mother* (London and New York: Routledge, 1999), pp. 205–21.

83 Winnicott, *Playing and Reality*, p. 62.

84 Winnicott, *Playing and Reality*, p. 62n. For Winnicott's complex and controversial attitude to the right to suicide (and its actual occurrence) on the part of deeply regressed patients, see F. Robert Rodman, *Winnicott: Life and Work* (Cambridge, MA: Perseus Books, 2003), pp. 162–63, 234–36, 333–37.

85 Winnicott, *Playing and Reality*, p. 62.

86 Winnicott, *Playing and Reality*, p. 63.

87 Winnicott, *Playing and Reality*, p. 63.

88 Winnicott, *Playing and Reality*, p. 63.

89 Winnicott, *Playing and Reality*, p. 64.

90 Winnicott, *Playing and Reality*, p. 64.

91 Winnicott, *Playing and Reality*, p. 35.

92 Winnicott, *Playing and Reality*, p. 64.

93 Winnicott, *Playing and Reality*, p. 63.

94 Winnicott, *Playing and Reality*, p. 64.

95 Austen, *Persuasion*, p. 212.

96 Austen, *Persuasion*, p. 96.

97 Austen, *Persuasion*, p. 97.

98 Austen, *Persuasion*, p. 162.

99 Austen, *Persuasion*, p. 162.

100 Austen, *Persuasion*, p. 149.

101 Austen, *Persuasion*, p. 206.

102 Austen, *Persuasion*, p. 215.

103 Austen, *Persuasion*, p. 213.

104 Austen, *Persuasion*, p. 219.

105 Austen, *Persuasion*, p. 219.

106 Austen, *Persuasion*, p. 212.

107 Austen, *Persuasion*, p. 215.

108 Austen, *Persuasion*, p. 170.

109 Austen, *Persuasion*, p. 211.

110 Austen, *Persuasion*, p. 26.

111 Austen, *Persuasion*, pp. 211–12.

112 Austen, *Persuasion*, p. 221.

CHAPTER TEN

Scholarly Revivals: Gothic Fiction, Secret History, and Hogg's *Private Memoirs and Confessions of a Justified Sinner*

INA FERRIS

Propelled by the unprecedented success of Walter Scott's Waverley novels, Romantic fiction assumed a new, more authoritative position in the literary field. It did so, as the example of Scott suggests, by way of an engagement with the past that answered to the period's widespread interest in questions of national history and national culture. Generic innovations such as Maria Edgeworth's and Sydney Morgan's national tales, along with Scott's more celebrated historical novel, placed the novel in new, more serious relation to scholarly and historical genres canvassing these questions, and moved novels themselves into the foreground of debates over national-cultural formation. Feeding into the innovations of the Romantic novel was the late-eighteenth-century genre of gothic, which itself saw a resurgence in the 1820s but whose relationship to scholarly and historical debates has largely been elided. Gothic novels may have scholarly trappings, but they are not generally read in relation to scholarly discourses and debates. These trappings are mostly seen as musty devices to launch the fiction's move into the more glamorous zone of romance, where the political, psychological and philosophical resonances that have attracted most critical attention achieve their fullest play. But the genre's explicit, if mischievous, positioning of itself on the terrain of learning deserves more serious attention, pointing to an intersection in the Romantic period between gothic fiction and questions of historical practice and publication that bears centrally on key debates in the period.

From the outset, gothic fiction had typically framed its texts through a trope of scholarly retrieval, presenting itself as the rediscovery, translation, transcription, or piecing together of obscure documents from the past. The following work was found in the library of an ancient catholic family in the north of England. It was printed in Naples, in the black letter, in the year 1529.'[1] So opens *The Castle of Otranto* in a gambit that was already well worn by the time of Walpole's writing, but over the course of the next half century this fiction of a 'found manuscript' was to assume an increasingly literal charge, as masses of manuscripts from private collections found their way into new public collections, and scholars scoured the repositories of Europe for medieval and early modern texts. As Joep Leerssen wryly observes in his discussion of this phenomenon: 'at the time a lot of manuscripts *were* being found in attics'.[2] Leerssen, like most literary historians, is interested primarily in the period's recovery of early literary texts, which came to serve doubly as both cultural 'heirlooms' and historical-anthropological documents in a national history. But obscure historical documents were equally turning up, part of a less noticed historical revival, and it was these that raised in especially acute form one of the most widely canvassed issues in the period: how can we or how should we *approach* the past?

In response to this question, the upsurge of European interest in the printing of old and obscure historical manuscripts in the late eighteenth and early nineteenth century threw the spotlight on figures of mediation such as editors and translators, so that when Walpole framed the publication of *The Castle of Otranto* (ostensibly a translation by an eighteenth-century English canon of a sixteenth-century Italian publication) with a preface by the supposed translator, he was not simply indulging in a hoary literary joke but evoking a very current debate. Striking a mock scholarly note, Walpole's preface argues for a probable date of composition of the supposed manuscript, but the pertinent historiographic point is the modern translator's position in relation to the text he is translating: his ready assumption of his own (and the reader's) progressive distance from the 'dark ages' in which the manuscript was written.[3] By the early decades of the nineteenth century, however, the question of how to read the 'remains' of the past had become at once more prominent (under history's own increasingly archival turn) and more problematic (under an emergent historicism that defined the past as at once alien to the present and accessible through its records). In the process national culture itself came to be understood largely in terms of revival, and much of the recent attention to gothic fiction has been prompted by a sharpened recognition of the importance of the late-eighteenth-century romance revival to British national formation.[4] Foregrounding literary revivalism, scholars have placed gothic novels within a nativist generic matrix (e.g. ballad collection, national literary history, translations of ancient originals), which was instrumental in giving imaginative and affective energy to the heritage model of the nation taking hold in the culture. As Deidre Lynch has argued, the form and literariness of gothic novels helped to shape their readers as national subjects by functioning as a kind of 'national library' to underwrite a canonical 'tradition'.[5] But at the same time libraries – even national ones – also contain less organized archives: vast heaps of manuscripts, printed ephemera, disregarded documents. Out of these emerged the genre of secret history that Isaac D'Israeli called 'subterraneous history' in a pioneering essay on the subject in 1823.[6] The alliance of gothic fiction with this genre, although signalled by Walpole, has remained an obscured thread in accounts of its genealogy. But this alliance, I want to suggest, means that gothic novels belong as much to the historical as the literary revival, and this double belonging complicates the standard story of their implication in national culture, placing them in more fractious and equivocal relation to notions of heritage and national history.

If the historical and literary revivals underway at the turn of the nineteenth century went hand in hand, they did not always go in step.[7] Certainly, the discourses of history and literature witnessed a new convergence at the end of the eighteenth century with the expansion of the historical field to include much of what had been formerly understood as 'private' or non-historical. As the authority of established historiographical modes such as political history and military history began to be dislodged, the relations among the various genres of representation of the past, including literary genres, were reshuffled and redefined. But in an important way the literary and historical modalities of representation tended to pivot on quite different temporalities, engendering a division in the thinking of historical and national being in the period. Where the literary modality posited a temporality guaranteeing continuity, one in which the past could be interiorized as an active 'tradition' or more radically as a 'now' (as in Blake's sense of Milton as a current presence), the historical modality assumed, by contrast, a highly differentiated time, setting the past at a distance and activating a temporality marked by disjunction rather than continuity.[8] Neither modality, however, was fully at ease with itself, hence that saturated focus on the past characteristic of Romantic writing that the editors underscore in their introduction to this collection. Such saturation points to a widespread, powerful sense of the past as a *problem* in the period, its status as the subject of intense debate, controversy, and conflict.

The Romantic gothic novel entered this debate through its longstanding alliance with antiquarian forms of secret history, an alliance that reaches a telling culmination in James Hogg's *Private Memoirs and Confessions of a Justified Sinner* (1824). Under the pressure of contention over what it meant to 'do' history (propelled in no small part by the extraordinary popular success of Walter Scott's historical novels), apparently esoteric matters of scholarship and antiquarianism took on new charge and assumed a public profile in post-Waterloo Britain. If the first phase of Romantic gothic owed its explicitly political edge to its immersion in the revolutionary ferment of the 1790s, in the process opening up insular English forms to continental influences, as Markman Ellis has shown earlier in this volume, the period after Waterloo witnessed an inward turn that moved into the foreground internal tensions within the (less than) United Kingdom. It is no accident that Irish and Scottish novels flourished in these years nor that what they tended to make political was the question of historiography itself. To track gothic's alliance with secret history is thus to move into the foreground a debate over the writing of history that activated fault lines in the whole notion of revival pivotal to the making of national culture in the period.

Secret History and the 'Appetite for Remains'

Secret history is only now beginning to emerge from invisibility in literary history. As Robert Mayer has noted, for most of its long history is has been ignored by both critics and historians.[9] Recently, however, literary scholars such as Michael McKeon have rediscovered the genre, impelled in large part by interest in its paradoxical status as the publication of privacy.[10] Secret histories publish secrets or, at least, what has not been readily known, and they typically operate in the informal and often shady realms outside the protocols of public history. When they flourished in the late seventeenth and early eighteenth century, Mayer points out, such publications assumed at least three forms: historical, polemical, fictive. Contemporary readers easily distinguished among these, even as they tolerated their interanimation (or contamination). Perhaps for this reason eighteenth-century critics tended to dismiss all three, lumping them together as sensationalist, biased, and anecdotal. What made secret history suspect was not simply the often dubious claim to be 'true' (the 'true secret history of X') but the duplicity whereby it promised the pleasures of both fiction and history. While its secrets and anecdotes yielded the pleasures of fiction, secret history attracted readerly attention in the first place with the lure of historical revelation: an account of what 'really' went on in royal courts, diplomatic circles, and other high public venues. Well aware of its appeal, early-eighteenth-century novelists from Daniel Defoe to Delariv-iere Manley and Eliza Haywood exploited this generic doubleness, styling their fictional texts 'secret histories' and often producing actual secret histories themselves. Haywood, for example, subtitled her novels 'true secret history' (e.g. *Double Marriage* and *Mercenary Lover*) and also published a secret history of Mary Queen of Scots, whose title underlines the unique revelations promised by the genre: *Mary Stuart, Queen of Scots: being the secret history of her life and the real causes of all her misfortunes. Containing a relation of many particular transactions in her reign; never yet published in any collection. Translated from the French, by Mrs Eliza Haywood* (London, 1725).

In both fictional and non-fictional forms, secret history opened out spaces for alternative histories or counter-histories, and it remained in play as a popular genre throughout the eighteenth century and into the nine-teenth, gradually but never entirely losing its identification with salacious chronicles of sexual scandal while continuing to posit scandal in high places. Sophia Lee's *The Recess* (1783) is exemplary. Lee's highly sensational gothic tale of the (fictional) twin daughters of Mary Queen of Scots exploits the long-circulating rumours that the queen had borne children to the Duke of Norfolk, and it explicitly aligns itself with secret history from the start by presenting itself as based on a manuscript whose provenance cannot be revealed. However, in contrast to earlier similar 'histories' of ille-gitimate royal births, illicit marriages, adultery, and so on, Lee's narrative aims not to titillate readers with prurient details of transgressions in court society but to write an underground and sentimental history of the nation, which functions literally as a counter-Elizabethan history of the English nation. Decades later, Mary Shelley was to make similarly critical and spec-ulative use of the conjunction of women and secret history in *Valperga* (1823), which inserts into the documented life of the fourteenth-century Tuscan ruler Castruccio Castracani, Prince of Lucca, the fictional figures of betrayed women, deploying the 'private chronicles' linked to their exis-tence to enact a feminist critique of dominant models of public history.

Thus turned to more critical and intellectual ends, novels presenting themselves as secret histories in the late eighteenth and early nineteenth century took their place alongside other historical genres in the critical reorientation of the whole historical field away from 'general history'. In this reorientation the antiquarian inflection of secret history was pivotal, as the generic term was broadened to include informal first-person accounts of historical events, not simply scandalous revelations. Moreover, such accounts were increasingly collected and published by an antiquarian-editor anxious to preserve and mediate the 'remains' of the past. Meanwhile, 'remains' themselves achieved new prominence as classical models of history were destabilized both by a scientific turn towards documentary 'sources' (heralding the emergence of the modern discipline of history) and by a 'sentimental' turn, which sought for a more intimate and affective relationship to life as experienced in the past.[11] No matter how opposed in other ways, both the scientific and sentimental turns agreed in valorizing the witness-narrative, and understood historiography less as a synthetic mode of explanation and evaluation than as the collection and collation of primary documents through which access to the lived past could be gained. In an important way, history's business was coming to be seen to be the 'real' as much as the 'true'; or, more precisely, the true now had to take the real into account, as had not been the case when new histories were mostly derived from previous ones. Under an emergent historicism that posited historical change as substantial rather than superficial, the reality of the past was understood to inhere in an alterity to which material 'remains' provided access. At the same time, the truth of the past continued to be (as it always had been) a matter of present determination, that is, a function of the judgement of the historian.

These two imperatives of history – the real and the true – implied different kinds of authorship and different formal protocols. Two histories published by James Macpherson (of Ossianic fame) will help to illustrate. In 1775 Macpherson published a continuation of Hume's famous national history, *The History of Great Britain, From the Restoration, To the Accession of the House of Hanover*, along with a secret history whose full title reads *Original Papers; Containing the Secret History of Great Britain, From the Restoration, to the Accession of the House of Hannover. To Which are Prefixed Extracts from the Life of James II. As Written By Himself. The Whole Arranged and Published by James Macpherson, Esq; In Two Volumes.*[12] The latter underlines the antiquarian redefinition of secret history as no longer a scandalous revelation of the dubious motives informing events in public history but a collection of unofficial and mostly unpublished contemporary writings, which might or might not work to the same revelatory end. Macpherson's is a chronological compilation of Jacobite documents (letters, anecdotes, speeches, dispatches, etc.), most of which had been gathered in collections in Paris and not previously published. They are linked together with little commentary but referenced by elaborate footnotes and citations. The introduction sets up Macpherson as an 'Editor' of historical 'materials', and it insists (understandably enough in light of the Ossianic scandal) on his adherence to the responsibilities of the scholar. Hence it cites the provenance of documents; details research gaps; and emphasizes Macpherson's diligent activities as translator, editor, and transcriber.[13] The materials themselves, notably the memoirs of James II written 'in his own hand', are presented as windows on the historical characters and their times. 'If the Memoirs of King James cannot raise their author to the rank of a fine writer,' Macpherson comments, 'they certainly do him credit as a man.'[14] By contrast, the preface to Macpherson's national history, while equally insistent on his thorough scholarly preparation (including reliance on the manuscripts printed in the *Original Papers*) presents him rather as a detached 'Author' than as a busy scholar in intimate contact with manuscripts in the archive. As 'Author' the historian focuses on the construction of his narrative, discussing the difficulty of how to balance an allegiance to 'evidence' with concern for the reading convenience of 'the Public', and declaring his impartiality and judiciousness: 'He considered himself throughout in the light of a judge upon mankind and their actions; and, as he had no object but truth, he trusts he has attained his end'.[15]

Where authors (and national histories) seek to achieve the wholeness of narrative form, editors (and secret histories) stay in the partial and plural mode of collected 'materials'. The important point for the relationship between the two – a relationship that remained contestatory even as it was necessarily complementary – is the doubleness inherent in the category of 'materials'. At one level materials are secondary: inert 'bits' requiring the synthetic and hermeneutic powers of narrative to give them semantic value. At the same time, however, they constitute the ground of historical narrative, which cannot operate without them, and this gives them a certain primacy that brings along with it the power to discomfit and destabilize narrative configurations. Exposing the limits and lacunae of general history, the informal narratives of secret history act as a corrective, dislodging the received structures of general history by virtue of their status as concrete 'remains' that provide both a tangible relationship to the past (one holds the very document once held by a figure in the past) and a close-up view unavailable to general history: 'From the fulness of their accounts [those of secret history] we recover much which had been lost to us in the general views of history, and it is by this more intimate acquaintance with persons and circumstances, that we are enabled to correct the less distinct, and sometimes the fallacious appearances in the page of the popular historian.'[16]

D'Israeli's defence in his essay on secret history of the often-derided 'appetite for *Remains* of all kinds' reminds us that 'remains' are at once what the dead leave behind (traces) and what cannot be gathered into a structure of some kind (the unassimilable or not-yet-assimilated). Hence it is 'remains' that provided the secret historian with a lever to tilt official versions of the past, and they constitute the positive side of secret history's negative relationship to standard historical genres. Targeting both the 'popular historian' and 'theoretical writers of history', D'Israeli critiques in particular those historians such as Hume and Robertson whom he regards as indolent scholars, producing histories that either simply reproduce earlier ones or remain parasitic on the antiquarian researches of others. Hume comes in for special scorn, castigated for remaining satisfied with 'the common accounts, and the most obvious sources of history' despite the opportunities for research available to him in his post in the Advocates' Library in Edinburgh. 'One single original document has sometimes shaken into dust their palladian edifice of history', D'Israeli claims, and his satisfaction at this outcome underscores the degree to which for him the negative rather than positive powers of secret history are the key to its value.[17] His is the typical antiquarian distrust of achieved form, especially of the narrative form sustaining national histories, and he is quick to attribute the reluctance of 'popular historians' to do archival research to their concern that details they found 'would be so many obstructions in the smooth texture of a narrative'.[18]

The status of secret history thus hinged on two things: an intellectual power activated by its sceptical relationship to the forms of general history and an imaginative/affective power activated by its attachment to the 'remains' of the past. But the historicist assumption of the past as substantive difference complicated the latter claim. In contrast to literary remains, historical remains possessed a recalcitrant exteriority that made them resistant to interiorization, less capable of activating the sympathies allowing for the ready assimilation of scraps of the literary past. In Radcliffean gothic, for example, the protagonists (along with Radcliffe's readers) could internalize old literary texts with only minimal effort, turning them into aspects of their own consciousness, because the literary text was understood to occupy a transtemporal aesthetic realm confirming identification across time. Faculties of sentiment and sympathy, along with the powers of imagination, provided the bridge linking disparate times and spaces. More heretical gothic fictions may have challenged this assumption, as does Charles Robert Maturin in *The Milesian Chief* (1812), which casts a cynical eye on the Radcliffean model of sensibility and sympathy in rejecting the sentimental aesthetic of its cosmopolitan heroine, who claims to 'feel' the music and song of dispossessed Irish bards.[19] But it was historical rather than literary 'remains' that most acutely posed for the period the question of sympathy across distance. The reproduction of historical manuscripts, whose archaic idiom made strange the English language itself, made apparent that there was no ready passage between 'now' and 'then'. To speak to the present, then, the past had to be not only mediated but continually reframed, as it receded into ever more opaque dimensions of historical difference. An enthusiast for antiquarian activities such as D'Israeli stepped lightly around this problem, preferring to concentrate on secret history's critical powers of negation vis-à-vis established history. But the Scottish James Hogg, writing on the peripheries of both English culture and literary culture, made it a central issue in his *Private Memoirs and Confessions of a Justified Sinner*. Living out a decidedly more edgy relationship to print culture than D'Israeli, as well as contending with the powerful proximity of Walter Scott (as Ian Duncan shows in the following essay), Hogg saw the question of how one approached national historical materials as at once more urgent and more problematic

Hogg and the Double-Voicing of the Past

The Private Memoirs and Confessions of a Justified Sinner identifies two genres – memoirs and confessions – but the novel is familiarly known by a short title that names only the latter, dropping the former altogether. Critics typically refer to *Confessions of a Justified Sinner* or, more simply, the *Confessions*. This elision of 'private memoirs' in favour of 'confessions' underlines the way in which, for most of its critical history, discussion of Hogg's novel has privileged a certain modality of the sinner's narrative, reading it as a secularized version of the old spiritual form of 'confession' and hence as an instance of modern self-writing.[20] Attention has turned on the text's articulation of interiority, on writing as the externalization of a subjectivity understood in terms of inner crises, emotions, psychic patterns, and so forth. Recent years have seen a broadening of the models of both subjectivity and confession, along with a restoration of Hogg's novel to its discursive and cultural matrix in early-nineteenth-century Edinburgh.[21]

But the 'private memoirs' have not returned to visibility. Memoirs evoke a historical rather than theological (or psychological) pole of discourse, while to qualify them as *'private* memoirs' is to align them with traditional secret history. The suggestion of scandalous, notably sexual, revelations induced by the juxtaposition of 'private memoirs', 'confessions', and a 'sinner', however, is contained (if not necessarily deflected) by the scholarly, antiquarian model invoked in the full title of the work: *The Private Memoirs and Confessions of a Justified Sinner: Written By Himself: With a Detail of Curious Traditionary Facts, and Other Evidence, By the Editor.*

Secret histories in the form of edited historical memoirs proliferated in early-nineteenth-century Edinburgh. In one form they appeared as (usually) heterogeneous collections of contemporary documents, as in the *Secret History of the Court of James the First* anonymously edited by Walter Scott in 1811 or Thomas McCrie's edition of various seventeenth-century texts in *Memoirs of Mr. William Veitch, and George Brysson, Written by Themselves. With Other Narratives Illustrative of the History of Scotland, From the Restoration to the Revolution* (1825). In another guise, they were printed as single texts, as in the various memoirs from turbulent periods of Scottish history printed by the Bannatyne Club, an antiquarian printing club founded by Scott the year before Hogg's novel was published. Often advertising themselves as 'from the original manuscript', the publications of the Bannatyne included titles such as *Memoirs of His Own Life by Sir James Melville of Halhill... From the Original Manuscript* (1827), a sixteenth-century memoir by a prominent member of the Stuart court written in retirement for his children, and *Memoirs of His Own Life and Times by Sir James Turner... From the Original Manuscript* (1829), a seventeenth-century memoir by a mercenary from Aberdeen notoriously involved in the oppression of radical Presbyterians after the Pentland Rising.[22] In the context of such scholarly and publishing activities, the anonymous first edition of Hogg's work looks very much like a secret history. It not only signals its double authorship in identifying both the Sinner and the Editor in the title but follows standard practice in including a frontispiece reproducing a passage of the Sinner's original manuscript with a notation to the page in the printed text corresponding to the manuscript sample. Drawing attention to the fact of printing – the transformation of a text from one medium to another – this frontispiece announces itself as a translation *with* an original. A Dedication to an actual lord provost of Glasgow is then followed by a lengthy introduction titled 'The Editor's Narrative', which opens in conventional scholarly fashion by citing authorities (records, local traditions) and providing the family background of the memoirist (including a scholarly fussing over the spelling of the family surname).

The scholarly model structures Hogg's entire text, albeit with a distinct irony. The Editor concludes his long introductory account by returning to the question of authorities: 'this is all with which history, justiciary records, and traditions, furnish me relating to these matters'.[23] Advising readers that he will now present 'an original document of a most singular nature', he states that he will offer no remarks but leave each reader 'to judge for himself'. However, he cannot quite forbear giving advance notice that what follows will cast in the shade whatever readers may have heard of 'the rage of fanaticism in former days'. A new title page then announces 'Private Memoirs and Confessions of a Sinner. Written by Himself', and the biblical rhythms and language of this text immediately establish its archaic nature and distinguish its language from that of the modern editor's narrative: 'Therefore, in the might of heaven I will sit down and write: I will let the wicked of this world know what I have done in the faith of the promises, and justification by grace, that they may read and tremble.'[24] Continuing the documentary thread but giving it a bizarre twist, the Editor himself returns in a coda to offer an account of how he came to possess the Sinner's manuscript. Two documents are featured: an 'authentic letter' printed in *Blackwood's* in August 1823 on the uncovering of a mummified corpse and signed by James Hogg; and the partially printed/partially written text found by the Editor and fellow members of the Edinburgh literati in the grave alongside the same recently (and repeatedly) uncovered corpse when they go in search of the phenomenon reported in the *Blackwood's* letter. A parody of notions of scholarly search and discovery, the coda transforms the standard account of discovery in dusty libraries into a macabre comedy of clumsy grave robbing. 'With the scenario of a document unearthed from a grave,' Ian Duncan comments, 'Hogg literalizes the central metaphor of modern antiquarian romance revival: the recovery of "remains," "reliques," or "fragments" of a departed, organic culture'.[25] When read in the light of secret history rather than romance revival, however, what comes to literal ground in this scene is not so much the literary antiquarian notion of an organic culture as the scholarly dream of tangible access to the past.

But in pointing his readers (and critics) to his 1823 letter on 'A Scots Mummy' printed in *Blackwood's*, Hogg in fact effects another of the canny diversionary moves that mark his entire literary career, for he leaves unmentioned an earlier letter to *Blackwood's* far more central to the genesis of the *Private Memoirs and Confessions*: 'A Letter to Charles Kirkpatrick Sharpe, Esq. On his Original Mode of Editing Church History' published in the December 1817 issue of the magazine.[26] Hogg's letter attacks Charles Kirkpatrick Sharpe, a well-known and outspoken Edinburgh antiquary of flamboyantly Tory views, who had recently published an irreverent edition of a seventeenth-century memoir of the persecution of Scottish Presbyterianism titled *The Secret and True History of the Church of Scotland, From the Restoration to the Year 1678* (1817), which was written by the Reverend James Kirkton, one of the signatories of the Solemn League and Covenant. Sharpe's own name was also prominently displayed on the title page: *Edited from the MSS. by Charles Kirkpatrick Sharpe, Esq.* Not only Hogg responded to the incongruity of so unlikely a match of author and editor. Walter Scott, himself a friend of Sharpe, drew immediate notice to the oddity in his review for the *Quarterly Review*: 'After remaining for more than a century in manuscript, [Kirkton] has been edited [...] by a gentleman who, although a curious enquirer into the history of that calamitous period, and therefore interested in the facts recorded in the text, seems neither to feel nor to profess much value for the tenets, nor respect for the person, of his author.'[27] Almost obsessively, the review keeps returning to the matter of 'our ingenious editor', whose very visible and clearly partial presence in the volume obviously discomfits Scott. If he shared Sharpe's conservative politics, his own investment in the protocols of modern scholarship made him wary of his friend's personal and performative notion of editorship, a notion ever more out of step with the depersonalized and professionalized practices being developed for historical editing and publishing in the period.

Early-nineteenth-century bookish associations of antiquarian bent such as the Bannatyne Club, along with learned societies, were beginning to establish the standards of notation, collation, and commentary that were to shape editing practices for much of the rest of the century. Central to these standards was a commitment to 'presenting' the author's manuscript. Thus Thomas Thomson, vice-president of the Bannatyne Club, insists in his introduction to *Memoirs of His Own Life by Sir James Melville of Halhill* (Edinburgh, 1827) on a scrupulous presentation of the authorial manuscript, no matter its errors, promoting a model of editorial fidelity and transparency.[28] Sharpe, however, refused simply to display Kirkton's text. Instead, he constantly engages with it, contesting, taunting, and overturning Kirkton in long and spiky footnotes that frequently overwhelm the latter's own text. Repeatedly, the pages of the volume literally divide into text and counter-text, as when Kirkton's encomium on the Presbyterian 1st Marquis of Argyle as 'a man of singular piety, prudence, authority, and eloquence' prompts an extended and breathless footnote invoking a rash of counter-authorities to argue that, on the contrary, Argyle was treacherous, cruel, disloyal, selfish – not to mention 'red-haired, and with squinting eyes'.[29] Clearly, Sharpe regarded himself as in no sense bound either to enter sympathetically into the document he was publishing or to allow it to speak 'for itself'. Moreover, he prefaces Kirkton's 'True and Secret History' with a lengthy 'Biographical Notice', equally contentious and opinionated, along with two sermons by Kirkton about which he remarks: 'it is truly astonishing, with such models of pulpit eloquence as England and France could then furnish, that the Scottish clergy, even in the reign of William, continued their old vulgar method of preaching, derived from Knox, Henderson, Rutherford, and other ministers, almost totally devoid of sound doctrine, solid learning, common sense, or the slightest glimmer of imagination'.[30]

Hogg's own indignation was aroused less by Sharpe's breach of scholarly decorum than by his detached approach to the past. In his letter to *Blackwood's* mocking Sharpe's 'original mode of editing', he casts Kirkton's narrative as both an 'authentic record' of its time and 'a true and domestic portrait of the way and manner in which the persecuted Covenanters felt and thought with regard to their oppressors'. 'Certainly,' he adds, 'no one, whose heart is not prejudiced, can take a near view of this portrait without increasing reverence and esteem.'[31] But Sharpe challenged the assumption that 'a near view' of the past necessarily released a flow of sympathy for the actors therein, remaining locked into his own 'prejudiced' heart and indulging in the irreverent 'waggish' commentary that arouses Hogg's ire. Herein, rather than at the level of specific ideological difference, lies his most telling deficiency as editor for Hogg. Indeed, the most striking aspect of Sharpe's edition is not the energy of his disputation with Kirkton, which is predictable enough, but the sheer abundance of digressive footnotes occasioned by a habit of reading that yields less a reading *of* than a reading *alongside* the text. This editor, that is, refuses secondariness and subordination. Over and over again, a casual remark in Kirkton's narrative launches an elaborate footnote providing anecdotes that veer off from the original authorial context. At one point, for instance, Kirkton's passing reference to advice that a woman keep a poniard to protect her chastity from rapacious episcopal clergymen generates a footnote, several pages long, detailing a case taken from late-seventeenth-century Scottish criminal records involving an adulterous merchant's wife, who 'carried a similar weapon of defence, though probably not to protect her chastity'.[32] Sharpe recounts with relish the lurid (proto-gothic) tale: the woman's murder of her aristocratic lover in Corstorphine on 16 August 1679; her hiding in a castle garret until discovered by a stray slipper; her abortive escape from prison dressed in male clothes; her execution at the Cross in Edinburgh; and the local tradition of her ghostly haunting of the spot where she killed her lover, 'wandering and wailing' with a bloody sword in her hand.

In thus overriding scholarly protocols, Sharpe's 'original mode of editing' offends by approaching the past as a mental object of 'curiosity', treating its texts a discursive trigger for the editor's own investigations and preoccupations. While he had a stake in ideas about and from the past, that is, he had little interest in the experience of the past (the feelings and thoughts valorized by Hogg). This lack of interest accounts for the way in which editorial and authorial texts rarely intersect, more typically sliding past each other to form the 'contrast' that arrests Hogg's attention for much of the *Blackwood's* letter. Dwelling on this contrast, he tips it decisively in favour of the 'manly narrative' of Kirkton: 'There we have all along the upper part of the page, the manly narrative of honest Kirkton, speaking of his suffering friends with compassion, but of his enemies as became a man and a Christian. And below that, such a medley of base ribaldry, profane stuff, and blasphemous inuendos [*sic*], as at one view exhibits the character of both parties.'[33] Playing the 'wag', Sharpe generates what is literally a subversive sub-text.

Suggestively, however, when Hogg comes to write his mock secret history in *Private Memoirs and Confessions*, what he transfers is less the subversive relation of the two texts than the *fact* of contrast between editorial and authorial voices. He picks up from Sharpe's edition of Kirkton the symptomatic nature of the friction between the texts, which speaks to an inevitable divergence of horizons under a historicist model that posits disjunction as the modality of historical time. The texts in Sharpe's volume do not talk to one another, and neither do the texts in Hogg's own fictional secret history. Mounting a double-pronged critique of historical thought, *Private Memoirs and Confessions* attacks general history (as was conventional in secret histories) but it also interrogates the motivating assumptions of secret history itself. On the one hand, as often noted, the novel undermines the mediating concepts through which a modern mind makes sense of and surmounts the past to produce the present as the kind of synthesis exhibited most famously in the period by Scott's Waverley novels.[34] On the other

– and this has been less often remarked – it places in question the antiquary's conviction that, once suspect mediating concepts have been
ditched, the past can be authentically approached through the concreteness and intimacy of its fragmentary 'remains'. Hogg's point in
manipulating the laminated texts of antiquarian secret history is not primarily that editorial objectivity is an illusion: objectivity is never the issue. His
Editor may present himself as 'unprejudiced', but he does not represent
himself as impartial. Like Charles Kirkpatrick Sharpe, he makes apparent
from the beginning where he stands, condemning 'severe and gloomy
bigots', heaping sarcasm on 'the profound Mr. Wringhim's sermons', and
parodying the idiom of the ultra-Presbyterians.[35] Hogg's trickier and more
pertinent point is that while textual 'remains' may make the past more
visible, they also make it more visibly alien.

'[The] past is at once closer to us and, at the same time stranger', says F.
R. Ankersmit, speaking of the implications of a similar rejection of bridging
concepts in the writing of history in our own time.[36] Confronting the
immediacy of documents from the past, especially its informal and intimate documents such as memoirs and journals, one comes face to face
with opacity. 'What can this work be?' the Editor exclaims at the conclusion of the Sinner's narrative, and he is no more enlightened when he
comes to the conclusion of the entire volume: 'With regard to the work
itself, I dare not venture a judgment, for I do not understand it.'[37] Intimate
contact with the words of the past has produced not the cognition that
would yield firm judgement but rather its bafflement. Trying out one term
after another from his generic taxonomy (allegory, parable, mad dream),
the Editor finally leaves the undecidable text to revolve in the unbridge-
able difference between 'this day' and 'that age'.[38] In doing so he secures
the authenticity of the past – its distinct reality – but at the expense of its
legibility, as the authentic increasingly comes to stand in inverse relation to
the intelligible. Moreover, in preserving the trace of the past (the Editor
follows the Sinner's injunction to reproduce his memoir without alteration), he leaves it floating, hence open to the very 'waggishness' Hogg
deplored in Sharpe's reading of Kirkton. Indeed, Hogg himself finally
proves a wag, entering the final pages of his text to turn his back, ostenta-
tiously, on historical investigation of the past: 'I hae mair ado than I can
manage the day, foreby ganging to houk up hunder-year-auld banes'.[39] In
the final pages, the impertinent figure of the blunt shepherd begins
strangely to cross with that of his antagonist, the mannered antiquary-
dandy from the city, who similarly turned his back on the protocols of

modern understanding. Rooted in secret history's suspicion of historical reason and dignity – 'An historian,' pronounced James Mackintosh in the *Edinburgh Review* 'is not a jester or a satirist'[40] – Hogg's prankish text brings to culmination the gothic novel's scandalous relation to the historiographic enterprise. In its wayward enactment and critique of the attraction to 'remains' that was redefining what it meant to do history and to publish the past in the early decades of the nineteenth century, *Private Memoirs and Confessions of a Justified Sinner* confirms gothic's investment in debates central to the making of Romantic culture but equally ensures that it keeps a heretic (gothic) distance from its consolidations.

Notes

1 Horace Walpole, *The Castle of Otranto* (Oxford: Oxford University Press, 1998), p. 5. On the found manuscript as a gothic trope, see in particular Fiona Robertson, *Legitimate Histories: Scott, Gothic, and the Authorities of Fiction* (Oxford: Clarendon Press, 1994), pp. 86–93 and Meg Russett, *Fictions and Fakes: Forging Romantic Authenticity, 1760–1845* (Cambridge: Cambridge University Press, 2006).

2 Joep Leerssen, 'Literary Historicism: Romanticism, Philologists, and the Presence of the Past', *Modern Language Quarterly* 65 (2004), pp. 221–43 [p. 226].

3 Walpole, *Otranto*, p. 6.

4 Such studies are too numerous to cite, but for influential accounts that pay special attention to the question of gothic romance and national formation, see Ian Duncan, *Modern Romance and Transformations of the Novel: The Gothic, Scott, Dickens* (Cambridge: Cambridge University Press, 1992); and Katie Trumpener, *Bardic Nationalism: The Romantic Novel and the British Empire* (Princeton: Princeton University Press, 1997). Other recent studies of gothic fiction in the Romantic period include Marshall Brown, *The Gothic Text* (Stanford: Stanford University Press, 2005); Michael Gamer, *Romanticism and the Gothic: Genre, Reception, and Canon Formation* (Cambridge: Cambridge University Press, 2000); Robert Miles, *Gothic Writing 1750–1820* (1993) (Manchester and New York: Manchester University Press, 2nd edn, 2002); James Watt, *Contesting the Gothic: Fiction, Genre and Cultural Conflicts, 1764–1832* (Cambridge: Cambridge University Press, 1999). Also exemplary are the essays in Jerrold E. Hogle, ed., *The Cambridge Companion to Gothic Fiction* (Cambridge: Cambridge University Press, 2002) and David Punter, ed., *A Companion to Gothic* (Oxford: Blackwell, 1999).

5 Deidre Lynch, 'Gothic Libraries and National Subjects', *Studies in Romanticism* 40 (Spring, 2001), pp. 29–48. See also Miranda Burgess, *British Fiction and the Production of Social Order 1740–1830* (Cambridge: Cambridge University Press, 2000).

6 Isaac D'Israeli, 'True Sources of Secret History', in *Curiosities of Literature* (London: Edward Moxon, 12th edn, 1841), p. 517.

7 For suggestive comments on the connection between the literary and the historical revivals, see Ann Rigney, *Imperfect Histories: The Elusive Past and the Legacy of*

Romantic Historicism (Ithaca and London: Cornell University Press, 2001), especially chapter 4.

8 Wai Chee Dimock uses the example of Blake and Milton in a discussion of the deserialized time of Romantic literary history, 'Nonbiological Clock: Literary History against Newtonian Mechanics', *South Atlantic Quarterly* 102 (Winter 2003), pp. 153–77. For a fascinating (and gothic) discussion of how literary forms in the period attempted to overcome the disjunctions of historicist time, see Ted Underwood, 'Romantic Historicism and the Afterlife', *PMLA* 117 (March 2002), pp. 237–51.

9 Robert Mayer, *History and the Early English Novel: Matters of Fact from Bacon to Defoe* (Cambridge: Cambridge University Press, 1997), pp. 95–96.

10 See Michael McKeon, *The Secret History of Domesticity: Public, Private, and the Division of Knowledge* (Baltimore: Johns Hopkins University Press, 2005). For other recent perspectives on secret history, see April London, 'Isaac D'Israeli and Literary History: Opinion, Anecdote, and Secret History in the Early Nineteenth Century', *Poetics Today* 26 (2005), pp. 351–86; and Kathryn Temple, *Scandal Nation: Law and Authorship in Britain, 1750–1832* (Ithaca and London: Cornell University Press, 2003), chapter 3.

11 On the 'sentimental' turn, see in particular Mark Phillips, *Society and Sentiment: Genres of Historical Writing in Britain, 1740–1820* (Princeton: Princeton University Press, 2000), and his 'Relocating Inwardness: Historical Distance and the Transition from Enlightenment to Romantic Historiography', *PMLA* 118 (May 2003), pp. 436–49.

12 Despite renewed interest in Macpherson, his work as a historian has not attracted a great deal of attention from either historians or literary scholars. The most useful account remains D. B. Horn's 'Some Scottish Writers of History in the Eighteenth Century', *The Scottish Historical Review* 40 (April 1961), pp. 1–18.

13 Not all were convinced. The *Edinburgh Review* refers slightingly to Macpherson's introduction in the course of a review of a later life of James II, remarking on 'that unsatisfactory vagueness – that indisposition to state the sources of his information fully and candidly – that tone of disregard for the public, and defiance of the most reasonable demands of criticism, which have thrown so deep a shade over his literary probity', [James Mackintosh?], 'Life of James II.', *Edinburgh Review* 16 (1816), p. 406.

14 *Original Papers; Containing the Secret History of Great Britain, From the Restoration, To the Accession of the House of Hannover*, 2 vols. (London, 1775), Vol. 1, p. 6.

15 *The History of Great Britain, From the Restoration to the Accession of the House of Hanover*, 2 vols. (London, 1775), Vol. 1, p. vii.

16 D'Israeli, 'True Sources', p. 512.

17 D'Israeli, 'True Sources', p. 514. The negative power of antiquarian history is memorably summed up by Walter Scott, who remarks in a survey of Scottish historians: 'Father Innes, it must be observed, was an antiquary, not a historian. His Essay was of a negative nature, merely showing what parts of the apocryphal history of Scotland could not possible be true'; review of Joseph Ritson's *Annals of the Caledonians*, *Quarterly Review* (July 1829), repr. in *Miscellaneous Prose Works* (Edinburgh, 1835), Vol. 20, p. 313.

18 D'Israeli, 'True Sources', p. 514.

19 On Maturin's novel, see Ina Ferris, *The Romantic National Tale and the Question of Ireland* (Cambridge: Cambridge University Press, 2002), chapter 4.

20 Admittedly, there is a pragmatic reason for the choice of *Confessions* over *Memoirs* as a short title, for Hogg wrote actual memoirs (*Memoirs of the Author's Life*, 1806, 1821), but the generic point holds.

21 Peter Garside offers the most complete restoration of the historical and publishing contexts of Hogg's novel to date in the introduction to his edition, *Private Memoirs and Confessions of a Justified Sinner* (Edinburgh: Edinburgh University Press, 2002), pp. i–xcix. My references to the novel are to this edition.

22 I discuss this point at greater length in 'Printing the Past: Walter Scott's Bannatyne Club and the Antiquarian Document', *Romanticism* 11.2 (2005), pp. 143–60.

23 Hogg, *Private Memoirs*, p. 64.

24 Hogg, *Private Memoirs*, p. 68.

25 Ian Duncan, 'Authenticity Effects: The Work of Fiction in Romantic Scotland', *South Atlantic Quarterly* 102 (Winter 2003), p. 111.

26 [James Hogg], 'A Letter to Charles Kirkpatrick Sharpe, Esq. On his Original Mode of Editing Church History', *Blackwood's Magazine* 2 (December 1917), p. 306. Peter Garside draws attention to this letter in one of the few references to a link between Sharpe's edition and Hogg's novel; Introduction, *Private Memoirs*, pp. xxxvi.

27 [Walter Scott], 'Kirkton's Church History', *Quarterly Review* (January 1818), repr. in *Miscellaneous Prose Works*, Vol. 19, pp. 213, 264.

28 On Thomson's extraordinary and influential career as editor and researcher in Scottish public records, see Marinell Ash, *The Strange Death of Scottish History* (Edinburgh: Ramsay Head Press, 1980).

29 Charles Kirkpatrick Sharpe, ed., *The Secret and True History of the Church of Scotland, From the Restoration to the Year 1678. By the Rev. Mr. James Kirkton…* (Edinburgh, 1817), p. 104.

30 Sharpe, ed., *Secret and True History*, p. xvi.

31 Hogg, 'Letter', p. 306.

32 Sharpe (ed.), *Secret and True History*, p. 182n.

33 Hogg, 'Letter', p. 307.

34 For a compelling recent reading along these lines, see Duncan, 'Authenticity Effects'.

35 Hogg, *Private Memoirs*, pp. 4–5.

36 F. R. Ankersmit, *Historical Representation* (Stanford: Stanford University Press, 2001), p. 155.

37 Hogg, *Private Memoirs*, pp. 165, 174.

38 Hogg, *Private Memoirs*, p. 175.

39 Hogg, *Private Memoirs*, p. 170.

40 [James Mackintosh], 'Sismondi's *History of France*', *Edinburgh Review* 35 (July 1821), p. 491.

CHAPTER ELEVEN

Sympathy, Physiognomy, and Scottish Romantic Fiction

IAN DUNCAN

1

In a fatal hour Robert Wringhim, the protagonist of James Hogg's novel *The Private Memoirs and Confessions of a Justified Sinner* (1824), meets a stranger who bears an uncanny physical resemblance to himself. Not only to himself: 'I observed several times, when we were speaking of certain divines and their tenets, that his face assumed something of the appearance of theirs; and it struck me, that by setting his features into the mould of other people's, he entered at once into their conceptions and feelings'. The stranger, who calls himself Gil-Martin, explains the 'cameleon art [...] of changing [his] appearance':[1]

> 'My countenance changes with my studies and sensations,' said he. 'It is a natural peculiarity in me, over which I have not full control. If I contemplate a man's features seriously, mine own gradually assume the very same appearance and character. And what is more, by contemplating a face minutely, I not only attain the same likeness, but, with the likeness, I attain the very same ideas as well as the same mode of arranging them, so that, you see, by looking at a person attentively, I by degrees assume his likeness, and by assuming his likeness I attain to the possession of his most secret thoughts.'[2]

Such a virtuoso pitch of observation assumes 'likeness' in order to empty it: draining the other person's interiority, rendering him as a set of surface effects, erasing his integrity and uniqueness.

Gil-Martin's declaration recalls a passage in Edmund Burke's aesthetic treatise *A Philosophical Inquiry into the Origin of Our Ideas of the Beautiful and the Sublime* (1756), in which Burke relates 'a curious story of the celebrated physiognomist', Tommaso Campanella:

This man, it seems, had not only made very accurate observations on human faces, but was very expert in mimicking such as were any way remarkable. When he had a mind to penetrate into the inclinations of those he had to deal with, he composed his face, his gestures, and his whole body, as nearly as he could into the exact similitude of the person he intended to examine; and thus carefully observed what turn of mind he seemed to acquire by this change. So that, says my author, he was able to enter into the dispositions and thoughts of people as effectually as if he had been changed into the very men.[3]

Hogg may have read Burke's treatise, or he may have come across the citation of this passage in Dugald Stewart's *Elements of Philosophy of the Human Mind* (based on his influential lecture course at Edinburgh University).[4] To enter into other people's conceptions and feelings: the aim of this physiognomic technique echoes, in turn, one of the key discourses of Scottish Enlightenment moral philosophy. In his *Treatise of Human Nature* David Hume defines sympathy as the mental operation by which 'we enter [...] deep into the opinions and affections of others, whenever we discover them'.[5] 'By the imagination we place ourselves in [another person's] situation', Adam Smith develops Hume's account in *The Theory of Moral Sentiments*: 'we enter as it were into his body, and become in some measure the same person with him'.[6] The 'cameleon art', in short, is a sympathetic art, and Robert duly acknowledges Gil-Martin as his 'friend'.

This essay explores Scottish Romantic fiction's engagement with a set of discourses about gaining access to the 'dispositions and thoughts of people' in a modern society made up of strangers. Criticism has recognized the key role played by sympathy, the dialectical medium of sentimental and social formation, in the 'rise' of eighteenth-century narrative genres, including history and biography as well as the novel.[7] The literary uses of physiognomy, the most elaborate of a range of Enlightenment techniques for interpreting, representing and thus fully socializing the embodied self, are less well studied. If Smith's *Theory of Moral Sentiments* undertakes the age's most ambitious codification of sympathy as the foundation of a modern moral technology, Johann Kaspar Lavater's *Essays on Physiognomy*, current in Great Britain from the 1790s, expresses, in the attempt to solve, this project's ethical and epistemic crisis. *The Private Memoirs and Confessions of a Justified Sinner* puts drastic moral pressure on the ambition to enter another person's thoughts and feelings, common to the various discourses that interpret the human countenance, the legible page of the socialized body. Through the language of physiognomy Hogg's novel mounts something like a Nietzschean critique of the liberal politics of sympathy, revealing the will-to-power that charges its imaginary dynamic of senti-mental exchange. The outsider's view of the cultural formations of the Scottish Enlightenment, articulated through the tormented utterance of a 'fanatic', does not spare the dominant post-Enlightenment literary genre of the novel itself, and the modes of sympathetic identification activated in its reading. To understand the novelistic legacy of the Smithian model of sympathy that is at stake I shall turn to Walter Scott's *Redgauntlet*, published in Edinburgh in the same month as the *Confessions of a Justified Sinner*. This most profound and subtle of the Waverley novels makes the emergence of modern ways of imagination and sentiment its historical topic. In the complexity of its representation, Scott's novel no less strin-gently than Hogg's recognizes the 'Romantic' crisis of an Enlightenment project.

2

Jacob Spon, Burke's source for the anecdote about Campanella, describes 'physionomie' as a technique practised by learned men who observe the principle that the image of the soul is depicted on a person's external coun-tenance: 'cette regle generale, que la nature tire souvent le portrait de nôtre ame sur nôtre visage, & que certains airs & certaines conformations ont accoûtumé de suivre le temperament & marquer les inclinations de l'homme'.[8] The 'general rule' of a correspondence between an essential identity (a soul), with its domain of thought and feeling contained in the body, and a system of signs imprinted on the body's external surface, in gestures, vocal tones, and facial expressions, recurs insistently throughout the period of the Enlightenment. It informs a range of disciplines of inter-pretation, self-representation and self-regulation through the body and its attributes, such as acting and elocution, which claim to give access to internal states of feeling by the management of external physical proper-ties. At the same time, the insistence on a correspondence between inward being and outward appearance betrays an anxiety about the reliability and status of that correspondence and its constituent semiotics. The anxiety stems less from a potential opacity or instability of the correspondence than from the opposite: the prospect of an excessive legibility, a trans-parency in which the inner, private self is written on the body's surface, leaving no residue of being apart from its material manifestations.

Burke cites the anecdote about Campanella to illustrate a claim 'that when the body is disposed, by any means whatsoever, to such emotions as it would acquire by the means of a certain passion, it will of itself excite something very like that passion in the mind'. In other words, the disposition of the body (for example, of the muscles that control facial expression) can produce by itself the inward state of feeling that it signifies (or 'something very like' it). Burke echoes claims made in eighteenth-century acting manuals. 'To act a passion well,' writes Aaron Hill in his *Essay on the Art of Acting*, 'the actor never must attempt its imitations 'till his fancy has conceived so strong an image, or idea, of it, as to move the same impressive springs within his mind, which form that passion, when 'tis undesigned, and natural'. Hill instructs the aspiring actor to observe his own appearance in a mirror: 'let him not imagine the impression rightly hit, till he has examined both his face and air, in a long, upright looking glass; for there, only, will he meet with a sincere and undeceivable test of his having strongly enough, or too slackly, adapted his fancy to the purpose before him'.[9] The repertoire of gestures and expressions, rather than the inner quality of feeling, provides the guarantee of authenticity.

Similar claims appear in elocution manuals, which proliferate in the second half of the eighteenth century, especially in the British provinces and colonies. With the standardization of spoken as well as written forms of English, elocution supplies an important technique for provincial subjects ambitious for advancement in the imperial professions and administration. Elocution manuals codify, sometimes in great detail, the repertoire of expressions, gestures and intonation which speakers can draw on, not just to imitate a particular emotion or attitude but to produce it within themselves. In his influential lectures on elocution, which instructed virtually an entire generation of Scottish Enlightenment literati, Thomas Sheridan affirmed the technique's philosophical principles. The authors of modern treatises on taste and the passions 'forget that the passions and fancy have a language of their own, utterly independent of words, by which only their exertions can be manifested and communicated'.[10] Sheridan identifies the body as the medium of this language, which he denominates a 'hand-writing of nature' and a 'written language of nature', expressively more genuine than the artificial writing systems developed by civilization.[11]

Sheridan's breezy optimism has darkened to anxiety in Lavater's monumental attempt to systematize physiognomy. Lavater defines his theme as 'the Science of discovering the relation between the exterior and the interior – between the visible surface and the invisible spirit which it covers –

between the animated, perceptible matter, and the imperceptible spirit which impresses this character of life upon it – between the apparent effect, and the concealed cause which produces it'.[12] Self-questionings and reassertions proliferate:

> Does the Human face, that mirror of the Deity, that master-piece of the visible creation, present no appearance of cause and effect, no relation between the exterior and the interior, the visible and invisible, the cause, and what it produces? […] What is universal Nature but Physiognomy? Is not every thing surface and contents? body and soul? external effect and internal faculty? invisible principle and visible end? […] This tacit but universal acknowledgment, that the exterior, the visible, the surface of objects, indicates their interior, their properties; that every external sign is the expression of internal qualities; – this acknowledgment, I say, appears to me decisive.[13]

Lavater's almost panicky insistence expresses the urgency of his task: to weld together metaphysical and scientific ways of knowledge, split apart in the projects of Enlightenment. Hume, for example, had deconstructed the binary terms – visible and invisible, matter and spirit, body and soul, form and content, effect and cause – that Lavater now seeks to reaffirm. Accordingly, Lavater conceives of his 'science' as a missionary intervention, the response to a categorical ethical crisis. 'The Physiognomy, taken in the most extensive or the most restrictive sense, is the soul of all our opinions, of our efforts, our actions, our expectations, our fears and our hopes […] It is our guide, and the rule of our conduct'.[14] Physiognomy will save civilization.

However, Lavater must defend his discipline against sinister constructions of it. 'With secret ecstasy the benevolent Physiognomist penetrates into the interior of his fellow-creature':[15] the formulation admits the prospect of a penetration that might not be benevolent. Lavater acknowledges what he calls the potential 'inconveniences' of physiognomy:

> Is not the rage for detecting, censuring, exposing the failings of others already too general? Is it fit to assist this propensity by teaching a method of drawing from the inmost recesses of the heart, the secrets, the thoughts, the infirmities which lie there concealed? Behold, observers starting up in every corner, with penetrating looks, with eyes armed against their fellow-creatures. In societies, in private Parties, in Churches – every where Physiognomists – employed in nothing, affected with nothing, interested in nothing, but studying the faces, and diving into the hearts of their neighbours.[16]

The whole of civil society is convulsed, in this visionary spasm, by an epidemic of obsessive, invasive face-reading. Supposed to counter the alienated activity of 'criticism', physiognomy instead unleashes a scopic warfare of all against all.

Lavater's paranoid glimpse of the moral obverse of his system antici-pates the doings of 'Mr Spy', the editorial persona that James Hogg devised for the weekly magazine he launched in Edinburgh in 1810. Mr Spy is a mischievous mutation of Addison and Steele's 'Mr Spectator', monitor of the emergent eighteenth-century public sphere, as well as of Adam Smith's imaginary 'impartial spectator', the superego supposed to regulate the moral transactions of modern life. A stranger in the city, uprooted from the customary relations that fix identity, Mr Spy seeks to accumulate onto-logical capital through observation of his fellow citizens:

> I am now become an observer so accurate, that by contemplating a person's features minutely, modelling my own after the same manner as nearly as possible, and putting my body into the same posture which seems most familiar to them, I can ascertain the compass of their minds and thoughts, [...] not precisely what they are thinking of at the time, but the way that they would think about any thing.[17]

The qualification echoes Lavater: 'You will not know beforehand all that a man means to say, write, or do, in general; but you will be able to foresee of what he is *capable* or *incapable*, how he will act or express himself in such and given circumstances'.[18] Mr Spy's propensity, as commentators have noticed, looks forward to the 'cameleon art' professed by Gil-Martin in the *Confessions of a Justified Sinner*. That novel includes several scenes in which a malevolent observer starts up 'with penetrating looks, with eyes armed against [his] fellow-creatures [...] [in] societies, in private Parties, in Churches'. The gaze of a fraternal *doppelganger* haunts George Colwan everywhere he goes in Edinburgh, from the tennis court and golf links to Greyfriars church; later, Robert falls under Bell Calvert's inconvenient eye, as well as the supernatural surveillance of Gil-Martin.

Lavater tries to avert such alarming declensions of his science by appealing to the stabilizing medium of intersubjective feeling that Scottish moral philosophy called sympathy. 'Physiognomy unites hearts: it alone forms intimate and lasting connections; and friendship, that heavenly sentiment, has no foundation more solid'.[19] The claim grants physiognomy the socializing function assigned to sympathy by the Scottish philosophers; but rather than being supplementary to sympathy, it takes its place as friendship's 'foundation' or constituent technique. If Hogg presents Gil-Martin as a diabolical maestro of the physiognomic art, it is within the larger context of the Scottish account of sympathy as a moral technology for the maintenance of social bonds in a modern, implicitly urban, society of strangers – persons whose knowledge of one another is not predicated upon customary relations, such as kinship.

3

'I was born an outcast in the world,' Robert Wringhim declares at the beginning of his memoir.[20] Robert's upbringing disciplines his sense of estrangement into an extremist deformation of the Calvinist psychology that recurs throughout Scottish moral philosophy and fiction, which confer upon it – secularized and historicized – the exemplary status of a modern structure of feeling.[21] Hume's *Treatise of Human Nature* provides the classic account of this sentimental formation. In the conclusion to the first book, the author steps back from his argument, to complain:

> I am at first affrighted and confounded with that forelorn solitude, in which I am plac'd in my philosophy, and fancy myself some strange uncouth monster, who not being able to mingle and unite in society, has been expell'd all human commerce, and left utterly abandon'd and disconsolate.[22]

The problem implies its solution. Hume has translated the epistemological crisis of an evacuation of metaphysical relations from the world into a social crisis of exile and solitude. Society thus holds the cure for what Hume calls his 'philosophical melancholy and delirium'. It constitutes the illusory yet irresistible field of 'custom' which reabsorbs the alienated imagination. 'I dine, I play a game of backgammon, I converse, and am merry with my friends': not by rational choice, but by a natural, instinctual imperative. The philosopher finds himself 'absolutely determin'd to live, and talk, and act like other people in the common affairs of life'[23] – until nature, in the form of intellectual curiosity, shall urge him once more to resume his lonely ratiocination. Hume goes on to analyse the natural force that integrates us into common life in the second book of the *Treatise*, where he gives it the name of sympathy.

The protagonists of both *Redgauntlet* and the *Confessions of a Justified Sinner* find themselves in a Humean predicament of melancholy solitude. Appearing 'an unaccountable monster' in others' view, Robert Wringhim flees across country, shunned by the common folk among whom he seeks refuge.[24] Nature – sympathy – cannot cure him since no society will take him in. Instead of a destiny regulated by sociability, the 'Memoirs and Confessions' narrates the totalization of the sinner's solitude in a logic of extinction: the fall of the house of Colwan by fratricide, matricide, suicide. Scott's novel, however, attempts the comic narrative of socialization that the *Confessions of a Justified Sinner* refuses. Darsie Latimer, the novel's dejected step-brother, complains of his exile from family origins:

> I am affected with a sense of loneliness, the more depressing, that it seems to me to be a solitude peculiarly my own. In a country where all the world have a circle of consanguinity, extending to sixth cousins at least, I am a solitary individual, having only one kind heart to throb in unison with my own. [...] I am in the world, as a stranger in the crowded coffee-house, where he enters, calls for what refreshments he wants, pays his bill, and is forgotten so soon as the waiter's mouth has pronounced his 'Thank ye, sir.'[25]

The simile of 'the crowded coffee-house' informs Darsie's melancholy with the historical and anthropological theme of modernization: he is exemplary in the very conviction that he is unique. The coffee-house, prototypical setting of the eighteenth-century public sphere, specifies its commercial ethos as well as the disappearance of an organic web of kinship relations.[26] Unlike Hogg, Scott accepts the wager of the modern republic of letters to make good the substitution. *Redgauntlet* will justify literature itself – Scott's historical fiction – as the commercial institution that provides a sentimental and aesthetic replenishment of traditional relations threatened with oblivion in modern society: but by advertising, rather than trying to conceal, the sceptical knowledge that these are imaginary relations and not real ones.

Hume's philosopher is delivered from the melancholy that attends his intellectual adventure by being 'merry with my friends'. *Redgauntlet* unfolds a complex meditation on friendship as the customary relation that replaces kinship ties in commercial society: sustaining individual identity against modern anomie, on the one hand, and against atavistic coercions of kinship, on the other. Scott's novel explores the ambivalent ascendancy of the new sociology of friendship, a voluntary, equal association among strangers, over the pre-modern usage of the term (in Scots) to designate extended, hierarchical kinship relations. Friendship must bear the Smithian charge of an active, horizontal relation of sympathetic exchange through which both the desiring individual and the social group can reproduce themselves. Darsie's intimation of 'one kind heart to throb in unison with my own' picks up a musical metaphor from Smith's *Theory of Moral Sentiments*, which holds, however, that 'unison' may not be necessary, nor even desirable, as a condition of sympathy: in the mixed relations of modern society 'concord' will suffice.

Both *Redgauntlet* and the *Confessions of a Justified Sinner* novelize the Humean logic that a metaphysical relation, once sceptical reason has expelled it from the world, reasserts its lost authority in the 'fanatical' mode of delusion – as the literalizing reiteration of an obsolete cultural system. The 'cause' returns, in other words, as an ideology – Jacobite absolutism, Calvinist antinomianism – that justifies itself in a language of predestinarian fatalism. 'I was now a justified person, adopted among the number of God's children – my name written in the Lamb's book of life,' Wringhim announces: 'no bypast transgression, nor any future act of my own, or of any other man, could be instrumental in altering the decree'.[27] 'The privilege of free action belongs to no mortal,' sneers Darsie Latimer's uncle Hugh Redgauntlet: 'our most indifferent actions are but meshes of the web of destiny by which we are all surrounded'.[28] Latimer and Wringhim are both stepsons astray from a natural and social origin defined by biological paternity, divested now of its traditional symbolic integrity. Ancient kinship ties, paternal authority, fatality and literalism all predicate one another as symptoms of a sublime but deathly cultural apparatus that reasserts itself, beyond the breach of modernity, in the utterance of a sentence of extermination. 'His skull is yet standing over the Rikargate, and even its bleak and mouldered jaws command you to be a man', Redgauntlet ventriloquizes the dead father in his attempt to conscript Darsie into the Jacobite cause.[29] It is here that Scott invokes physiognomy. The imprint of a horseshoe on the brow, the hereditary birthmark of the Redgauntlets, signifies the traumatic reiteration of an original paternal speech-act: 'It was said that his father cursed, in his wrath, his degenerate offspring, and swore that, if they met, he should perish by his hand'.[30] The sentence is fulfilled when the father rides over the body of his fallen son. Paternal authority reproduces itself in the discontinuous structure of a repetition of antagonistic violence: the son reiterates the father's will in rebelling against him, and, in a hideous literalization of genetic imprinting, the father stamps on the son's brains. The 'fatal mark of our race' reappears on Darsie's brow when, in an involuntary spasm of resentment, he returns his uncle's frown and glimpses his own reflection in a mirror. Physiognomy, the somatic symptom of a patriarchal regime of hierarchical coercion, thus represents the antithesis of a sympathetic dynamic of mutual elective affinity in Scott's novel.

Throughout *Redgauntlet* friendship and paternal authority form, respectively, the modern (horizontal) and traditional (vertical) axes of the core social-ethical value of *pietas* or loyalty (flagged in the novel's epigraph from

As You Like It). Alan Fairford equivocates between the claims of his father and his friend Darsie Latimer, and Darsie yearns for Alan while his uncle commands him to embody his dead father's cause. At first glance the values of this opposition seem clear enough. After the fall of the old regime, the word of the father can no longer reproduce the vital relations of culture. Modern friendship flourishes in sympathetic exchange, while the prescriptive, top-down vector of paternal authority threatens to provoke, instead, antipathy, the motor of an uncanny, inhuman and mechanical conflict typified by the family curse. By insisting on the subjective component of loyalty, in the contractarian language of sympathy-based moral sentiment, Scott's first-person narration has already rewritten it as modern:

> I am, and have all along been, the exclusive object of my father's anxious hopes, and his still more anxious and engrossing fears; so what title have I to complain, although now and then these fears and hopes lead him to take a troublesome and incessant charge of all my motions?[31]

Alan uses the language of friendship to justify filial piety: his affections are bound to his father by the sympathetic insight into his 'fears and hopes'. Filial piety now relies on an imaginative apprehension of the father's vulnerability rather than his strength – investing the relation with a measure of sympathy's contractual charge, and founding sympathy on a shared affect of anxiety. Unmitigated strictness on the father's part, it is implied, would license the son's revolt. The novel does allow a brief idyll of father–son friendship, significantly a professional one, when the Fairfords collaborate to sort the chaotic archive of the Peebles lawsuit ('the specimen of all causes') into a transparent narrative.[32] But Alan deserts the lawsuit once he realizes that their collaboration has been resting upon his father's betrayal of his friendship with Darsie. The anxious synthesis of paternal authority, filial piety and mutual sympathy splinters under stress.[33]

At the same time, Darsie Latimer yearns for a lost world of kinship. This yearning drives the plot of *Redgauntlet*, until it is overwhelmed by the reciprocal force of Hugh Redgauntlet's effort to graft the dead cause onto a living heir. It seems that the new bonds of friendship cannot by themselves assuage what the novel represents as a profound psychic need; their horizontality, covering a historyless present, is by definition superficial. The obliterated scutcheon of the Quaker Joshua Geddes expresses a willed sublimation of ancestral ties that is at once excessive and incomplete. It seems we need those 'deep' relations of kinship and fealty: but they must be recovered in the mode of friendship. They must, in other words, be imaginary and sentimental relations before they can be 'real' ones. (Heterosexual difference produces a strange inversion of this logic: Darsie's dangerous desire for Lilias is reconstituted as friendship by the revelation that they are brother and sister.) Darsie's adventures in the first volume, in what turns out to be an unwitting quest for origins, trace the pattern of an inadvertent reconstitution of ancient 'friendship' through the sentimental techniques of sympathy. Wandering across the countryside, he falls in with a series of representatives of communities dwelling outside civil society: Jacobites, rural vagrants, and Quakers (a self-designated 'Society of Friends'). Darsie's dislocation from paternity seems to endow him with a compensatory talent for invoking their sympathy. The new friendships revive old family relations – father, sister, feudal retainer – but in disguise, unrecognized. The plot withholds from them the 'metaphysical' logic of causality. The Quaker Geddes can indulge in a paternal kindness towards Darsie because he is not his father; the plot, however, does not allow him to play a father's part. The case of the folk minstrel Wandering Willie is still more instructive. Willie turns out (unbeknownst to either of them) to be Darsie's ancestral vassal. In one of the novel's comic set pieces, Willie and the captive Darsie exchange messages encoded in the titles of national airs that they play and whistle to one another. The episode alludes to a legendary adventure of Richard Coeur de Lion, and it seems as though a romance plot is being hatched: Darsie's sympathetic connoisseurship of popular culture will surely bear fruit in a rescue. Strikingly, though, no such attempt follows. The episode leads nowhere.

The plot of *Redgauntlet*, then, establishes patterns of friendship in which the sentimental reconstitution of an ancient kinship relation follows its divorce from causality. Friendship is the subjective constituent of a tangled web of affiliations, coincidences and recognitions in which narrative consequences are suspended – as becomes clear in the final chapters at Father Crackenthorpe's inn, the maze in which all plots and characters accumulate. The inn, like the coffee-house, is a commercial space of hospitality, but one that lies outside civil society (on the disputed margin between national and historical regimes), where it is presided over by false fathers – the carnivalesque Crackenthorpe, the pathetic Bonaventura. Everyone in the novel turns up, but in order that their diverse agencies *not* converge into a unified narrative engine. Bathos and confusion reign. Here Redgauntlet's invocation of a fatal, literal, material paternity is emptied at last of its metaphysical charge. 'Then, gentlemen, […] the cause is lost for ever!'[34]

The Hanoverian general Colin Campbell exorcizes 'the cause' with the most powerful speech-act in the Waverley novels. Campbell's authority does not rest solely on the army that backs up his presence; the modern state apparatus has so permeated and colonized the lateral relations of friendship that it no longer needs to issue a paternal command – even as its utterance continues to rely on the disposition of material force. Campbell designates the social regime of friendship with a set of interlocking recognitions and refusals of recognition. Thus he can banish friendship's uncanny opposite, that antipathetic compulsion signified by the horseshoe mark: the involuntary, uncontrollable recognition of a genetic identity that has already imprinted itself on the body:

> He had passed through their guards, if in the confusion they now maintained any, without stop or question, and now stood, almost unarmed, among armed men, who, nevertheless, gazed on him as on the angel of destruction.
>
> 'You look coldly on me, gentlemen,' he said. 'Sir Richard Glendale – My Lord – we were not always such strangers. Ha, Pate-in-Peril, how is it with you? And you, too, Ingoldsby – I must not call you by any other name – why do you receive an old friend so coldly?'[35]

The angel of destruction assumes the form of a private gentleman who, in hailing the conspirators as friends, declines to recognize them as historical agents. The death this angel deals is a social death, that of Jacobitism's public, historical identity. The General dismisses them to the oblivion of private life:

> 'Come, do not be fools, gentlemen; there was perhaps no harm meant or intended by your gathering together in this obscure corner, for a bear-baiting, or a cock-fighting, or whatever other amusement you may have intended [...] I have come here, of course, sufficiently supported both with cavalry and infantry, to do whatever might be necessary; but my commands are – and I am sure they agree with my inclination – to make no arrests, nay, to make no farther inquiry of any kind, if this good assembly will consider their own interest so far as to give up their immediate purpose, and return quietly home to their own houses.'[36]

Charles Edward Stuart himself admits the power of the sentence: 'I bid you farewell, unfriendly friends – I bid *you* farewell, sir, (bowing to the General,) my friendly foe'.[37] The paradoxes acknowledge that the Jacobite revival has already fallen apart through its failure to control the categories of friendship and authority that frame historical agency.[38]

4

The opening of *Redgauntlet*, with its epistolary and dialogic division of the narrative between two friends, simulates the 'imaginary change of situation upon which', according to Adam Smith, 'sympathy is founded'. Scott's *Tale of the Eighteenth Century* models Smith's account of the moral psychology of civil society as a formal principle of the novel as a genre, and not only as a thematic principle, as it has been in many of Scott's earlier works. The exchange of letters binds the reader into the structure of sympathetic exchange, as we assume the place of each of the novel's protagonists in turn. This formal disposition of the narrative highlights (via Scott's allusions to Richardson) a distinctively novelistic tradition of sentimental reading.[39] Scott stylizes and historicizes the institutional basis of sympathy as a work of reading, so that we may reflect upon our own participation in the liberal culture of modernity that the novel invokes.

Sympathy is a work of the imagination in *The Theory of Moral Sentiments*. Willed, laborious and negotiated, it requires as well as offers reciprocity, but of a curiously negative kind. What is shared is not the expression of feelings but their alienation. Sympathy arises not so much 'from the view of the [other person's] passion, as from that of the situation which excites it'.[40] This requires a painstaking work of observation, reflection and conjectural narration, in which the 'imaginary change of situation' is crafted as a 'case'. The spectator must 'endeavour, as much as he can, to put himself in the situation of the other, and to bring home to himself every little circumstance of distress which can possibly occur to the sufferer. He must adopt the whole case of his companion with all its minutest incidents; and strive to render as perfect as possible, that imaginary change of situation upon which his sympathy is founded'.[41] For this to take place, the sufferer must have first sympathized with the spectator – muting the expression of his joy or anguish to approximate a social norm of 'insensibility', since onlookers will be repelled by a violent outcry. The social function of sympathy is thus to maintain a cool or neutral affective medium of 'propriety'.[42] Reciprocally, we imagine ourselves as objects in the point of view of others: society is the 'mirror' in which we observe and regulate our 'countenance and behaviour'.[43] 'When I endeavour to examine my own conduct,' Smith prescribes, 'I divide myself, as it were, into two persons,' he who acts and he who observes and judges.[44] The work of imagination appropriates other to self and at the same time converts self to other, stabilizing both terms through a strenuous labour of internal estrangement and self-division.[45]

The exchange between self and other undoes both categories in *The Private Memoirs and Confessions of a Justified Sinner*. In a parody of Smith's trope of socializing self-division, Robert Wringhim wants a friend but finds a demonic double. 'You think that I am your brother,' Gil-Martin introduces himself, 'or that I am your second self': immediately posing the problem of a friendship that falls catastrophically between, instead of subsuming, kinship and self-consciousness.[46] Ideology, or the imaginary relation of belief, constitutes the new bond: 'I am indeed your brother, not according to the flesh, but in my belief of the same truths.' The claim on an imaginary brotherhood sustained by 'belief of the same truths' subverts the sceptical basis of sympathy, which posited, in Smith's account, likeness rather than identity, harmonized difference rather than unison, as the condition of a working social order. The idea of 'a collective made of individuals' is foundational to *The Theory of Moral Sentiments*, as Nancy Armstrong has insisted.[47] Sympathy is the moral instrument through which civil society regulates itself as a homeostatic system of differences of degree, between individuals, rather than differences between social classes or ethnic or religious communities. Identity through belief constitutes a fantasy of excessive socialization, called 'fanaticism' by Enlightenment historiography, which postulates a society without internal otherness. Lord Kames, in *Sketches of the History of Man*, argues that evangelical conversion, the promotion of belief of the same truths, destroys the 'necessary variety in sentiment and opinion' that supplies a basic principle of social cohesion:

> Different countenances in the human race, not only distinguish one person from another, but promote society, by aiding us to chuse a friend, an associate, a partner for life. Differences in opinion and sentiment have still more beneficial effects: they arouse the attention, give exercise to the understanding, and sharpen the reasoning faculty. With respect to religion in particular, perfect uniformity, which furnisheth no subject for thinking nor for reasoning, would produce languor in divine worship, and make us sink into cold indifference. How foolish then is the rage of making proselytes? Let every man enjoy his native liberty, of thinking as well as acting.[48]

Wringhim's new friend, who appears to be 'the same being as myself', systematically erases other people's difference, beginning with difference of countenance: 'by looking at a person attentively, I by degrees assume his likeness, and by assuming his likeness I attain to the possession of his most secret thoughts.' Collapsing the binary terms reaffirmed in Lavater's treatise (surface and depth, inside and outside, likeness and identity, self and other), Gil-Martin's physiognomy evacuates the liberal domain of interiority that it was supposed to secure. '[We] were incorporated together – identified with one another', writes Wringhim of his friend; and of himself: 'I generally conceived myself to be two people [...] The most perverse part of it was, that I rarely conceived *myself* to be any of the two persons'.[49]

Armstrong contrasts Smith's account of sympathy, an ethical discipline for the maintenance of individuals, with the earlier theory of sympathy as an involuntary, contagious, transpersonal force that dissolves the bounds between self and other, proposed by David Hume. In Hume's account sympathy is triggered by physiognomic observation: 'When any affection is infus'd by sympathy, it is at first known only by its effects, and by those external signs in the countenance and conversation, which convey an idea of it'.[50] What interests Hume is the force or vector that transforms this 'idea', derived from observation, into an equivalent state of feeling within the observer. 'This idea is presently converted into an impression, and acquires such a degree of force and vivacity, as to become the very passion itself, and produce an equal emotion, as any original affection'.[51] The sign, that is, becomes the condition it signifies. 'In sympathy there is an evident conversion of an idea into an impression':[52] as Adela Pinch notes, the claim reverses the normal priority of impression and idea in Hume's argument.[53] 'This is the nature and cause of sympathy; and 'tis after this manner we enter so deep into the opinions and affections of others, whenever we discover them'.[54] Sympathy is realized, in short, in the conversion of an idea of another person's feeling into a feeling of our own, rooted in our own psychosomatic organization.

Hume's account of sympathy yields the imperial logic of Gil-Martin's 'cameleon art' in the *Confessions of a Justified Sinner*. Indeed, Gil-Martin's physiognomy devolves the Smithian model of sympathetic exchange into the Humean; or rather, Gil-Martin uses a Smithian hermeneutic discipline to harness the involuntary, contagious force of sympathy for a diabolical will to power. He executes a Humean set of 'conversions' – between surface and content, outside and inside, likeness and identity – in which the thoughts and dispositions of others are interpreted, replicated, and taken over as 'impressions' of his own. This drive to re-embody the idea of the other's feeling as a feeling of one's own runs counter to the moralistic project of *The Theory of Moral Sentiments*, with its emphasis on the abstraction of feeling. Smith at first acknowledges that sympathy involves the epistemological urge to 'enter as it were into' another person's being:

> By the imagination we place ourselves in his situation, we conceive ourselves enduring all the same torments, we enter as it were into his body, and become

in some measure the same person with him, and thence form some idea of his sensations, and even feel something which, though weaker in degree, is not altogether unlike them.[55]

However, Smith's insistence on the (Humean) principle that 'it is by the imagination only that we can form any conception of what are [another person's] sensations' attenuates to a figure of speech ('as it were [...] in some measure [...] not altogether unlike') the Gil-Martian scenario of bodily invasion and identity theft. Indeed Hume's wild sympathy – spontaneous, passionate, embodied – is the disciplinary target of *The Theory of Moral Sentiments*. Smith the civic moralist (in Nicholas Phillipson's phrase) seeks to domesticate the free-range model of sympathetic contagion, with its anarchic dissolution of the boundaries of self and other, through a complex interactive labour of reflection that demarcates those boundaries and produces the ethical subject of civil society. Smith forestalls the 'conversion of an idea into an impression', Hume's 'nature and cause of sympathy', with the argument that sympathy can only be sustained upon the disembodiment of passion and sensation.[56] The 'passions which take their origin from the body' are far less susceptible to sympathy than those that take their origin from the imagination, 'because our imaginations can more readily mould themselves upon [another man's] imagination, than our bodies can mould themselves upon his body'.[57] Physiognomy, with its fixation on the body's expressive surfaces, accordingly plays little or no part in the Smithian work of sympathy, with its refinement of the 'imaginary change of situation' through a conjectural reconstruction of 'the whole case' of the other person's predicament.[58]

Hogg's devolution of the Smithian model of sympathy into its wild Humean prototype in *Confessions of a Justified Sinner* resonates with recent comparisons between Smith and his Irish contemporary Edmund Burke, drawn by Luke Gibbons and Seamus Deane. While Smith sought 'to found the notion of a civil society on a doctrine of social sympathy which was predicated on a concept of distance', Burke's *Philosophical Inquiry* 'challenged and disrupted the integrationist narratives of the Scottish Enlightenment', based on tropes of abstraction and exchange, with an 'aesthetics of terror and disintegration'.[59] In sharp contrast to Smith's moral blueprint for Scottish assimilation into the British Union, Burke evokes the psycho-political regime of a 'colonial sublime' constituted by a passionate identification with distress and suffering. Where Smithian moral sentiment would 'purge the body and its discontents from the public sphere', Burke (following Hume) mobilizes 'the contagion of our passions' for an ethical identification that Gibbons calls 'the sympathetic sublime'.[60] Burke's citation of the physiognomic skills of Campanella, echoed in Gil-Martin's explanation of his 'cameleon art', occurs in a discussion of the 'cause of pain and fear': the physiognomist uses his powers of facial control to abstract himself from the agonies of torture by the Inquisition. Hogg's devil however assumes the role of inquisitor – contemplating the other person's countenance with such skill that he possesses his 'most secret thoughts'.

Burke's alternative declension of the Humean model of sympathy illuminates the crisis that shook the authority of *The Theory of Moral Sentiments* during the French Revolution controversy. It also suggests a genealogy for Hogg's recourse, in *Confessions of a Justified Sinner*, to what we might call Irish or colonial tropes of physiognomy and the sympathetic sublime, in stark antithesis to Scott's reaffirmation of Smithian codes of moral sentiment in *Redgauntlet*. Dugald Stewart, the main interpreter of Scottish Enlightenment thought to Scott's generation, dismissed Smith's model of sympathetic exchange as 'an illusion of the imagination', and rehabilitated, instead, Hume's account of the 'inexplicable contagion of sympathetic imitation', grounded in the 'mimical powers connected with our *bodily frame*'.[61] 'When we assume any strongly expressive look, and accompany it with appropriate gestures, some degree of the correspondent emotion is apt to arise within us'.[62] Citing Burke's anecdote about Campanella, Stewart notes the 'very close connection' between the 'two talents, of mimickry and physiognomy':[63]

> the effect of mimickry cannot fail, of itself, to present to the power of Conception, in the strongest and liveliest manner, the original which is copied; and therefore, it is not surprising, that, on such an occasion, the mimic should enter more completely into the ideas and feelings he wishes to seize, – to identify himself in imagination for the moment (if I may use the expression) with the archetype he has in view.[64]

However, for Stewart, writing in the turbulent wake of the French Revolution, sympathetic imitation betrays the imagination's vulnerability to 'the contagious nature of convulsions, of hysteric disorders, of panics, and of all the different kinds of enthusiasm', especially 'the infectious tendency of religious enthusiasm' and the sublime energy of crowds.[65] The counter-revolutionary context informs not only Stewart's reversion from Smith to Hume but the Burkean associations with which the reversion is charged. Fanaticism and the crowd, figures for the dissolution of individuality into an undifferentiated, asocial collectivity, are topoi of the Burkean sublime, shaped now by Burke's late politicization of them in the *Reflections on the Revolution in France*. They portend an appalling loss of identity and agency, rather than their sympathetic enhancement. Sympathy, promising fraternity, brings terror.

With the surmise that his uncanny friend must be 'the Czar Peter of Russia [...] travelling through Europe in disguise',[66] Wringhim names a fantasy of enlightened despotism haunting the politics of sympathy. Peter the Great would found the most grandiose of eighteenth-century New Towns upon the corpses of his subjects. If Scott's *Redgauntlet* reaffirms an Enlightenment cultural history in which the sympathetic imagination (instantiated in the work of fiction) may replace archaic, authoritarian bonds with civil relations of sentimental exchange, *Confessions of a Justified Sinner* parses Smithian sympathy as a sublime technique that colonizes the other's difference and undoes the self itself – the basis of civil society as a formal system of regulated differences. At the same time Hogg's novel recuperates, with shocking moral force, the Burkean 'sympathetic sublime' of an involuntary identification with terror and anguish. The book presents itself as a collection of documents comprising 'the whole case' of Robert Wringhim, a case so extreme that even his editor shares the 'detestation' in which Wringhim seems universally to be held.[67] Hogg however exploits the formal mechanism of novelistic sympathy to pose a radical challenge to his readers' apprehensions of sympathy's moral content. The very act of reading a first-person narration – a confession – forges the contagious sympathetic link whereby we find ourselves in Robert's situation, beyond the pale of civil society: 'an outcast in the world'.[68]

Notes

1   James Hogg, *The Private Memoirs and Confessions of a Justified Sinner*, ed. P. D. Garside (Edinburgh: Edinburgh University Press, 2001), pp. 119, 124.
2   Hogg, *Confessions of a Justified Sinner*, p. 86.
3   Edmund Burke, *A Philosophical Enquiry into the Origin of Our Ideas of the Beautiful and the Sublime*, ed. Adam Phillips (Oxford: Oxford University Press, 1990), p. 120. See also Dugald Stewart, *Elements of Philosophy of the Human Mind*, 3 vols. (London: Strahan, 1792; Edinburgh: Ramsay, 1814; London: Murray, 1827).
4   It is unlikely that Hogg knew Burke's source, an antiquarian compilation by the seventeenth-century Huguenot humanist and physician Jacob Spon: *Recherches curieuses d'antiquité, contenues en plusieurs dissertations* (Lyon, 1683). Burke accurately cites Spon (p. 358), although his most Gil-Martian formulation, 'he was able to enter into the disposition and thoughts of people', exaggerates the original, 'pour

juger [...] ce que ces personnes avoient dans le coeur' ('to judge [...] what people had in their hearts').

5   David Hume, *A Treatise of Human Nature*, ed. Ernest C. Mossner (Harmondsworth: Penguin, 1984), p. 369.

6   Adam Smith, *The Theory of Moral Sentiments*, ed. D. D. Raphael and A. L. Macfie (Oxford: Clarendon Press, 1976), p. 9.

7   See, e.g., David Marshall, *The Surprising Effects of Sympathy: Marivaux, Diderot, Rousseau, and Mary Shelley* (Chicago: University of Chicago Press, 1988); Catherine Gallagher, *Nobody's Story: The Vanishing Acts of Women Writers in the Marketplace 1670–1820* (Berkeley: University of California Press, 1994); Julie Ellison, *Cato's Tears and the Making of Anglo-American Emotion* (Chicago: University of Chicago Press, 1999); Adela Pinch, *Strange Fits of Passion: Epistemologies of Emotion, Hume to Austen* (Stanford: Stanford University Press, 1996); and Mark Salber Phillips, *Society and Sentiment: Genres of Historical Writing in Britain, 1740–1820* (Princeton: Princeton University Press, 2000).

8   Spon, *Recherches curieuses d'antiquité*, pp. 357–58.

9   Aaron Hill, *An Essay on the Art of Acting* (London, 1754), Vol. 4, p. 339.

10   Thomas Sheridan, *A Course of Lectures on Elocution: Together with Two Dissertations of Language; and some other tracts relative to these subjects* (London: W. Strachan, 1762), p. x.

11   Sheridan, *A Course of Lectures on Elocution*, pp. 113, 116.

12   John Caspar Lavater, *Essays on Physiognomy, Designed to Promote the Knowledge and the Love of Mankind*, trans. from the French by Henry Hunter, 3 vols. (London: John Murray, 1789–92), Vol. 1, p. 20.

13   Lavater, *Essays on Physiognomy*, Vol. 1, pp. 29, 32, 24–35.

14   Lavater, *Essays on Physiognomy*, Vol. 1, pp. 32–33.

15   Lavater, *Essays on Physiognomy*, Vol. 1, p. 77.

16   Lavater, *Essays on Physiognomy*, Vol. 1, p. 80.

17   James Hogg, *The Spy*, ed. Gillian Hughes (Edinburgh: Edinburgh University Press, 2000), p. 4.

18   Lavater, *Essays on Physiognomy*, Vol. 2, p. 422.

19   Lavater, *Essays on Physiognomy*, Vol. 2, p. 51.

20   Hogg, *Confessions of a Justified Sinner*, p. 97.

21   Susan Manning, *The Puritan-Provincial Vision: Scottish and American Literature in the Nineteenth Century* (Cambridge: Cambridge University Press, 1990), p. 44.

22   Hume, *A Treatise of Human Nature*, p. 311.

23   Hume, *A Treatise of Human Nature*, p. 316.

24   Hogg, *Confessions of a Justified Sinner*, p. 19.

25   Walter Scott, *Redgauntlet: A Tale of the Eighteenth Century*, ed. D. Hewitt and G. M. Wood (Edinburgh: Edinburgh University Press, 1995), p. 4.

26   See, classically, Jürgen Habermas, *The Structural Transformation of the Public Sphere: An Inquiry into a Category of Bourgeois Society* (Cambridge, MA: MIT Press, 1988), pp. 32–33, 43–51.

27   Hogg, *Confessions of a Justified Sinner*, p. 79.

28   Scott, *Redgauntlet*, p. 193.

29   Scott, *Redgauntlet*, p. 317.

30 Scott, *Redgauntlet*, p. 190.
31 Scott, *Redgauntlet*, p. 11.
32 Scott, *Redgauntlet*, p. 138.
33 On Scott's treatment of patriarchy and contract see Alexander Welsh, *The Hero of the Waverley Novels; With New Essays on Scott* (Princeton: Princeton University Press, 1992), pp. 213–41; on *Redgauntlet* see pp. 227–31.
34 Scott, *Redgauntlet*, p. 373.
35 Scott, *Redgauntlet*, p. 371.
36 Scott, *Redgauntlet*, pp. 372–73.
37 Scott, *Redgauntlet*, p. 374.
38 Charles Edward Stuart cannot sustain either the paternal logos, in its ideological form of Divine Right absolutism, or the new ethos of homosocial friendship, to both of which he appeals in vain. Charles invokes the doctrine of the king's two bodies to defend his dalliance with Clementina Walkinshaw: a private indulgence of the sexual body should not compromise the public authority of the sovereign body. But the appeal fails through its contamination by the modern relation it actually invokes, the distinction between public and private life: in fact Charles's liaison does compromise his role as father of the nation, since his mistress is betraying him to the government (*Redgauntlet*, pp. 355–58). See also Judith Wilt's argument that the liaison terminates a fatal feminization of Stuart patriarchy ('a feminine influence predominates'); Judith Wilt, *Secret Leaves: The Novels of Walter Scott* (Chicago, University of Chicago Press, 1985), pp. 126–29.
39 See Leah Price, *The Anthology and the Rise of the Novel: From Richardson to George Eliot* (Cambridge: Cambridge University Press, 2000), pp. 54–66; Nicola Watson, *Revolution and the Form of the British Novel, 1790–1805: Intercepted Letters, Interrupted Seductions* (Oxford: Clarendon Press, 1994), pp. 149–53.
40 Smith, *Theory of Moral Sentiments*, p. 10.
41 Smith, *Theory of Moral Sentiments*, p. 21.
42 Smith, *Theory of Moral Sentiments*, pp. 31–48.
43 Smith, *Theory of Moral Sentiments*, p. 110.
44 Smith, *Theory of Moral Sentiments*, p. 110.
45 For the resonance of this term in Smith and Scott, see James Chandler, *England in 1819: The Politics of Literary Culture and the Case of Romantic Historicism* (Chicago: University of Chicago Press, 1998), pp. 229–30, 307–20.
46 Hogg, *Confessions of a Justified Sinner*, p. 117.
47 Nancy Armstrong, *How Novels Think: The Limits of Individualism from 1719–1900* (New York: Columbia University Press, 2005), pp. 14–15.
48 Henry Home, Lord Kames, *Sketches of the History of Man*, 4 vols. (Edinburgh: Strahan, Cadell, Creech, 2nd edn, 1788), Vol. 2, pp. 438–39.
49 Hogg, *Confessions of a Justified Sinner*, p. 106.
50 Hume, *A Treatise of Human Nature*, p. 367.
51 Hume, *A Treatise of Human Nature*, p. 367.
52 Hume, *A Treatise of Human Nature*, p. 370.
53 Pinch, *Strange Fits of Passion*, p. 34; on Hume's contagious, 'transpersonal' model of the feelings, see also pp. 3–7, 17–44.
54 Hume, *A Treatise of Human Nature*, p. 369.

55 Smith, *Theory of Moral Sentiments*, p. 9.
56 See John Mullan's comparison between Hume's contagious model of sympathy and Smith's version predicated upon 'spectatorial aloofness': *Sentiment and Sociability: The Language of Feeling in the Eighteenth Century* (Oxford: Clarendon Press, 1988), pp. 25–56; 43; and Nicholas Phillipson's account of 'Adam Smith as Civic Moralist', in Istvan Hont and Michael Ignatieff, eds., *Wealth and Virtue: The Shaping of Political Economy in the Scottish Enlightenment* (Cambridge: Cambridge University Press, 1983), pp. 179–202.
57 Smith, *Theory of Moral Sentiments*, p. 29.
58 Smith, *Theory of Moral Sentiments*, p. 21.
59 Seamus Deane, *Strange Country: Modernity and Nationhood in Irish Writing since 1790* (Oxford: Clarendon Press, 1997), pp. 1–27; 37.
60 Luke Gibbons, *Edmund Burke and Ireland: Aesthetics, Politics and the Colonial Sublime* (Cambridge: Cambridge University Press, 2003), pp. 83–120; 11, 84, 105–106.
61 Stewart, *Elements of Philosophy*, Vol. 2, pp. 171–72, 208, 154.
62 Stewart, *Elements of Philosophy*, Vol. 2, p. 185.
63 Stewart, *Elements of Philosophy*, Vol. 2, p. 186.
64 Stewart, *Elements of Philosophy*, Vol. 2, p. 191.
65 Stewart, *Elements of Philosophy*, Vol. 2, pp. 195–96, 203, 209.
66 Hogg, *Confessions of a Justified Sinner*, p. 89.
67 Hogg, *Confessions of a Justified Sinner*, p. 175.
68 Hogg, *Confessions of a Justified Sinner*, p. 67.

Works Cited

Adultery Anatomized: in a select collection of tryals, for criminal conversation (London: 2 vols., 1761)

Advertisement for *A Select Collection of Old Plays* (London: R. Dodsley, 14 January 1744) [*The Eighteenth Century*; reel 9720, no. 12]

Advertisement for *A Select Collection of Poems, The Gazetteer and New Daily Advertiser* No. 15, 929 (2 March 1780 [Page 1])

Advertisement for *A Select Collection of Poems, The Morning Chronicle, and London Advertiser* No. 3, 332 (22 January 1780 [Page 1])

Advertisement for *Sir Charles Grandison* for *The Novelist's Magazine* (London: Harrison, 1783)

Advertisement for *Supplement to Bell's British Theatre, The World*, no. 4. (5 January 1787 [Page 1])

Advertisement for *The New Novelist's Magazine* (London: Harrison, 1786)

Allestree, Richard, *The Gentleman's Calling* (London: Printed for T. Garthwait, 1660)

Alliston, April, 'Transnational Sympathies, Imaginary Communities', in Margaret Cohen and Carolyn Dever, eds., *The Literary Channel: The Inter-National Invention of the Novel* (Princeton and Oxford: Princeton University Press, 2002)

Anderson, Benedict, *Imagined Communities: Reflections on the Origins and Spread of Nationalism* (London: Verso, rev. edn, 1991)

Ankersmit, F. R., *Historical Representation* (Stanford: Stanford University Press, 2001)

Aravamudan, Srinivas, 'Fiction/Translation/Transnation: The Secret History of the Eighteenth-Century Novel', in Paula R. Backscheider and Catherine Ingrassia, eds., *A Companion to The Eighteenth-Century English Novel and Culture* (Oxford: Blackwell, 2005)

Armstrong, Nancy, *Desire and Domestic Fiction: A Political History of the Novel* (Oxford: Oxford University Press, 1987)

— 'Writing Women and the Making of the Modern Middle Class', in Amanda Gilroy and W. M. Verhoeven, eds., *Epistolary Histories: Letters, Fiction, Culture* (Charlottesville: University Press of Virginia, 2000)

— *How Novels Think: The Limits of British Individualism from 1719–1900* (New York: Columbia University Press, 2006)

Ash, Marinell, *The Strange Death of Scottish History* (Edinburgh: Ramsay Head Press, 1980)

Astell, Mary, *Political Writings*, ed. Patricia Springborg (Cambridge: Cambridge University Press, 1996)

Aubert de Vertot D'Auberf, Réné, *The History of the Revolution in Portugal in the year 1640* (London: Matt. Gilliflower, Tim. Goodwin, Mat. Wotton, Rich. Parker, and Benj. Tooke, 1700)

Austen, Jane, *Pride and Prejudice*, ed. James Kinsley (Oxford: Oxford University Press, 1970)

— *Northanger Abbey*, ed. John Davie (Oxford: Oxford University Press, 1971)

— *Mansfield Park*, ed. James Kinsley (Oxford: Oxford University Press, 1980)

— *Sir Charles Grandison*, ed. Brian Southam (Oxford: Clarendon Press, 1980)

— *Letters*, ed. Deirdre Le Faye (Oxford: Oxford University Press, 3rd edn, 1997)

— *Persuasion*, ed. Linda Bree (Peterborough, Ontario: Broadview Press, 1998)

— *Persuasion*, ed. Gillian Beer (Harmondsworth: Penguin, 1998)

— *Pride and Prejudice* (New York and London: Norton and Company, 2001)

Austen-Leigh, William, and Richard Arthur Austen-Leigh, *Jane Austen: A Family Record* (Boston: G. K. Hall, 1989)

Austin, Andrea, 'Between Women: Frances Burney's *The Wanderer*', *English Studies in Canada*, 22.3 (1996)

Austin, Susan, *Fragments from German Prose Writers* (London: John Murray, 1841)

Ballantyne's Novelist's Library (London: Hurst, Robinson & Co.; Edinburgh: J. Ballantyne, 10 vols., 1821–24)

Barbauld, Anna Letitia, 'On the Origin and Progress of Novel-Writing', in Barbauld, ed., *The British Novelists* (London, 1810), Vol. 1

— *The Poems of Anna Letitia Barbauld*, ed. William McCarthy and Elizabeth Kraft (Athens and London: The University of Georgia Press, 1994)

Barbauld, Anna Letitia, ed., *The British Novelists* (London: F. C. and J. Rivington and others, 50 vols., 1810)

Barclay, Florence L., *Returned Empty* (London: G. P. Putnum's Sons, 1920)

Barker-Benfield, G. J., *The Culture of Sensibility: Sex and Society in Eighteenth-Century Britain* (Chicago: University of Chicago Press, 1992)

Barrow, John, *Some Account of the Public Life, and a Selection from the unpublished Writings, of the Earl of Macartney, the latter consisting of extracts from an account of the Russian Empire; a sketch of the political history of Ireland; and a journal of an embassy from the King of Great Britain to the Emperor of China* (London: Cadell, 1807)

Barruel, Augustin, *Memoirs, Illustrating the History of Jacobinism,* trans. Robert Clifford (London: T. Burton, 4 vols., 2nd edn, 1798)

Barthes, Roland, *Mythologies*, trans. Annette Lavers (New York: Hill and Wang, 1972)

Baudrillard, Jean, 'The System of Collecting', in John Elner and Roger Cardinal, eds., *The Cultures of Collecting* (London: Reaktion Books, 1994)

Bell's British Theatre, consisting of the most esteemed English plays (London: John Bell; York: C. Etherington, 20 vols., 1776–78)

Bell's Edition of Shakespeare's Plays … with notes critical and illustrative (London: J. Bell, 9 vols., 1774)

Benedict, Barbara, *The Making of the Modern Reader: Cultural Mediation in Early Modern Anthologies* (Princeton: Princeton University Press, 1996)

Benis, Toby, '"A Likely Story": Charlotte Smith's Revolutionary Narratives', *European Romantic Review* 14.3 (2003), pp. 291–306

Bhabha, Homi, 'Of Mimicry and Man: The Ambivalence of Colonial Discourse', in *The Location of Culture* (London: Routledge, 1994)

Blackburn, Robin, *The Overthrow of Colonial Slavery, 1776–1848* (London: Verso, 1989)

Blair, Hugh, *Lectures on Rhetoric and Belles Lettres* (London: W. Strahan; T. Cadell, 2 vols., 1783)

Blair, Hugh, ed., *The Works of Shakespear, in which the beauties observed by Pope, Warburton, and Dodd are pointed out* (Edinburgh: W. Sands and others, 1753; reprinted Edinburgh: A. Donaldson, 8 vols., 1771)

Bradshaw, Penny, 'Gendering the Enlightenment: Conflicting Images of Progress in the Poetry of Anna Laetitia Barbauld', *Women's Writing* 5.3 (October 1998), pp. 353–71

Brokey, Dorothy, *The Minerva Press, 1790–1820* (London: The Bibliographical Society at the University Press, Oxford, 1939)

Brooke, Charlotte, *Reliques of Irish Poetry: Consisting of Heroic Poems, Odes, Elegies, and Songs, Translated into English Verse* (Dublin, 1789)

Brooks, Peter, 'Virtue and Terror: *The Monk*', *ELH* 40 (1973), pp. 249–63

— *Realist Vision* (New Haven: Yale University Press, 2005)

Brown, Charles Brockden, *Carwin the Biloquist*, in *Wieland or The Transformation. An American Tale*, ed. Jay Fliegelman (New York: Penguin Books, 1991)

Brown, Homer Obed, *Institutions of the English Novel from Defoe to Scott* (Philadelphia: University of Pennsylvania Press, 1997)

Brown, Julia Prewitt, *Jane Austen's Novels: Social Change and Literary Form* (Cambridge, MA: Harvard University Press, 1979)

Brown, Marshall, *The Gothic Text* (Stanford: Stanford University Press, 2005)

Burgess, Miranda, *British Fiction and the Production of Social Order 1740–1830* (Cambridge: Cambridge University Press, 2000)

— 'The National Tale and Allied Genres, 1770s–1840s,' in John Wilson Foster, ed., *The Cambridge Companion to the Irish Novel* (Cambridge: Cambridge University Press, 2006)

Burke, Edmund, *Reflections on the Revolution in France*, ed. Conor Cruise O'Brien (Harmondsworth: Penguin, 1976)

— *A Philosophical Enquiry into the Origin of Our Ideas of the Beautiful and the Sublime*, ed. Adam Phillips (Oxford: Oxford University Press, 1990)

— *First Letter on a Regicide Peace*, in R. B. McDowell, ed., *The Writings and Speeches of Edmund Burke* (Oxford: Clarendon Press, 1991), Vol. IX

Burney, Frances, *Cecilia, or Memoirs of an Heiress*, ed. Peter Sabor and Margaret Anne Doody (Oxford: Oxford University Press, 1988)

— *The Wanderer; or, Female Difficulties*, ed. Margaret Anne Doody, Robert Mack, and Peter Sabor (Oxford: Oxford University Press, 1991)

— *Evelina, or, A Young Lady's Entrance into the World*, ed. Susan Kubica Howard (Peterborough: Ontario: Broadview Literary Texts, 2000)

Butler, Marilyn, *Jane Austen and the War of Ideas* (Oxford: Clarendon Press, 1975)

Butler, Marilyn, Heidi Van de Veire, and Kim Walker, 'Introduction', in *The Novels and Selected Works of Maria Edgeworth*, general eds. Marilyn Butler and Mitzi Myers, 12 vols. (London: Pickering & Chatto, 1999), Vol. 5 (ed. Van de Veire and Walker with Butler)

Byrne, Paula, 'A Simple Story: From Inchbald to Austen', *Romanticism* 5.2 (Fall, 1999), pp. 161–71

Byron, George Gordon, *The Corsair*, in *Byron: Poetical Works*, ed. Frederick Page and John Jump (Oxford: Oxford University Press, 3rd edn, 1975)

— *Childe Harold's Pilgrimage*, in *Lord Byron: The Major Works*, ed. Jerome J. McGann (Oxford: Oxford University Press, 1986)

— *The Giaour*, in *Byron*, ed. Jerome J. McGann (Oxford: Oxford University Press, 1986)

Cabinet of Poetry, The, Containing the best entire pieces to be found in the works of the British Poets (London: Richard Phillips, 6 vols., 1808)

Carlson, Julie, *In the Theatre of Romanticism: Coleridge, Nationalism, Women* (Cambridge: Cambridge University Press, 1994)

Cassirer, Ernst, *The Philosophy of the Enlightenment*, trans. Fritz Koelln and James Pettegrove (Princeton: Princeton University Press, 1951)

Cavell, Stanley, 'The Avoidance of Love: A Reading of *King Lear*', in *Must We Mean What We Say?* (New York: Cambridge University Press, 1976)

— 'In Quest of the Ordinary', in Morris Eaves and Michael Fischer, eds., *Romanticism and Contemporary Criticism* (Ithaca: Cornell University Press, 1986)

Chandler, James, *England in 1819: The Politics of Literary Culture and the Case of Romantic Historicism* (Chicago: University of Chicago Press, 1998)

Christensen, Jerome, *Romanticism at the End of History* (Baltimore: Johns Hopkins University Press, 2000)

Clark, Robert, ed., *New Casebooks: Sense and Sensibility and Pride and Prejudice* (London: St Martin's Press, 1994)

Clark, Stuart, 'Scientific Status of Demonology', in Brian Vickers, ed., *Occult and Scientific Mentalities in the Renaissance* (Cambridge: Cambridge University Press, 1984)

Classic Tales, Serious and Lively. With Critical Essays on the Merits and Reputation of the Authors (London: John Hunt & Carew Reynell, 5 vols., 1806)

Cohen, Ralph, ed., *Studies in Eighteenth-Century British Art and Aesthetics* (Berkeley: University of California Press, 1985)

Coleman, Deirdre, 'Conspicuous Consumption: White Abolitionism and English Women's Protest Writing in the 1790s', *ELH* 61.2 (Summer 1994), pp. 341–62

Coleridge, Samuel Taylor, 'Rime of the Ancyent Marinere', in *Lyrical Ballads*, ed. W. J. B. Owen (New York: Oxford University Press, 2nd edn, 1969)

— *Biographia Literaria*, ed. James Engell and Walter Jackson Bate (Princeton: Princeton University Press, 2 vols., 1983)

Collection of Novels, A, Selected and Revised by Mrs. Griffith (London: G. Kearsley, 3 vols., 1777)

Colley, Linda, *Britons: Forging the Nation, 1707–1837* (New Haven: Yale University Press, 1994)

Connolly, S. J., 'Eighteenth-Century Ireland: Colony or Ancien Régime?', in D. George Boyce and Alan O'Day, eds., *The Making of Modern Irish History: Revisionism and the Revisionist Controversy* (London: Routledge, 1996)

Constable, Thomas, *Archibald Constable and his Literary Correspondents* (Edinburgh: Edmonston & Douglas, 3 vols., 1873)

Cooper, Anthony Ashley, Third Earl of Shaftesbury, *Characteristics of Men, Manners, Opinions, Times*, ed. Lawrence E. Klein (Cambridge: Cambridge University Press, 1999)

Corbett, Mary Jean, 'Affections and Familial Politics: Burke, Edgeworth, and the "Common Naturalization" of Great Britain', *ELH* 61.4 (1994), pp. 877–97

Court of Queen Mab, The: Containing a select collection of only the best, most instructive, and entertaining tales of the fairies (London: M. Cooper, 1752)

Cox, Jeffrey N., *Poetry and Politics in the Cockney School: Keats, Shelley, Hunt and their Circle* (Cambridge: Cambridge University Press, 1998)

Critical Review; or, Annals of Literature (London: 1756–1817)

Curran, Stuart, ed., *The Poems of Charlotte Smith* (New York and Oxford: Oxford University Press, 1993)

D'Israeli, Isaac, 'True Sources of Secret History', in *Curiosities of Literature* (London: Edward Moxon, 12th edn, 1841)

Deane, Seamus, *Strange Country: Modernity and Nationhood in Irish Writing since 1790* (Oxford: Clarendon Press, 1997)

Decremps, M., *The Conjurer Unmasked; or, La Magie Blanche Dévoilée: being a clear and full explanation of all the surprising performances exhibited by the most eminent and dextrous professors of slight of hand* (London: T. Denton, 1785)

Defoe, Daniel, *The Compleat English Gentleman*, ed. Karl D. Bülbring (London: David Nutt, 1890)

della Casa, Giovanni, *Galateo: or, A Treatise on Politeness and Delicacy of Manners* (London: Printed for J. Dodsley, 1774)

Deresiewicz, William, *Jane Austen and the Romantic Poets* (New York: Columbia University Press, 2004)

Derrida, Jacques, *Of Grammatology*, trans. Gayatri Chakravorty Spivak (Baltimore: Johns Hopkins University Press, 1998)

Dimock, Wai Chee, 'Nonbiological Clock: Literary History against Newtonian Mechanics', *South Atlantic Quarterly* 102 (Winter 2003), pp. 153–77

Doody, Margaret Anne, 'Jane Austen's Reading', in J. David Grey, ed., *The Jane Austen Companion* (New York: Macmillan, 1986)

— *Frances Burney: The Life in the Works* (New Brunswick, NJ: Rutgers University Press, 1988)

Driver, Felix, *Geography Militant: Cultures of Exploration and Empire* (Oxford: Blackwell, 2001)

Duckworth, Alistair M., *The Improvement of the Estate: A Study of Jane Austen's Novels* (Baltimore: Johns Hopkins University Press, 1971)

Dülmen, Richard van, *The Society of the Enlightenment: The Rise of the Middle Class and Enlightenment Culture in Germany*, trans. Anthony Williams (Cambridge: Polity Press, 1992)

Duncan, Ian, *Modern Romance and Transformations of the Novel: The Gothic, Scott, Dickens* (Cambridge: Cambridge University Press, 1992)

— 'Authenticity Effects: The Work of Fiction in Romantic Scotland', *South Atlantic Quarterly* 102 (Winter 2003), pp. 93–116

DuPlessis, Rachel Blau, *Writing Beyond the Ending: Narrative Strategies of Twentieth-Century Women Writers* (Bloomington: Indiana University Press, 1985)

Eagleton, Terry, *The Function of Criticism* (London: Verso, 1984)

— *The English Novel: An Introduction* (Oxford: Blackwell Publishing, 2005)

Eberle, Roxanne, 'Amelia Opie's *Adeline Mowbray*: Diverting the Libertine Gaze; or, the Vindication of a Fallen Woman', *Studies in the Novel* 26.2 (1994), pp. 121–52

Echard, Siân, *Printing the Middle Ages* (Philadelphia: University of Pennsylvania Press, 2008)

Edgeworth, Maria, *Castle Rackrent and Ennui*, ed. Marilyn Butler (London: Penguin Books, 1992)

— *The Absentee*, in *The Novels and Selected Works of Maria Edgeworth*, general eds. Marilyn Butler and Mitzi Myers, 12 vols. (London: Pickering & Chatto, 1999), Vol. 5 (ed. Heidi Van de Veire and Kim Walker, with Marilyn Butler)

— *The Absentee*, ed. Heidi Thomson and Kim Walker (London: Penguin, 1999)

— *Belinda*, ed. Kathryn J. Kirkpatrick (Oxford: Oxford University Press, 1994, reissued as Oxford World's Classics, 1999)

— *The Absentee*, ed. W. J. McCormack and Kim Walker (Oxford: Oxford's World Classics, 2001)

Einige Originalschriften des Illuminatensordens (Munich: Johann Baptist Strobl, 1787)

Elias, Norbert, *The Civilizing Process: Sociogenetic and Psychogenetic Investigations*, trans. Edmund Jephcott (Oxford: Blackwell, 2000)

Ellis, Markman, *The History of Gothic Fiction* (Edinburgh: Edinburgh University Press, 2000)

Ellison, Julie, *Cato's Tears and the Making of Anglo-American Emotion* (Chicago: University of Chicago Press, 1999)

Emsley, Sarah, 'Radical Marriage', *Eighteenth-Century Fiction* 11.4 (July 1999), pp. 477–98

Epstein, Julia, *The Iron Pen: Frances Burney and the Politics of Women's Writing* (Madison: University of Wisconsin Press, 1989)

Erdman, David, ed., *The Complete Poetry and Prose of William Blake* (New York: Anchor Books, 1988)

Fanon, Frantz, *Black Skin, White Masks*, trans. Constance Farrington (New York: Grove Press, 1994)

Fenwick, Eliza, *Secresy; or, The Ruin on the Rock,* ed. Isobel Grundy (Peterborough, Ontario: Broadview Press, 1994)

Ferguson, Frances, 'Legislating the Sublime,' in Ralph Cohen, ed., *Studies in Eighteenth-Century British Art and Aesthetics* (Berkeley: University of California Press, 1985)

— 'Rape and the Rise of the Novel', in R. Howard Bloch and Frances Ferguson, eds., *Misogyny, Misandry, and Misanthropy* (Berkeley: University of California Press, 1989)

Ferguson, Moira, '*Mansfield Park*: Slavery, Colonialism, and Gender', *Oxford Literary Review* 13 (1991), pp. 118–39

— *Colonialism and Gender Relations from Mary Wollstonecraft to Jamaica Kincaid: East Caribbean Connections* (New York: Columbia University Press, 1993)

— *Subject to Others: British Women Writers and Colonial Slavery, 1670–1834* (London: Routledge, 1992)

Ferris, Ina, *The Achievement of Literary Authority: Gender, History, and the Waverley Novels* (Ithaca and London: Cornell University Press, 1991)

— 'Scholarly Revivals', *William & Mary Quarterly*, no. 34.2 (2001), ppooo

— *The Romantic National Tale and the Question of Ireland* (Cambridge: Cambridge University Press, 2002)

— 'Printing the Past: Walter Scott's Bannatyne Club and the Antiquarian Document', *Romanticism* 11.2 (2005), pp. 143–60

Flammenberg, Lawrence, *The Necromancer: or, The Tale of the Black Forest,* trans. Peter Teuthold *[Der geisterbanner, eine Wundergeschichte aus mündlichen und schriftlichen Traditionen gesamnelt]* (London: Minerva Press, 1794)

Fordyce, James, *Sermons to Young Women* (London: Millar, 2 vols., 1794)

Foster, John Wilson, ed., *The Cambridge Companion to the Irish Novel* (Cambridge: Cambridge University Press, 2006)

Fraiman, Susan, 'Jane Austen and Edward Said: Gender, Culture and Imperialism', in Deidre Lynch, ed., *Janeites: Austen's Disciples and Devotees* (Princeton: Princeton University Press, 2000)

Fried, Michael, *Absorption and Theatricality: Painting and Beholder in the Age of Diderot* (Chicago: University of Chicago Press, 1980)

Fulford, Tim, *Landscape, Liberty and Authority: Poetry, Criticism and Politics from Thomson to Wordsworth* (Cambridge: Cambridge University Press, 1996)

Gailhard, Jean, *The Compleat Gentleman: Or, Directions for the Education of Youth as to their Breeding at Home and Traveling Abroad* (London: Printed for Thomas Newcomb, 1678)

Gallagher, Catherine, *Nobody's Story: The Vanishing Acts of Women Writers in the Marketplace, 1670–1920* (Berkeley: University of California Press, 1994)

Galperin, William, 'What Happens When Austen and Burney Enter the Romantic Canon?', in Thomas Pfau and Robert Gleckner, eds., *Lessons of Romanticism: A Critical Companion* (Durham, NC: Duke University Press, 1998)

— *The Historical Austen* (Philadelphia: University of Pennsylvania Press, 2003)

Gamer, Michael, *Romanticism and the Gothic: Genre, Reception, and Canon Formation* (Cambridge: Cambridge University Press, 2000)

— 'Maria Edgeworth and the Romance of Real Life', *Novel: A Forum on Fiction* 34.2 (Spring 2001), pp. 232–66

Garside, Peter, 'Walter Scott and the "Common" Novel, 1808–1819', *Cardiff Corvey: Reading the Romantic Text* 3 (September 1999), available at http://www.cf.ac.uk/encap/corvey/articles/cc03_no2.html, accessed 21 June 2003

Garside, Peter, Raven, James and Schöwerling, Rainer, general eds., *The English Novel 1770–1829, a Bibliographic Survey of Prose Fiction Published in the British Isles* (Oxford: Oxford University Press, 2 vols., 2000)

Gibbons, Luke, *Edmund Burke and Ireland: Aesthetics, Politics and the Colonial Sublime* (Cambridge: Cambridge University Press, 2003)

Gilpin, William, *Observations Relative Chiefly to Picturesque Beauty, Made in the Year 1772, on Several Parts of England; Particularly the Mountains, and Lakes of Cumberland, and Westmoreland* (London: Blamire, 2 vols., 1788)

Gilroy, Amanda and Wil Verhoeven, eds., 'Introduction', in 'The Romantic-Era Novel: A Special Issue', *Novel: A Forum on Fiction* 34.2 (Spring 2001), pp. 147–62

Gisborne, Thomas, *An Enquiry into the Duties of the Female Sex* (London: Cadell, 1797)

Glanvill, Joseph, *Sadducismus triumphatus: Or, A full and plain Evidence, Concerning Witches and Apparitions* (London: A. Bettesworth and J. Batley, 4th edn, 1726)

Godwin, William, *The British Critic* (London: F. and C. Rivington, July 1795), pp. 94–95

— *Enquiry Concerning Political Justice*, 1793, 1796, 1798, Vols. 3 and 4 of *Political and Philosophical Writings of William Godwin*, ed. Mark Philp (London: William Pickering, 1993)

— *Caleb Williams*, eds. Gary Handwerk and A. A. Markley (Peterborough, Ontario: Broadview Press, 2000)

Goldfinch, The. Being a Select Collection of the Most Celebrated English Songs (London: R. Baldwin, 1748)

Goldstein, Bill, 'Publishers Give Classics a Makeover', *The New York Times* (10 February 2003) [Section A, page 9, column 1]

Gray, Thomas, 'Elegy Written in a Country Church Yard', in David Fairer and Christine Gerrard, eds., *Eighteenth-Century Poetry: An Annotated Anthology* (Oxford: Blackwell Publishing Ltd, 2nd edn, 2004), pp. 354–58

Green, André, 'The Intuition of the Negative in *Playing and Reality*', in Gregorio Kohon, ed., *The Dead Mother* (London and New York: Routledge, 1999), pp. 205–21

Grey, J. David, ed., *The Jane Austen Companion* (New York: Macmillan, 1986)

— *Jane Austen's Beginnings: The Juvenilia and Lady Susan* (Ann Arbor: UMI, 1989)

Guillory, John, *Cultural Capital: The Problem of Literary Canon Formation* (Chicago: The University of Chicago Press, 1993)

Guthke, Karl S., 'C. M. Wieland and M. G. Lewis', *Neophilologus* 40 (1956), pp. 231–33

Habermas, Jürgen, *The Structural Transformation of the Public Sphere: An Inquiry into a Category of Bourgeois Society*, trans. Thomas Burger (Cambridge, MA: The MIT Press, 1989)

Hamilton, Alastair, *Heresy and Mysticism in Sixteenth Century Spain: The Alumbrados* (Cambridge: James Clarke & Co., 1992)

Hamilton, Elizabeth, *Translations of the Letters of a Hindoo Rajah*, ed. Pamela Perkins and Shannon Russell (Peterborough, Ontario: Broadview Press, 1999)

Hartley, Lucy, *Physiognomy and the Meaning of Expression in Nineteenth-Century Culture* (Cambridge: Cambridge University Press, 2001)

Hawkins, Laetitia Matilda, *Letters on the Female Mind, its Powers and Pursuits, Addressed to Miss H. M. Williams, with particular reference to her Letters from France* (London: Hookham, 2 vols., 1793)

Hays, Mary, *The Victim of Prejudice*, ed. Eleanor Ty (Peterborough, Ontario: Broadview Press, 2nd edn, 1998)

— *Memoirs of Emma Courtney*, ed. Marilyn Brooks (Peterborough, Ontario: Broadview Press, 2000)

Hazlitt, William, *The Collected Works of William Hazlitt*, ed. A. R. Waller and Arnold Glover (London: J. M. Dent, 1903)

Hechter, Michael, *Internal Colonialism: The Celtic Fringe as a Subject of British Colonial Development, 1536–1966* (London: Routledge, 1975)

Helsinger, Elizabeth K., *Rural Scenes and National Representation: Britain, 1815–1850* (Princeton: Princeton University Press, 1997)

Hemlow, Joyce, 'Fanny Burney and the Courtesy Books', *PMLA* 65.5 (September 1950), pp. 732–61

Henderson, Andrea, *Romantic Identities: Varieties of Subjectivity, 1774–1830* (Cambridge: Cambridge University Press, 1996)

— 'Burney's *The Wanderer* and Early-Nineteenth-Century Commodity Fetishism', *Nineteenth-Century Literature* 57.1 (2002), pp. 1–30

Heydt-Stevenson, Jill, '"Unbecoming Conjunctions": Mourning the Loss of Landscape and Love', *Eighteenth-Century Fiction* 8.1 (October 1995), pp. 51–71

— 'Liberty, Connection, and Tyranny: The Novels of Jane Austen and the Aesthetic Movement of the Picturesque', in Thomas Pfau and Robert Gleckner, eds., *Lessons of Romanticism: A Critical Companion* (Durham, NC: Duke University Press, 1998)

— '"Changing her Gown and Setting her Head to Rights": New Shops, New Hats, New Identities', in Jennie Batchelor and Cora Kaplan, eds., *Women and Material Culture, 1660–1830* (Basingstoke: Palgrave Macmillan, 2007)

Hill, Aaron, *The Works of the Late Aaron Hill ... In Four Volumes. Consisting of Letters on Various Subjects, And of Original Poems, Moral and Facetious. With An Essay on the Art of Acting* (London: Printed for the Benefit of the Family, 1753)

Hofkosh, Sonia, *Sexual Politics and the Romantic Author* (Cambridge: Cambridge University Press, 1998)

Hofman, Amos, 'Opinion, Illusion and the Illusion of Opinion: Barruel's Theory of Conspiracy', *Eighteenth-Century Studies* 27.1 (1993)

Hogg, James, 'A Letter to Charles Kirkpatrick Sharpe, Esq. On his Original Mode of Editing Church History', *Blackwood's Magazine* 2 (December 1917)

— *The Spy*, ed. Gillian Hughes (Edinburgh: Edinburgh University Press, 2000)

— *The Private Memoirs and Confessions of a Justified Sinner*, ed. Peter Garside (Edinburgh: Edinburgh University Press, 2001)

Hogg's New Novelist's Magazine (London: Alex. Hogg, 1794)

Hogle, Jerrold E., ed., *The Cambridge Companion to Gothic Fiction* (Cambridge: Cambridge University Press, 2002)

Home, Henry, and Lord Kames, *Sketches of the History of Man* (Edinburgh: Strahan, Cadell, Creech, 4 vols., 2nd edn, 1788)

Horn, D. B., 'Some Scottish Writers of History in the Eighteenth Century', *The Scottish Historical Review* 40 (April 1961)

Howard, George Elliott, *A History of Matrimonial Institutions* (Chicago: University of Chicago Press, 2 vols., 1904)

Hume, David, *A Treatise of Human Nature*, ed. Ernest C. Mossner (Harmondsworth: Penguin, 1984)

Hunter, J. Paul, *Before Novels: The Cultural Contexts of Eighteenth-Century English Fiction* (New York and London: W. W. Norton & Company, 1990)

Hushahn, Helga, 'Sturm und Drang in Radcliffe and Lewis', in Valeria Tinkler-Villani, Peter Davidson, and Jane Stevenson, eds., *Exhibited by Candlelight: Sources and Developments in the Gothic Tradition* (Amsterdam: Rodopi, 1995)

Hutter, Albert, 'Poetry in Psychoanalysis: Hopkins, Rossetti, Winnicott', in Peter Rudnytsky, ed., *Transitional Objects and Potential Spaces: Literary Uses of D. W. Winnicott* (New York: Columbia University Press, 1993)

Irigaray, Luce, 'The Blind Spot of an Old Dream of Symmetry', in *Speculum of the Other Woman*, trans. Gillian C. Gill (Ithaca: Cornell University Press, 1985)

Jacob, Margaret, *The Radical Enlightenment: Pantheists, Freemasons and Republicans* (London: George Allen & Unwin, 1981)

Jacobus, Mary, *Psychoanalysis and the Scene of Reading* (Oxford: Oxford University Press, 1999)

James, C. L. R., *The Black Jacobins* (New York: Vintage, 1989)

Jameson, Fredric, *The Political Unconscious: Narrative as a Socially Symbolic Act* (Ithaca: Cornell University Press, 1981)

Johnson, Claudia, *Jane Austen: Women, Politics, and the Novel* (Chicago: University of Chicago Press, 1988)

— *Equivocal Beings: Politics, Gender, and Sentimentality in the 1790s: Wollstonecraft, Radcliffe, Burney, Austen* (Chicago: University of Chicago Press, 1995)

— '"Let Me Make the Novels of a Country": Barbauld's *The British Novelists* (1810/1820)', *Novel: A Forum on Fiction* 34 (Spring 2001), pp. 163–79

Johnson, Samuel, *The Rambler*, no. 4 (31 March 1750), in Frank Brady and W. K. Wimsatt, eds., *Samuel Johnson, Selected Poetry and Prose* (Berkeley: University of California Press, 1977)

Jones, C. B., *Radical Sensibility: Literature and Ideas in the 1790s* (New York: Routledge, 1993)

Kant, Emanuel [sic], 'An Answer to the Question, What is Enlightening?', in *Essays and Treatises on Moral Political and Various Philosophical Subjects*, trans. William Richardson (London: printed for the translator by William Richardson, 2 vols., 1798)

Kant, Immanuel, 'An Answer to the Question: What is Enlightenment?', in *On History*, trans. Lewis White Beck et al. (New York: Macmillan, 1963)

— *Critique of Judgment*, trans. Werner S. Pluhar (Indianapolis: Hackett, 1987)

— 'An Answer to the Question: What is Enlightenment?', in *Political Writings*, trans. Hans. S. Reiss (Cambridge: Cambridge University Press, 1996)

Kaufmann, David, 'Law and Propriety, Sense and Sensibility: Austen on the Cusp of Modernity', *ELH* 59.2 (1993), pp. 385–408

Kaul, Suvir, *Poems of Nation, Anthems of Empire: English Verse in the Long Eighteenth Century* (Charlottesville: University of Virginia Press, 2000)

Kelly, Gary, *Women, Writing, and Revolution, 1790–1827* (New York: Oxford University Press, 1993

Kent, Christopher, 'Learning History with, and from, Jane Austen', in J. David Grey, ed., *Jane Austen's Beginnings: The Juvenilia and Lady Susan* (Ann Arbor: UMI, 1989)

Kiely, Robert, *The Romantic Novel in England* (Cambridge, MA: Harvard University Press, 1972)

Kirkham, Margaret, *Jane Austen: Feminism and Fiction* (Sussex: Harvester, 1983)

Kirsch, Irving, 'Demonology and Science during the Scientific Revolution', *Journal of the History of the Behavioural Sciences* 16 (1980), pp. 359–68

Knigge, Adolf Franz Friedrich Ludwig von, *Practical Philosophy of Social Life; The Art of Conversing with Men: after the German of Baron Knigge*, trans. Peter Will (London: T. Cadell and W. Davies, 2 vols., 1799)

Knight, David, 'Chemistry on an Offshore Island: Britain, 1789–1840', in David Knight and Helge Kragh, eds., *The Making of the Chemist: The Social History of Chemistry in Europe, 1789–1914* (Cambridge: Cambridge University Press, 1998)

Kucich, Greg, 'Charlotte Smith and the Political Uses of Women's Educational History', paper given at the BARS/NASSR Conference, 'Emancipation, Liberation, Freedom' (Bristol, 26 July 2007)

Labbe, Jacqueline, Introduction to Charlotte Smith, *The Old Manor House*, ed. Jacqueline M. Labbe (Peterborough, Ontario: Broadview Press, 2002)

Langan, Celeste, *Romantic Vagrancy: Wordsworth and the Simulation of Freedom* (Cambridge: Cambridge University Press, 1995)

— 'Venice', in James Chandler and Kevin Gilmartin, eds., *Romantic Metropolis: The Urban Scene of British Culture, 1780–1840* (Cambridge: Cambridge University Press, 2005)

Lascelles, Mary, *Jane Austen and her Art* (Oxford: Oxford University Press, 1939)

Lavater, John Caspar, *Essays on Physiognomy, Designed to Promote the Knowledge and the Love of Mankind*, trans. Henry Hunter (London: John Murray, 3 vols., 1789–92)

Leask, Nigel, *British Romantic Writers and the East: Anxieties of Empire* (Cambridge: Cambridge University Press, 1992)

— '"Wandering through Eblis": Absorption and Containment in Romantic Exoticism', in Tim Fulford and Peter J. Kitson, eds., *Romanticism and Colonialism: Writing and Empire, 1780–1830* (Cambridge: Cambridge University Press, 1998)

Lee, Debbie, *Slavery and the Romantic Imagination* (Philadelphia: University of Pennsylvania Press, 2002)

Lee, Yoon Sun, 'A Divided Inheritance: Scott's Antiquarian Novel and the British Nation', *ELH* 64 (1997), pp. 537–67

Leerssen, Joep, *Mere Irish and Fíor-Ghael: Studies in the Idea of Irish Nationality, its Development and Literary Expression prior to the Nineteenth Century* (Cork: Cork University Press, 1997)

— *Remembrance and Imagination: Patterns in the Historical and Literary Representation of Ireland in the Nineteenth Century* (Cork: Cork University Press, 1997)

— 'Literary Historicism: Romanticism, Philologists, and the Presence of the Past', *Modern Language Quarterly* 65 (2004), pp. 221–43

Leisure Hours' Amusements. Being a select collection of One hundred and fifty of the most diverting Stories dispersed in the writings of the best English Authors (London: M. Cooper, 1744)

Leisure Hours Amusements for Town and Country: Being a select collection of the most humourous and diverting stories ... To which is now added, A Collection of Characters, copied from the original drawings of the greatest masters (London: R. Dodsley, 2 vols., 1750)

Levine, Robert S., *Conspiracy and Romance: Studies in Brockden Brown, Cooper, Hawthorne, and Melville* (Cambridge: Cambridge University Press, 1989)

Levinson, Marjorie, *Wordsworth's Great Period Poems: Four Essays* (Cambridge: Cambridge University Press, 1986)

Lewis, Matthew, *The Monk*, ed. Emma McEvoy (Oxford: Oxford University Press, 1995)

Linebaugh, Peter, and Rediker, Marcus, *The Many-Headed Hydra: The Hidden History of the Revolutionary Atlantic* (New York: Beacon Press, 2001)

Liu, Alan, 'Local Transcendence: Cultural Criticism, Postmodernism, and the Romanticism of Detail', *Representations* 32 (1990), pp. 75–113

Locke, John, *Some Thoughts Concerning Education,* ed. Ruth Grant and Nathan Tarcov (Indianapolis: Hackett, 1996)

London, April, 'Isaac D'Israeli and Literary History: Opinion, Anecdote, and Secret History in the Early Nineteenth Century', *Poetics Today* 26 (2005), pp. 351–86

Lukács, Georg, *The Historical Novel,* trans. Hannah and Stanley Mitchell, Introduction by Fredric Jameson (Lincoln: University of Nebraska Press, 1983)

Lynch, Deidre Shauna, *The Economy of Character: Novels, Market Culture, and the Business of Inner Meaning* (Chicago: University of Chicago Press, 1998)

— 'Gothic Libraries and National Subjects', *Studies in Romanticism* 40 (Spring 2001), pp. 29–48

Lynch, Deidre Shauna, ed., *Janeites: Austen's Disciples and Devotees* (Princeton: Princeton University Press, 2000)

Lynch, Deidre Shauna, and William B. Warner, eds., *Cultural Institutions of the Novel* (Durham, NC: Duke University Press, 1996)

Macaulay, Thomas, *Minute on Indian Education,* in Barbara Harlow and Mia Carter, eds., *Archives of Empire, vol. 1: From the East India Company to the Suez Canal* (Durham, NC: Duke University Press, 2003)

MacCarthy, Fiona, *Byron: Life and Legend* (New York: Farrar, Straus, Giroux, 2002)

Mackintosh, James, 'Life of James II', *Edinburgh Review* 16 (1816)

— 'Sismondi's *History of France*', *Edinburgh Review* 35 (July 1821)

Macpherson, James, *Original Papers; Containing the Secret History of Great Britain, From the Restoration, To the Accession of the House of Hanover,* Vol. 1 (London, 2 vols., 1775)

Makdisi, Saree, *William Blake and the Impossible History of the 1790s* (Chicago: University of Chicago Press, 2003)

Mandell, Laura, 'Sacred Secrets: Romantic Biography, Romantic Reform', *Nineteenth-Century Prose* 28.2 (2001), pp. 28–54

Manning, Susan, *The Puritan-Provincial Vision: Scottish and American Literature in the Nineteenth Century* (Cambridge: Cambridge University Press, 1990)

Marcet, Jane, *Conversations on Chemistry* (London: Longman, 9th edn, 1824)

Marshall, David, *The Surprising Effects of Sympathy: Marivaux, Diderot, Rousseau, and Mary Shelley* (Chicago: University of Chicago Press, 1988)

Mason, John E, *Gentlefolk in the Making; Studies in the History of Courtesy Literature and Related Topics from 1531 to 1774* (Philadelphia: University of Pennsylvania Press, 1935)

Maturin, Charles, *Melmoth the Wanderer* (Oxford: Oxford University Press, 1968)

Mayer, Robert, *History and the Early English Novel: Matters of Fact from Bacon to Defoe* (Cambridge University Press, 1997)

McCarthy, William, 'We Hoped the *Woman* Was Going to Appear', in Paula R. Feldman and Theresa M. Kelley, eds., *Romantic Women Writers: Voices and Countervoices* (Hanover and London: University Press of New England, 1995)

McCormack, W. J. and Kim Walker, Introduction, in *The Absentee*, ed. W .J. McCormack and Kim Walker (Oxford: Oxford University Press, 1988, 2001)

McGann, Jerome, *The Romantic Ideology* (Chicago: University of Chicago Press, 1983)

McGann, Jerome, ed., *Lord Byron: The Major Works* (Oxford: Oxford University Press, 1986)

McKeon, Michael, *The Origins of the English Novel* (Baltimore: Johns Hopkins University Press, 1987)

— *The Secret History of Domesticity: Public, Private, and the Division of Knowledge* (Baltimore: Johns Hopkins University Press, 2005)

McMaster, Juliet, 'The Silent Angel: Impediments to Female Expression in Frances Burney's Novels', *Studies in the Novel* 21.3 (1989), pp. 235–52

Meek, Ronald L., *Social Science and the Ignoble Savage* (Cambridge: Cambridge University Press, 1976)

Mellor, Anne K., *Mothers of the Nation: Women's Political Writing in England, 1780–1830* (Bloomington: Indiana University Press, 2000)

— Embodied Cosmopolitanism and the British Romantic Woman Writer', *European Romantic Review* 17.3 (July 2006), pp. 289–300

Miles, Robert, 'What is a Romantic Novel?', *Novel* 34.2 (Spring 2001), pp. 180–201

— *Gothic Writing 1750–1820* (Manchester and New York: Manchester University Press, 2nd edn, 2002)

Miller, D. A., 'Closure and Danger', in Robert Clark, ed., *New Casebooks: Sense and Sensibility and Pride and Prejudice* (London: St Martin's Press, 1994)

— *Jane Austen, or The Secret of Style* (Princeton: Princeton University Press, 2003)

Miller, Julia Anne, 'Acts of Union: Family Violence and National Courtship in Maria Edgeworth's *The Absentee* and Sydney Owenson's *The Wild Irish Girl*', in Kathryn Kirkpatrick, ed., *Border Crossings: Irish Women Writers and National Identities* (Tuscaloosa and London: University of Alabama Press, 2000)

Milton, John, *Paradise Lost*, ed. Gordon Teskey (New York and London: W.W. Norton & Company, 2005)

Modern Novels (London: R. Bentley and S. Magnes, 12 vols., 1681–91)

Mooneyham, Laura G., *Romance, Language and Education in Jane Austen's Novels* (New York: St Martin's Press, 1988)

Moore, Lisa, *Dangerous Intimacies: Toward a Sapphic History of the Novel* (Durham, NC: Duke University Press, 1997)

Morison, Stanley, *John Bell, 1745–1831* (Cambridge: Cambridge University Press, 1930)

Morning Chronicle, The (London, 1770–1864)

Morse, Jedidiah, *A Sermon, Delivered... May 9, 1798* (Boston, 1798)

Mudrick, Marvin, *Jane Austen: Irony as Defence and Discovery* (Berkeley: University of California Press, 1968)

Mullan, John, *Sentiment and Sociability: The Language of Feeling in the Eighteenth Century* (Oxford: Clarendon Press, 1988)

Myers, Mitzi, 'De-Romanticizing the Subject: Maria Edgeworth's "The Bracelets", Mythologies of Origin, and the Daughter's Coming to Writing', in Paula R. Feldman and Theresa M. Kelley, eds., *Romantic Women Writers: Voices and Countervoices* (Hanover and London: University Press of New England, 1995), pp. 88–110

— '"We Must Grant a Romance Writer a Few Responsibilities": "Unnatural Incident" and Narrative Motherhood in Maria Edgeworth's *Emilie de Coulanges*', *The Wordsworth Circle* XXVII.3 (1996), pp. 151–57

New English Theatre, The (London: J. Rivington and others, 12 vols., 1776–77)

New Novelist's Magazine, The (London: Harrison, 2 vols., 1786–87)

Novelist, The: or, A Choice Selection of the Best Novels. [Ed. J. H. Emmert] (Göttingen: Vandenhoeck and Ruprecht, 1792–93)

Novelist, The; or Tea-Table Miscellany. Containing select tales of Dr. Croxall (London: T. Lowndes, 2 vols., 1766)

Novelist's Magazine, The (London: Harrison, 23 vols., 1779–88)

Opie, Amelia Alderson, *Adeline Mowbray; or, the Mother and the Daughter*, ed. Miriam L. Wallace (Glen Allen, VA: College Publishing, 2004)

Owenson, Sydney, *Patriotic Sketches, written in Connaught* (London: Phillips, 1807)

— *The Wild Irish Girl*, ed. Kathryn Kirkpatrick (Oxford: Oxford University Press, 1999)

Park, Suzie, 'Resisting Demands for Depth in *The Wanderer*', *European Romantic Review* 15.2 (June 2004), pp. 307–15

Park, You-me, and Rajan, Rajeswari Sunder, eds., *The Post-Colonial Jane Austen* (London: Routledge, 2000)

Pascoe, Judith, *Romantic Theatricality: Gender, Poetry, and Spectatorship* (Ithaca: Cornell University Press, 1997)

Payson, Seth, *Proofs of the real existence and dangerous tendency of Illuminism* (Charlestown: Samuel Etheridge, 1802)

Pearce, Susan M., *On Collecting: An Investigation into Collecting in the European Tradition* (London: Routledge, 1995)

Peck, Louis F., *A Life of Matthew G. Lewis* (Cambridge, MA: Harvard University Press, 1961)

Penton, Stephen, *The Guardian's Instruction, or, The Gentleman's Romance* (London: Printed for Simon Miller, 1688)

Phillips, Mark, 'Relocating Inwardness: Historical Distance and the Transition from Enlightenment to Romantic Historiography', *PMLA* 118 (May 2003), pp. 436–49

Phillips, Mark Salber, *Society and Sentiment: Genres of Historical Writing in Britain, 1740–1820* (Princeton: Princeton University Press, 2000)

Phillipson, Nicholas, 'Adam Smith as Civic Moralist', in Istvan Hont and Michael Ignatieff, eds., *Wealth and Virtue: The Shaping of Political Economy in the Scottish Enlightenment* (Cambridge: Cambridge University Press, 1983)

Pinch, Adela, *Strange Fits of Passion: Epistemologies of Emotion, Hume to Austen* (Stanford: Stanford University Press, 1996)

'Pleasing Publication, A', Advertisement for *The Novelist's Magazine* (London: Harrison, 1779)

Plotz, John, *The Crowd: British Literature and Public Politics* (Berkeley: University of California Press, 2000)

Pocock, J. G. A., *Virtue, Commerce, and History* (Cambridge: Cambridge University Press, 1985)

Poets of Great Britain Complete from Chaucer to Churchill, The (London: John Bell; Edinburgh: Apollo Press, 109 vols., 1777–82)

Poovey, Mary, *The Proper Lady and the Woman Writer: Ideology as Style in the Works of Mary Wollstonecraft, Mary Shelley, and Jane Austen* (Chicago: University of Chicago Press, 1984)

—— *A History of the Modern Fact: Problems of Knowledge in the Sciences of Wealth and Society* (Chicago: University of Chicago Press, 1998)

Pope, Alexander, 'Epistle to a Lady: Of the Characters of Women', in Roger Lonsdale, ed., *The New Oxford Book of Eighteenth-Century Verse* (Oxford: Oxford University Press, 1992)

—— *The Dunciad*, in David Fairer and Christine Gerrard, eds., *Eighteenth-Century Poetry* (Oxford: Blackwell Publishing, 2nd edn, 2004)

Popular Romances: Consisting of Imaginary Voyages and Travels (Edinburgh: John Ballantyne; London: Longman, Hurst, Rees, Orme, and Brown; and John Murray, 1812)

Price, John Vladimir, 'The Reading of Philosophical Literature', in Isabel Rivers, ed., *Books and their Readers in Eighteenth-Century England* (New York: St Martin's Press, 1982)

Price, Leah, *The Anthology and the Rise of the Novel: From Richardson to George Eliot* (Cambridge: Cambridge University Press, 2000)

Punter, David, ed., *A Companion to Gothic* (Oxford: Blackwell, 1999)

Quere, Ralph W., 'Changes and Constants: Structure in Luther's Understanding of the Real Presence in the 1520s', *Sixteenth Century Journal* 16.1 (1985), pp. 45–78

Radcliffe, Ann, *The Mysteries of Udolpho*, ed. Bonamy Dobrée (Oxford: Oxford University Press, 1998)

Raven, James, *The British Novel 1750–1770: A Chronological Checklist of Prose Fiction Printed in Britain and Ireland* (Newark, DE: University of Delaware Press, 1987)

Render, William, *The Armenian; or, The Ghost-Seer* (London: C. Whittingham for H.D. Symonds, 1800)

Repository, or General Review, The: consisting chiefly of a select collection of literary composi-tions, extracted from all the celebrated periodical productions now publishing (London: C. Corbett, 1756)

Richards, Thomas, *Knowledge and the Fantasy of Empire* (London: Verso, 1993)

Richardson, Alan, *Literature, Education, and Romanticism* (Cambridge: Cambridge University Press, 1994)

Richardson, Samuel, *A Collection of the Moral and Instructive Sentiments… Contained in the Histories of* Pamela, Clarissa, *and* Sir Charles Grandison (London: Printed for Samuel Richardson, 1755)

— *Pamela: Or, Virtue Rewarded* (Boston: Houghton Mifflin, 1971)

— *Clarissa or the History of a Young Lady*, ed. Angus Ross (New York: Penguin, 1985)

— *The History of Sir Charles Grandison*, ed. Jocelyn Harris (Oxford: Oxford University Press, 1986)

Rigney, Ann, *Imperfect Histories: The Elusive Past and the Legacy of Romantic Historicism* (Ithaca and London: Cornell University Press, 2001)

Roberts, Marie Mulvey, and Hugh Ormsby-Lennon, *Secret Texts: the Literature of Secret Societies* (New York: AMS Press, 1995)

Robertson, Fiona, *Legitimate Histories: Scott, Gothic, and the Authorities of Fiction* (Oxford: Clarendon Press, 1994)

Robison, John, *Proofs of a Conspiracy Against all the religions and governments of Europe, carried on in the secret meetings of Free Masons, Illuminati, and Reading Societies* (London: T. Cadell and W. Davies, 1797)

Rodman, F. Robert, *Winnicott: Life and Work* (Cambridge, MA: Perseus Books, 2003)

Rogers, Katherine, *Frances Burney: The World of 'Female Difficulties'* (New York: Harvester Wheatsheaf, 1990)

Rose, Mark, *Authors and Owners: The Invention of Copyright* (Cambridge, MA: Harvard University Press, 1993)

Ross, Marlon, 'Romantic Quest and Conquest: Troping Masculine Power in the Crisis of Poetic Identity', in Anne K. Mellor, ed., *Romanticism and Feminism* (Bloomington: Indiana University Press, 1988)

Ross, Trevor, *The Making of the English Literary Canon: From the Middle Ages to the Late Eighteenth Century* (Montreal: McGill-Queen's University Press, 1998)

Russell, Jeffrey B., *A History of Witchcraft: Sorcerers, Heretics, and Pagans* (London: Thames and Hudson, 1980)

Russett, Meg, *Fictions and Fakes: Forging Romantic Authenticity, 1760–1845* (Cambridge: Cambridge University Press, 2006)

Said, Edward, *Culture and Imperialism* (New York: Vintage, 1993)

Saunders, Julia, '"The Mouse's Petition": Anna Laetitia Barbauld and the Scientific Revolution', *The Review of English Studies* 53 (2002), pp. 500–16

Schiller, Friedrich, *The Ghost-Seer; or Apparitionist*, trans. Daniel Boileau [*Der Geis-terseher*] (London: Vernor & Hood, 1795)

Schmidt, James, 'The Question of Enlightenment: Kant, Mendelssohn, and the Mittwochsgesellschaft', *Journal of the History of Ideas* 50.2 (1989), pp. 269–91

— 'Inventing the Enlightenment: Anti-Jacobins, British Hegelians, and the *Oxford English Dictionary*', *Journal of the History of Ideas* 64.3 (2003), pp000

Scott, Walter, *Lay of the Last Minstrel* (London: Longman, 1805)

— 'Mrs Radcliffe', in *Lives of the Novelists* (Paris: A. and W. Galignani, 2 vols., 1825)

— *Miscellaneous Prose Works of Walter Scott* (Edinburgh: R. Cadell, 1835)

— *Marmion*, in *Scott: Poetical Works*, ed. J. Logie Robertson (London: Oxford University Press, 1904, repr. 1967)

— *The Lady of the Lake*, in *Scott: Poetical Works*, ed. J. Logie Robertson (London: Oxford University Press, 1904, repr. 1967)

— *The Letters of Sir Walter Scott*, ed. H. J. C. Grierson (London: Constable, 12 vols., 1932)

— *Waverley* (Harmondsworth: Penguin, 1972)

— *Redgauntlet: A Tale of the Eighteenth Century*, ed. D. Hewitt and G. M. Wood (Edinburgh University Press, 1995)

— *Ivanhoe* (Oxford: Oxford University Press, 1996)

Select Collection of English Songs, A (Belfast: James Magee, 1751)

Select Collection of English Songs, A (London: J. Johnson, 3 vols., 1783)

Select Collection of Epitaphs, A (London: M. Cooper; W. Owen; and R. Davis, 1754)

Select Collection of Modern Poems, A. By the most eminent hands (Glasgow: J. Gilmour, 1744)

Select Collection of Novels, A, ed. Samuel Croxall (London: John Watts, 6 vols., 1720–21)

Select Collection of Old Plays, A (London: R. Dodsley, 12 vols., 1744)

Select Collection of Oriental Tales, A (London: J. Bell and others; Edinburgh: W. Gordon and others, 1776)

Select Collection of Original Letters, A; written by the most eminent persons, on various entertaining subjects, and on many important occasions: from the reign of Henry the Eighth, to the present time (London: J. & J. Rivington and R. and J. Dodsley, 2 vols., 1755)

Select Collection of Plain, Rational Arguments against the Tenets of an Athanasian Trinity, A (London: C. Henderson, 1755)

Select Collection of Poems, A (London: John Nichols, 8 vols., 1780–82)

Select Collection of Remarkable Trials, A (London: Henry Anderson, 1744)

Select Collection of Songs, A, sung in the several lodges of the most antient and noble order of Bucks (London: T. Legg, 1753)

Sha, Richard C., *The Visual and Verbal Sketch in British Romanticism* (Philadelphia: University of Pennsylvania Press, 1998)

Sharpe, Charles Kirkpatrick, ed., *The Secret and True History of the Church of Scotland, From the Restoration to the Year 1678. By the Rev. Mr. James Kirkton* (Edinburgh, 1817)

Shelley, Mary, *Lodore*, ed. Lisa Vargo (1835; Peterborough, Ontario: Broadview Press, 1997)

— *Matilda*, in *Mary and Maria/Matilda*, ed. Janet Todd (London: Penguin Books, 1992)

Shelley, Percy, Letter to Leigh Hunt, 23 December 1819, in *Letters*, ed. Frederick L. Jones, 2 vols. (Oxford: Clarenden Press, 1964), Vol. 2

Sheridan, Thomas, *A Course of Lectures on Elocution: Together with Two Dissertations of Language; and some other tracts relative to these subjects* (London: W. Strachan, 1762)

Simmel, Georg, 'The Sociology of Secrecy and of Secret Societies', trans. Albion Small, *The American Journal of Sociology* XI.4 (1906), pp. 441–98

Simpson, David, *Romanticism, Nationalism, and the Revolt against Theory* (Chicago: University of Chicago Press, 1993)

Siskin, Clifford, *The Historicity of Romantic Discourse* (Oxford: Oxford University Press, 1988)

— *The Work of Writing: Literature and Social Change in Britain 1700–1830* (Baltimore: Johns Hopkins University Press, 1998)

Smiles, Samuel, *A Publisher and his Friends: Memoir and Correspondence of the Late John Murray, with an account of the origin and progress of the house, 1768–1843* (London and New York: John Murray and Charles Scribner's Sons, 2 vols., 1891)

Smith, Adam, *The Theory of Moral Sentiments*, ed. D. D. Raphael and A. L. Macfie (Oxford: Clarendon Press, 1976)

Smith, Barbara Herrnstein, *Contingencies of Value* (Cambridge, MA: Harvard University Press, 1988)

Smith, Charlotte, *The Banished Man* (London: printed for T. Cadell, Jun., and W. Davies, 1794)

— *The Poems of Charlotte Smith*, ed. Stuart Curran (New York and Oxford: Oxford University Press, 1993)

— *Desmond*, ed. Antje Blank and Janet Todd (Peterborough, Ontario: Broadview Press, 2001)

— *The Old Manor House*, ed. Jacqueline M. Labbe (Peterborough, Ontario: Broadview Press, 2002)

Smith, Elihu Hubbard, *The Diary of Elihu Hubbard Smith*, ed. James E. Cronin (Philadelphia: American Philosophical Society, 1973)

Sokolsky, Anita, 'The Melancholy Persuasion', in Maud Ellmann, ed., *Psychoanalytic Literary Criticism* (London: Longman, 1994)

Southam, Brian, *Jane Austen and the Navy* (London and New York: Hambledon and London, 2000)

Speier, Hans, 'Historical Development of Public Opinion', *American Journal of Sociology* 55.4 (January 1950), pp. 376–88

Spon, Jacob, *Recherches curieuses d'antiquité, contenues en plusieurs dissertations* (Lyon: Thomas Amaulry, 1683)

Sports of the Muses, The. Or a minute's mirth for any hour of the day. Containing a select collection of only the best and most approved English and Scotch songs, ballads, and tales (London: M. Cooper, 1752)

St Clair, William, *The Reading Nation in the Romantic Period* (Cambridge: Cambridge University Press, 2004)

Stauffer, Vernon, *New England and the Bavarian Illuminati* (New York: Faculty of Political Science, Columbia University, 1918)

Staves, Susan, *Married Women's Separate Property in England, 1660–1833* (Cambridge, MA: Harvard University Press, 1990)

Sterne, Laurence, *A Sentimental Journey Through France and Italy*, ed. Ian Jack (Oxford: Oxford University Press, 1984)

Stevenson, John Allen, '"A Geometry of His Own": Richardson and the Marriage-Ending', *Studies in English Literature, 1500–1700* 26.3 (Summer 1986), pp. 469–83

Stewart, Dugald, *Elements of Philosophy of the Human Mind*, 3 vols. (London: Strahan, 1792; Edinburgh: Ramsay, 1814; London: Murray, 1827)

Stewart, Maaja, *Domestic Realities and Imperial Fictions: Jane Austen's Novels in Eighteenth Century Contexts* (Athens: University of Georgia Press, 1993)

Stewart, Susan, *On Longing: Narratives of the Miniature, the Gigantic, the Souvenir, the Collection* (Durham, NC and London: Duke University Press, 1993)

Stone, Lawrence, *Broken Lives: Separation and Divorce in England 1660–1857* (New York: Oxford University Press, 1993)

Straub, Kristina, *Divided Fictions: Fanny Burney and Feminine Strategy* (Lexington: University of Kentucky Press, 1987)

Supplement to Bell's British Theatre, consisting of the most esteemed farces and entertainments, now performing on the British stage (London: John Bell, 4 vols., 1784)

Swift, Jonathan, *The Writings of Jonathan Swift*, ed. Robert Greenberg and William Piper (New York: Norton, 1973)

Swineburne, Henry, *A Treatise of Spousals, or Matrimonial Contracts wherein all the questions relating to that subject are ingeniously debated and resolved* (London: Robert Clavell, 1686)

Taylor, Richard C., 'James Harrison, *The Novelist's Magazine*, and the Early Canonizing of the English Novel', *Studies in English Literature 1500–1900* 33 (1993), pp. 629–43

Temple, Kathryn, *Scandal Nation: Law and Authorship in Britain, 1750–1832* (Ithaca and London: Cornell University Press, 2003)

Temple of Fame, The; or The Sc—D—L—S Chronicle for the Year 1748. Being a select collection of such late pieces of secret history, lampoons, satires, &c. (London: H. Carpenter, 1749)

Thomas, Keith, *Religion and the Decline of Magic* (London and New York, 1968)

Thompson, Helen, 'How the Wanderer Works: Reading Burney and Bourdieu', *ELH* 68 (Winter 2001), pp. 965–89

— *Ingenuous Subjection: Compliance and Power in the Eighteenth-Century Domestic Novel* (Philadelphia: University of Pennsylvania Press, 2005)

Thompson, R., *The Atalantis Reviv'd: Being a select collection of Novels, of illustrious persons of both sexes. Taken from the best authors who have wrote on this subject* (London: Charles Corbett and Tho. Harris, 2 vols., 1745)

Thomson, James, 'Autumn', in *The Seasons*, ed. James Sambrook (Oxford: Clarendon Press, 1981 [1744 edn])

Todd, William B. and Ann Bowden, *Tauchnitz International, Editions in English 1841–1955: A Bibliographical History* (Bibliographical Society of America, 1988)

'To the Public', Prospectus for *Bell's British Theatre* (London: John Bell, 1774)

Trilling, Lionel, *The Opposing Self* (New York: Viking, 1955)

Trumpener, Katie, *Bardic Nationalism: The Romantic Novel and the British Empire* (Princeton: Princeton University Press, 1997)

Tschink, Cajetan, *The Victim of Magical Delusion; or, The Mystery of the Revolution of P— —L: a magico-political tale. Founded on historical facts*, trans. Peter Will (London: G.G. and J. Robinson, 3 vols., 1795)

Tuite, Clara, 'Cloistered Closets: Enlightenment Pornography, The Confessional State, Homosexual Persecution and *The Monk*', *Romanticism on the Net 8* (November 1997), available at http://www.ron.umontreal.ca

— 'Domestic Retrenchment and Imperial Expansion: The Property Plots of *Mansfield Park*', in You-me Park and Rajeswari Sunder Rajan, eds., *The Post-Colonial Jane Austen* (London: Routledge, 2000)

— *Romantic Austen: Sexual Politics and the Literary Canon* (Cambridge: Cambridge University Press, 2002)

Tutor, or Youths Companion, The: Being a select collection of questions and answers (London: M. Cooper, 1753)

Ty, Eleanor, *Unsex'd Revolutionaries: Five Women Novelists of the 1790s* (Toronto: University of Toronto Press, 1993)

Underwood, Ted, 'Romantic Historicism and the Afterlife', *PMLA* 117 (March 2002), pp. 237–51

Vallancey, Charles, *Collectanea de Rebus Hibernicis*, 6 vols. (Dublin: Marchbank, 1770–1804)

Varma, Devendra, *The Gothic Flame. Being a History of the Gothic Novel in England: Its Origin, Efflorescence, Disintegration, and Residuary Influences* (1957; repr. New York: Russell & Russell, 1963)

Wallace, Miriam L., 'Introduction', in Miriam L. Wallace, ed., Mary Hays, *Memoirs of Emma Courtney*, and Amelia Alderson Opie, *Adeline Mowbray; or, the Mother and the Daughter* (Glen Allen, VA: College Publishing, 2004), pp. 1–41

— 'Mary Hays's "Female Philosopher": Constructing Revolutionary Subjects', in Adriana Craciun and Kari Lokke, eds., *Rebellious Hearts: British Women Writers and the French Revolution* (Albany: SUNY Press, 2001)

Walpole, Horace, *The Castle of Otranto*, ed. W. S. Lewis (Oxford: Oxford University Press, 1998)

— *The Impenetrable Secret* (London: Strawberry Hill, n.d.) [BL: C.31.b.32.]

Warner, Michael, *The Trouble with Normal: Sex, Politics, and the Ethics of Queer Life* (New York: Free Press, 1999)

Warner, William, *Licensing Entertainment: The Elevation of Novel Reading in Britain, 1684–1750* (Berkeley: University of California Press, 1998)

Watson, Nicola, *Revolution and the Form of the British Novel, 1790–1805: Intercepted Letters, Interrupted Seductions* (Oxford: Clarendon Press, 1994)

Watt, Ian, *The Rise of the Novel: Studies in Defoe, Richardson and Fielding* (Berkeley: University of California Press, 1957)

Watt, James, *Contesting the Gothic: Fiction, Genre and Cultural Conflicts, 1764–1832* (Cambridge: Cambridge University Press, 1999)

Watten, Barrett, *The Constructivist Moment: From Material Text to Cultural Poetics* (Middletown, CT: Wesleyan University Press, 2003)

Wellek, René, *Immanuel Kant in England, 1793–1838* (Princeton: Princeton University Press, 1931)

Welsh, Alexander, *The Hero of the Waverley Novels; With New Essays on Scott* (Princeton: Princeton University Press, 1992)

Wieland, Christoph Martin, 'A Couple of Gold Nuggets', in James Schmidt (ed.), *What is Enlightenment? Eighteenth-Century Answers and Twentieth-Century Questions* (Berkeley: University of California Press, 1996)

Williams, Eric, *Capitalism and Slavery* (Chapel Hill: University of North Carolina Press, 1994)

Wilt, Judith, *Secret Leaves: The Novels of Walter Scott* (Chicago: University of Chicago Press, 1985)

Winnicott, D. W., 'Ego Distortion in Terms of True and False Self' (1960), in *The Maturational Processes and the Facilitating Environment* (London: Hogarth Press, 1965), pp. 140–52

— 'The Location of Cultural Experience', in *Playing and Reality* (London and New York: Routledge, 1971)

Wolfson, Susan, 'The Speaker as Questioner in Lyrical Ballads', *Journal of English and Germanic Philology* 77 (1978), pp000

— *Formal Charges: The Shaping of Poetry in British Romanticism* (Stanford: Stanford University Press, 1997)

Wollstonecraft, Mary, *Original Stories from Real Life* (London: Joseph Johnson, 1791)

— *Mary and The Wrongs of Woman*, ed. Gary Kelly (New York: Oxford University Press, 1976, 1980)

— *A Vindication of the Rights of Woman*, ed. Carol Poston (New York: Norton, 2nd edn, 1988)

— *A Vindication of the Rights of Men*, in Janet Todd, ed., *A Wollstonecraft Anthology* (New York: Columbia University Press, 1989)

— *Maria*, in *Mary and Maria / Matilda*, ed. Janet Todd (London: Penguin Books, 1992)

— *A Vindication of the Rights of Men; A Vindication of the Rights of Woman*, ed. D. L. Macdonald and Kathleen Scherf (Peterborough, Ontario: Broadview Press, 1997)

— *A Vindication of the Rights of Woman*, ed. Anne Mellor and Noelle Chao (New York: Longman, 2007)

Wollstonecraft, Mary, and William Godwin, *A Short Residence in Sweden* and *Memoirs of the Author of 'The Rights of Woman'*, ed. Richard Holmes (New York: Penguin, 1987)

Wood, Gordon S., 'Conspiracy and the Paranoid Style: Causality and Deceit in the Eighteenth Century', *William & Mary Quarterly* 3.39 (1982), ppooo

Wordsworth, Dorothy, *The Journals of Dorothy Wordsworth*, ed. Mary Moorman (Oxford: Oxford University Press, 1971)

Wordsworth, William, *Poems*, ed. Thomas Hutchinson (London: Oxford University Press, 1911)

— *William Wordsworth*, ed. Stephen Gill (Oxford: Oxford University Press, 1990)

Works of the English Poets (London: J. Nichols and others, 68 vols., 1779–81)

Young, Edward, *Conjectures on Original Composition in a Letter to the Author of Sir Charles Grandison* (London: A. Millar; R. & J. Dodsley, 1759)

World, The: Fashionable Advertiser (London, 1787–94)

Zonitch, Barbara, *Familiar Violence: Gender and Social Upheaval in the Novels of Frances Burney* (Newark: University of Delaware Press, 1997)

Index